Sydney Harbour

A history
Ian Hoskins

IAN HOSKINS has worked as an academic and public historian in Sydney for over 30 years. The original edition of *Sydney Harbour: A history* won the Queensland Premier's Literary Prize for History in 2010 and *Coast*, his history of the New South Wales coast, won the New South Wales Premier's Prize for Community and Regional History in 2014. His most recent work, *Australia & the Pacific: A history* was shortlisted for the Australian History Prize in 2022. He was the CH Currey Fellow at the State Library of NSW in 2019 exploring the Library's extensive Pacific collections.

To Lisa, Hal and Ariel,
and my parents who guided
me to the harbour

Sydney Harbour

A history
Ian Hoskins

NEWSOUTH

A NewSouth book

Published by
NewSouth Publishing
University of New South Wales Press Ltd
University of New South Wales
Sydney NSW 2052
AUSTRALIA
https://unsw.press/

© Ian Hoskins 2022
First published 2009

10 9 8 7 6 5 4 3 2 1

A catalogue record for this book is available from the National Library of Australia

ISBN: 9781742237794 (paperback)
        9781742238623 (ebook)
        9781742239545 (ePDF)

Design Josephine Pajor-Markus and Di Quick
Cover design Peter Long
Cover image Nick Jones / Unsplash
Printer Griffin Press

All reasonable efforts were taken to obtain permission to use copyright material reproduced in this book, but in some cases copyright could not be traced. The author welcomes information in this regard.

This book is printed on paper using fibre supplied from plantation or sustainably managed forests.

UNSW
SYDNEY

CONTENTS

Introduction *vi*

ONE The harbour people *1*

TWO An unexpected harbour *16*

THREE From convicts to commerce *48*

FOUR Possession secured *79*

FIVE Foreshore defenders *109*

SIX A harbour of wonder, a harbour of filth *141*

SEVEN Big plans and a bridge *176*

EIGHT Workers and warriors *207*

NINE Modern harbour *230*

TEN The people's harbour *258*

Afterword *294*

Acknowledgments *313*

Notes *314*

Bibliography *331*

Index *333*

INTRODUCTION

I first saw Sydney Harbour as a four-year-old boy, arriving with my family on a ship called the *Australasia*. The epic name conjures images of a vessel to rival the *Great Western* of previous times. The reality was a little more prosaic – the MV *Australasia* was a 16-year-old 10 000-ton cargo liner that combined comfortable passenger berths with the derricks and winches needed for removing cargo from holds fore and aft. In this respect it was not unlike the practical motor vessels that had linked Australia's coastal cities to each other, the Pacific and Asia for the previous 40 years. Our ship plied the Sydney–Brisbane–Singapore route. Still, to come in anything with such a name was richly symbolic. My mother, sisters and I were travelling to join my father, who had already arrived by plane. We were leaving the cosseted life of British ex-pats in Singapore and about to make a new one in a somewhat more egalitarian society in Australia. It was 1966.

My family must have been among the last immigrants to come to Sydney by sea. Had I been a little older it might have been a formative experience, but the recollections of early childhood are as random as a lucky dip. While odd things from that fifth year have lodged in my memory – a Malay wedding and green tree snakes – our entry to the harbour is not one of them. How I wish it were different for I might have had first impressions to compare with the myriad of artists and writers who came before and were awed by the unfolding vistas. Instead, an historical imagination tells me that we passed by green and buff headlands kept free of development because of their strategic significance, and foreshores made cubic and red by the roof tiles and bricks of thousands of houses and flats. Between the points were crescents of sand. There were yachts on swing moorings but nothing like the number that crowd the coves today.

The naval base at Garden Island had been crowned by its huge hammerhead crane for just over a decade. After such a stretch of forest and homes, the arm and tower suggested the beginning of the working harbour – although it was something of a false start for the gardens and groves of the Domain and Botanic Gardens lay just beyond. On the next point along sat an extraordinary shell-like structure partially complete. It was the Sydney Opera House with concrete ribs still exposed. The AMP Building towered behind, recently installed as the country's tallest skyscraper. Shiny and new, its glass and metal contrasted with the soot-stained sandstone of old Sydney.

We might have docked in Sydney Cove: cargo ships still did in the 1960s, some on the east side, some at the long jetty protruding on the west. Instead, the *Australasia* continued a little farther to Walsh Bay, under the Sydney Harbour Bridge – monolithic and a little dour with its granite blackened by 30 years of car exhausts and coal smoke. There the long, timber finger wharves were already half a century old, showing their age and nearing the end of their working lives. From then on, along both north and south shores, were the docks, cranes and fuel tanks of a working port.

That was a place I knew nothing of, for we settled back in the east around Middle Harbour. As children we sneaked into yacht clubs to which we did not belong, to peer over jetties at fish we rarely caught. For a while the harbour loomed large, just as it did for most who lived around it – a defining presence and a watery common. Yet for all its egalitarianism there were still strata in this harbour society: those with boats and those without, those with smart waterfronts and those in the modest streets beyond. There were the fishers, the swimmers, the workers, the city commuters. Eventually we moved away and the harbour's relevance receded. For though the place is a national icon, recognised around the world, it still means most to its locals.

The waterway I entered in 1966 was a landscape in transition, beginning the shift from a port of wharves, coal-loaders and shipbuilding slips to a harbour city of banks, services, restaurants and tourists. Walsh Bay was part of the former, the AMP Building and the Opera House were symbols of the latter. But then Sydney Harbour had been a place of quickening change since Europeans first arrived to 'take possession' for an empire and upset the relative ecological, social and political equilibria that existed with the Aboriginal clans. The open-air gaol, with water for walls, gradually filled with boats and became a commercial port, which then cast off its convict past. The officiously titled Port Jackson evolved into Sydney Harbour, a waterway of world renown visited by the likes of Anthony Trollope and Joseph Conrad. In the early 1900s the demands of efficiency and the emergency of plague erased much of the old waterfront. Then a bridge was built – long heralded – that changed the scale of the place and created its first enduring icon.

Along the way Sydneysiders constructed waterfront homes, both huge and humble. They worked and played around their harbour, recognised its beauty, invested it with new meanings expressed in words and pictures and, all the while, treated it as an economic resource. They fought over ownership and access, defended it from outsiders and each other. *Sydney Harbour: A history* is my attempt at telling these stories.

Exploring the full breadth of the harbour's history is a huge and daunting task. The first attempt to do so in a comprehensive way appeared, coincidentally, in the year of my arrival. The author of *The History and Description of Sydney Harbour* – the writer, publisher and ardent nationalist Percy Reginald Stephensen – had been observing the changes around the waterway for 30 years. During this time he made the not-uncommon intellectual shift from the politics of the left to those of the right. However, his love of Australian history remained a constant. Most of what he wrote was published under the name of his friend and some-time employer Frank Clune but, in his last years, Stephensen tackled the subject of the harbour. For him the place symbolised, as his biographer suggested, 'a fresh, clean image of a new Australia'.[1] The story had not been told, Stephensen thought, for fear of its complexity and the scorn of 'idealists and carping critics'. Despairing of the possibility of writing a 'complete' history of such a place, Stephensen adopted a narrative approach. Unable, however, to resist the temptation to get as much in as possible, his study became something of a compendium, with the story of each cove and building following one upon another. Perhaps for this reason there was a faint sense of exhaustion in the introduction: 'anyone who in the future may decide to write a better book on Sydney Harbour than this one will at least find the channels lit and buoyed'.[2] Indeed, Stephensen died in 1965 before he finished the book to his own satisfaction. It was published anyway, updated in 1980 and then went out of print. Tellingly, the histories that followed tended to focus on particular facets of the harbour's story: its ferries, forts, personalities or precincts.

I became engrossed in the history of Sydney Harbour as a public historian working for North Sydney Council, in an area with a long and intimate connection to the water. There is, therefore, a considerable amount of North Sydney's history here and, of course, much else besides. But I make even fewer claims to comprehensiveness than Stephensen because, in the interest of readability, I have tried to construct a continuous and chronological narrative and, in doing so, have necessarily eschewed 'completeness'. My harbour is essentially the fairway that runs from the Heads to the beginning of the Parramatta River at Balmain. I have explored episodes and themes which, from my reading, were significant at particular moments. Some, such as the sinking of the *Dunbar* in 1857 and the Japanese submarine attack in 1942, are well known. Others – such as the concern over the harbour's fish stocks in the late 1800s – are less so. Undoubtedly there are many other places, events and people that might have been selected. I hope the story that unfolds covers some essential themes, if not every detail.

This book was written in the midst of a passionate and often pessimistic debate about the future of the harbour, prompted by the departure of waterfront industry and its possible replacement by residential development. Container ships, car carriers, even the harbour pilot, have recently gone. The sight of a tanker heading to Gore Cove just west of the Bridge is now exceptional. Such occasional vessels seem only to underline the fact that much work on the waterway now is given over to fun – cruise ships, tourist boats, yachts, waterfront restaurants. An entire book could be written on that topic alone and, as there are centuries of history to explore beforehand, my brief discussion of the contemporary harbour raises more questions than it answers. I hope, nonetheless, it provides some useful perspectives.

The postindustrial harbour makes many who have known the place for an age uneasy. As an historian, I find such changes both interesting and confronting, but at the risk of sounding complacent see hope in the optimism of Kenneth Slessor – poet, journalist and harbour resident. Few loved the place more. He had grown up with the 'dazzle of the Harbour' in his eyes, its smell in his nose, its 'bells and whistles' in his ears and its spray on his 'doorstep'. When he lost a friend to the waterway's depths, Slessor penned one of the country's best-loved poems – 'Five Bells' – in response. In 1962 he acknowledged that much of what he had experienced had passed into history, but found comfort in the waterway's perpetual 'loveliness': 'For the pleasures that have gone there are the pleasures that renew themselves each time the wind shifts or the clouds move or the moon rises. They are to be had free of charge by looking out of a window.'[3]

ONE

THE HARBOUR PEOPLE

'THE RETURN OF AN OLD FRIEND'

It is water that gives a foreshore its shape on the map. Balls Head juts out into the western end of Sydney Harbour just before the waterway divides into the Lane Cove and Parramatta rivers. It resembles the little White's seahorse that might still be found in the seagrass beds of nearby Balls Head Bay and the coves to the east. Fifteen thousand years ago, while the oceans were held back in glacial ice, the head was simply the top of one of the steepest escarpments of a river valley. That water course, joined by another from the north, drained into an ocean some 15 kilometres east of the present coastline. As the glaciers melted, the sea advanced up to the sandstone cliffs that ran north and south of the river, then through the hole in the wall that became known as the Heads, and along the main valley and the northern tributary. As they filled, the headlands, points and bays of present-day Port Jackson and Middle and North harbours were defined. Thirteen hills within the valley became harbour islands.

The extent of Sydney's waterway can be seen in this early aerial photograph
Sydney Harbour looking east by Hall and Co. The Sydney Harbour Bridge is
nearing completion with the arch joined so the date is 1930 or 1931.

State Library of New South Wales

The water off Balls Head filled to over 35 metres – second in depth only to the channel between Blues and Dawes points. There, the old valley floor is under nearly 50 metres of water and another 15 metres of mud. In evolutionary terms the inundation was recent and rapid. Only 8500 years ago the water was 15 metres below its present level. When the sea rise stopped some 2500 years later, schools of tailor and jewfish could swim where parrots and cuckoos may once have flown.

Sydney's harbour became a temperate waterway and, in parts, an estuarine environment where freshwater mixes with sea. It sits between tropical and cold waters and still has one of the largest and most diverse range of fish in the world. In summer the East Australian Current brings species down from the tropical north. That is when the abundance is greatest. Snapper move through the deep water off Balls Head and elsewhere, sometimes schooling near the surface as they have done for centuries or more. Translucent whiting inhabit waters off the sand beaches that formed at the water's edge where the incline was not too steep. Around other gentle slopes, and farther up where the harbour has split and narrowed along its estuarine rivers and tributaries, there were mudflats. Plate-sized mud oysters lived there in abundance but they have now gone. Their smaller relations continue to cling to the rock platforms that had once been terrestrial ledges. Black bream swim across the rocks, cracking the shellfish open with their teeth. Smaller rocky peaks have become reefs, supporting kelp beds, inhabited by moray eels and navigated by huge blue groper and delicate sea dragons. Crusty, mottled red rock cod – camouflaged to look like pieces of reef – still sit motionless in wait for prey around the lower harbour. Like much of the fauna that gradually colonised the developing ecosystem, the cod can be found elsewhere along the coast. The similarly spiny Sydney scorpionfish is the only known species to have evolved or survived to become an exclusive resident of the harbour. The creature exists nowhere else in the world.

The sandstone cliffs and headlands were created by layers of river sand laid down around 220 million years ago. The soil that developed over the stone was thin and infertile, yet along the harbour's northern foreshore and slopes it supported forests of large trees – smooth, sinewy red angophoras that wrapped their roots around the rocks, rough-trunked bangalays growing tall to catch the sun like the Sydney peppermints that dangled strips of bark from glowing cream-coloured upper limbs. Below there were grevilleas and wattles. Subtropical rainforest with coachwood and tree fern grew in sheltered pockets. At the high North Head there was low heath swept by wind and salt spray. On the southern shore the slopes and heads were less dramatic, and forests of scribbly gum, blueberry ash, lillypilly and cheese tree gave way to patches of foreshore wetland and coastal heath to the east. The forest canopy was a dull green from a distance but beneath it grew shrubs that bore tiny flowers of yellow, red, pink and white.

People were living on the ridges, escarpments and foreshores even as the sea was rising. A site at Cammeray, near Middle Harbour, contains the remains of shellfish meals that are at least six thousand years old and is the most ancient of the known camps around the harbour. But habitation in the area was almost certainly older. Many more sites must lie beneath the harbour. Some time after the water stabilised the people began naming places that we know today. The delicate tip of present-day Blues Point was called Warrungareah and the more bulbous Dawes Point diagonally opposite was Tar-ra. The headland to the east of that was Tu-bow-gule and the deep-water cove in between was Warrane. Freshwater streams emptied into many of the bays but the one at Warrane was the most reliable.

There are ochre stencils and pictograph carvings on Balls Head that were created hundreds, if not thousands, of years ago. The sandstone is ideal for inscribing, being hard but brittle. Engraved images were started with a series of shallow holes picked out by an even harder stone point. These were then joined together in a process that probably took several weeks. The biggest and best known of those at Balls Head shows a marine creature with a human figure inside. It was one of a small group containing a shoal of fish and two spirit men or ancestral figures recorded in the late 1800s. WD Campbell, who surveyed the engravings of the greater Sydney region in the late 1890s, found one of a man inside a fish at Manly 'flat rocks' on the spur of a hill with a view to the ocean. Nearby was a group of whales. At Muston Street, Mosman, Campbell identified a large group of fish with a shark pursuing a man. There were also fish cut into flat rock some 21 metres above the sea near the Hornby Lighthouse on South Head. He saw a fish on a boulder at Watsons Bay. At Point Piper the outline of a large shark contained several smaller fish.[1]

There were many more images, forming one of the largest open-air collections of rock art in the world. But when Campbell was conducting his survey they were already disappearing, built over as houses and roads spread across the foreshores. In the 1950s the writers Ruth Park and D'Arcy Niland moved into a 19th-century stone manse above Neutral Bay and discovered that the old rector's home stood matter-of-factly over a gallery of images: 'The tail of a sacred snake vanished under the toilet and beneath the house itself, for the golden rock was richly engraved with pictures of whales, hammerhead sharks, wallabies and lizards. In the concavities under the house, sculpted by wind and rain, were dim paintings of human beings ...'[2]

At Balls Head, 30 years after Campbell made his notes and sketches, a road was laid down to provide access to the new coal-loader built in the western side of the headland. The road ran over the fish engravings, then soil and grass gradually spread across the spirit figures so that only the great sea creature remained. At some point in the following years that was duly surrounded by a North Sydney Council fence and its outline reiterated with white paint to create a historic landmark and a reminder of what once was.

In June 2008 the road was dug up and all that remained of the fish and spirits revealed. It was a significant event for the Aboriginal community of Sydney, some of whom call the harbour Birra Birra, and some who identify with its original clans and the Eora Nation they comprise. The people gathered at Balls Head were from far and wide – saltwater people, sweetwater people, rainforest people and inland people – and all with a shared heritage of Aboriginality. One of those present, from the dry northwest of New South Wales, referred

The carving at Balls Head is one of the largest surviving around the harbour.
It depicts a marine creature, possibly a whale, with a human figure within.
This photograph dates to around 1900.

North Sydney Heritage Centre Collection, Stanton Library

to the revelation of the pictographs as 'the return of an old friend'.
For Professor Michael McDaniel, the symbolism of the road works
was obvious. Few commodities exemplified the history of European
dominance over land, sea and other people more than coal. Where once
people trod lightly across the ground, there came the heavy footprint of
its infrastructure. Coal reflected a 'value system' that held small regard
for the art of the dispossessed. Scraping away the road, by contrast, was
an expression of respect for people and earth.[3]

'The man in the whale is a clever fella'

The people who lived around the harbour when Europeans arrived in 1788 called themselves Eora. Today, the name is used to refer to a specific political or social entity: the Eora Nation of the Sydney regions. Previously, it was probably a general term for humanity. The clans had specific names that more directly associated them with their place. At least seven of these groups lived around the waterway when Europeans arrived. Each may have comprised as many as a hundred men, women and children.[4] Much of what is understood of the territories derives from accounts made soon after contact and during the upheaval of colonisation and may be imperfect. The Gayamaygal occupied Kay-ye-my (Manly Cove) and the Borogegal were from Booragy (Bradleys Head). The Gamaragal's territory, Cammeray, encompassed a large area to the east and west of Balls Head. The territory to the west again, along the Lane Cove and Parramatta rivers, was Wallumede – the land of the Wallumedegal. At the head of the estuary were the Boromedegal: the name Parramatta was an early European pronunciation of their Country's name. The Wangal occupied the land called Wane along the southern shores of the river and harbour to Tumbalong (Darling Harbour). The Gadigal lived along Cadi, the southern shore from Tumbalong to the Heads. They may have shared the lucrative fishing spot near the mouth of the harbour with a clan called the Birrabirragal. There were other groups identified by the colonists, but their territories were not recorded.

Whereas the clan groups were known from their territories, some individuals took names from the animals around them. Among those who encountered the first Europeans was an elderly woman called Mau-ber-ry, whose name referred to a fish like the gurnard. Bal-loo-der-ry was Aboriginal for leatherjacket. Bennelong, a Wangal man who became the most important mediator between the harbour people and the newcomers, took his name from 'a large fish'. His child Dilboong 'was named after a small bird'. The young woman who helped a young lieutenant called William Dawes compile a list of Aboriginal words was known by the word for 'large grey kangaroo', Pat-ta-go-rang.[5]

This naming possibly entailed a totemic relationship of a person to a particular animal. The intrinsic significance of the harbour's animals for its people was also suggested in the art that covered the rock platforms. There were kangaroos and the occasional emu. But it is the preponderance of fish and whales, as well as people, that is striking. Campbell noticed that engraved sites around the foreshores he explored were usually elevated cleared platforms with 'commanding views' over the water.[6] At the high Balls Head site you could look up and down the harbour. The Mosman engravings were located where there was a 'very fine view of Middle Harbour and the Heads'. The elevation is much lower and more gradual at Point Piper but the position on the bend in the harbour makes for equally remarkable views to the west and up to the northeast. The rock images may have related to the totems of an individual or group. They may have helped in the passage of lore. Some might have illustrated creation stories explaining the formation of the harbour, which followed incremental sea rise and climate change, in terms of the actions of mythical beings. And although they were obviously not casual scratchings, the engravings may simply have been a record of observation – a depiction of the creatures that were seen in the waters below.

The uncertainty stems from the social collapse that was caused by colonisation. For within two years of the arrival of Europeans, the Aboriginal population was devastated by the impact of disease – called *galgalla* by the local people. Dispossession followed rapidly. Knowledge of the harbour people and their place, therefore, comes mediated through the first colonial accounts of a culture still intact and subsequent descriptions of the groups who coalesced in the wake of the rupture. Later writings of surviving groups along the coast have provided important comparisons. More recent understanding of culture has been passed down through community and families. All of this was useful to Gerry Bostock, a Bundjalung man from the rainforest and saltwater Country of northern New South Wales, when he interpreted the Balls Head site in 1992:

8

> I go to white sources to find out about these people, but
> I put an Aboriginal meaning onto what they say ... This is
> a place of learning, a place of ceremonies, a place where the
> whales were sung in to shore. Whales beaching themselves
> in the Harbour were a great source of food. The man in the
> whale is a clever fella. It looks like he's got a club foot, but
> that represents the feathers that he wore on his feet so he
> did not make footprints ... Having no neck he was also the
> Creator ...[7]

The power of a clever man was important because corralling and killing a migrating whale would have been very difficult while throwing shell-tipped spears and riding fragile canoes propelled by paddles. Possibly the act of killing a whale was anathema to the clans. But effort and skill obtained most everything else necessary for life next to the water. The weather-worn rock gave shelter with its overhangs. Where these were unsuitable, tree bark was used for huts. The same material provided torches to light the night and illuminate nocturnal fishing parties. It was used for bedding and clothing. Long lengths of she-oak or Bangalay bark could be shaped into canoes, or nowey, that were essential to passage around the waterway – these were then used at the end of life to fuel funeral biers. Bark baskets or net bags carried the catch. Cockle and oyster shells were used as tools for working plants and wood. Sandstone was a useful abrasive for working shells, stone and wood, and harder stones such as quartz and silcrete were ideal spear barbs, drills and cutting blades. The grass tree provided the shaft for spears and resin that could be used to adhere barbs.[8]

Technologies changed over the millennia. The discovery, or introduction, of fishing hooks almost a thousand years ago was momentous. Turban shells were ground down to create the sharp crescent hooks that were fastened to the ends of lines made by stripping and twisting fibrous tree bark. It must have greatly increased the yield from the harbour and may also have led to a reorganisation of social roles. By the time the Europeans were observing and making notes, it was women who manufactured and used the hooks and lines.

The foreshore forest gave sustenance by way of rushes that could be ground to make 'flour' for native bread. There were geebung fruit, native currants and figs. Medicines and balms could be found among the trees and shrubs. Kangaroos and possums were hunted for red meat and skin, although it was the woods people to the west who had the most dexterous methods of hunting tree-dwelling animals. They also used fire to flush out these creatures and, in the process, promote certain species. As a result they maintained a forest that the Europeans described as 'in general entirely free from underwood'. This occurred around the harbour as well. The result was more varied, depending upon the presence and density of large trees. In 1788 Governor Arthur Phillip noted, 'There are several parts of the harbour in which the trees stand at a greater distance from each other than in Sydney Cove.' Where fire was used it created particular habitats through the promotion of certain fire-resistant or dependent varieties of plants. So the harbour clans actively shaped their environment.[9]

However, for saltwater people, it was water that was central to physical and spiritual sustenance. The name Wallumede, the land of the Wallumedegal, was derived from the word for the snapper fish, wallumai. Captain John Hunter observed, 'All the human race, which we have seen here, appear to live chiefly on what the sea affords.'[10] As Governor Phillip's second-in-command, Hunter spent many hours charting the waterway and observing its people and animals. David Collins, judge-advocate for the new colony and its first historian, was so struck by the amount of fish consumed by the clans that he attributed their itchy skin disorder, 'djee-ball djee-ball', to the singularity of the diet. The 'woods,' he remarked, 'afford them but little sustenance'.[11]

In the warmer months the brightly coloured fish called wrasses were speared or hooked. Snapper and bream were probably staples. Shellfish were continuously gathered and middens of discarded shells lined the foreshores, but finned fish were more nutritious. The spears for catching these, called callarr and mooting, were men's equipment.

Their multiple prongs increased the target area and held a writhing fish, pulled from the harbour, without the need to completely impale it. Women fished from canoes using hook and line. They attracted their quarry with chewed-up mussels thrown out as floating bait or berley while chanting for 'hour after hour … inviting the fish beneath them to take their bait'. Fish could be sung to the hook just as whales might be lured through the Heads. The women cooked some of the catch on board in order to prolong the quest, so their canoes streamed smoke from the small fires burning on clay pads, seagrass or sand.[12] The oil from the catch was smeared on the skin to ward off mosquitoes and flies.[13]

Women would have caught deep-water fish such as snapper with their lines and men speared the bream that poked about in the rocky shallows for shellfish. But even the sheer number of fish in the harbour, and the ocean around it, does not compare with the vast shoals that inhabit the nutrient-rich cold waters of the northern hemisphere. Finding fish in winter required endurance and perseverance.[14]

'[A] very powerful people'

The harbour clans probably remained within their territories through good times and bad. Arthur Phillip remarked upon the 'beaten paths' between Port Jackson and Botany Bay but in that first year of contact did not see any 'regular migrations to the northward in the winter months, or to the south in summer'.[15] There was, however, frequent interaction between the groups, with established protocols for visiting each other's Country. Marriage laws facilitated this by demanding that men and women marry outside their clan. So Bennelong, from the land west of Tumbalong, married a woman called Barangaroo, who came from the north shore around Balls Head. Barangaroo and her Gamaragal people may have spoken Guringai, a language shared with the groups farther north. If so, there must have been words commonly understood with clans to the south. It is more probable that all those around the harbour and westward up the estuary spoke a dialect of the same language: coastal Dharug. Words and custom were apparently shared with the woods people to the west. When the Gadigal man Colbee ventured beyond Parramatta with a party of Europeans in 1791, he knew to 'whoop' a warning to the local Buruberongal people and, having made contact, could converse and understand the local language 'perfectly'.[16]

The harbour and its islands were a common zone belonging to no one group or person. Water was at once a territorial boundary and an avenue for communication along which people travelled for cultural business. The best documented of these occasions occurred in 1795 at the bay called Woggan-ma-gule, present-day Farm Cove. On the foreshore there an oval-shaped ceremonial space called Yoolahng was cleared. Men and boys gathered for a ritual that would initiate the youths into manhood. The culmination was the removal of a front tooth – an ordeal that required bravery and self-control. The ceremony was presided over by the north shore Gamaragal who arrived in the evening, presumably by canoe, only after the Yoolahng had been prepared. Tooth evulsion bound 'those who lived on the sea coast' in a common rite of manhood. It was apparently not practised by the woods people to the west.[17] Nonetheless, others travelled from beyond the waterway to attend. Some of the participants were painted with the white clay found on the shoreline. In this instance kangaroo-hunting scenes and ceremonial dances were enacted in front of the boys, before each was taken to have his tooth knocked out with a bone mystically produced earlier by Gamaragal clever men. Blood was allowed to flow freely and, where the wound was severe, 'broiled fish' was applied as a dressing. The teeth extracted in these ceremonies possibly symbolised an irretrievable boyhood for, once removed, they were not to be retained. Bennelong had buried his after he became a man. Others threw theirs into the sea.[18]

By the time this particular ceremony was performed, the world of the harbour clans was being upturned in the wake of European contact. David Collins, who attended some stages of the ritual and later wrote up a description in his journal, prevailed upon Bennelong's sister and another woman, Daringa, to give him three of the extracted teeth as scientific curios. They did so 'with great secrecy and dread', fearing retribution from the Gamaragal men in charge.[19] Daringa was moved, it seems, by sentiment because she requested that one of the teeth, from a boy raised by Surgeon White, be given to that officer in appreciation for his kindness. More profound than this transgression, however, was the wholesale dispossession already underway. By 1795 more than 8500 hectares of land around Sydney had been appropriated by colonists. Even as the Gamaragal were mustering enough initiated men to carry on the culture, 12 hectares of their land on the harbour had simply been given away and sold by the newcomers – first to a convict, then to a political exile. The latter, Thomas Muir, had built a 'neat little house' on the shore 'for the purpose of seclusion' and become the first European to reside on the north shore.

The symbolism and significance of this small incursion were all the greater because the Gamaragal were acknowledged as 'a very powerful people' in the realm of the harbour clans – possessed of a 'muscular and robust' appearance and the right to preside over initiation. Bennelong had told David Collins that they could 'oblige' any 'to attend wherever or whenever they directed'.[20] As the Gadigal were reduced to a few individuals by disease, the Gamaragal had survived to carry on cultural business well into the 1790s. Yet within another generation this clan too had ceased to exist as a separate entity. From the 1820s the carvings at Balls Head, and more than 200 hectares of foreshore and forest around them, were owned by a white man – part of a grant given in recognition of past and future services to commerce. In the absence of the clan's regular burning, the surrounding forest changed. Underbrush grew thick and fires regularly swept across the foreshore. The land was near useless for farming, and the forest became the haunt of smugglers and deserters, much to the annoyance of the new owners. In time others touted the potential of bays 'so admirably adapted for wharfs, warehouses and stores of every description'.[21] The

DA-RING-HA,
Colebee's Wife.

Convict artist Thomas Watling observed the harbour's people and animals closely. His portraits show a humanity that is absent from the naive renderings executed by other First Fleet artists such as the anonymous 'Port Jackson Painter'. This one is entitled *Da-ring-ha Colebee's Wife*. Daringa had a close relationship with Barangaroo. Years earlier she had had her fishing tackle stolen by a convict and had wept when the thief was flogged on Phillip's orders.

© *Natural History Museum, London*

jetties and slipways came gradually, for most of the development was on the southern side. It was a century before Balls Head got its great waterfront coal-loader.

In fact, the foreshore there was one of the last camping grounds on the harbour for Aboriginal people, but in the late 1870s these were probably displaced people from the south coast. Local knowledge of the inscriptions almost certainly faded, just as some of the carvings and stencils themselves had disappeared. White residents looked on this as an easy metaphor for the fate of the people who had created them. An 1889 excursion to a cave near Middle Harbour in search of 'hieroglyphics' ended in disappointment because the images 'had long since disappeared like the Cammera tribe that traced them'.[22] The 'clever fella' and the whale, however, survived to be reclaimed two hundred years later.

TWO

AN UNEXPECTED HARBOUR

'THERE APPEARED
TO BE SAFE
ANCHORAGE'

There was a well-worn track between the harbour and the large bay to the south that Aboriginal people called Ka-may. The two groups living around that waterway – the Gameygal and Gweagal – shared a saltwater culture with the harbour clans. Life revolved around the bounty of the sea. Unlike the drowned river valley to the north, this bay was formed as rising water filled a shallow basin. Its sandy floor was covered with sediment carried west with the ocean swells and waves that washed ashore through the southeast-facing entrance. Mangroves were prolific around the western shores and submarine meadows of strapweed seagrass filled the smaller coves along the south. That was a delicately balanced ecosystem near the northern extent of its range.[1] Fish thrived in the sandy bay. It was an especially important habitat for stingrays and it is likely that they had a totemic significance for the local people and probably were not hunted.

On 28 April 1770 Aboriginal men were so 'totally engaged' in fishing that they apparently did not notice the 400-ton barque *Endeavour* turn with the wind and slip into the bay.[2] The vessel was 21 months into a voyage of discovery under the command of James Cook. He had stopped at Tahiti to observe the transit of Venus, then proceeded west in the hope of finding *terra australis*, a land mass whose presence had exercised imaginations in the northern hemisphere for centuries. The circumnavigation of New Zealand ruled those islands out of contention. Sailing west again, Cook and his company encountered the east coast of Australia – the first Europeans to do so. Among them was the gentleman naturalist Joseph Banks, who had paid handsomely for the opportunity to gather specimens for his collection. He likened the country to the back of a 'lean cow', its shrubs and trees being the 'long hair' and the rocks and outcrops 'the scraggy hips'.[3] The wide bay they entered at the end of April was a welcome anchorage and a place to get freshwater, fish and interesting plants for Mr Banks. Cook was impressed by the remarkable number of the great flat fish he saw and called the place 'Sting Ray's Harbour'. When later he looked about at the collection of plants brought on board, the navigator changed the name to Botany Bay.

The Europeans were quick to exploit the abundance of seafood. They had landed 135 kilograms of fish two days after arriving. On 5 May they caught several huge stingrays that had followed the tide into shallow water. These were gutted, weighed and then eaten. On Sunday, 6 May, with a perfect northwest breeze, the white men left. The Gameygal and Gweagal had avoided contact throughout their nine-day stay and they probably watched the *Endeavour's* departure from the line of trees before resuming their fishing. A fragmentary insight into the local impression of this extraordinary intrusion was related 75 years later by a surviving member of one of the clans: 'They thought they was the devil when they saw them landed first, they did not know what to make of them. When they saw them go up the masts they thought they was oppossums.'[4] The Europeans, by contrast, left detailed accounts of their adventure. In his journal, Banks remarked that the meal of stingray was 'excellent'.⁵ Some three leagues (about 15 kilometres) north of the bay, Cook noted that they were 'abreast a bay or harbour, in which there appeared to be safe anchorage'. He casually called it Port Jackson and kept sailing. Having charted the coast to its northernmost point, the navigator named the land New South Wales and claimed it for the English king, George III.⁶

'Where the deuce is Port Jackson?'

The *Endeavour* returned to England in 1771, with Banks's collection having taken over much of the ship's interior. The idea of actually colonising the new possession in the South Seas took some years to ferment. Banks was preoccupied for some of the time with developing the botanical gardens for the king at Kew, just outside London. But in 1779 he suggested sending convicts to New South Wales since the American colonies had been lost as an overflow for Britain's crowded gaols – the Americans had declared independence three years earlier and were still fighting to realise that desire. One New World dumping ground for felons might usefully replace another. Banks's proposal was followed in 1783 by another from James Mario Matra, the well-born and ambitious son of an American loyalist who had seen the place first-hand sailing as a midshipman on the *Endeavour*. In the first instance, Matra suggested, New South Wales would be a place of asylum for 'unfortunate American loyalists' displaced during the colonial war. Matra went on to emphasise – and embellish – the commercial and strategic advantages of settlement. There was 'every variety of soil' to be found for agriculture, and the north might support the cultivation of sugar cane, coffee, tea, cotton, tobacco 'and the other articles of commerce that have been so advantageous to the maritime power of Europe'. The country was close to New Zealand and that land's flax plant, which was thought to have potential for sailmaking. Its strategic position would assist in any future conflict with Holland

18

or Spain: 'we might with equal facility invade the coast of Spanish America, and intercept the Manilla ships, laden with the treasures of the west'.[7]

The 'few black inhabitants' Matra had observed were dismissed as inconsequential. The American colonists would be assisted with 'useful inhabitants from China' and Polynesians ('as many women as may serve for the men'). A conversation with the home secretary Lord Sydney led Matra to add the humane disposal of felons to the list of advantages. Their crimes could be forgiven and they would be given land to farm – never to return to Britain. It was a 'beautiful union' of 'economy to the publick, and humanity to the individual'. In 1786 Sydney reported on the matter to the lords commissioner of the Treasury. It was not quite the proposal Matra had put forward. Where the American had outlined the potential of the entire coastline, Sydney noted that His Majesty 'has thought it advisable to fix upon Botany Bay, situated on the coast of New South Wales in the latitude of about 33 degree south'. The possibility of cultivating tropical products was mentioned in the accompanying 'Heads of a Plan', as was the use of New Zealand flax and timber. Matra's casual anticipation of the sexual utility of Pacific women was followed up as a precaution against homosexuality: 'to preserve the settlement from gross irregularities and disorders', in Sydney's words. But it was the permanent relocation of convicts that was of most importance. Gone was any mention of loyalists and commerce.[8]

This was a less expansive vision, but nonetheless it entailed an enormous logistical effort. Eleven ships were to be obtained to transport 759 convicts with the marines and officers to manage them – over a thousand people in all – 19 000 kilometres away. The first orders were placed in August 1786. Food and equipment was provided for two years, after which it was supposed the colony would be self-sufficient. It was a colonising venture that had no precedent in terms of distance and scale.[9]

Though this was to be a penal colony, Lord Sydney had to gain the co-operation of the East India Company before the undertaking could begin.[10] With its own army and fighting ships, the company was a powerful partner in Britain's imperial endeavours. Its charter guaranteed a monopoly of English trade and navigation in Asia and the Pacific. Accordingly, the king's instructions to the 'Governor in Chief' of the colony confirmed that 'every sort of intercourse' between any settlement in New South Wales and China or other European outposts 'should be prevented by every possible means'.[11]

Lord Sydney thought Captain Arthur Phillip the best person to be governor-in-chief. Phillip was well travelled and acknowledged as a 'humane' and 'resolute' servant of the king.[12] In May 1787 they were ready to sail. The plans and preparations had not been kept secret. On the contrary, interest was so high that several of the principals signed contracts for the publication of their journals. The name Botany Bay had gained currency in the popular mind and would remain synonymous with permanent exile for decades to come. In song and broadside it was a place of both misery and hope. One of the earliest verses, written five months before the fleet sailed, conjured up images of a paradise in which a bountiful nature offset the inequities of civilisation. At Botany Bay the convicts would find:

> Food that's as good as heart can wish,
> Soon may be there acquir'd,
> Finest of FOWL, and sweetest of FISH,
> What can be more desir'd?
> Labour-apart- where every day
> Nature is kindly giving,
> Plenty to have, and nothing to pay,
> That is the land to live in! …[13]

The fleet sailed on 13 May. The world was becoming small as Europe's trade routes multiplied. Leaving the Canary Islands, David Collins, a marine officer of some eight years' experience, noted that 'the track which we had to follow was too beaten to afford us anything new or interesting'.[14] At the beautiful harbour town of Rio de Janeiro they took on orange seeds and banana plants. At the Cape of Good Hope Phillip bought more seeds and plants to 'introduce to the new settlement' – pear, apple, strawberry, quince and oak. Cattle, horses, sheep, goats and pigs to stock the farms of the new colony were also loaded. Now they were about to leave the 'beaten' track. Collins described it later: 'All communication with families and friends now cut off, we were leaving the world behind us, to enter a state unknown'.[15] The ships sailed again on 12 November.

The fleet split up. Phillip went ahead in the *Supply,* accompanied by three transports full of male convicts whom he intended to set to work immediately. Hunter followed in the flagship *Sirius* leading seven other transports, and on 7 January 1788 he sighted the Australian coast, just as 'the journals of the celebrated Cook' had indicated they would. On the morning of 20 January, Hunter and his ships sailed into Botany Bay. Phillip had arrived in the *Supply* two days earlier, followed by the three transports. Forty-eight people had died along the way; of these, all but three were convicts and their children. It was agreed this was better than it might have been.

Cook's cartography may have been accurate but the assessments of the bay based on descriptions from his voyage were not. Relief gave way to disappointment. It was a 'commodious' waterway, as Phillip's instructions had suggested, but it possessed none of the 'other advantages' alluded to. There was little shelter for ships and little water for the settlement. The ground was 'damp and spungy'. Before the ships began to unload their human cargo, Phillip decided to explore the harbours Cook had glimpsed a short way to the north – Port Jackson and, beyond that, Broken Bay. Three small boats made the trip, carried along on a 'mild swell'. Some hours later they entered the heads of Port Jackson. The northern shoreline of the harbour was unpromising but as they followed the waterway southwest they realised its extent and potential. The published account of Phillip's reaction, which was sold in Britain the following year, included one of the enduring descriptions of the place; it was 'one of the finest harbours in the world, in which a thousand sail of the line [warships] might ride in perfect security'.[16]

After two days exploring the harbour's coves, the boats returned to Botany Bay where the convicts were still aboard their transports. As the British prepared to leave for the northern harbour, two French ships appeared. They, too, had been guided to the bay by Cook's extraordinary charts and anticipated a British settlement already established. Instead, the First Fleet was hastening to the other unexpected harbour. The conditions as they exited confirmed Phillip's decision to abandon the bay: the 'wind blowing so hard we cannot get out', wrote a desperate Lieutenant Ralph Clark. They left behind the French ships, some felled trees and a sawpit. The people of Ka-may, upset at the destruction of their forest, were pleased to see them go.[17] It was a time of surprises all round. The very first thing the surgeon George Worgan wrote in his letter and journal account of the settlement was: 'Dear Richard. I think I hear You saying, "Where the D--ce is Sydney Cove Port Jackson?"'[18]

'[T]aking possession of Nature'

Phillip choose to make his settlement on a small streamed cove some two hours row down the harbour on the southern shore – quite secure from surprise attack. It was not the only place with freshwater but Phillip thought it the best. The creek, later named the Tank Stream, entered the cove off to one side and there was a beach and rocks near its mouth. On either side the shore sloped into the water with patches of sand between rocks. The cove was deep enough to allow ships to be unloaded close to shore. It was the place the Gadigal had known as Warrane. Phillip named it Sydney Cove, after the home secretary who had championed the expedition and his own appointment as governor. When a makeshift observatory was set up on the western point this became Point Maskelyne in honour of the astronomer royal. Ultimately it would bear the name of the young lieutenant who worked there – William Dawes. The other side was simply Cattle Point, for that was where the livestock were coaxed ashore. They stayed until they had 'cropped the little pasturage it afforded' and were then herded to the next little bay along – the ceremonial ground the Aboriginal people called Woggan-ma-gule and the colonists renamed Farm Cove.[19] To the west, Tumbalong became Long Cove and later Darling Harbour.

The shore was heavily forested. The trees came down so close to the deep water that David Collins wrote 'every man stepped from the boat literally into a wood'.[20] Those on the foreshore were probably swamp oaks, their needle-like foliage resembling pine trees from Europe. There was the tall swamp mahogany, with its dark leaves and thick coarse bark. There were angophoras and bangalays. Taller hardwoods such as the blackbutt could be found farther back along the valley of the stream, and among these were turpentine trees. The shaggy paperbarks were flowering. Bangalow and cabbage palms added to the diversity of the foliage. Scattered throughout the wood were smaller trees and shrubs. These included grevilleas, acacias and the blueberry ash, whose delicate perfumed flowers may still have been blooming in late January.[21]

Ralph Clark was delighted with the new prospect. It eclipsed Rio de Janeiro and all other harbours. To his beloved wife Betsey, embodied in his journal, he wrote, 'blessed be to god that we have got Save to ane Anchor in one of the finest harbours in the world – I never Saw any like it – the river Thames is not to be mentioned to it and that I thought was the finest in the world'.[22] Surgeon White was just as impressed: 'Port Jackson I believe to be, without exception, the finest and most extensive harbour in the universe, and at the same time the most secure, being safe from all the winds that blow.'[23]

Refuge was understandably important after such a long voyage but the uncertain newcomers also responded to the harbour's appearance. As he moved slowly up the south arm on 26 January, Surgeon Arthur Bowes projected elements of an English landscape garden upon the scenery. Its varied features and contours were picturesque whereas the 'awful' rocks and headlands inspired awe in the manner of the Sublime. Nature had achieved here, with water and forest, what the best gardener might only dream of contriving:

the finest terras's, lawns, and grottos, with distinct plantations
of the tallest most stately trees I ever saw in any nobleman's
grounds in England, cannot excel in beauty those w'h nature
now presented to our view. The singing of the various birds
amongst the trees, and the flight of the numerous parraquets,
lorrequets, cockatoos, and macaws, made all around appear
like in enchantment; the stupendous rocks from the summit
of the hills and down to the very water's edge hang'g over
in a most awful manner from above, and form'g the most
commodious quays by water, beggar'd all description.[24]

The newcomers had already begun clearing the 'stately trees'. David
Collins witnessed that with an eye for the historic and an acute
awareness of beginnings and endings. His contemplation of the moment
also contained some Romantic regret, as noise replaced silence and vice
threatened nature's purity. He was reminded of Milton's *Paradise Lost*.
He wrote of 'the rude sound of the labourer's axe, and the downfall of
its ancient inhabitants'. The 'stillness and tranquillity' gave way 'to the
voice of labour, the confusion of camps and towns'. Collins hoped that
the convict minds might be reformed so that 'on taking possession of
Nature … we might not sully that purity by the introduction of vice,
profaneness, and immorality'.[25]

That evening Phillip had the Union Jack run up a newly erected
flagstaff and drank to the health of the king with his officers and men.
The following day, 27 January, there was more clearing, and tents were
set up by the male convicts. From his vantage aboard the *Friendship*,
Ralph Clark thought these looked 'prety [*sic*] amongst the Trees'.[26]
Even before a plan was drafted, the outlines of a town were drawn
upon the ground itself. In the absence of real enclosures these served
also as figurative walls: 'the provost marshall, aided by the patrole, had
orders to take into custody all convicts that should be found without
the lines', noted Surgeon White on the second day.[27]

The forest and the harbour were the effective walls of this open-
air prison. The lines were the first part of Phillip's attempt to imprint

'order and useful arrangement' upon a 'savage coast', but the cove's topography played a part in the intended and actual layout of his settlement. A hospital was placed on the west side, where it attracted fresh air. The marines were also positioned there, facing east down the harbour and any threats that might enter. Their encampment was close to two vital food stores. Any piece of terraced land that could usefully accommodate a tent or hut was considered. Most of the male and female prisoners were put on the western side, a place that would be called the Rocks. The remaining convicts, the governor's temporary accommodation and other officers were situated on the eastern slopes with the commissary store.[28]

The landscape itself was also quickly turned to the primary purpose of delivering instruction and discipline. The first church service was held under a 'great tree' by Parson Richard Johnson. On 11 February the convict Thomas Hill was found guilty of stealing a biscuit and exiled for a week to the rocky island near the mouth of the cove that the Gadigal called Mat-tew-na-ye and the newcomers would name Bare Island and then Pinchgut. A second trial, on 27 February, found Thomas Barrett guilty of stealing from the public store and sentenced him to death. In the absence of a gallows, the 'fatal tree' from which he was 'launched into eternity' was a living specimen growing 'between the male and female convicts Camp'. Three months later that tree, or another of similar usefulness, served the dual purpose of gallows and whipping post: 'A Convict was executed for robbing a Tent & some other Convicts who had been guilty of Theft, were flogged at the Tree while the other was hanging over their heads, to endeavor if possible to strike these abandon'd wretches with terror.'[29]

In March more lines were marked out for later development.[30] There was still a great deal of clearing to be done. Drawing upon planning models for Greenwich on the River Thames and Rio de Janeiro, Phillip envisioned a wide street running from the mouth of the Tank Stream as it opened into the southwest corner of the cove, back up to the permanent governor's house on an elevated site. Some 70 metres above the water, this would command 'a capital view of

Long Cove [Darling Harbour]' and, conversely, be the primary focus for ships moored in Sydney Cove. Phillip never resided on this site but gardens laid out in front of the 'temporary' building to the east extended down to the waterfront, creating a similar, if less grandiose, impression. The small tent observatory, erected to record the passage of comets, also established the local time so critical for navigational calculations. The new settlement was, thereby, drawn 'into the world' of European sailing routes.

The first wharf was quickly built directly below the governor's house on a small protuberance jutting out to the east of the stream mouth. A second was later positioned along the straight western shore to service the hospital. They were almost certainly the first artificial structures placed in the harbour. Their vertical supports were quite unlike the uneven and mainly horizontal surfaces that occurred naturally on rocks and the occasional fallen log along the foreshore. They had the potential to host animals and plants not otherwise found at the water's edge, species that might arrive encrusted on the bottom of ships. The wharves signalled the beginning of fundamental ecological change in the harbour.[31]

Phillip's first home was an elaborate tent. With a timber frame, it could support some of the 'squares' of window glass imported for more substantial dwellings, but the tent leaked and let in the wind. The marines' tents were open to 'spiders and vermin'. Soon the foreshore and forest gave up materials for other, more or less permanent, structures. Cabbage palms were easily felled, their soft trunks used for walls and their foliage for roofs. In a cove to the east, which the Gadigal called Kogerah and the colonists would know simply as Rushcutters Bay, there were rushes that could be cut and thatched. The swamp oak made good shingles. The thin trunks of the acacia were cut and combined with mud to become the wattle-and-daub walls for the huts that sheltered most of the population. That conditions were crude and confronting was clear from the letter of one anonymous but highly literate female convict:

> I take the first opportunity that has been given us to acquaint
> you with our disconsolate situation in this solitary waste of
> the creation … the inconveniences since suffered for want of
> shelter, bedding, &c., are not to be imagined by any stranger.
> However, we now have two streets, if four rows of the most
> miserable huts you can possibly conceive of deserve that name.
> Windows we have none, as from the Governor's house, &c.,
> now nearly finished, no glass could be spared: so that lattices
> of twigs are made by our people to supply their places.[32]

Clay found back beyond the valley about a kilometre from the cove
was turned into bricks, using a mould that had been brought out from
England. The convict James Bloodworth supervised that operation.
Female prisoners were sent to Cattle Point to gather shells, which were
burned down for lime mortar. The sandstone upon which all else sat
was quickly appreciated for its structural qualities and plasticity but its
widespread use was still years away. Surgeon Worgan wrote:

> Here is plenty of Materials for the Mason & Stone-Cutters
> to practice their art on; and they speak very highly of the
> Quality of the Stone, as being well-adapted for Buildings. As
> a Cement for these Materials, Nature has provided a whitish
> Marl, which, the Masons think will answer tolerably well; if
> it should not, they have no resource but in burning Oyster, &
> Cockle Shells, for no Stone has been yet discovered that will
> do for Lime.[33]

The 'whitish marl' was the clay that the local Gadigal people and
others used for body paint. Smeared on the outside walls of the huts it
would give the settlement a whitewashed appearance.

Extraction was one way to take possession of nature; observing and
collating was another. To describe and relate plants and animals brought
those organisms within a framework of European understanding.
Both Phillip and Surgeon White had committed to publishing their

accounts of the settlement before leaving England. There, interest in natural history was high among the wealthy and learned. When natural wonders were combined with travel narratives and the exoticism of the Pacific and Antipodes, book sales were assured. Phillip's published account listed 453 subscribers and White's *Journal of a Voyage to New South Wales with 65 Plates of Non-descript Animals, Birds, Lizards, Serpents, Curious Cones of Trees, and Other Natural Productions* had 288, many of whom ordered multiple copies.

White's book became, for a time, the standard reference on Australian natural history.[34] He had arrived with some expectation of what might be encountered. There were, for instance, some one hundred Australian bird species already known in England as a result of Cook's voyage.[35] In April 1788 White could compare his own observations with the descriptions of the 'King's Fisher', 'Banksian Cockatoo' and 'Blue-bellied parrot' in John Latham's *General Synopsis of Birds*, published between 1781 and 1786. The engravings and descriptions in the published accounts of both White and Phillip included some of the harbour's many fish species. The 'Old Wife' was compared with a fish listed in Francis Willughby's 'Icthyologia': *De Historia Piscium* published in 1686. The Port Jackson shark was described and accurately drawn, possibly from a specimen sent to England. 'Watt's Shark', the spotted wobbegong, was thought to be 'a species which has hitherto escaped the researches of our Icthyologists'. The monstrous, bearded creature which appeared in Phillip's book suited the description that accompanied it. This shark was

> supposed to be full as voracious as any of the genus, in proportion to its size; for after having lain on the deck for two hours, seemingly quiet, on Mr. Watts's dog passing by, the shark sprung upon it with all the ferocity imaginable, and seized it by the leg; nor could the dog have disengaged himself had not the people near at hand come to his assistance.[36]

However, the nature encountered around the harbour came to frustrate more than it fascinated. The 'labourer's axe' was quickly blunted by the swamp oak and red gum, and the timber itself was often 'refractory' and apparently rotten in the middle. Summer and autumn thunderstorms had been frightening and almost apocalyptic in their violence. The soaking rains penetrated the shelters and turned the cleared land to mud. Having observed the effects of the felling, Phillip followed up with the first attempts at environmental protection. A 15-metre exclusion zone was established around the Tank Stream in an attempt to protect its clear water. The plants and seeds collected at Rio de Janeiro and the Cape were sown in front of the governor's house. The sight of favourite and familiar species growing in a new garden brought some optimism: 'we soon had the satisfaction of seeing the grape, the fig, the orange, the pear, and the apple, the delicious fruits of the Old, taking root and establishing themselves in our New World'. But despite the rain, the plants withered in the summer heat and sandy soil.[37] Scurvy and dysentery spread as fresh food became scarce.

While it had been assumed that agriculture would underpin the settlement's self-sufficiency, there was also an expectation that the bounty of the sea would help. Fishing equipment was duly loaded alongside the saws, ploughs, grindstones and other 'utensils' that were purchased for the colony. Doubtless, the accounts of the prolific fish stocks at Botany Bay that flowed from Cook's voyage informed this assumption. Suitably equipped, the Europeans lost no time exploring the piscine potential of the harbour. For a while the expectations were realised: summer and autumn are good seasons for fishing in Port Jackson. On 27 January Surgeon John White noted that the '[t]he boats sent this day to fish were successful', and they went out regularly after that.[38] The work was not without its dangers. Lieutenant William Bradley wrote the following month that 'We found Fish plenty altho' the Harbour is full of sharks.' The pickings were easier on the foreshore: 'there is a great quantity of shell fish in the Coves that have mud flats at the bottom, Oysters very large'.[39] This was probably the mud oyster.

WATTS'S SHARK.

Published Nov. 2, 1789, by J. Stockdale.

Front View of the Mouth the size of Life.

British readers were able to see and read about the fauna
of Sydney Harbour within two years of colonisation.
The London-based engraver Peter Mazell produced this
likeness of a Wobbegong shark, he labelled 'Watt's Shark',
for the 1789 account of Phillip's voyage.

Image courtesy of the State Library of South Australia

Marine Captain Watkin Tench was delighted with the seafood pulled
from the water:

> I shall not pretend to enumerate the variety of fish which
> are found. They are seen from a whale to a gudgeon. In the
> intermediate classes may be reckoned sharks of a monstrous
> size, skait, rock-cod, grey-mullet, bream, horse-mackarel,
> now and then a sole and john dory, and innumerable others
> unknown in Europe, many of which are extremely delicious,
> and many highly beautiful. At the top of the list, as an article of
> food, stands a fish, which we named light-horseman [snapper]
> … No epicure in England could pick a head with more glee
> and dexterity than they do that of a light-horseman.[40]

But just as with the land around it, the harbour came to disappoint. As winter arrived, the water turned cold and the fish either left or found deep holes away from the seine nets. Tench was despondent: 'fish, which our sanguine hopes led us to expect in great quantities, do not abound. In summer they are tolerably plentiful, but for some months past very few have been taken.' Ironically, the bay they had abandoned was a better fishing ground than Port Jackson. Tench noted grimly that the French sailors who arrived at Botany Bay as the British were weighing anchor had caught as many as two thousand 'grouper' and 'light horseman' in a single day.[41]

From the first days of disembarkation, Phillip hoped that 'fish and other fresh provisions' might combat the scurvy that was spreading 'with a virulence which kept the hospital tents generally supplied with patients'.[42] But the disease continued to spread. There was very little vitamin C left in what remained of the fruit and vegetables obtained at Rio and the Cape. Convicts and marines alike suffered from vitamin deficiency and the difficult task of building a settlement was magnified by the physical and psychological effects of illness.

In the absence of a trained botanist, John White and the other medical officers foraged for fresh food and medicines in the forest around the harbour. Paperbark leaves were used for tea and as a remedy for scurvy. Surgeon Denis Considen wrote to Joseph Banks in November 1788, noting that 'an infusion' of leaves from these members of the myrtle family 'was a mild and safe astringent for the dysentery'.[43] These became known collectively as tea trees. Surgeon Worgan sampled the fruit of a 'small Fig, and Berries of unknown, species'.[44] This may have included the small creeping native sarsaparilla, which was used as a 'sweet tea'. There were attempts to harvest the wildlife. In February 1788 an emu was shot and brought into the settlement. John White dissected the bird, made some notes on its physiology and then ate it: 'The flesh of this bird was very good, and tasted not unlike young tender beef.' The animals were, however, 'exceedingly shy' and 'faster than a greyhound'.[45] The kangaroo was even more evasive. The female letter-writer who wrote home with her piteous description of convict living conditions also outlined the diet that had evolved over nine months: 'our kangaroo rats are like mutton, but much leaner; and there is a kind of chickweed so much taste like our spinach that no difference can be discerned. Something like ground ivy is used for tea; but a scarcity of salt and sugar makes our best meals insipid.'[46] As unappetising as this obviously was, it was probably healthier than the diet of dried pork, rice and flour that was the staple for the colonists for several years to come.[47]

John White accompanied Governor Phillip on excursions around the harbour in search of land that might support crops. In April of the first year they endured both cold and mosquito attacks while moving through various landscapes, from coastal heath to plateaus of blue gum forest, on the north shore. White's description of the country around Middle Harbour mixed a Romantic appreciation of the Sublime with the practical stoicism required of the coloniser: 'Here in the most desert, wild, and solitary seclusion that the imagination can form any idea of, we took up our abode for the night, dressed our provisions, washed our shirts and stockings, and turned our inconvenient situation to the best advantage in our power.'[48] Failing to find any arable land, they made their way back to the main harbour where a waiting boat carried them down to Sydney Cove.

Shortly afterwards, Phillip and his surgeon took a boat west up the estuary. They landed at a place called Arrowanelly by the local Wangal people and Homebush by a later colonist. White described country 'covered with enormous trees, free from underwood'. They explored a branch of the river 'along the bank of which the grass was tolerably rich and succulent, and in height nearly up to the middle, interspersed with a plant much resembling indigo'. Although they encountered no Aboriginals, their presence was obvious with trees and grass still burning in the aftermath of hunting. The party continued west in their boats until 'the tide ceased to flow; and all further progress for boats was stopped by a flat space of large broad stones, over which a fresh-water stream ran'. From a large hill they sighted the hazy blue mountains to the west that would be a psychological and physical barrier to the coastal settlement for nearly 30 years.[49]

Phillip was conscious of the diminishing prospects around the cove and came to regret his decision to establish the colony there. 'Had I seen the country near the head of the harbour I might have been induced to have made the settlement there,' he admitted in a later despatch to England.[50] In September 1788 he had decided to do just that. The colony's second town was initially named Rose Hill and then Parramatta, a reference to an Aboriginal word for the eels that thrived in the shallow estuary. Cultivation began there at the end of the first year and a second residence for the governor was erected in 1790. A year later two-thirds of the hungry European population were living at Parramatta or on distant Norfolk Island, which had been tentatively settled shortly after the first arrival. In the lower harbour, nature continued to confound and it seemed the settlement at Sydney Cove might wither like the seedlings that had been planted in the first summer. At the end of 1791 Watkin Tench wrote of it: 'This place had long been considered only as a depot for stores. It exhibited nothing but a few old scattered huts and some sterile gardens. Cultivation of the ground was abandoned, and all our strength transferred to Rose Hill.'[51] Taking possession of nature, at least around the harbour, was harder than David Collins could have imagined.

'Fish they always accept very eagerly'

Taking possession was made difficult for another reason: the place was already occupied by the Gadigal, Wangal, Gamaragal and others. The colonial project had been devised without a clear understanding of how many people lived in Botany Bay, let alone Port Jackson. Accounts from Cook's voyage suggested there were not many. And so Phillip's instructions simply proclaimed him governor-in-chief of a territory that stretched from South Cape to Cape York and halfway across a continent as yet unexplored. He was to establish an 'intercourse with the natives' that might be encountered and 'conciliate their affections'.[52]

David Collins explained the British claim to the land by reference to the 'right of discovery' established when Cook sailed up the coast in 1770.[53] That justification was predicated on an understanding that the land was empty or unowned. The occupants of the *Endeavour* had clearly observed people, or the evidence of their presence, all along the Australian coast, but Enlightenment philosophers such as John Locke maintained that tenure was established only when labour was 'mixed' with the land by way of agricultural activity or construction.[54] Both Joseph Banks and James Matra were, therefore, able to dismiss the relevance and rights of the local people because their saltwater culture was grounded in a 'state of nature' which apparently held land and sea in a common ownership without permanent settlements. The country's 'few black inhabitants', wrote Matra, '... knew no other arts than such as were necessary to their mere animal existence, and [were] almost entirely sustained by catching fish'.[55] If cultivation were known inland, Banks argued, surely the coastal people would have imitated the practice. Instead, it was the sea that was 'universaly found to the cheif source of supplys to Indians ignorant of the arts of cultivation [*sic*]'.[56] These assumptions were all implied in Collins's description of that first day of clearance around the cove. Europeans were 'taking possession' by shaping the land. The silence of the forest confirmed its effective emptiness. New South Wales was *terra nullius*.

Some doubts about the validity of this position may have begun entering Phillip's mind even before his company started pegging their tents at Sydney Cove. As he explored the waterway on 23 January 1788, Phillip passed the land of the Gayamaygal people on the north side just inside the harbour. Twenty men 'waded into the water unarmed' to inspect the boat and receive gifts. Their 'confidence, and manly behaviour' impressed the governor and prompted him to name the place Manly Cove. When he and his men came up on the beach to prepare a meal, the local people were, not surprisingly, very curious. If they had heard stories of the 'devils' and human 'oppossums' who had visited Kay-may (Botany Bay) to the south a generation earlier, they were not obviously frightened by this reappearance. Phillip's Enlightenment sensibility was such that he responded by giving a graphic lesson in territory, boundaries and British manners. He 'drew a circle round the place where the English were, and without much difficulty made the natives understand that they were not to pass that line; after which they sat down in perfect quietness'. It was 'proof how tractable these people are, when no insult or injury is offered, and when proper means are to influence the simplicity of their minds'.[57]

That interaction, and another preceding it at Camp Cove just within South Head, set a pattern for encounters between the newcomers and the harbour clans. The foreshores were the stages upon which the dramas of contact and then negotiation were acted out. It was hardly surprising: beaches and coves were the natural meeting places between marine peoples. They were open places where people could be easily seen and situations assessed. They were the first point of contact in a cultural and natural landscape so dominated by the presence of the harbour.

Aboriginal people were encountered repeatedly on the various explorations of the waterway that began within days after arriving. In August of the first year, Phillip set off with John Hunter and others determined to conduct a water-borne count of the local population. The flotilla of two longboats, a cutter and gig spread out and sighted 137 men, women and children and 67 canoes. Hunter knew that this was a fraction of the total, 'for I have seen in one part of the harbour more than that number'.[58] Phillip would conclude that there were nearly fifteen hundred people from Botany Bay to Broken Bay and, significantly, that these people lived in defined territories.

Phillip and the other officers had quickly appreciated the significance of seafood for the harbour clans. 'Fishing,' remarked Tench, '... seems to engross nearly the whole part of [their] subsistence.'[59] With that revelation there developed a strategy to 'conciliate' the clans and deal with the reality of a resident Aboriginal population not accounted for in the governor's instructions. Around the harbour, baubles and tools were handed over, but it was fish that became the most frequent currency for exchange and an important point of

Aboriginal people no doubt had mental maps of the harbour but John Hunter's *Plan of Port Jackson New South Wales* is probably the first image of the entire waterway. It was drafted in the first year of British colonisation. The map's accurate charting of shorelines and water depth is evidence of the European determination to measure and record landscapes so that they might be put to a 'rational' use. The plan was published in John Stockdale's 1789 book *The Voyage of Governor Phillip*.

Rex Nan Kivell Collection, National Library of Australia

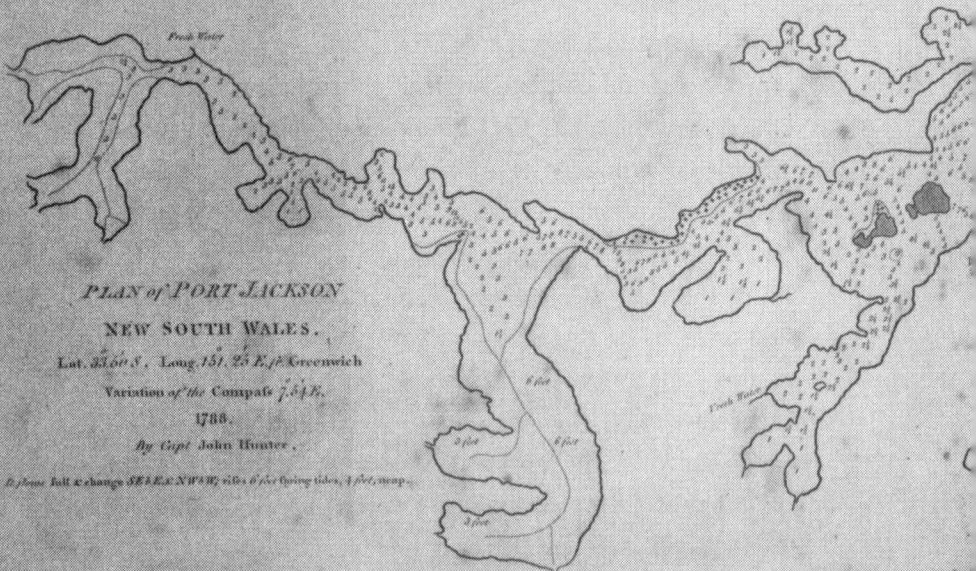

Fresh Water

PLAN of PORT JACKSON

NEW SOUTH WALES.

Lat. 33.50 S , Long. 151. 25 E. ʳ Greenwich

Variation of the Compass 7.54 E.

1788.

By Capt John Hunter .

It flows full & change SEsE & NW&W; rises 6 feet Spring tides, 4 feet, neap .

Fresh Water

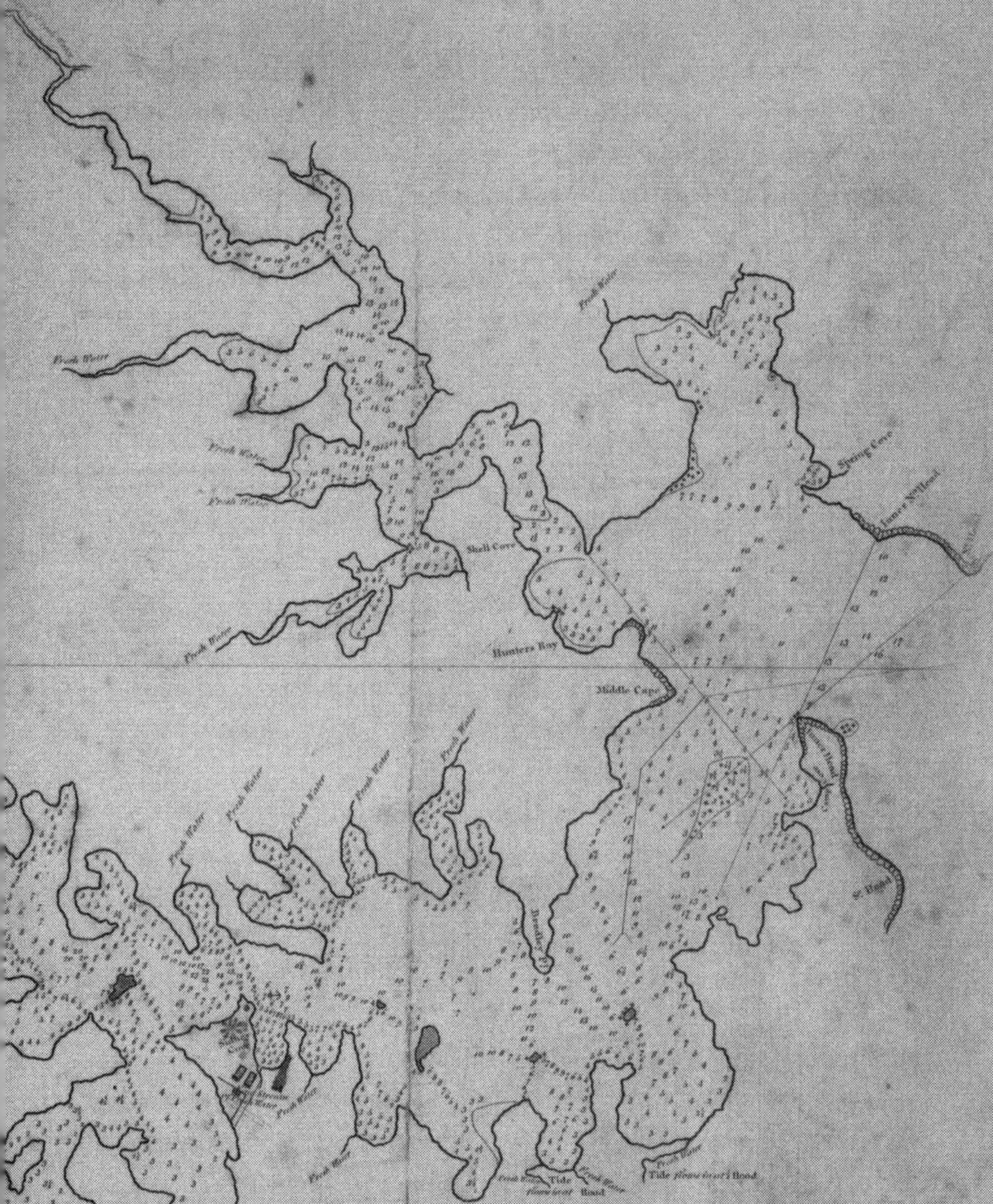

Fresh Water

Fresh Water

Fresh Water

Fresh Water

Shell Cove

Hunters Bay

Middle Cape

Spring Cove

Fresh Water

Tide flows to
Road

Tide flows to
Road

Tide flows to ... Head

Miles.

common interest. Doubtless that would have been the case in Botany Bay had the Europeans stayed there. The colonists had come prepared for diplomatic exchange and Aboriginal people had a well-established system of tribute and trade. Aboriginal people were present at the first of the harbour hauls and their assistance was 'rewarded' with a share of the catch. They were apparently pleased and satisfied with the transaction.[60] The local people showed 'strong marks of distaste' when offered pork and threw away the bread they were given, but 'Fish,' noted Phillip, 'they always accept very eagerly.'[61]

The governor-in-chief soon passed orders forbidding the appropriation of the fishing tackle and canoes that were routinely left around the foreshore by their Aboriginal owners. Theft of equipment was rare among the harbour clans and their honesty impressed the governor. Phillip's orders, however, were largely ineffectual among the convicts and marines and the easily procured fishing spears were traded among the Europeans, both for personal use and for the souvenir trade back in England. Watkin Tench was particularly conscious of the impact of the latter. He made the extraordinary observation that each 'addition to the cabinet of the virtuosi, from this country, had wrung a tear from the plundered Indian'.[62]

The movement of goods was not all one way. Fishing gear was willingly exchanged for hatchets and when they were introduced to the pleasures of European barbering, Aboriginal men gave fish in return for a clean shave. In May 1788 Bradley wrote that 'Several Canoes came down the Harbour & passed within the Ship, some of the Men came alongside we gave them some fish & several other things, they were much pleas'd & gave us some Oysters in return, these people seem'd to suffer much from the Cold.'[63] These were either Gadigal people who had been fishing nearer the Heads or men from one of the north shore clans. They were satisfied with the transaction because there were not many fish around at the time. That same month Bradley observed another group from 'some of the Coves down the Harbour'. They were 'friendly' but 'seem'd to be very badly off for food not having any Fish'. Bradley's boat stopped at another cove where they met an 'Old Woman with a Child' and some men who 'had two fires under a very large hollow rock'. Neither they nor the Europeans could find any fish. The Aboriginal people 'were most of them chewing a root much like fern' while continuing the vigil for seafood: 'we passed close to two Men on a rock who were so intent upon fishing that they did not notice us, nor did they strike a fish the whole of the time that we were near them.'[64]

The scarcity of fish in that first year may have been exacerbated by the severe El Niño Southern Oscillation event, a cyclical climate and sea change that can bring extremes of wet or dry weather and replace cold water with nutrient-poor warm currents. The presence of the Europeans may also have impacted upon fish numbers.[65] Their arrival had suddenly increased the human population, and the continual netting undertaken since January had removed hundreds of fish from the harbour. Aboriginal spears and hooks took out one fish at a time. A single haul of the seine netted dozens. In 1788 the fish were disappearing as early as April. The competition for fish brought on an assertiveness among some of the local people. They simply took from the Europeans what before they had been offered. In July of that first year Phillip reported that a group of about 20 armed men 'came down to the spot where our men were fishing, and without any previous attempt to obtain their purpose by fair means, violently seized the greatest part of the fish which was in the seine.'[66] Phillip condemned their behaviour, but also acknowledged the sense of property and trespass that might have motivated the action: 'they very highly resent the incroachments [*sic*] made upon their fishing places'.[67] He was probably aware, as Tench certainly was, that the Europeans had been quick to identify and appropriate the best fishing spots in the harbour.

The incident recalled an earlier episode in Ka-may where the local people had simply helped themselves to the seine haul. Of that occasion Surgeon White wrote:

> No sooner were the fish out of the water than they began to lay hold of them, as if they had a right to them, or that they were their own; upon which the officer of the boat, I think

> very properly, restrained them, giving however, each of a part.
> They did not at first seem very well pleased with this mode
> of procedure, but on observing with what justice the fish was
> distributed they appeared content.[68]

That was summer and the fish were plentiful. The local people could perhaps afford to indulge the newcomers and their unusual customs. With fewer fish, the strangers were almost certainly overstaying their welcome.

Apparently oblivious to any proprietary right to the catch, White was simply irritated at what he thought were bad manners. Phillip's ambivalence about his own people's trespassing and the reaction it provoked from the local clans went to the heart of the contradictory task that confronted him: to both dispossess a resident people and 'conciliate their affections'. A humane paternalist, he hoped at least he might be able to teach them something that would make 'amends for our encroachments upon their fishing places'.[69]

Relations with the harbour people in the first year had oscillated between 'sociable' exchanges, such as the shaving sessions, and violence. Some of this, like the killing of convict rush-cutters in the cove that provided thatching materials, was probably related to retribution. The dead men, in that instance, had apparently stolen a canoe. On another occasion, two 'Convalescent Convicts' gathering 'greens for the Hospital' were attacked with stones and fishing spears. This happened close to Warrane – Sydney Cove – and may have been prompted by trespass, competition for resources, payback or simply malice. Unable to communicate his intentions and stabilise the relationship, Phillip decided to kidnap some of the local people and use them as mediators.

'[T]hat love for the place of our birth'

In December of that first year two marine lieutenants, Lidgbird Ball and George Johnston, rowed to the beach where Phillip had earlier drawn his educational line in the sand. There they seized two men. One escaped into the water, the other was taken to Sydney Cove and manacled. The captive was immediately surrounded by convicts and marines, few of whom had been close to an Aboriginal person. He was an object of curiosity and fear, for the Europeans had a tenuous foothold in the harbour and stories of attacks and killings in the forest and on the foreshore were commonplace. They named the captive Manly and placated him with meals of seafood and duck. He consumed as many as eight fish at one sitting. In January 1789 Manly was rowed down the harbour 'to convince his countrymen that he had received no injury'. Along the way he told his captors the names of the various coves and headlands. Again, the beach and the harbour were perfect places for liaison and negotiation. At Kay-ye-my, the Gayamaygal assembled and shouted at their clansman as he floated offshore. Manly sobbed and repeated the name 'Weerong' (Warrane) in order, as Tench concluded, 'to inform his countrymen of the place of his captivity; and perhaps invite them to rescue him'.[70]

Manly was not rescued. Instead, he lived with the Europeans for the next four months, learning about their customs and teaching them about his people and his language. He became very close to Watkin Tench, who wrote of him at length in his journal. A breakthrough was made in February when Tench noted: 'His reserve, from want of confidence in us, continued gradually to wear away: he told us his name, and Manly gave place to Arabanoo. Bread he began to relish; and tea he drank with avidity: strong liquors he would never taste, turning from them with disgust and abhorrence.'[71]

In April Arabanoo was taken down the harbour again. This time there was no greeting from the Gayamaygal for, by then, the disease the clans called galgalla had spread through the harbour and few of Arabanoo's people were alive. David Collins recorded his reaction: 'those who witnessed his expression and agony can never forget either ... he lifted up his hands in silent agony for some time; at last he exclaimed "All dead! All dead!"'[72] Bodies were being found around the harbour for months afterwards, 'in excavations of the rock, or lying upon the beaches and points of the different coves which they had been in'.[73] Arabanoo contracted the disease himself and died in May. He was buried in the governor's garden surrounded by the struggling orange and lemon trees. Phillip was in attendance.

The Europeans were genuinely appalled by the impact of the disease, but the awful reality of the epidemic was that it halved the Aboriginal population and facilitated the dispossession that the success of their project depended upon. There were survivors enough, however, to attack wayward colonists and fishing boats. Phillip therefore decided to kidnap another mediator. In November 1789 officers and men were sent again to Manly to carry out the capture. Having learned the efficacy of giving fish, they stopped along the way to pick up their gifts from a passing seine boat. They then proceeded to 'North Cove' and, seeing a great number of natives on the water and the beach, Bradley and his crew held up 'two large fish' – the bait for their trap. The gifts were taken 'eagerly' and a dance ensued. During the brief celebration two men were seized and dragged back to the longboat. William Bradley took the captives back to Sydney Cove and shackled and shaved them. 'It was', he confessed, 'by far the most unpleasant service I ever was ordered to Execute.'[74]

The two captives were from the south side of the harbour – a Gadigal man called Colbee and Bennelong, a Wangal man. Colbee escaped within two weeks. Bennelong stayed for six months. During that time he established a close relationship with Phillip, eating at the governor's house and warming to British comforts. He became aware that his position as mediator might afford him a position of importance among both Europeans and Aboriginals and developed a particular fondness for the red braided marine's jacket he was given.

Bennelong eventually escaped but frequently returned to the European encampment, straddling both cultures. In September 1790 he asked Phillip to build him a house at Sydney Cove and the governor did so at Tubow-gule, the place the colonists had originally called Cattle Point but would soon rename Bennelongs Point.

Bennelong's wife Barangaroo was not so keen on acculturation. A Gamaragal woman, she displayed that clan's fierce independence, refusing to wear the clothes offered by the Europeans and discouraging her husband's fraternisation. The couple spent a great deal of time together on Me-Mel, one of the harbour islands just off the eastern boundary of Wangal territory.[75] But it was a fractious relationship. On one occasion in October Barangaroo destroyed Bennelong's fishing tackle in protest at his continual visits to the cove. To a fisherman it was an emphatic expression of displeasure.

He may have been a mediator, but Bennelong's political acumen also complicated Phillip's efforts to understand and cultivate the harbour clans. The expectations of the local people remained opaque and Bennelong's behaviour could be unpredictable and self-serving.[76] Phillip tried to recruit another man, Bal-loo-der-ry, as a commercial fishermen. In June 1791 Bal-loo-der-ry and others sold and bartered mullet, bream and other species found in the Upper Harbour to the people of Parramatta. But his canoe was stolen while he was selling his catch and he immediately lost interest in the venture. Despite hearing that the thief had been hanged, Bal-loo-der-ry took his own traditional revenge upon the Europeans, spearing and wounding one of the colonists. As a result he was banished from the settlements.

The most dramatic of the encounters between Phillip and the people he was trying to 'conciliate' occurred in September 1790 – again on a beach. It was initiated by arrival of a whale, possibly 'sung' into the harbour from Balls Head. The semi-literate journal of Marine Private John Easty contains a distilled account of a whale's appearance on Friday, 23 July 1790:

> Last night Thos Harp Jn° Wilkins Marines belonging to the
> Detachment
> and Jn° Bates a marine and Mr fargerson
> midshipman belonging the Sirous went Down the harbour a
> fishing and this morning
> being a fishing a whaile over Set the boat
> when the 3 Latter was all drownd
> but Wilkins was Saved by Swiming.[77]

The mishap occurred off Bradleys Head, the point that protruded most into the harbour from the north. The animal was possibly a southern right whale swimming north on its winter breeding migration. It may have entered the harbour to give birth. Curiosity is a characteristic of the species but Daniel Southwell, who also described the event, could not decide whether it was 'mischievous or playful'. It 'no sooner espied the boat than he pursued and never left her till he had overturned and sent her to the bottom'. It must have been a substantial impact for the sunken craft had been a flat-bottomed punt and not easily capsized. The colonists pursued the whale and harpooned it either in reflexive response or retribution. The appearance of the 'monstrous creature' was also a reminder that the harbour was not necessarily a sanctuary from all the horrors of the sea.

The whale escaped but was almost certainly mortally wounded because a carcass, 'in the most disgusting state of putrefaction', was washed up at Manly Cove in early September.[78] Despite its condition, the creature was a windfall for the Aboriginal group there, who may now have consisted of individuals from various clans. Bennelong joined the feast and he invited Phillip to partake. The conciliatory governor arrived but, in the course of approaching one of the Aboriginal men, was speared in the shoulder. It may have been a case of nervousness or possibly an orchestrated payback wounding, planned by a canny Bennelong to settle grievances against the British and enhance his own standing with his people.[79] It took nearly two hours to row Phillip back to Sydney Cove where he could be treated for his wound. He survived and decided that the episode was, indeed, the result of an unfortunate misunderstanding. Relations with Bennelong were restored with the further provision of fish tributes. Later, when the Wangal man complained of the theft of fishing tackle and other items, Phillip ensured the return of these.

The friendship stumbled on for another two years. There were episodes of apparent betrayal and dishonesty and others of 'great service'. Among the latter was the rescue, 'in a squall', of a European fishing party and the salvage of their boat by Bennelong and other Aboriginal men.[80] When Phillip left the colony in December 1792 he took Bennelong and another young man, Yem-mer-ra-wan-nie (Imeerawanyee), with him to England. He also packed a great many specimens of animals, plants and rocks for the delight and interest of the cognoscenti at home. The party boarded the *Atlantic* before dawn. It took two hours for the wind to carry them through the Heads. Bennelong might have made this exit once before on a trip to Norfolk Island. Yem-mer-ra-wan-nie may have seen his harbour from the seaward side while riding the swell in a canoe. But for the first harbour people to cross an ocean this view of a receding coastline must have been profound. The *Atlantic* sailed east to Cape Horn, passing icebergs and enduring bad weather along the way. It proceeded up to Rio de Janeiro and then to England, making landfall by May 1793.

Bennelong and Yem-mer-ra-wan-nie were presented to George III and were probably feted for a time. Many of those they met would still have been more familiar with the name of the original destination, Botany Bay, than Port Jackson. Neither of the men enjoyed London and both pined for home. Even David Collins, who had regarded Phillip's attempt to assimilate the harbour people with scepticism, acknowledged their homesickness in terms of a universal 'love for the place of our birth ... where we have lived and grown from infancy to manhood'.[81] Yem-mer-ra-wan-nie never saw his harbour home again. He died of a chest cold a year after arriving. Bennelong returned in November 1795.

The harbour may not have changed much in appearance but the society that occupied it had. Under the interim governments of Major Francis Grose and Captain William Paterson, at least 8600 hectares of land had been granted to Europeans.[82] Several stretches of waterfront, particularly in the Upper Harbour on the way to Parramatta, were being farmed – much of this in the territory of Bennelong's Wangal people. Aboriginal people were now a common sight on the streets of Sydney town although they were yet to adopt European garb. The forest stream that had once provided the settlement with freshwater had become a filthy drain but the food shortages were less frequent and less acute. The commercial and foreign ship visits begun before Phillip departed had increased in his absence so that, by 1795, the future of the town as a port seemed assured.

Bennelong took pride in the clothes he brought back from England. 'His dress appeared to be an object of no small concern with him,' Collins observed acerbically. But Bennelong's position as a diplomat was largely redundant and his status among his own people was precarious.[83] Barangaroo had died before he left and now Bennelong's new wife abandoned him for another man. The beating he gave the interloper at Rose Bay did nothing to rectify the situation. He hovered around the governor's house but more and more turned to alcohol, leaving the settlement and his clothes behind on trips around the harbour. One of these was to a large initiation ceremony held at Middle Harbour – among the last recorded in the harbour region. Bennelong's house on the point had deteriorated in his absence and was demolished shortly after his return. Decrepit and abandoned, its precious bricks were taken to improve the signal marker erected at South Head.[84] Me-Mel was by now generally known as Goat Island. Had he gone back there, Phillip's old confidant would have shared the place with bothersome livestock exiled from the mainland. Bennelong died on 3 January 1813 and was buried in the riverside orchard of ex-convict brewer James Squire at Kissing Point, some 7 kilometres west of the point that now bore his name. It had once been the territory of the Wallumedegal, the 'snapper fish' clan. With its oranges and open acreage, Squire's property symbolised the successful possession of nature and the dispossession of a people as well as anywhere. But although it was not his country, Bennelong may have simply been grateful of a resting place by the harbour.

THREE

FROM CONVICTS TO COMMERCE

'EVERYTHING THAT
WAS NECESSARY
FOR MAKING THEIR
ESCAPE'

William Bryant was a man of the coast. In 1784 the fisherman from Cornwall had been found guilty of resisting arrest while allegedly in possession of smuggled goods. William probably met the already-pregnant Mary Broad on board the old prison hulk they shared on the Thames. They sailed together on the *Charlotte* bound for Botany Bay. William and Mary spent nine months at sea wondering what new life lay ahead for them. She gave birth to one of the 22 children born en route and named the little girl after the boat that carried them both. Mary too was a native of the Cornish coast, a sailor's daughter who had escaped the noose after assault and robbery, only to find herself on a very different shore.[1] William and Mary were married four days after Phillip's fleet anchored in Sydney Cove.

As one 'bred from his youth to the business of a fisherman', William was a valuable human resource in a settlement on the edge of a harbour and the brink of a famine. He was only one of three fishermen listed among the First Fleet arrivals and the harbour did not give up its bounty easily: 'The universal voice of all professed fishermen is, that they never fished a country where success was so precarious and uncertain,' wrote Watkin Tench.[2] The food William provided could mean the difference between life and death. Nine hundred kilograms of fish, a good month's take, equated to a saving of 225 kilograms of pork from the diminishing public store.[3] William was given extra rations and a percentage of his catch to encourage his productivity. He and Mary and little Charlotte were provided with a hut, specially built. In February 1789 William was caught selling some of the catch and the family lost their privileges. He was flogged but kept his job. The fisherman was, as David Collins ruefully admitted, 'too useful a person to part with'.[4] Others had been hanged, exiled or sent to hard labour for depleting the public store and so the punishment might be considered light. However, the episode, or at least the hardship that followed, convinced William and Mary of the need to escape.

Isolation compounded the effects of hunger and poor shelter. The convict transports had all left by the end of the first year, leaving only the flagship *Sirius* and the *Supply* as reliable links with the outside world. In March 1790 the *Sirius* was wrecked on Norfolk Island and the *Supply* was later dispatched to the disease-ridden Dutch port of Batavia to secure supplies. The harbour was empty of ships. The literate among the desperate colonists already compared themselves with castaway characters from fiction. Four days after news of the shipwreck of the *Sirius* broke in Sydney Cove, one wrote:

> In all the Crusoe-like adventures I ever read or heard of, I do not recollect anything like it … if you was to see with what ardent expectations some of the poor wretches watch an opportunity of looking out to sea, or the tears that are often

shed upon the infants at the breast, you must have feelings
that otherwise you never could have any experience of.[5]

There was momentary relief when the Second Fleet entered the
harbour during June 1790. Collins bemoaned the arrival of elderly
women he thought 'unnecessary and unprofitable' aboard the *Lady
Juliana*.[6] That vessel brought with it more bad news: the large store
ship, the *Guardian,* had hit an iceberg and returned to the Cape of
Good Hope, having lost much of its cargo. The supplies that reached
the cove were offset by three transport loads of sick convicts. The
attrition rate on this disastrous voyage – some 273 people had died at
sea – highlighted the relative success of Phillip's ships. The harbour
foreshores were strewn with corpses as the most recently deceased were
simply heaved overboard. Reverend Richard Johnson wrote: 'some
of these unhappy people died after the ships came into the harbour,
before they could be taken on shore – part of these had been thrown
into the harbour, and their dead bodies cast upon the shore, and were
seen laying naked upon the rocks'.[7] The remaining dead and dying
were rowed ashore to the Hospital Wharf on the west side of the cove.
Collins, who had already witnessed the spread of pestilence among
the clans, thought that no more 'horrid spectacles ... had ever been
witnessed in this country'. The governor ordered that the bodies be
'carried to the opposite north shore' and buried.[8] The response of the
Gamaragal people, who were still living there, is not known.

Phillip was furious. He wrote to the home secretary Lord Grenville,
pointing to the greed of the private contractors responsible for the
passage: 'it would be a want of duty not to say that it was occasioned by
the contractors having crowded too many on board those ships'.[9] But
transportation was a business opportunity. The enterprising master
of the *Lady Juliana* set aside space for trade goods and a shop was
opened on the waterfront in the cove to sell 'articles of grocery, glass,
millinery, perfumery, and stationery' at inflated prices.[10] However,
he misjudged his market and his timing and little was sold. Having
disgorged their human cargoes, the masters of several ships sailed on

to the markets of China, via Norfolk Island, in the service of the East India Company.

Drought-affected gardens yielded little during the remainder of the year and the haul from the harbour did not offset the hunger. 'Fish is by no means Plenty', wrote a miserable Captain William Hill in July 1790, '… should one be Offer'd for Sale, 'tis by far too dear for an Officers Pocket.'[11] There might have been more as summer approached, but then in November a precious fishing boat sank. That was the worst year for the colony.[12]

William Bryant nearly lost himself and his boat in March 1791 when the heavily laden vessel was swamped in a squall. It was only the timely intervention of Bennelong that saved them. Bryant had apparently established a relationship with the Wangal man, or at least with his sister, for she and her children were in the fisherman's boat when it floundered. Possibly she was there to guide him to the best harbour fishing spots in exchange for wind-powered transportation. In any case she was a good swimmer and made it to shore with a child on her shoulders.[13] Within a generation acclimatised colonists would be bathing and diving in the harbour themselves, but swimming was not a skill widely shared by the newcomers – even those possessed of maritime abilities – so it was possible that William was saved by clinging to a bark canoe. Bennelong and other Aboriginal men salvaged the cutter and dragged it up on a beach, along with its precious oars and mast. That 'great service' earned the grudging gratitude of David Collins, and it also kept William and Mary's hopes for escape alive. They had been secreting supplies for their flight for months – a seine net, fishing line, flour, rice, tools and sails. Mary also picked and stored the native sarsaparilla she knew could help stave off sickness. But it was the fishing boat that would carry them to freedom.

Bryant must have continued to sell fish illegally for he had saved enough money to buy a compass, quadrant, a chart and weapons from the master of the Dutch ship *Waaksamheyd*, which had been contracted in Batavia by the master of the *Supply* to deliver provisions and arrived in the harbour in December 1790. William and Mary had, as Marine

Private John Easty wrote later, 'Evrey thing that was nesarry for Making thare Escape'.[14] The night of 28 March 1791 was moonless: ideal for fishing or fleeing. So instead of hauling his seine, William ran to the boat with Mary, their two children and seven other convicts and sailed out of the Heads, past the signal station and lookout that had been built on the southern headland in February. They headed north. There were no vessels in the harbour that could catch the cutter. The *Waaksamheyd* had sailed for England the previous morning with John Hunter and the manuscript of Phillip's journal aboard. The *Supply* had left for Norfolk Island the day before that.

William, Mary, the children and the others made the remarkable trip up the coast and around to Dutch Timor in nine weeks. There the escapees passed themselves off as shipwreck survivors for a time before being found out and imprisoned. William and his son Emmanuel died of disease in Batavia. Charlotte, too, succumbed before Mary was returned to England in June 1792. She was befriended by the lawyer and biographer James Boswell and, with his help, was pardoned in May 1793. In return Mary gave Boswell some of the native sarsaparilla picked along the harbour. He kept it in a packet marked 'leaves from Botany Bay used as Tea'.[15] Mary's remarkable escape elevated her to the status of a minor celebrity and kept 'Botany Bay' alive in the popular imagination as a place of exile and, it might be said, of adventure. The names Sydney Cove and Port Jackson had less currency. Mary's feat also highlighted the power of liberty and freedom within British thinking, and newspapers celebrated the tenacity of the escapees.

Back on the harbour, where the loss of a boat and a fisherman was keenly felt, there was also sympathy and admiration. Watkin Tench followed his journal description of the escape with the confession that 'I never looked at these people without pity and astonishment. They had miscarried in a heroic struggle for liberty after having combated every hardship and conquered every difficulty.'[16] John Easty empathised:

> ... thoughts of Liberty from Such a place as this is
> Enoufh to induce any Convicts to try all Skeemes to obtain it

as thay are the Same as Slaves all the time thay are in this
Country allthough thare times
are Expired for which thay are sentenced
by Law thare is no difference between them and a Convict that
is jest Cast for transportation.[17]

When Matra and then Lord Sydney had suggested sending felons away
– preferably forever – they imagined a system that provided the means
of survival, improvement and happiness.[18] John Easty thought he was
witnessing slavery. For his part, William Bryant was convinced that he
had served his time. Mary just wanted to go home.

The escape of William and Mary was not the first in the early
years of settlement, but it was the most remarkable. They followed in
the wake of John Tarwood and others who, five months earlier, had
somehow made their way down the harbour from Parramatta to South
Head, where they stole a 'wretched weak boat' and sailed off. Tarwood
got as far as Port Stephens, about 200 kilometres up the coast, and took
refuge with Aboriginals there. These episodes highlighted a dilemma
for Phillip and his successors. An open-air prison in a distant harbour
was only secure while the sea served as a moat. This was the case for
most of those 'poor wretches' who daily gazed out to the Heads. For
them, the sea existed as a physical and psychological barrier and its
terrors must have compounded the awful distance between the harbour
and home. But for the desperate, the intrepid and those with maritime
skills, ocean-going vessels promised liberty.

Emancipists took the opportunity to go home afforded by convict
transports heading back via China. Phillip regretted the loss of 'able-
bodied men' but was unclear about what to do with expirees who
demanded and seized their 'liberty'.[19] Some serving convicts headed
off on foot, possibly in search of China, but the majority left by sea,
in stolen boats, as stowaways or deckhands on convict ships. The
creation of a separate anchorage for non-British ships as early as 1789,
in the so-named 'Neutral Bay', did little to stem these departures
after American vessels started arriving in port to refit and offer their

merchandise. Several convicts, including the political exile Thomas Muir who had enjoyed the solitude of Gamaragal land, fled in a Yankee ship called the *Otter* late in the summer of 1796. The penal settlement at Sydney Cove was a porous prison. It leaked like an old longboat.

Conditions there – where rows of unguarded convict huts perched on the ridges and pathways – were the antithesis of the architecture of punishment and reform outlined by the English philosopher Jeremy Bentham in the very year that the Botany Bay expedition was being fitted out. His panopticon, or circular prison, had at its centre an observation tower for permanent surveillance, or at least the illusion of it. Such control of the prisoner was, in Bentham's opinion, far more humane and conducive to reform than the system of exile implemented in New South Wales. He remained one of the most trenchant critics of transportation. The uncertainty entailed in the sentencing, control and future of those prisoners was the very opposite of the bureaucratic and protoscientific penology of Bentham's ideal. 'I sentence to you but to what I know not', declared his imaginary judge, 'perhaps to storm and shipwreck, perhaps to infectious disorders, perhaps to famine, perhaps to be massacred by savages, perhaps to be devoured by wild beasts. Away – take your chance; perish or prosper, suffer or enjoy; I rid myself of the sight of you.'[20]

The harbour prison would not get a convict barracks until 1819. And then it was self-surveillance and betrayal, rather than the all-seeing eye of authority, which foiled the escapes that were continually planned: 'conspiracies to cut out vessels from the harbour, or to effect escape, are frequently made there; but the accumulation of numbers seem rather to have afforded means of timely detection'.[21]

'[N]o wood in this country … will float'

In the year following the Bryants' escape a permanent fishing station was established at South Head to provide food for the sick. A man named Barton was appointed to oversee the operation. He was a ship's pilot and knew the harbour as well as any.[22] Phillip responded more immediately to the escape by tightening up procedures and creating check lists. It was a step along the way to the certainty of penal bureaucracy. Sentries were placed on the wharves at night. The departure of every vessel required the approval of the officer of the guard. A register of those authorised to use the boats after sunset 'for fishing or other services' was to be kept and checked by that officer. No privately built boats could be more than 4.25 metres long – too small, it was hoped, to make another escape by sea at all tempting.[23]

By this time the government gangs had constructed a ferry: a flat-bottomed 'hoy' called the *Rose Hill Packet*, which took people and supplies between Parramatta and Sydney Cove. It was little more than a 'bed of timber' and made its way up and down the harbour in time with the tide. Two other boats had been pieced together from parts brought out 'in frame' aboard the *Supply*. The *Supply* and the *Sirius* had been the means of communication between the colony and Norfolk Island, and beyond if need be, but no interim-sized vessels had been provided, probably because the planners had imagined a single settlement on a bay rather than two or more sites within a harbour and on a river that stretched for 20 kilometres.

In any case, this was a penal settlement not a commercial port. Phillip was compelled to ask repeatedly for ocean-going ships of 30 and 40 tons to be sent out with trained shipwrights to tend them. A vessel finally arrived 'in frame' aboard the convict transport *Pitt* in February 1792. Unfortunately, the space it occupied displaced bundles of new clothing intended for the convicts.[24] With little skilled labour to draw upon, it took 12 months to assemble and launch the ship.

Phillip's instructions regarding the private construction of vessels that could negotiate an ocean were explicit. It was not allowed. This was not so much a precaution against escape as further reassurance to the East India Company. The restrictions subsequently imposed by Phillip on the size of locally built boats suggest there was a demand for harbour craft, if not boats that could travel beyond the Heads. Before the formal issuing of land grants in 1792 and the consequent establishment of farms along the harbour's estuary, the course of everyday life depended upon the harbour. As early as September 1789 David Collins noted that a boat 'belonging to a gentlemen of the settlement' had overturned while returning from 'down the harbour' laden with cabbage trees, presumably for the purposes of building. The harbour was a highway. The colonists, free and convict, were building, operating and trading from the boats that they made for themselves.

Ralph Clark dealt with his homesickness by exploring the harbour in his 'own boat'. He regularly rowed down to the little island he had sown with potatoes, corn and other crops. But the planting of a garden out on Clark Island was no guarantee against theft – it was akin to sowing a garden beside the roadside – and the lieutenant's corn crop was regularly raided. As the harbour clans had yet to develop a taste for European food, the thieves were probably European. On 1 March 1790, before he left for a posting on Norfolk Island, Clark sold his boat for the considerable sum of 10 guineas and a pig. By then there was something of a private fleet on the harbour, part of which was commandeered by the authorities for fishing.[25]

Cook and Matra had placed great hope in the worth of the Norfolk Island pine as a marine timber: a mast made from a single trunk was preferable to one composited from several, and the pines they had seen were tall and straight. Exploitation of these trees, and of the island's flax plants for sailcloth and rope, was the only commercial or strategic imperative in the final 1786 plan to settle 'Botany Bay'. However, on closer inspection the colonists found the trees 'unfit for large masts' and too brittle even for an oar.[26] Instead, the Port Jackson boatbuilders looked to the local forest for their materials. Even there the initial assessments were not good. Surgeon White found yet more evidence for the contrariness of the new land when he experimented with the buoyancy of the native timber: 'Strange as it may be imagined, no wood in this country, though sawed ever so thin, and dried ever so well, will float … it sinks to the bottom like a stone.'[27] While they were mystified by this, the Europeans blamed the poor structural qualities of the timber on the regular burning of the forest practised by the harbour clans. Tench noted that 'more than forty of the choicest young trees were cut down' to find enough useful timber to replace a single mast on the *Supply*.

There was a type of 'light wood' found that was 'excellent for boat building'. Unfortunately, these trees, probably coachwood, were small and scarce.[28] In any case, Daniel Paine, the colony's first specialist boatbuilder, preferred turpentine and stringy bark. He used the curvy limbs of the mangrove trees found in the coves and swamps of the harbour 'for cutting into Boats timbers', as they grew 'in every shape for the purpose'.[29] Paine was particularly fond of the mahogany that grew up on the Hawkesbury River. Recognising the value of this species, John Hunter, who had taken over as governor in September 1795, attempted to curtail indiscriminate clearing by ordering that the 'King's mark' be placed upon specimens useful for 'Naval purposes'. Land grants were issued upon the provision that maritime timber would be reserved for government use.[30] In 1798 the schooner *Sydney* was sent from the harbour to the Hawkesbury to seize the good wood that had been cut for private sale. These logs were used to begin a replacement brigantine for the now-condemned First Fleet ship *Supply*.

Exploration of the southwestern reaches of Broken Bay to the north in 1798 had revealed flood plains along the freshwater Hawkesbury River. The first land grants had been issued there in late 1794, during the interim rule of the lieutenant governors Grose and Paterson between the departure of Phillip and the return of Hunter in 1795. The number of small landholders jumped after Phillip left: from 72 to 213 in late 1795. A handful were newly arrived free migrants, the rest were ex-convicts or militiamen.[31] Arable land was handed out along the banks of the harbour estuary at Kissing Point and Liberty Plains, where sandstone bedrock met shale and the soil was relatively rich and well drained. It was far more attractive than the sandy, rocky waterfront in the lower harbour. Land around Parramatta at the head of the harbour was also being granted. The unplanned occupation of Hawkesbury land, so far from either Sydney or Parramatta, reflected the desperate need for more grain to feed a colony attempting to achieve self-sufficiency. In the absence of roads, these farms were linked to the primary settlement by river and sea. The clearing of the Hawkesbury further stimulated boat-building in Port Jackson.

Daniel Paine was writing in 1795 and 1796 as confidence in local timber was growing. Captain Henry Waterhouse was another enthusiast. He had sailed to Botany Bay and Port Jackson in 1788 with Phillip in the *Sirius*. In 1794 Henry was the commander of the *Reliance* which brought Daniel Paine to the colony, returned Bennelong to his harbour home and delivered John Hunter as the new governor. A naval man with a good eye for commercial opportunities on land, Waterhouse was the first to import merino sheep to the country. Some of these he sold to John Macarthur on whose estuarine estate, Elizabeth Farm, they would begin to multiply and seed the flocks that came to cover the colony in the next century.

Waterhouse was very impressed with the quality of the wood used to repair his decrepit *Reliance* as it lay 'alongside the Rocks in the town of Sydney' in 1796. Both straight and crooked timbers were easily obtained 'close to the Water's edge … through the whole Harbour of Port Jackson'. The planking wood was so hard that nails 'drove in' could not be removed. The timber's essential oils and gums were good for more than medicines and balms, giving remarkable protection against rot. Unlike northern hemisphere naval timbers such as black birch, this wood could survive voyaging in warm and cold waters. Responding to the demand for new sources of naval timber in 1802, Waterhouse wrote about his own observations of the first wood that had been felled around the harbour and his incidental experiments conducted over two tours of duty in the colony. He examined the trunks that had been cut and rolled into the harbour to create the first clearings back in 1788. They had apparently survived a decade in saltwater unaffected: 'Logs when taken up again in 1798, were as sound as when cut down – not the smallest appearance of decay.'[32] The peculiarities of this perverse nature were at last delivering benefits.

The official activity on the harbour occurred in the government boatshed built on the eastern side of Sydney Cove in 1788 and the new yard laid out on the west side in 1797. By the end of that year there were

16 shipwrights, boatbuilders, labourers and watchmen working. These men built a pinnace and other small craft for the *Reliance* and the *Supply*. Repairs were carried out on the boat that came out with the *Pitt*. Several small boats used at the South Head fishery and by the hospital were also reconditioned. The boatyard had been improved further with various sheds and a 'steamer' erected for seasoning planks.[33]

For the settlement up at Parramatta they had also built a 'whaleboat', a long rowing boat often fitted with a sail. This was probably the 'excellent' cedar-and-banksia craft made available to the adventurous surgeon George Bass so that he might explore the south coast while his ship the *Reliance* was being overhauled in Sydney Cove. Bass had proved his 'active disposition' in 1796 by attempting – unsuccessfully – to cross the mountains that confined the settlement to the harbour and hinterland. He had already investigated Botany Bay and the Georges River with Lieutenant Matthew Flinders in an 2.4-metre boat called *Tom Thumb*. A similarly small craft, also called *Tom Thumb* and built in Port Jackson, took Bass into Port Hacking farther south.[34] He would later explore the coastal coal seams at what would be called Coalcliff. In December 1797 Bass and six others took the harbour-built whaleboat down past Point Hicks, the place where James Cook had first sighted the Australian coast. The 1900-kilometre trip took 12 weeks and along the way Bass found Jervis Bay, Shoalhaven River, Twofold Bay, Wilsons Promontory and Western Port. So great were the swells off the southernmost tip of the mainland that Bass thought he was in a strait of water separating the mainland from Van Diemen's Land. He would prove this with Flinders later in 1798 when the pair circumnavigated the island.[35]

In this way the vast colony of New South Wales was slowly consolidated: ships and small boats setting out from Port Jackson naming bays and interesting rivers and claiming distant islands. Bass's discovery – which promised to shorten the trip from Britain's South African Cape colony to Port Jackson – was named Bass Strait in the surgeon's honour by Governor Hunter in 1799. The whaleboat survived for a time as a waterside shrine: 'preserved in the harbour with a kind of religious respect', in the words of the visiting scientist François Péron. A few snuff boxes were made from its keel and treasured as 'relics' by those lucky enough to obtain them. On the French map of Sydney Cove, the position of 'Chaloupe de M. Bass' – Mr Bass's rowboat – was expressly marked sitting below the Rocks. Its inclusion placed it alongside other noteworthy sites, such as the granary, the defensive battery and the governor's house. A fragment of its timber was decorated with a silver band engraved with the details of Bass's discoveries. Hunter's successor as governor, Philip King, presented this to Nicholas Baudin, Péron's commander, in 1802.[36]

It was a poignant gift for a Frenchman. Enacted in a brief moment of peace between the two nations, the act was undoubtedly a gesture of conciliation. King had already extended extraordinary hospitality to the crew of the two French ships – providing fresh food and care for the many suffering from scurvy, and even approving the sale of a locally built schooner to the expedition (the *Casuarina*, so-named after the useful she-oak that lined the harbour's edge). King knew the presence of these ships was a temptation for would-be stowaways and he ordered that a government cutter be rowed round and round the little fleet all the while it was in the harbour. Yet there was suspicion of the French as well. Baudin's ships were sharing the harbour with the *Investigator*, captained by Matthew Flinders and sent to chart the Australian coast in response to the French expedition.[37] With its cartographic inscription, the embellished chunk of wood from Mr Bass's rowboat might also, therefore, have served as a subtle reminder to the French of who had been quick enough to claim the spoils of discovery in 1788.

For his part, Matthew Flinders sailed out from Port Jackson and turned left as Baudin went right and headed south. George Bass's little harbour-built boat still lay near the place where the colony had been declared in January 1788: a memorial to the imperial endeavour and, perhaps, the skill of the local boatbuilders. Flinders continued his circumnavigation around the northern coastline and returned to Sydney's harbour in June 1803. He named the continent he had circled 'Australia'.[38]

'All this vast activity, all this movement of ships ...'

In 1797 the *Cumberland* was the 'largest and best' of the government's harbour-built boats. It was used to transport stores and grain between Port Jackson and the Hawkesbury farms. As a result of this trade, there were some who were outside government employment willing and able to build vessels 'for any person who chose to employ them'.[39] That this private boat-building industry was developing without permission or regulation bothered Governor Hunter, who could foresee more escapes. He ordered all private craft to be taken to the boatyard where Daniel Paine 'cut a number on their stern', which was then entered into a register. The owners were told to whitewash the numbers so they could be easily read from a distance. Unregistered boats were liable to be seized.

In September 1797 Hunter's fears were realised. The prized *Cumberland* was pirated en route to the Hawkesbury by exiled Irish political prisoners They escaped to who knows where. Their feat prompted a spate of similar attempts in private boats – some successful, some not. An exasperated Hunter again tried to regulate the construction and traffic around the harbour. More lists were demanded. Boats that were left at night with their oars and sails aboard were to be scuttled. Anyone going to the Hawkesbury had to show a pass. And the governor expressly forbade 'the building of any boat whatever for the use of private persons'. In a harbourside settlement, however, such an industry was difficult to curtail.[40]

New South Wales was huge but the group of Europeans laying claim to it was tiny. There were, therefore, many more crossed paths and connections between people and events than one might think plausible. The desperate pursuit of the *Cumberland* had taken Lieutenant John Shortland about 170 kilometres north, where he discovered a navigable river and a seam of coal. It was the northern edge of a deposit that continued down under Port Jackson itself to the south coast. The

Hunter, or 'Coal' River, would provide the colony with an early export. Its mines became a place of exile for recalcitrant convicts from Port Jackson. Later, the coal would provide the gas to light the harbour city's lights and then the fuel for its electrical power stations.

For his part, George Bass had come across some survivors of one of the post-*Cumberland* escapes on his way back from 'discovering' Bass Strait. They were on an island far to the south, near Wilsons Promontory. Bass took pity on them but his whaleboat was not big enough for everyone and five of the escapees were left on the mainland to make their own way by land to Port Jackson. The surgeon was as humane as he was intrepid and the moment of parting was emotional. All realised the probable fate that awaited the castaways.[41] The convicts were never seen again.

David Collins attributed this and the other escape attempts to the leniency shown Mary Bryant after her flight and recapture. News of Mary's release in London must have drifted down to Sydney via the shiploads of convicts who had disembarked since 1792. Stories and ideas spread quickly in a culture that was still grounded in a tradition of spoken, rather than written, words. The men whom Bass found in February 1798 may well have been inspired by the Bryants' exploits, but Collins also acknowledged that their escape in October 1797 had been more directly motivated by the relatively recent news of the wreck of the merchant ship *Sydney Cove* off the far south coast the previous February. In this case, the convicts simply hoped they might find the wrecked vessel, salvage it and sail away.[42]

The monopoly of the East India Company and the restrictions of the protective Navigation Acts, which forbade trade between British colonies and foreign ships, were as permeable as the ocean 'walls' of the penal colony. Necessity had forced Governor Phillip and his successors to accept cargoes from visiting American ships, which should not have been selling their wares in a British port. And since 1793 the harbour-side colony had been visited by Bengal-based merchant ships loaded with speculative cargo. The *Sydney Cove* was carrying 32 000 litres of spirits and a variety of other goods sent out by the Calcutta firm of

Campbell and Co. Damaged by storms in the Indian and Southern oceans, the ship limped to an island off the coast of Van Diemen's Land, later named Preservation Island after the incident, where it ran aground. The weather was fierce enough but the ship had probably been weakened by its own flawed technology: the copper sheathing protecting its Indian teak planks against worms reacted with the iron nails securing the timbers. The ship would have leaked regardless of the weather.

The crew survived by eating the greasy meat of the mutton birds that inhabited the island in their thousands. These numbers were matched by the fur seals, adults and maturing pups, which wriggled around the beach and slipped through the water. Seventeen of the crew made the extraordinary trek north to Port Jackson to get help – first by boat, then by land – but only three survived the ten-week ordeal and were picked up in May by a fishing boat venturing south of the Heads. Two boats were despatched in June to rescue the remainder of the crew and bring the cargo to Sydney. Not all of it was loaded and what remained stayed to tempt the desperate men of Parramatta. One thing leads to another. The saga not only motivated the convicts to flee southwards, it probably encouraged Hunter to let George Bass investigate the existence of the strait that he had suspected might provide an alternative to the route south of Van Diemen's Land.

The brothers John and Robert Campbell, of Campbell and Co., understood the vagaries and potential of maritime commerce, having grown up in the Scottish port of Greenock. Their naming of the *Sydney Cove* had about it both an optimism and a geographic precision born of commercial audacity. 'Botany Bay' might do as an imaginative destination in broadsides and songs, but the Campbells knew exactly where this new market was developing. Despite the wreck on Preservation Island, they persevered, encouraged by the possibility of deriving a profit, with a return cargo of fur and oil taken from the seals their stranded men had seen to the south.[43] In any case, a reciprocal Indian trade had already begun in cedar and mahogany, which were cut around the harbour and the Hawkesbury and shipped to Bengal.

Robert Campbell had only recently joined his older brother there. In April 1798 he left Calcutta – in another opportunistically named vessel, the *Hunter*, a deferential gesture to the presiding governor – to investigate Port Jackson for himself and the company. Much would happen over the next decade to transform Sydney Harbour from penal port to an outpost of commerce and Campbell would figure prominently in these changes.

The ship's appearance would have been signalled from the flagstaff on South Head. It was probably guided up the harbour by the Port Jackson pilot, using instructions written by John Hunter himself after his survey of 1788. Once inside the Heads navigation depended upon a familiar eye rather than the sextant and chronometer. 'In coming in with Port Jackson, you will not immediately discover where the harbour is,' wrote Hunter.

> Steer right in for the outer points, for there is not any thing in the way but what shows itself by the sea breaking on it, except a reef on the south shore which runs off a small distance only: when you are past this reef and are a-breast the next point on the same side, you will open to the southward of you an extensive branch of the harbour, into which you will sail.[44]

The headlands and coves were still 'wild and uncultivated' but the forest around the town had gone. Resilient stumps beside the huts and tracks were an indication of what had been. On approaching Sydney Cove, the *Hunter* passed the gibbeted body of the murderer Francis Morgan, which had been hanging in chains from a frame on Pinchgut Island since November 1796 – a spectacle that horrified Aboriginal people but amused the Europeans. Campbell's vessel shared the waterway with many other smaller craft, including canoes. The convict transport *Barwell* was anchored in the cove. Two other ships, the *Buffalo* and the *Porpoise*, were being refitted for colonial service. Within days the *Hunter* was joined by three whaling vessels, the *Cornwall*, *Eliza* and *Sally*. From the lonely outpost of Phillip's years, the harbour was becoming a convenient port of call in an ocean that was getting busier and 'smaller'. As traffic increased, the governor instituted new harbour regulations dictating that no one was permitted to board a new arrival until its 'master had been with the governor and received the port orders'.[45] A register of shipping arrivals followed in 1799.

The settlement that confronted Campbell was also undergoing a building program. High on 'the rocks' above the new dockyard was the recently completed stone windmill, situated so as to catch the harbour wind and process the grain being grown upstream and north on the Hawkesbury. A sandstone granary was being built on the western side of the Tank Stream, not far from the Hospital Wharf. Habitations in this part of Sydney town had appeared somewhat more organically than the official buildings. An assembly of small huts dotted the hillside, connected by winding pathways rather than streets. There were homes, shops, pubs and even a theatre. Seamen lived alongside convicts and emancipists – some had leases, but many did not.

All the houses faced the Heads, the gateway to the world to which the town was increasingly connected after a decade of settlement. While some may have looked out to sea longing for escape, many now looked forward to what the sea might deliver. And for those who had endured months in a transport hold or weeks at sea slaughtering whales, the harbour was the sanctuary it had been to the First Fleeters. As each convict transport arrived, the local people took to the water in small 'bumboats' to tout fresh fish and vegetables and re-establish links with anticipated or unexpected friends and relatives. Transported Irish rebel Joseph Holt remarked upon the reception after he arrived in Sydney Cove on a Sunday morning in January 1800:

> In the course of half-an-hour, fifty boats were alongside; all the robbers, pickpockets, and thieves had plenty of acquaintance, but I did not see a soul to whom I was known … Next morning there were twice as many boats alongside as on the previous day, every one bringing presents to their acquaintance.[46]

It was to the Rocks, also, that the whaling crews went while their foul-smelling ships were in port. The crews' masters and the authorities on land were seemingly powerless to stop their men from indulging the settlement's 'two temptations': alcohol and sex. When these ships sailed, 'the town was freed from the nuisance'.[47]

In 1798, goods imported to augment the supplies held at the commissariat store were channelled through the hands of the officers of the New South Wales Corp and some civil officials who had organised to form a trading cartel. Governor Hunter hoped that Robert Campbell's shipment of 'India goods and a few cows and horses' might be used to break this monopoly. To this end he commanded that it should not be sold until the settlers in the different districts had been given an opportunity to purchase the goods directly through an agent. The monopolists, however, convinced the governor that no proper agent could be found and that they would act in this capacity 'for the general benefit of the whole colony'. Campbell's cargo was duly sold to the cartel of officers and officials.

Farmers had the option of selling their produce to the official commissariat store, from whence those dependent upon public stores were fed and clothed, or trading directly with the monopoly for goods bought by the military and officials using their paymaster's bills. Many chose the latter option. Having exchanged farm goods for imports – often at a highly inflated value – officers sold their newly acquired grain or beef to the government for treasury bills. These two forms of bills, paymaster and treasury, gave them an almost-exclusive access to the hard currency needed to buy the cargoes. It was, for a time, a near-perfect circle. Settlers complained that the spirits bought from the *Hunter* for 8 shillings a gallon (4.5 litres) were being sold for the equivalent of between 20 and 60 shillings.[48]

The English and the Irish had brought with them a love of drinking. Small farmers were particularly keen to exchange their produce for the liquor that was generically referred to as rum. It was consumed in huge amounts, partly to deaden the effects of discomfort and hard work, and thereby it also became currency among the people in the absence of sterling. Hunter was appalled by the economy and culture that developed around grog. The botanist George Caley was more sanguine. In 1803 he rationalised the use of spirits to Joseph Banks: 'As a test, is not the drudgery or laborious work of the great towns in England done by the use of spirits or other fermented liquor?' Caley could not avoid the rum economy. He later paid 5 gallons of the drink for an echidna he hoped to send back to England, but the animal escaped before it could be despatched.[49]

The officers had begun their venture into commerce in 1792 when they chartered the store ship *Britannia*. That vessel had landed a cargo of clothes and food for the government and was supposed to continue on to hunt whales under licence to the East India Company. The winds outside the Heads, however, refused to carry the ship south to where the sperm whales swam, so its captain, William Raven, returned it to the harbour. The officers seized the opportunity presented by the ill wind and contracted Raven to purchase goods and cattle from the Cape of Good Hope on the pretext that the public store could not 'tend to the comfort of themselves and the soldiers of the Corp'. That comfort was increased exponentially when the imported 'Cape brandy' was exchanged for six times its value.[50] The arrangement almost certainly contravened the East India Company monopoly but nothing was done to prevent it. Indeed, Raven and the *Britannia* became regular visitors to the harbour, serving both the government and the officers. For his assistance, William Raven was granted a lease at the Rocks overlooking Sydney Cove.

Although Robert Campbell was compelled to sell his first cargo to the Corp, it must have been apparent to him that the officers' monopoly was not watertight. Emancipist traders were already entering the market as agents and auctioneers. Port Jackson, therefore, was a place that might also accommodate a free merchant. Three months after Campbell arrived, emancipist Simeon Lord purchased the lease of another ex-convict dealer, Shadrach Shaw, at the head of the cove, next to the Tank Stream and the bridge that forded it. Its waterfront situation was evidence that any plan Phillip may have entertained to keep the shoreline there for government or public use was no longer operative. Lord built a warehouse and, in 1803, a four-storey home, the largest in the town. He used local sandstone for the house walls. Two floors were lined with cedar. The ground-floor rooms were given over to business, the others were private. Instead of facing the water, Lord's house overlooked Bridge Street and back up the hill towards Government House, which was somewhat smaller and shabbier than his home. Its deliberate aspect might have reflected deference or hubris.

Lord was partner to two other ex-convicts, Henry Kable and James Underwood. They too would obtain leases in the cove. Kable's was in the Rocks. Underwood's was directly opposite Lord's establishment, on the other side of the Tank Stream. He built a large squarish building with a 'captain's watch' on top – a fenced rooftop walkway looking out to the water. As a boatbuilder, Underwood especially had a connection with the water. But all three men would derive their fortunes from the sea – by harvesting the bounty of seals and whales within it or shipping merchandise across it. These men, and some others, built and operated the colony's first merchant fleet.

Robert Campbell bought a waterfront lease at the Rocks from the convict baker John Baughan and lived in the house with a garden until returning to India in 1799. Before leaving he added two adjoining leases belonging to Henry Waterhouse. It was here that Campbell enjoyed 'East India breakfasts' and the luxury of an 'eastern style of living' – food and furnishings that would become more prevalent in the colony with the consolidation of the India–China trade.[51] It was to here, also, that Campbell returned as the colony's first free merchant to build a wharf-and-warehouse complex sited in an indentation on the foreshore, which became known as Campbells Cove. The wharf was capable of accommodating Campbell and Co.'s huge 'cattle ship', the 1000-ton *Castle of Good Hope,* which in 1803 brought 300 Calcutta cows and 63 500 litres of spirit (of which only 18 000 were landed). Campbell could land livestock, merchandise and barrels of seal and whale oil at his establishment. After the unloading, sulphur was burned to flush out the rats that infested the vessels. Presumably those that were not killed as they attempted to escape the fumes ran ashore to infest the Rocks.

At the 14-year-old Hospital Wharf, by comparison, flat-bottomed lighters were still required for transporting goods and people to and from the shore.[52] Captain James Colnett of the naval ship *Glatton* thought the facility so bad that he disembarked at Campbell's place to avoid 'crawling on all-fours' along the public wharf. Colnett was equally dismissive of the surrounding town, which he likened to 'a miserable Portuguese settlement'.[53] Campbell's home, Wharf House, was, in his opinion, the only 'respectable' dwelling in the settlement. The 19-room colonnaded building was finished with Australian cedar shipped from the Hunter River and furnished with pieces made from Indian teak and Burmese blackwood. Many of Campbell's rugs, linen, silverware and china came from India and the Orient. Peacocks and emus are reputed to have wandered around the gardens.[54] Surrounding this enclave in the Rocks were houses assembled in a 'total absence of order' – a place described as 'the abode of a horde of savages'.[55]

Captain Colnett had set his mind against the harbour colony, and its governor, from the moment he sailed through the Heads and encountered an unresponsive signal station, unmarked shoals and an indifferent pilot. His experience suggests that there might be a gap between the posting of a regulation and its implementation. For Governor King had, in fact, introduced the most comprehensive set of port regulations yet drafted for Port Jackson. The governor tried to balance the functions of a penal colony and commercial port with its own civil society. He told the watermen who now plied the estuary to Parramatta that they had to 'treat the passengers with civility' and keep a 'tight' boat with a spare set of oars should the passenger wish to assist. Security was still pre-eminent and the monitoring of embarkations and arrivals was improved. The position of naval officer was created, a non-military post that primarily involved the collection of duties.[56] The surgeon William Balmain, who had pulled the spear from Phillip's shoulder a decade earlier, was the first to hold the lucrative job which was remunerated by a commission on duties collected.

Between 1801 and 1806 there was an average of 24 ship visits a year to the harbour. François Péron was amazed at the commerce: 'All this vast activity, all this movement of ships gave these shores an air of importance and industry that we were not in the least expecting to encounter on a coast not long since unknown to Europe, and our interest grew with our admiration …'[57] Most vessels were under 300 tons so the arrival of the *Castle of Good Hope* must have been a remarkable sight. Sixteen of the 21 ships that entered in 1801 carried general merchandise, not all of which were intended for colonial consumption. Four American ships passed through to resupply before carrying their cargo on to China, thereby complying with the Navigation Acts and the dictates of the East India Company.[58] There were seal and otter skins from South America, also on their way to Canton. Barrels of whale oil came from the South Seas headed for Britain. Simeon Lord bought a Spanish ship, captured by a British whaler as a war prize, renamed it the *Anna Josepha* in honour of Governor King's wife and used it to ship coal and timber boat spars to the Cape of Good Hope.

Campbell's harbour-side residency exploited a concession in the East India Company monopoly. His own firm's vessels now qualified as 'country ships' and, therefore, could trade within the area bounded by the Cape, China and the Pacific. Others, such as Simeon Lord, had to circumvent the regulations or establish alliances that would allow them to trade legally. Some of these were successful but many failed because of seizure, pirating, shipwreck and fluctuating markets. Nonetheless, the Port Jackson merchants made money by moving local timber, Pacific sandalwood, Hunter River coal, Tahitian pork, South Seas whale oil, Indian rum and British manufactured goods through the harbour on their way to local buyers or markets overseas. That the colony imported more than it exported remained a constant. The colonists were convinced also that the sea itself held resources for exploitation.

Fishing was not an option. The harbour catch was hopelessly unreliable and Governor Hunter had also discounted the possibility of establishing a deep-water – pelagic – fishing industry that could sustain the local population, let alone supply an export market: 'we have no fishing-banks upon this coast like those of the North Sea or Newfoundland', he reported to the Duke of Portland, then home secretary, in 1797. The attempts of one free settler, Mr Boston, to set up a fish curing business had come to nothing.[59]

Rather, when the colonists spoke of 'fisheries' they meant whaling and sealing. Sperm whaling was capital intensive and required large ships that stayed at sea for months. Port Jackson was a useful place for these British and American ships to refit and recruit. As they migrated and calved to the south, 'black whales' – like the southern right that may have tipped over the colonists' barge and fed the Manly clan in 1791 – could be hunted by harbour-based ships. But fur seals best promised to provide an export commodity that would gain credit with the London merchants to fund imports. Seal skins were, in the words of Governor King, 'among the very few natural productions of the country that can be esteemed commercial',[60] and they were sought after in China and then England for use as wearable furs, for leather and for milliners' felt. Seal oil was a lighter, less odorous alternative to boiled-down whale blubber for cooking, lighting, lubrication and soap-making.

The ripples spreading out from the harbour were many and profound. Port Jackson's commercial growth had repercussions for ecologies and communities along the coast and out into the Pacific. The local merchants and shipowners had an advantage of proximity over their far-ranging British and American counterparts. The sealing 'mother ships' were free to return to port or continue on to other islands for the sandalwood or pork trade after dropping men at the sealing stations, often on remote islands. They stayed at the sealing grounds for months of killing. The industry had its human victims as well. Gangs could be left for years or even forgotten. Rival gangs sometimes fought and killed each other. Aboriginal women were kidnapped from Van Diemen's Land and the mainland and taken as 'wives' to these semi-permanent settlements.

William Raven on the *Britannia* had opened up the sealing grounds of New Zealand in 1792 after the first of his visits to Sydney Harbour.

The Australian seal colonies, the existence of which were confirmed in 1797 by the stranded crew of the *Sydney Cove*, were made up of four species: the Australian and New Zealand fur seals, the subantarctic fur seal and the Australian sea lion. They give birth usually to a single pup in the summer months. Seals are weaned around six months old, but the sea lion pups stay with their mothers for as long as 18 months. Five thousand skins and 1600 litres of oil were brought back to Sydney from Cape Barren Island in Bass Strait in 1799 before being shipped off to the profitable Chinese market. In less than six years, between November 1800 and August 1806, 118 721 seal skins came back to Port Jackson, 98 280 of which were then exported.[61] The Bass Strait colonies were seriously depleted by 1810 but new islands and new colonies were being discovered. In that year Campbell's ship *Perseverance* came across huge seal and 'sea elephant' populations on the subantarctic Campbell and Macquarie islands – so-named in honour of the merchant and a new governor. When news of the find broke in Sydney, six ships left immediately for the new territory which, in turn, was soon exploited to the point of collapse.

Robert Campbell had as many as 180 men in his sealing gangs by 1804. At the same time Kable and Underwood employed 63 men,[62] some of them recruited through advertisements in the *Sydney Gazette*. One of these, in late summer 1804, called for 'twenty-four able men, to proceed to the Islands in Bass's Strait upon a Sealing voyage, in the schooner *Governor King* on her return from Hunter's River; also, Two steady, active men, capable of taking the Charge of separate gangs'.[63] The men were typically paid with 'lays', or shares of the takings, an incentive to maximise the kill. Kable and Underwood probably found a good number of their 'able' men in the Rocks area behind the company's warehouse, dock and boatyard. Aboriginal men also joined the crews. The enticement of sailors prompted regulations limiting the amount of alcohol on sealers and whalers to 365 litres per 26 men. The sealing exodus created social problems and difficulties for surveillance of convict escapees. Shipowners were compelled, therefore, to pay bonds of £500 to prevent illegal departures and ensure the support of families left behind.[64]

The seal skins were either air dried or salted for preservation. The latter technique used crystals shovelled up from evaporated harbour water. There was already an industry in place to cater for the need: salt manufacture had been carried out on the foreshores of Sydney Cove, Rose Bay and other locations since 1792 and the product was used mainly for the preservation of pork and some fish. At the Hospital Wharf a man called Miller sold the fish he caught and cured down south at Port Aiken.[65] From 1806 private enterprise became involved to meet the demands of sealing and food preservation. The one-time officer monopolist and now trader and grazier, John Macarthur, set up an evaporation works at Pyrmont, on Cockle Bay. Sixteen hectares of ground were cleared for salt pans at an estate called Newington up the harbour estuary.

The 75-ton schooner *Governor King*, referred to in Kable and Underwood's *Sydney Gazette* advertisement, was the largest of the company's fleet of four. It was built and launched in Sydney Cove, probably under the supervision of James Underwood, in 1803. Two years later the company built the 185-ton *King George*, the largest vessel then constructed in the harbour, 'ship-rigged' with three masts. Campbell's 170-ton *Perseverance* was launched with much ceremony before 'many persons of the first respectability' in January 1807.[66] The ship's name might have been a motto for the business. All were seagoing vessels and all contravened the restriction on boat-building that had been issued by Phillip and subsequent governors up to 1809.

King was keen to open up commerce in general and sealing in particular. Fostering boat-building was an ideal way 'to give every possible encouragement to so beneficial a pursuit'.[67] And while expressing necessary respect for the East Indian monopoly, the governor presumably gave Campbell permission in 1805 to send the *Lady Barlow,* loaded with seal skins and oil, to London, where it was nonetheless seized as an illegal trader. Of all the governors, William Bligh adhered most to the intent of the colonial instructions. Accordingly, he supported the development of a self-sufficient agricultural economy rather than a commercial port. Boat-building fell away after his arrival in 1806 and was not revived until Lachlan Macquarie assumed the governorship in 1810 and the East Indian monopoly was partially dismantled three years later. Then colonial ships of up to 350 tons were granted permission to trade with Britain. The restriction, and the duty on colonial seal and whale products, was lifted completely in the 1820s.[68]

By then the sealing industry had collapsed in the wake of unsustainable slaughter and a glutted market. The southern Australian colonies of seals, sea lions and elephant seals never fully recovered. But the ecological devastation had stimulated boat-building in the harbour and this, in turn, helped the colonists find other things to harvest and sell.[69] When the *Perseverance* sailed in 1813 with the expert Sydney ropemaker Robert Williams aboard, it was looking for flax plants rather than seals. At the desolate Solander Island, south of New Zealand, it found a group of men dressed in seal skins and living off fish and the meat of seals and sea birds. They were sealers, dropped off and apparently forgotten years earlier.[70]

The Port Jackson schooners and sloops were too small to make the trip to the river Thames regularly, but they plied the Pacific, the Hawkesbury and the colonial coast carrying meat, grain, timber, sandalwood and coal back to Sydney Harbour for local consumption and export. The interaction was not always peaceable. Pacific Islanders were sometimes kidnapped and killed by crews sailing out of Sydney. Gardens were ransacked and property stolen. In 1814 Governor Macquarie imposed a £1000 bond on the masters of the trading ships 'to prevent the Continuance of a Conduct and Behaviour at once repulsive to Humanity and Interest'.[71]

The trade continued and the people of Port Jackson came to develop a special taste for Tahitian pork. They, and their visitors, also exhibited a fondness for Pacific souvenirs, manufactured artefacts and body parts. The French naval officer Hyacinthe de Bougainville expressed disgust at the trade in dried tattooed heads that came in on the whaling ships from New Zealand: 'most of the vessels which return from these islands carry several heads'.[72] For some, these symbols of 'savagery' may have confirmed the civility of the little settlement on this far-flung Australian coast. Others may have simply been amused. In the 1830s tattooed Māori oarsmen met immigrants and travellers as they rowed the harbour pilots out from their station at Watsons Bay. Their appearance added exoticism to what was already a spectacular entry through the Heads. The artist and writer Louisa Meredith was obviously impressed. She found the New Zealanders 'fairly outdid even my imaginings of the majestic'.[73]

The harbour was no longer the lonely coastal prison imagined by Lord Sydney. Rather, it more closely resembled James Matra's original vision of a commercial port filled with enterprising people making good after serving their time. And although Pacific women were never taken en masse as wives, as Matra had recommended, the harbour had become a place of many different voices. One observer painted a word picture of a Babel-like port where the Pacific connection was especially apparent: 'in the evening as you stroll along the picturesque shores of our harbour, you may be often melted with the wild melody of an Otheitean [Tahitian] love song from one ship, and have your blood frozen by the horrific whoop of the New Zealand war dance from another'.[74]

The gradual removal of Britain's protective duties on colonial products had come too late for the seal industry, but it encouraged graziers to export wool to English mills from the vast sheep runs created to the west of the mountains. The spread of pasture also meant that the people of Sydney often chose to eat cheap meat rather than the fish that swam in their harbour.[75] Local fishermen may have learned the habits of the elusive fish that frustrated Tench and others in the early years. Now, it seemed, marketplace competition confounded the development of a large-scale commercial fishery. The red meat of farmed animals was cheaper than the wild fish of the harbour and sea. In his enthusiastic account, written to attract prospective migrants, naval surgeon Peter Cunningham described an abundance of fish for anglers, but suggested that those sold by the street vendors were caught mainly by 'native blacks' using 'hooks and lines' near the Heads.[76] A decade later Louisa Meredith noted the impact of culinary fashion and conspicuous consumption among the upper class with whom she associated: 'I never saw native fish at a Sydney dinner table – the preserved or cured cod and salmon from England being served instead.'[77]

But the end of British protection stimulated that other 'fishery'. Local whalers started to chase the sperm and southern right whales found off Australia's eastern and southern coasts. For a period, colonists were looking out to the sea and inwards to the hinterland for wealth: Port Jackson was both a conduit for agricultural produce and the centre for a saltwater economy. In 1828, as a record 530 000 sheep wandered about grassland and cleared forest, applications were made for harbour-side allotments on which to build whaling stations. In 1830 the *Sydney Gazette* reported, 'At this moment we have 22 [whaling ships] actually at sea and several in the harbour preparing to join them.' From 1830 to 1832 whaling earned more than wool – as much as 29 per cent of the colony's total export income.[78] When the brig *Norval* left the harbour for the Port of Liverpool in April 1831, it carried with it 262 bales of wool, 106 pieces of cedar, 67 pieces of blue gum, 200 loose hides, 112 casks of sperm oil, 21 casks of black (right whale) oil, 3 casks and 1 bale of seal skins, 148 bales of flax, and 8 'hundredweight [405 kilograms]' of 'old copper'.[79] Seventy-six ships headed out from Sydney in 1835 to kill deep-sea whales and bring their oil back to port.[80]

Darling Harbour, next to Sydney Cove, was a favoured wharfage, but the presence of so many whaling ships near the town prompted the surveyor-general to note cautiously that, while 'in an infant colony consideration of comforts, pleasure and Gratification' should not interfere with the pursuit of prosperity, 'establishments connected with Whale Fishery might prove a nuisance to the inhabitants of that part of Sydney'.[81] The stench and the mess might be better situated on the harbour's undeveloped north side. Accordingly, Archibald Mosman bought 1.6 hectares in Great Sirius Bay and constructed a station for the deep-sea sperm whalers to heave down, boil blubber and store their product: oil for cooking, ambergris for perfumes and waxy spermaceti for candles. The convenience and economy of town wharfage, however, proved too great and those 'engaged in the fisheries' continued to moor in Darling Harbour and what would be called Walsh Bay between Dawes Point and Millers Point.

This proximity also appealed to the ships' crews. They easily made their way to the nearby Rocks for rest and recreation. 'The Whalers' Arms' was a name used repeatedly on public houses in the area.[82] Some sailors were waylaid by 'crimps' who then profited from the rewards paid by ships' captains attempting to recover their vanished crews. The intense activity also suited convicts, who sought to pass as seamen in order to escape. There were desertions from English ships: their crews were paid half the rates of their colonial counterparts sailing to and from India and the Pacific, and the rewards for whaling crews who shared in the profits of the voyage might be much better. The rate of desertion became so high that shipowners agreed to pay a levy of sixpence per shipping ton to offset the cost of maintaining a more effective water police. That small force had been established in 1830 at Longnose Point and then Goat Island to prevent smuggling and forestall convict escapes down the Parramatta River. By 1840, the year that transportation to New South Wales ended, it was the complexities of a busy commercial port that most concerned the authorities. A water police office was established in the heart of the commercial port, at the Rocks and then Cadman's Wharf on the west side of Sydney Cove. A second police rowboat was stationed near the pilots at Watsons Bay.

For his part, Archibald Mosman spent a prosperous decade on the north shore well away from the intensity of the Rocks. At a cove that was named after the First Fleet flagship *Sirius*, Mosman consolidated his whaling station and built a fine cottage called The Nest well above the stench his enterprise was creating around the beach below. Rotten blubber and barrels of oil caused the smell because the creatures were processed at sea rather than flayed and boiled down in the harbour. In fact, the sight of a whale in its entirety was a rare event for Sydneysiders in the 1840s. When, at that time, WJ Barry killed one just outside the Heads, he pulled the hapless creature into the waterway in the wake of his ship and 'turned it into oil' near Manly in front of a crowd of amazed onlookers.[83]

Mosman sold up in 1843. By then his place had become known as Mosmans Bay and there was still a colonial whaling fleet of 22 ships at sea.[84] They competed with free-ranging Americans who regularly visited the harbour in the latter years of the decade – as many as 46 ships in 1846. But the end of the industry in Sydney was near. Whale oil had already been eclipsed by wool as the colony's main export. The country's wealth was to be generated on land rather than at sea.

[FOUR]

POSSESSION
SECURED

'THE VISIT OF HOPE
TO SYDNEY COVE'

Charles Darwin sailed past Archibald Mosman's stinking whale station on 12 January 1836. By then Sydney Harbour was widely recognised as a waterway of superlative beauty. Yet Darwin's journal account of his arrival in Port Jackson contained none of the exultations that typified the early accounts or the latent tourism of more recent travelogues. Rather, the 'straight line of yellowish cliff' simply brought to mind 'the coast of Patagonia' and the 'thin scrubby trees' along the shore 'bespoke a useless sterility'. It was a dry summer and the harbour had probably lost some lustre. And Darwin was undoubtedly exhausted: he had been at sea in the *Beagle* for more than four years. Along the way he had begun to lose faith in the biblical account of creation and assembled the specimens and notes that would inform his own theory of evolution.

For a naturalist, Darwin was peculiarly preoccupied with the signs of civilisation in the harbour: the lighthouse and the 'beautiful villas and nice cottages'. If he noticed Mosman's whalers tucked back in the bay he did not record his thoughts. But the sight of so much commerce and construction around the harbour, in such a distant and unpromising place, was impressive. Darwin was moved to 'congratulate' himself that he 'was born an Englishman'. He stayed only a short time before heading off to Parramatta – by the 'excellent' macadamised road rather than the river. He went from there to the Blue Mountains and the sheep grazing country beyond. It was in the interior that Darwin really engaged with Australian nature and contemplated 'the strange character of the animals of this country'. But it was his inland stay that also convinced him there was no agricultural future for the colony. The soil was poor and the pasture 'thin'. The harbour, conversely, represented civilisation and a manufacturing and commercial future, one orientated to the sea rather than the dry interior: 'Possessing coal, she always has the moving power at hand. From the habitable country extending along the coast, and from her English extraction she is sure to be a maritime nation'.[1]

The harbour was a remarkably active place in 1836. There were now nearly twenty thousand people in Sydney. Relatively few lived on the foreshores but most depended in some way upon the port. Sixteen thousand of these were free and there was agitation to stop transportation of convicts altogether. The granting of free land had been abolished in 1831 and land sales now helped to raise money to assist free immigration. In 1836 the *Beagle* was one of 570 arrivals in Port Jackson, and only 16 of these were convict ships.[2] Of the rest, most were immigrant vessels, whalers, traders and local coasters carrying passengers and produce. The Sydney newspapers ran whole pages dedicated to shipping news; arrivals and departures to and from Newcastle, Norfolk Island, Launceston, Hobart, Liverpool and London. There were reports of wrecks, boats for sale, cargo unloaded.

Small commercial and residential complexes were even appearing on the otherwise undeveloped north shore. On the edge of Neutral Bay the boatbuilder HG Smith had constructed the harbour's first steamer, the *Surprise*. For six months in 1831 it ferried passengers to Parramatta before steaming to Van Diemen's Land. Others followed and in 1836 Charles Darwin may have seen the *William IV* or the *Sophia Jane* – paddle-wheelers that burned local coal on their way to and from the Hunter River.

Steam power promised control over the capriciousness of the wind, if not the sea. In February 1825 it had taken the outward-bound *Mangles* two days simply to reach the Heads and then, with no wind to counteract the swell, the ship was washed up on the Sow and Pigs, the reef that sat in the middle of the mouth of the south arm.[3] By 1841 there were 16 steamboats on the waterway – most connecting the harbour to Newcastle, Port Macquarie and the south coast. These vessels tied up in Darling Harbour where much of the boat-building was now occurring. The 'moving power' of coal was also in evidence on the foreshore there. John Dickson had set up the first powered flour mill at Darling Harbour in 1813. Barker's steam mill joined it in 1827. Both had their own wharfs for unloading coal and grain, and these extended out over the mudflats to deeper water. The illuminating power of coal would follow in 1841 when the Australian Gaslight Company built its first gasworks on the Darling Harbour waterfront.

Darwin's entrancement with Sydney and its working harbour had a familial link. Both his grandfathers – the naturalist and philosopher Erasmus Darwin and the potter Josiah Wedgwood – had celebrated the place *in absentia* back in 1789. Josiah had fashioned a medallion entitled *Hope, Art, Labour and Peace at Botany Bay* from marl collected on the foreshore of Sydney Cove by Arthur Phillip. It was the same clay that the Gadigal had used to decorate their bodies. Now it represented the arrival of European civilisation. A similar allegorical motif appeared on the title page of Phillip's published journal, with a reference also to practicality: 'The clay proves to be of a fine texture, and will be found very useful for the manufactory of earthern ware.' The intended symbolism of the harbour clay was profound; the incidental association with dispossession even more so. In Phillip's account of the First Fleet voyage, the image was followed by Erasmus Darwin's similarly themed poem, 'The Visit of Hope to Sydney Cove':

Where Sydney Cove her lucid bosom swells,
Courts her young navies, and the storm repels;
High on a rock amid the troubled air
HOPE stood sublime, and wav'd her golden hair;
Calm'd with her rosy smile the tossing deep,
And with sweet accents charm'd the winds to sleep;
To each wild plain she stretch'd her snowy hand,
High-waving wood, and sea-encircled strand.
'Hear me,' she cried, 'ye rising Realms! record
'Time's opening scenes, and Truth's unerring word. –
'There shall broad streets their stately walls extend,
'The circus widen, and the crescent bend;
'There, ray'd from cities o'er the cultur'd land,
'Shall bright canals, and solid roads expand. –
'There the proud arch, Colossus-like, bestride
'Yon glittering streams, and bound the chasing tide;
'Embellish'd villas crown the landscape-scene,
'Farms wave with gold, and orchards blush between. –
'There shall tall spires, and dome-capt towers ascend,
'And piers and quays their massy structures blend;
'While with each breeze approaching vessels glide,
'And northern treasures dance on every tide!' –
Then ceas'd the nymph – tumultuous echoes roar,
And JOY's loud voice was heard from shore to shore –
Her graceful steps descending press'd the plain,
And PEACE, and ART, and LABOUR, join'd her train.

The poem would be repeatedly cited a century later as Sydneysiders watched a huge structure, built of British steel by Australian hands, finally span the harbour. In 1932 the reference to 'the proud arch' was read as a remarkable prophecy of lineal progress. The Sydney Harbour Bridge was confirmation of Australia's place as a modern offshoot of empire. In 1789 Erasmus Darwin's poem was one of the clearest expressions of the classically inspired view of progress used to justify the appropriation of half the continent in accord with a natural law which dictated that 'savagery' would give way to agriculture, then commerce and, ultimately, to decadence and collapse.[4] Darwin's abstracted Sydney Cove, with its 'piers and quays' and 'approaching vessels' laden with 'northern treasure', was the birthplace of a new realm of empire. Civilisation would spread out from there like rays of sunshine.

Harbours were popular landscapes for evoking such allegorical visions of development because they recalled the ancient civilisations of the Mediterranean whose power and influence were built upon trading and naval fleets. The sequence of human development in this maritime setting was given one of its last and most graphic renderings by the American artist Thomas Cole, just as Darwin was sailing up to Sydney Cove in the mid-1830s. Each of Cole's five paintings was set in the same imaginary harbour. The viewer follows the cycle from *The Savage State*, through a virtuous 'pastoral' stage to the 'consummation' of imperial urbanity. The inevitable conflict and collapse follows in *Destruction* and the final scene, *Desolation*, is depicted by nature reclaiming the ruins – a salutary lesson in the dangers of hubris.

Cole's 'Course of Empire' series, painted between 1834 and 1836, was a contemporary critique of an expansive United States and its swaggering 'emperor', Andrew Jackson. For the younger Darwin, as for the first Australian colonisers themselves, the cautionary elements of the classical view were less apparent. He wrote to his sister at the time: 'this is really a wonderful colony; ancient Rome, in her imperial grandeur, would not have been ashamed of such as an offspring. When my Grandfather wrote the lines of "Hope's visit to Sydney Cove" on Mr Wedgwood's medallion he prophesised most truly.'[5]

'... *to the first dawn of youth and independence*'

Ironically it was the colony's first non-naval governor, Lachlan Macquarie – and his architecturally minded wife Elizabeth – who introduced to the harbour the structures that best evoked a 'civilised' port settlement. The Macquaries made tangible the 'charm'g seats, superb buildings, the grand ruins of stately edifices' imposed upon the harbour and its undeveloped foreshore by the fertile imagination of the First Fleeters. The major buildings of the era reflected the dominance of classical and the neo-Gothic building styles. Whereas the former was most evidently associated with the Enlightenment project of civilisation, the Gothic gave it a distinctly British feel.

Macquarie built the classically proportioned lighthouse that had caught Darwin's attention in 1836. He ordered a fort to be placed at Bennelong Point with matching castellated stables in the landscaped grounds of the Governor's Domain – in anticipation of a new government house built upon similar neo-Gothic lines. And it was Macquarie's appointed naval officer who would commission the harbour's first landmark waterfront home, Henrietta Villa. Erasmus Darwin's poem and Wedgwood's medallion better evoked the development of 'Sydney Cove' under this administration than in Phillip's first scrabbling months.

Governor Macquarie arrived in Sydney on the last day of 1809. The Dawes Point battery, which sat alongside Robert Campbell's warehouse and dock with its stores of seal skin and oil, fired a salute to the new governor in response to salvos from the arriving ships. Even then the harbour was an ideal arena and backdrop for pomp and celebration. The following night, 1 January 1810, ships in the harbour were lit up – the reflection on the water doubling the impact of the illumination. The spectacle continued throughout the month, with John Underwood contributing by projecting twin transparencies representing the Crown and commerce onto his waterfront house. A celebratory bonfire raged outside.

Macquarie was intent upon calming a colony rocked by mutiny and the deposition of his predecessor, William Bligh. That man had tried to implement London's vision of a penal colony sustained by an agricultural yeomanry of free and emancipated settlers. He discouraged boat-building and rescinded land grants within the town limits drawn up by Phillip. For this, and his belligerent demeanour, he was thought by many around the cove to be a despot. He was better liked at the Hawkesbury farms. As a naval commodore, he had difficulty imposing his will on the army men of the New South Wales Corps and, in a poisonous atmosphere of factional rivalry, he appointed Robert Campbell as naval officer responsible for collecting duties – despite the conflict of interest. Better a civilian merchant than an army acolyte. When robbed of power on land by Major George Johnston and others in 1808, Governor Bligh had contemplated exercising it to its fullest on the 'wooden world' of his ship *Porpoise* when it floated at the head of Sydney Cove. Then, he had instructed his acting commander to turn the ship's guns towards shore 'to Blow down the Town' that had rejected him.[6] He never gave the order to fire, sailing instead for the Derwent River. Bligh was not present when Macquarie arrived but he returned from his exile in Van Diemen's Land in January while the harbour was still illuminated. He stayed for four furious months before setting sail for England.

By contrast, Macquarie had a vision of a place that was far more that a prison. Imagining a civil society built upon the potential of reformed convicts, he set about aesthetic and practical improvements to the port town that would both reflect and facilitate the civic reformation. The old bridge over the Tank Stream was replaced in 1812. There would be a convict barracks and a new hospital on the ridge above the governor's house, which was improved in lieu of a larger grander Gothic pile planned for the garden-like Governor's Domain that extended down to Bennelong Point. The second governor's house at Parramatta was renovated in the classical style and a similarly symmetrical 'factory' for orphan girls built on the river bank nearby. Macquarie reserved enjoyment of the Sydney Domain, and the small botanical garden it contained, for himself, his wife and a respectable few. But ultimately it became public parkland and his defence of this swathe of green on the edge of the town would be one of the lasting legacies of his administration.

Again the harbour and its hinterland gave up much of the basic material for the new civic structures. Wood was floated down the estuary from forests up on the northwestern shore, and more of the yellow sandstone was cut from the building sites themselves. Some of the precious lime mortar used to bind the stone and brick came from the harbour bed. Scarcity of shells had been a problem since the beginning and the easily accessed Aboriginal shell middens, the discarded remains of millennia of waterside meals, had been dug and their contents burned years before. Now men in the 'shell gang' dredged for oysters – standing waist deep in water as the tide receded. Retrieving shells was also thought to have a punitive, if not reformative, effect and work on the 'shell gang' was 'generally reserved for the men of the worst character'. A construction fleet of no less than 12 boats, crewed by 52 men, was employed in ferrying these materials down the waterway to the town. This was joined by another eight vessels seeking out and cutting grass along the water for the governor's stables.[7]

A road leading from Hyde Park to South Head was pushed through the forest and heath in 1811. It would become one of the favourite carriage drives for Sydneysiders, providing picturesque glimpses of the harbour along the way. South Head was already the site of the signal station that communicated the arrival of ships via flag telegraph to the cove. In 1816 work began near there on a lighthouse, the first of the many Macquarie-era public works designed by the convict architect Francis Greenway, who had been transported for forgery in 1814. The symmetry of the structure, with a tower flanked by two domes, was classical in inspiration. It stood high on the cliffs that also provided the sandstone for its construction. The placement and proportions of the lighthouse recalled illuminated entrances to ancient ports. The tower's several oil-burning lamps each had a set of complex reflectors, replacing a simple beacon that had burned wood and coal since 1793. The new light was 108 metres above sea level and visible for 35 kilometres out to sea. The former harbourmaster and pilot Robert Watson was the first to keep the light shining above the bay that bore his name.

This portrait of Bennelong, titled *Native name Ben-nel-long, as painted when angry after Botany Bay Colebee was wounded,* is attributed to the Port Jackson Painter. Created around 1790, it shows the Wangal man in the body decoration created from the 'whitish marl' found around the foreshore.

© *Natural History Museum, London*

John Hunter was interested in all he saw and sought to draw or paint as much of it as he could. He titled this watercolour *Wolomy* – an Aboriginal name for the Snapper and origin of the clan name Wallumudegal. It is from Hunter's unpublished journal of paintings 'Birds and Flowers of New South Wales drawn on the spot in 1788, '89 and '90'.

National Library of Australia, PIC T1221 KN239/65 LOC MS SR

Above Francis Wheatley's oil painting of Arthur Phillip
on an imaginary Australian foreshore was painted in 1786,
as preparations for the penal colony began.
© *National Portrait Gallery, London, NPG1462*

Right Better known for his bird studies, John William Lewin also produced this
oil painting, *Fish Catch and Dawes Point Sydney Harbour*, around 1813.
It presented the diversity of species in the harbour but the suggestion of a
marine cornucopia ran counter to the experience of fishermen. The artist has
positioned his catch at Milsons Point opposite Dawes Point. In foreground are
brightly coloured wrasse surrounded by whiting. The centrepiece is a rock cod.
Above this is a snapper and behind is a hammerhead shark. The red fish to
the right is probably a nannygai.
Art Gallery of South Australia

Above Scrimshaw was both art and pastime for mariners. This detail of a carved walrus tusk depicts Port Jackson with a whaling ship in harbour. The tusk also features a section of the coast showing 'Jervy Bay' [Jervis Bay], Newcastle, Port Stephens and Port Macquarie. It is inscribed with the name William Grice, a member of the NSW Corp, and the date 1806, although Port Macquarie was not named until 1818.

Powerhouse Museum, Sydney. Photo: Scott Donkin; (detail) photographer unknown

Above This undated unsigned watercolour view of Henrietta Villa and Sydney town in the distance has been attributed to Joseph Lycett. A similar image appeared in his 1824 publication *Views in Australia*. As with Eyre's view of Sydney Cove the Aboriginal family in the foreground were included to indicate the 'natural' cycle of social change.

National Library of Australia, PIC R5676

Opposite John Eyre's four-part aquatint of Sydney Cove, viewed from both sides, was executed in 1808. The British reading audience saw it when John Heaviside Clark's engravings of Eyre's neat and vibrant Georgian settlement were first published in 1810. This pair shows the mouth and east side of the Cove. Government House is on the far left. A Norfolk Island pine has been planted to mark the site, starting a custom that would endure into the 20th century. Simeon Lord's house is shown partially obscured with four windows in the centre. James Underwood's flat roofed house sits on the waterfront below St Phillip's Church with its tower. The Government Wharf protrudes into the Cove beyond the trees. The gantry of the Hospital Wharf is detectable. The large waterfront building to the left of that is the warehouse of the ex-convict trader, Isaac Nichols. Robert Campbell's house, wharf and store complex is on the waterfront to the right of the picture. Eyre's picture is notable also for the number and variety of watercraft depicted. They were probably included to reinforce the impression of a vibrant settlement. The group of Aboriginal posed in the first part are almost certainly imaginary – serving an allegorical function as a reference to the state of nature superseded.

Rex Nan Kivell Collection, National Library of Australia

Portrait of Bungaree, a native of New South Wales,
with Fort Macquarie, Sydney Harbour in background,
oil on canvas by Augustus Earle, c. 1826.
Rex Nan Kivell Collection, National Library of Australia, NK118

Captain John Piper, oil on canvas by Augustus Earle, c.1826.
This portrait appears to have been painted with that
of Bungaree in mind.

Mitchell Library, State Library of New South Wales

C Martens

This Romantic watercolour view of South Head lighthouse was one of the
first works by Conrad Martens after his arrival in Sydney in 1835.
He would become the pre-eminent harbour artist of the 19th century.
State Library of New South Wales

Mrs Heriot Anley's 1840s watercolour of a scruffy Sydney Cove shows what is probably the steam dredge *Hercules* on the left and the new Government House on the right. The dredging presaged improvements that culminated in the stone-lined Circular Quay.

Mitchell Library, State Library of New South Wales

SYDNEY
GOVERNMENT HOUSE.
EMIGRANTS

To Oswald Blaxome. Esqre

H
AND
A
Range

BOUR, N.S.W.
ACQUARIE
VING.

rth Shore Sydney
respectfully dedicated by OW Brierly

Thomas Pickens' lithograph *Emigrants Arriving Sydney Harbour, NSW*, was published in London in 1853 and based on an artwork by Oswald Brierly. It shows a well-established post-convict port with Fort Macquarie on the waterfront and Government House above. Those who arrived after its publication would have disembarked from the wherry-like boats onto the new stone Circular Quay.

Rex Nan Kivell Collection, National Library of Australia, NK 6088

Edmund Thomas's 1857 watercolour *Entrance to Port Jackson* subtly
pointed to the dangers of sea travel to Sydney. The mast of the recently
wrecked vessel *Dunbar* can be seen above the waves.

Mitchell Library, State Library of New South Wales

Conrad Martens' 1851 view of Sydney from the heights of St Leonards, where he lived, shows a landscape and waterway in the process of change. The artist regularly used the elevated north shore to depict the town opposite. Here the uncleared bush in the foreground has a decidedly Italian feel. Note the ubiquitous goat.

Mitchell Library, State Library of New South Wales

Conrad Martens sketched and painted dozens of intimate scenes around the harbour. This 1850s watercolour is a rare image of fishermen with their seine net and boat.

State Library of New South Wales

The tower represented a major technological leap beyond the burning cauldron it replaced and was contemporaneous with the end of the great age of lighthouse construction in the United States. There, the towers demonstrated the power of a central government, which commissioned and controlled the towers, over the communities that accommodated them.[8] Macquarie's lighthouse, conversely, demonstrated decisiveness at the periphery of empire. The governor regarded his harbour as a major port – well before Britain's Colonial Office was willing to concede the point. Lighthouses had symbolised the sanctuary and civility of the harbour since the days of Ptolemy's tower at Alexandria and Claudius's lighthouse at Ostia on the mouth of the Tiber River. The Macquarie lighthouse would influence the design of Australian lighthouses for a century and earn the convict Greenway his pardon. When it was finally replaced in 1883, the government architect of the time copied the original.

In 1816 Macquarie gave his 'blessing' for another remarkable structure, Henrietta Villa. The owner, Captain John Piper, returned the favour by taking Elizabeth Macquarie's middle name for his fabulous house. It was built on a point the Gadigal had called Jerrowan and the colonists now knew as Eliza Point, also in honour of Mrs Macquarie. The many rock carvings there suggested its importance to the original owners – perhaps as a place where the harbour could be viewed from its mouth down to the west. The governor granted 77 hectares of land to the amiable Piper, an officer of the New South Wales Corp who had given up his commission to replace Robert Campbell as naval officer in 1813. It was a perfect harbour site for the man responsible for boarding new arrivals and receiving the official mail, co-ordinating departures, furnishing port regulation, collecting fees – and administering the function of the new lighthouse. Piper had already made money in the trading officers' monopoly in the 1790s but the £10 000 fortune needed to build his home over six years came from the commission on the imports he vetted as naval officer. Piper's villa was a direct product of harbour commerce: it was filled with imports and funded by the same. Fortunately, his appointment coincided with an upturn in shipping visits. In 1820 62 vessels came in, a tripling of the arrivals when he commenced his new job.[9] The Piper estate grew with the acquisition of adjoining properties and others around Sydney. In addition to the 727 hectares owned along the southeastern foreshore, he bought 285 hectares on the opposite shore, intended for his daughter and son-in-law – the so-called Thrupp Estate.[10]

Piper relished his harbour life and designed for himself a braided uniform with epaulettes. He brought an element of theatre to the position, proceeding up and down the waterway in a 13-metre gig propelled by ten oars or a 10-metre boat fitted with an awning, as the weather demanded. His crew were practised musicians and played military and naval tunes while out on the water.[11] When the house was finally finished, Piper continued the pantomime at home. Guests, both emancipists and free immigrants, were collected for parties by carriage or boat. They danced and chatted in the beautiful domed saloon, the banqueting hall or the gardens. Piper was extravagant but he was not exclusive. His equanimity in a society that still drew firm distinctions based upon birth and convict association did not please everyone, however. The deputy assistant commissary-general George Thomas Boyes referred to the locals as 'filth' and refused to attend functions at the 'fairy palace'. There was 'no honour in dining with Piper', he wrote to his wife, 'for he invites everybody who comes here indiscriminately'.[12]

Around 1826 Piper commissioned a full-length portrait of himself by Augustus Earle, the English-born son of an American who was travelling the world seeking landscapes and people to paint. Earle had arrived in the colonies in 1825 and stayed for three years before the urge to travel overtook him again. The year 1831 saw him aboard the *Beagle* with Charles Darwin, working as the expedition's artist. The Piper portrait was one of several commissioned by local notables while Earle was in town. It echoes the mid-18th-century paintings of the British landed gentry by Johann Zoffany, Thomas Gainsborough and others. Piper is standing resplendent in his self-styled naval officer uniform – in front of a placid harbour and rocky foreshore rather than the productive pasture of a country estate. But the symbolism is the same. He is in his landscape element: the harbour is the source of his social standing. The white domes of Henrietta Villa can be glimpsed like a temple amidst the forest. Two years spent in the Mediterranean must have familiarised Earle with idealised classical landscape and the scene resembles the Roman Campagna paintings made by the 17th-century Frenchman Claude Lorrain. Piper is even given a suggestive laurel as the oak leaf-shaped foliage of a nearby tree hovers over his distinguished head.

Henrietta Villa may have been started by Francis Greenway but was probably completed by the free immigrant architect Henry Kitchen. The sophistication of its neo-classical design was unprecedented in the colony, possibly reflecting the influence of the English architects Sir John Soane and John Wyatt. The two domes were a stylistic echo of the London metropolis but they also referenced the nearby light-house – the villa would have been the second substantial building viewed by new arrivals. It sat on a point jutting out just as the main 'south arm' of the harbour turned westwards. There, low on the water's edge with a backdrop of eucalypts, Henrietta Villa presented a startling impression. What was obvious to the Gadigal was also apparent to Piper and his architect/s. There were two frontages: one looking northeast towards the Heads, the other west to Sydney Cove.[13] It was a place to view and a place to be viewed.

The convicted forger and artist Joseph Lycett included the villa in his 1824 book of lithographs, *Views in Australia,* published for a British market interested in both grand houses and distant places. There, Henrietta Villa was the unequivocal symbol of civility on the harbour, described as the 'most superb residence in the colony'.[14] The book took the reader on a tour along the harbour and beyond to the Blue Mountains, Newcastle and down to Van Diemen's Land – following the path of Governor Macquarie's various vice-regal tours of the country. The 'noble harbour', Piper's villa, James Squire's productive farm at Kissing Point and John and Elizabeth Macarthur's park-like riverside property – where 'the land around the house and by the river is cleared of stumps, and is mown in the hay-season as in England' –

were all there as examples of the rising civilisation in and around the harbour. Beyond were outports and images of untamed nature. Lycett's pictures established a philosophical relationship between these places within the context of the classical view of empire. The point was explicitly made in the introductory text:

> In contemplating the progressive effects of Colonization, even slightly as they are sketched in these few pages, and exhibited in the following VIEWS, the mind is naturally led into reflections upon the origin and decay of nations. In these infant settlements of AUSTRALIA we might behold the germs of a mighty empire, which in future ages will pour forth its myriads to re-people future deserts.[15]

The state of nature was giving way to agriculture. Piper's villa and the port town indicated the consolidation of the next stage again: commerce and culture.

Ostentation was not to everyone taste. The merchant Edward Wollstonecraft was a wealthy and well-connected man who had been given 212 hectares of Gamaragal land on the north shore, including a headland, an offshore island and two bays. He used his waterfront for a warehouse and built a modest secluded Georgian house so far back on a ridge that it was called Crows Nest Cottage and would have been difficult to see from the harbour.

Others had lived by the water where and how they could – there was still enough foreshore for the poor. At Elizabeth Bay, a short way to the west of Point Piper, Macquarie had set up a row of simple huts for one of the surviving groups of Aboriginal people. That bay was also home to the fisherman Patrick Welch, who resided in a turf house with a stone chimney surrounded by a ditch and hedge. The tailor Thomas O'Neill lived nearby in a dwelling fashioned from an enormous burned-out blackbutt tree.[16]

The Macquaries understood the emotional and ideological power of architecture as well as Piper. To complement the staid order of

Georgian-style architecture, they imagined the cove as a place of turrets and towers where associations with a British heritage would be evoked. The foundation stone for Fort Macquarie was laid in December 1817 near the site of Bennelong's old house on the eastern point of Sydney Cove. It too was designed by Francis Greenway and built from sandstone quarried nearby. Greenway's plan placed the fort right on the water – lapped by waves at high tide and accessible from the land by a drawbridge. With its two-storied castellated tower, 15 guns and walls up to 3.7 metres thick, it was the largest fortification in the harbour. It was intended to prevent unauthorised departures rather than hostile arrivals.[17] Nonetheless, Macquarie's fort was disparaged as a piece of architectural confection. Greenway himself later likened it to the little garden forts built by the ridiculous Uncle Toby and Corporal Trim in Laurence Sterne's *Tristram Shandy*.[18] Taking a typically French interest in the harbour's defences, Hyacinthe de Bougainville was only slightly less dismissive:

> The fort has no garrison nor is it completely finished; it is merely an open square armed with three cannons on each of its turrets which are lashed by the sea … The walls of the fort overlook the beach and are so low that one could jump from them without risking injury.[19]

Augustus Earle thought it more 'ornamental than useful'.[20]

The fort was designed to work sympathetically with the castellations of Macquarie's new governor's house and stables located behind in the Domain. That house was never built but the stables were. So too were additions to the Dawes Point battery on the opposite peninsula. Earle thought the view to the west that encapsulated these structures was 'very pleasing'. A small octagonal cottage with little battlements was built for the ex-convict boatman Billy Blue behind the fort. The incomplete ramparts of Fort Phillip stood high on Windmill Hill and the turreted tower on St Phillip's Church, farther along the rise, completed the ensemble. It was a Romantic setting that might conjure for new arrivals and residents alike the works of Sir Walter Scott and the Gothick novelists. Certainly the architecture was readily associated with British heritage, although Bougainville found it 'garish'. Protruding out in front of Sydney Cove, Fort Macquarie was the defining element of the place and was featured as such in numerous paintings and drawings of the cove and harbour. Defensive effectiveness notwithstanding, it suggested British permanence and power amidst the busy scene of warehouses and ships. By 1828 Governor Ralph Darling added to the scene with a stone bathhouse on the Domain foreshore which had a 'Castellated Appearance to the Water to Correspond in some degree with Fort Macquarie'.[21] The effect was strengthened again with the completion of the new Gothic-style Government House in 1845.

For a decade, to the 1820s, this picturesque neo-Gothic was confined to Sydney Cove, where it contributed some drama to an ordered setting dominated by buildings of simpler classically inspired Georgian style. The symmetry of the original Government House was complicated by the addition of an east wing and verandah. But its original two-storey structure still related to the other buildings on the civic space that Macquarie had reinstated on the waterfront, Macquarie Place. These were the colonial secretary's office, his house and the chief judge's house. Simeon Lord's house also fronted the 'square' – an imposing but comparatively simple single-pile building. The governor had an obelisk erected in this place – a defining spot in the cove from which all road distances would be measured. A matching plinth was mounted near the water at Watsons Bay.

By 1822 Lachlan Macquarie had returned to Britain, having been forced to defend his administration against accusations of extravagance and leniency. The threat of transportation to New South Wales, it seemed to some, was no longer a deterrent for felons. The harbour prison and its offshoots had 'not been established with any view to territorial or commercial advantages', wrote the colonial secretary Earl Bathurst to JT Bigge, the man he sent to inquire into the colonial administration. Rather, they were to be viewed chiefly 'as receptacles for offenders'.[22] Lighthouses might be permissible but castles were not.

Five years after the Macquaries' departure, John Piper was bankrupt. He had mismanaged the collection of port fees, lived too well and bought too much land. Piper was a very public figure and he suffered a very public downfall. The whole town knew when he threw himself off a boat outside the Heads while his band played on. His crew hauled him out of the water to face the sell-off of his possessions. Piper's fate might have been seen as analogous to the cycle of imperial rise and fall – decadence before the inevitable decline. His collapse certainly presented an opportunity for others to build their own empires. The house and its grounds, and the Thrupp Estate over the water, were acquired by the Cooper family. The once-celebrated Henrietta Villa remained empty for a period; by 1860 it had been substantially altered, with the surviving structure referred to ignominiously as a 'temporary residence'. Its planned replacement was not completed until 1883. William Cooper's Italianate mansion, Woollahra House, was so vast that its owner subsequently offered it to the State as a potential Federal parliament house in 1898. The cyclical replacement of one symbol of wealth for another, more fashionable, would be repeated in the best waterfront locations around the harbour, where subdivision and immediate profit were not irresistible. The Coopers were not in a hurry. The break-up of Henrietta Villa's estate began after they left permanently for England in 1888. The subdivision of the relatively inaccessible Thrupp Estate across the water was even slower. Rows of cottages eventually sprang up there with the promise of a harbour bridge in the 1910s. A century after Piper had looked across at grey-green eucalypts and red-trunked angophoras, that side of the harbour thereby gained the character of low-rise, red-roofed suburbia by the water.

WC Wentworth – radical defender of colonial rights, newspaper proprietor and eventually an advocate of a local aristocracy – also recognised an opportunity. He righteously condemned the summary dismissal of his friend Piper and attacked Governor Ralph Darling for ignoring natural justice. Wentworth then bought 120 hectares of land with a tumbledown cottage called Vaucluse from Piper at the good price of £1500.

Wentworth was a believer in the cycle of empire and had written a patriotic reprise to Erasmus Darwin's poem in 1823. *Australasia* famously described an incipient antipodean power ready to emerge when 'bow'd by luxury' Britannia would 'cease to ride / Despotic Empress of old Ocean's tide.' The

> ... last-born infant then arise,
> To glad thy heart and greet thy parent eyes;
> And Australasia float, with flag unfurl'd,
> A new Britannia in another world.[23]

The poem was dedicated to Macquarie, whom Wentworth thought had nurtured the colony 'through the helplessness of infancy to the first dawn of youth and independence'. It was a defence of his vision for a rising colony. It laid out a story of continental conquest and the creation of agricultural wealth in the interior: 'soon, Australasia, may thy inmost plains, / A new Arcadia, teem with simple swains'. For its part, the harbour was the beautiful and busy maritime centre of this empire:

> ... Lo! Thickly planted o'er the glassy bay,
> Where Sydney loves her beauties to survey,
> And ev'ry morn delighted sees the gleam
> Of some fresh pennant dancing in her stream,
> A masty forest, stranger vessels moor,
> Charg'd with the fruits of ev'ry foreign shore.[24]

Wentworth's appreciation of the relationship between the harbour and hinterland came from experience. He had been one of three men Macquarie had sent across the Blue Mountains in 1813, and who had succeeding in making the 'inmost plains' known to the colonisers. In time he would become one of the colony's largest owners of sheep-grazing properties. The harbour was also the landscape of youthful memories. Wentworth was one of the first generation of native-born white Australians – and certainly one of the most accomplished. *Australasia* expressed the homesickness he felt while studying at Cambridge:

> Land of my birth! Though now, alas! No more
> Musing I wander on thy sea-girt shore,
> Or climb with eager haste thy barrier cliff,
> To catch a glimmer of the distant skiff,
> That ever and anon breaks into light,
> And then again eludes the aching sight,
> Till nearer seen she bends her foaming way
> Majestic onward to yon placid bay,
> Where Sydney's infant turrets proudly rise,
> The new-born glory of the southern skies …
>
> Where later too, in manhood's op'ning bloom,
> The tangled brake, th' eternal forest's gloom,
> The wonted brook, where with some truant mate
> I loved to plunge, or ply the treach'rous bait;
> The spacious harbour, with its hundred coves
> The fairy islets – seats of savage loves,
> Again beheld – restampt with deeper dye
> The fading visions of my infancy.[25]

In 1827 Wentworth was living at the very centre of the imagined empire, Macquarie Place, but with the sale of Piper's estate he was able to possess one of the 'hundred coves' of his beloved harbour – away from the masses with whom he had such an ambivalent relationship and the well-born snobs who sneered at his relationship with Sarah Cox, the daughter of a former convict. Vaucluse was rebuilt over the next decade, not as a 'stately mansion' with 'column'd front' as envisioned in the poem, but as a picturesque Gothic villa in a rugged cove setting. It was the ideal seat for a natural aristocrat and it renewed Macquarie's earlier vision of a Gothic harbour.[26] Wentworth had a classical view of civilisation and nature – he delighted in the establishment of order – but he clearly thought a Romantic architectural style better expressed his heritage. In the early 1840s the castellated Vaucluse joined the huge turreted Government House that now commanded the ridge above Bennelong Point. There had been more classically inspired villas built in the meantime – Elizabeth Bay House, Craigend and others high above the water in a new civil administrators' suburb stretching from Woolloomooloo to Darlinghurst – but the Gothic architecture of the lower harbour emphasised an 'ancient' British heritage. Other private castles were built – Grantham, Lindesay, Greenoaks among them. In 1858 directly opposite Fort Macquarie the merchant Adolph Feez built a two-storey picturesque villa that came to be called Kirribilli House. Sydney's 'infant turrets' had arisen.

The new Government House was designed at a distance by Edward Blore, an architect who never visited the harbour. The plan displayed little sensitivity to its site – the summer sun beat in through the huge unshaded windows – but the harbour vistas from the lawns were grand. In any case, like Piper's villa, this was a place to be seen as much as it was a platform for seeing. The great Gothic pile became another iconic waterfront structure, one that symbolised a place moving far beyond its role as a prison. The timing was perfect. Convict transportation to New South Wales ended in 1840 as the house was being built. A contemporary guide book expressed the effect: 'Who that has once felt can ever forget the sensation produced on his mind, on rounding Bradley's Head for the first time when this building burst unexpectedly on view … [immigrants] looked for a prison and behold a palace!'[27]

Such visual drama ensured that Government House and Fort Macquarie were pictured by many of the artists who depicted the harbour: John Skinner Prout, Robert Westmacott, ST Gill, Charles Rodius and Frederick Garling among them.[28] Conrad Martens, acknowledged in his own lifetime as the pre-eminent artist of the harbour, executed several paintings of the house. In his 1842 oil *View from the Window*, commissioned by then Governor George Gipps, the house appears on the east side of Sydney Cove as a luminescent castle, flanked on either side by Fort Macquarie and Greenway's stables. In the 1856 watercolour *Funeral of Rear-Admiral Phillip Parker King,* the castellated house and the fort are dramatic architectural elements within the spectacle unfolding on the harbour as a flotilla of small boats rows the dead naval hero and explorer across the water from his north shore home and a warship fires a broadside in salute.

Martens had arrived in Sydney nine months before Charles Darwin. The two were already friends. They had met on the *Beagle* when Martens replaced Augustus Earle as artist. The world was getting smaller and such crossed paths at the bottom of the globe were not unusual. Martens left the expedition in South America and, like Earle, came to Sydney to paint – 'in search of the picturesque', as one newspaper put it shortly after his arrival in 1835.[29] Martens' account of his arrival in the harbour epitomised the 19th-century quest for that aesthetic – the varied and exciting, the picture perfect scene:

> The appearance when off the heads is that of a wild and iron bound coast and the entrance that of a gigantic gateway, but the scene changes immediately upon entering to the calm and beautiful. Islands, bays, headlands of no great highs but covered with wood present themselves in succession ...[30]

Martens had not intended to stay in Sydney but he fell in love with the harbour and with a woman named Jane Carter. After their marriage in 1837 her parents gave the couple land at St Leonards – present-day North Sydney – and there they built a Gothic-style sandstone cottage called Rockleigh Grange. It was one of the many houses designed with the help of architectural pattern books by writers such as JC Loudon. Martens realised quickly that there was a market for harbour paintings among the middle and upper classes, just as there was a market for picturesque villas. Sydneysiders were in love with the harbour. Wealth was flowing from the wool and whale oil, and owners of prominent houses commissioned pictures of their waterfront properties, WC Wentworth among them. Others bought one of the multiple views Martens painted from Rose Bay, or one of the ten versions of *The Harbour from Craigend*. Printmaking followed, making the reproduction of single views easier and extending Martens' market. One of these works, a lithograph of Sydney and its harbour from above Lavender Bay at St Leonards, had sold at least 148 coloured and uncoloured copies by 1855.[31] From 1861 the auctioneer and woolbroker Thomas Mort bought several of Martens' paintings and made them available for regular public viewings in the gallery of his enormous Gothic home Greenoaks, which stood above the harbour at Darling Point.

Martens' harbour was like a lake – 'calm and beautiful' – and typically foregrounded by rugged scenery. The destructive power of the sea, in paintings such as *North Head Port Jackson*, finished in 1854, was only obvious at the harbour's 'gateway', emphasising the waterway's role as a sanctuary on 'a wild and iron bound coast'. His ability to represent water, rocks and sky was developed while on the *Beagle*. But Martens' Romanticism – his desire to capture the 'affect' of the natural – was almost always accompanied by a celebration of the 'civilised'. The steamers that plume white smoke on Martens' horizons are unthreatening machines in this aquatic garden. Even Archibald Mosman's whaling station, with its service road cutting down through the forested hillside, was depicted without obvious judgment of its destructive presence. The harbour was celebrated as a cultural place, with the presence of a boat or distant lighthouse and the sprawling skyline of the booming port town. The relatively undeveloped foreshores of St Leonards, so familiar to the local artist, served this latter purpose perfectly. His many views of town from the north shore replicate the hierarchy so apparent in the earlier colonial topographic works: a dark natural foreground giving way to the busy harbour and town illuminated by a brilliant sky.

'In the neighbourhood of Sydney the Natives are growing scarce'

In some of his earlier paintings Martens placed Aboriginal figures in this natural foreground. Their presence was another echo of the earlier allegorical depictions of the harbour. In Lycett's published *Views* and John Eyre's harbour vistas, rocky and bushy foregrounds were inhabited by Aboriginal individuals and groups who existed as an explicit counterpoint to the town, houses and ships beyond. They represented the state of nature being superseded.

Conrad Martens started painting Aboriginal characters out of his harbour pictures in the early 1840s. His popular lithograph of Sydney from St Leonards originally had two such figures in the foreground – one in European costume, one in traditional garb. Their place was taken by a European couple, holding hands, in a second version.[32] The alteration reflected changing artistic tastes and changing attitudes towards Aboriginal people. There were still 'natives' around Sydney in the early 1840s, as Martens was deleting them, but they no longer had a place in the art of the harbour. Images of 'noble savages' had given way to caricatures of tragic alcoholics and by the 1850s and 1860s they were a residual presence in lithographic reproductions of earlier works. Aboriginal people had virtually disappeared in popular imaginings of the waterway. Those who survived were written off as remnants of a disappearing 'race'.

Elsewhere in New South Wales Aboriginal people were very much in the minds of whites. Massacres, rape, captivity and disease followed in the wake of agricultural expansion from the southern highlands to the tropical north. The Mayall Creek massacre of 1838 and the subsequent execution of the European perpetrators divided white society between those who could justify the violence and those who condemned it. In 1845 a select committee reported on the condition of Aboriginal people. It was chaired by the lawyer Richard Windeyer, who had argued the preceding year that Aboriginal Australians had no claim to the land because they had no concept of property rights.[33] Windeyer was, nonetheless, concerned about their welfare and he thought it worth hearing their evidence. In the end the committee spoke to just one Black person. He was a harbour man called Mahroot. Some people called him 'the boatswain', presumably because of an affinity he had with the water.

The commissioners' questions ranged over matters of perennial interest to Europeans attempting to understand the people they had colonised: religion, morality, work ethics, social dislocation. Mahroot's evidence shed little light on the situation of the Aboriginal people in the interior but it did outline the story of social apocalypse and survival around the harbour. He was born at Botany Bay – sometime, he thought, during the time of the 'Governor before Macquarie'. Mahroot had also been told he was 49 years old, which placed him as an infant during Hunter's administration. Asked how many people were originally in his language group, he replied 'Four hundred I think in my recollection.' In 1845, however, 'the boatswain' was living at South Head with around 50 others. Only three of these people were from his language group; the remainder had come in from the Liverpool district to the southwest. Disease and dispossession had created social vacuums. Mahroot made it clear that things got worse when whites introduced alcohol.

Mahroot and his merged group of survivors spent their time fishing among the rocks and hunting possums – much as the Botany Bay people had done when he was a boy. But such had been cultural disruption that Mahroot had not undergone traditional initiation. Perhaps for this reason he provided little detail about his people's spirituality to his colonial questioners. Possibly Mahroot chose not to share his information. He was a man living between two worlds, adapting as best he could. He had simply run away rather than lose a tooth. He had a wife but no children and had worn trousers and a coat for as long as he could remember. As a young man Mahroot sailed with the whaling ships, earning £30 a voyage. Like the other sailors, he 'threw it away' back in port. In the 1840s he paid for his needs by catching fish for the Sydney market. He earned enough to 'keep going', but the fish were scarce in winter and the European nets had reduced the stocks even in the good season.

Mahroot's was a rare Aboriginal voice from the colonial harbour. He answered the committee's questions with a clarity and understanding that seemed to confound the expectations of the inquisitors.

> *Question* Do you quarrel with the black fellows of
> Liverpool now?
>
> *Answer* No.
>
> *Question* Do you think that black fellows would like
> their children to be taught like white people?
>
> *Answer* Some would, some would not.
>
> *Question* What do black fellows mean by devil devil?
>
> *Answer* Devil Devil is all over small pox like.

Asked why more Aboriginal men did not work on the whaling ships, he replied simply, 'Because it is dirty work and hard work and they do not fancy it at all.'[34]

Mahroot moves in and out of historical accounts. There were many Aboriginal people who remained around the harbour, despite the upheaval that was colonisation through the 19th century, but whose lives were not documented. That cannot be said of Bungaree whose utterances, actions and likeness were well recorded. He was painted and drawn and reported upon repeatedly in the 1820s and 1830s. Bungaree comes down through history as an important but highly mediated figure in the harbour landscape. We know him through the eyes and words of others.

Bungaree was not originally from the harbour but he knew life around the water. He was born at Broken Bay, the country of the Garigal people, and therefore he shared the language and some of the beliefs of the north shore clans. The thought of eating rays and sharks repelled him. By the late 1790s he had travelled down to the harbour and befriended Matthew Flinders. With what David Collins described as a 'good disposition and open and manly conduct', British officers and gentlemen saw in him traits they recognised and admired. Bungaree certainly possessed a character capable of traversing culture. In 1799 he joined Flinders' expedition of discovery and colonial consolidation north to Hervey Bay on the coast of present-day Queensland.[35] When the navigator sailed out of the harbour to circumnavigate the continent in 1802, Bungaree went with him, providing an Aboriginal presence in this unprecedented voyage. On the trip he liaised with other Aboriginal people with whom he had no shared language. But his Aboriginality and probably his understanding of coastal culture, made a difference on several occasions. At Sandy Cape on Fraser Island, for instance, he facilitated a conciliatory feast of porpoise blubber with local warriors.[36]

In this way Bungaree took up Bennelong's role as mediator and intermediary, enacting it around the coast and back in the harbour, where he assumed the position of an Aboriginal leader. The group around him was probably made up of people from different clans: reformation after so much dislocation. In 1815 Lachlan Macquarie called him 'Chief of the Broken Bay Tribe' and gave him an engraved brass gorget that said as much. Others around the harbour were given similar titles. A man called 'Kitten' became 'Chief of the Sydney Tribe'. Macquarie thought that Bungaree's 'good disposition' would also make him pliable, a model to other Aboriginal people who still showed a 'repugnance to civilisation'. To this end Bungaree and 15 others were given land 'on the northern shore of the Harbor' to farm. It was near a bay the Boregegal people called Koree, on ground that the Europeans came to call Georges Head. Macquarie supplied a fishing boat, tools and 'comfortable huts' and then reported to Earl Bathurst that he did not doubt 'they will become Industrious, and set a good Example to the other Native Tribes residing in the vicinity of Port Jackson'.[37] Aboriginal lifestyle might be doomed, but the paternal Macquarie thought that the people themselves could be 'civilised'. A year later white people were being killed on the Hawkesbury and Macquarie declared that no Aboriginal was to approach a settlement while armed. He sent soldiers to hunt down the attackers and ordered that their corpses be hung from trees – a far harsher lesson in British civility and justice.

Bungaree was not interested in fighting Europeans or farming. He was a negotiator. And as much as was possible for a 'colonised black man' and an alcoholic, he was his own person.[38] He abandoned the farm, but kept the boat and took it down to Kirribilli. This had been one of the favourite fishing places for the Gamaragal people and it provided Bungaree with both fish and easy access to the busy cove opposite, where he confronted newcomers and solicited money, grog and tobacco. It was from Kirribilli in April 1820 that he rowed out to the Russian ship *Vostok*, then visiting on a voyage of scientific discovery. Bungaree laid out his credentials to Captain Thaddeus von Bellingshausen: he had sailed with Matthew Flinders and, pointing back to the north, he said, 'This is my shore.' His wife Matora referred to herself as a queen. Then they asked for 'tobacco, old clothing, guineas and everything else that happened to catch their eye'.[39] In essence they were requesting tribute.

Bungaree continued his soliciting through the 1820s and became a regular sight on the waterfront. He and his group also maintained the traditions of the harbour clans. Fish were caught with spears around the rocky foreshore – to be eaten, sold or bartered. Hollow trees and rock ledges served as shelter in preference to the huts supplied by Macquarie. Matora covered herself in fish oil to deter insects and adorned her hair with animal teeth. The men gathered theirs in 'conical coiffures'. Ochre and paint were used as body paint. Music and dance remained important. IM Siminov described one ceremony at Kirribilli:

their music consisted of the sound of the two small sticks, which the single musician beat time with, and of his loud voice as he sang a dissonant song. The dancers stood before him in a single line. They jumped at each blow of the sticks, and hummed: prrs, prrs, prrss.[40]

It was around this time, just as he was painting John Piper, that Augustus Earle produced his portraits of Bungaree. By then the Aboriginal man had taken to wearing a cast-off military tunic, trousers and cocked hat – in part a self-conscious reference to his status as a 'chief' and a mariner and also, perhaps, in mimicry of the Europeans. So dressed, Bungaree became the subject of the colony's first lithographic print. This image and others were used to create a panorama of Sydney that toured England in 1829. With its many variations, Earle's representation of Bungaree became one of the iconic images of Sydney.

Earle also completed a version in oil paint, and the resonances between this and the Piper portrait are striking. That they were painted within months of each other suggests the formal similarities were intentional. In each the uniformed subject stands with left foot forward. The gently sloping point and the villa behind Piper have an equivalent in Bungaree's portrait with Bennelong Point and Fort Macquarie. Bungaree lifts his hat in greeting, Piper leans forward slightly in a gesture of patrician acknowledgment. The similarity is not surprising for both men were representative faces of the harbour, Piper in his capacity as naval officer and Bungaree in his as an Aboriginal 'chief'. Piper collected duties and fees to fund infrastructure – and his own lavish lifestyle – and Bungaree took it upon himself to ask for a few coins in the course of welcoming new arrivals 'to his country'.[41]

The use of oil paint to represent an Aboriginal person was probably unprecedented. By virtue of this, and the fact that the portrait is not a caricature, Earle appears to be according dignity to the Aboriginal man. But of course there could be no serious suggestion of equality between a poor Black man in a cast-off coat and a wealthy white administrator. Earle had a high regard for Piper, despite his subsequent fall from grace.[42] He may have been fond of Bungaree but any empathy or sympathy apparent in the oil painting was undermined by another lithographic version of the portrait published in 1830. There Bungaree is shown in the same gesture of greeting, joined this time by his second wife Caroo, who the whites called Cora or Queen Gooseberry. The impressive harbour background was replaced with one of a non-descript street, thereby robbing the 'chief' of his natural and noble context. The inclusion of two grog bottles in a nearby basket suggested to viewers that Bungaree and Caroo represented a tragic people doomed by their contact with civilisation. And for those who did not make the visual connection, Earle reported, 'In the neighbourhood of Sydney the Natives are growing scarce.'[43]

The shift from permitting Bungaree's nobility to denying it might be explained by Earle's intervening trip to New Zealand where the physique and culture of the Māori captured his imagination. They, rather than the first Australians, were 'the noble race of men' who might actually rise to the challenge of civilisation and inherit the future. In any case, Earle's view of Bungaree and his people was now widespread. The Ku-ring-gai man's refusal to settle and farm, his pointed and annoying parodies of European manners and dress, 'disproved' notions of a universal potential for individual improvement – the optimistic Enlightenment mindset that had spurred the 'civilising' impulse in Phillip and Macquarie. 'As in the eye of Nature he has lived / So in the eye of Nature let him die!' wrote Sydney magistrate Barron Field in 1825.[44] Around Sydney the Europeans 'humoured' Aboriginal people who remained and got on with the business of building wharves and boats and villas with views.

Bungaree, for his part, probably did not care whether he was being humoured or not. In his mind the harbour was his place and he went and did much as he pleased. But years of addiction and living rough took their toll and he died of an unspecified illness in 1830, the year Earle's condemnatory lithograph was published. Bungaree had been offered help at the public hospital and was taken in by the Catholic priest Roger Therry. But shortly before his death he was carried by his

people to Elizabeth Bay, where Macquarie had set up an Aboriginal
camp a decade earlier, and then to nearby Garden Island, the large
double-domed outcrop the clans had called Ba-ing-hoe. There he was
surrounded by members of his 'tribe' and others from Darling Harbour.
The island had been declared part of the governor's exclusive domain
by Macquarie, but for the Aboriginal people it had continued to be a
meeting place – out on the harbour but close to Woolloomooloo where
they had fished before the arrival of the Europeans and continued
their ceremonies during the 1820s. Bungaree's body was placed in a
coffin and taken to the grave of one of his wives – it was a burial rather
than a traditional cremation. Remarkably enough, the place was Rose
Bay, part of the old Piper estate. The *Sydney Gazette* noted Bungaree's
passing and burial but the graves were unmarked and their location
forgotten after a generation.

The 'King' was survived by his 'Queen'. Caroo was the daughter
of the prominent Aboriginal man Moorooboora, who led the Murro-
ore-dial clan from the beaches south of Botany Bay during the first
years of colonisation.[45] The Europeans gave her status some ironic
acknowledgment, presenting her with a gorget that read 'Gooseberry
/ Queen of Sydney to South Head' and was decorated with a crown, a
laurel and two fish.[46] Before her death in 1852, Caroo revealed something
of her knowledge of the lore of the harbour to George French Angas,
a naturalist, artist and collector of indigenous skulls. Angas was the
son of a wealthy shipowner and merchant, and – like Augustus Earle
before him – had travelled around the Mediterranean in pursuit of
views and other interests. The Angas family business brought George
to South Australia in the early 1840s and from there he began a
dutiful quest to record the culture of the 'fast disappearing' Aboriginal
people 'as may prove interesting to ethnologists at a future day'. He
enjoyed a 'ramble'. In Sydney he went to Camp Cove at South Head
and prevailed upon the Aboriginal people there to dive for delicately
coloured 'coralline' among the rocks. Mahroot may have been among
the men who speared fish by torchlight and provided Angas with 'a
wild and picturesque sight' to include in his account.

Caroo was also there at Camp Cove. Angas promised her tobacco and flour if she would accompany him around the harbour in a whaleboat in search of Aboriginal pictographs. She was chosen, rather than one of the men, because she was the oldest person in the 'Sydney Tribe' and her memory was good. That the old woman was reluctant to visit sacred sites reserved for men mattered little. Angas was more interested in the art of the dead than the sensitivities of the living. Caroo finally acquiesced and took Angas along the rocky headlands on the north shore. The extent of the artwork she revealed suggests a knowledge of the landscape and its special places that belies the contemporary impression of a life spent simply begging and drinking in the town. Caroo may also have accompanied Angas along to Middle Head and down to Lane Cove for he recorded many more engravings there of fish, kangaroos, people and shields.

The artist conducted his own investigations on the foreshore rocks of John Piper's old estate, where he was staying with the Coopers, and found at least ten engravings of life-sized male figures and huge fish. Angas was puzzled by what he saw and had difficulty reconciling the ancient rock art with the people still living around the harbour. He suggested an Asiatic or Celtic origin for the Australian art and the language, before concluding that 'By what event or means, or at what period New Holland was peopled by this now degenerate race, still remains clouded in obscurity ...'[47]

Angas ruminated less upon the reasons for the 'fast' disappearance of Aboriginal people. But by the 1840s thoughts of cycles of ascent and decline were being replaced by ideas of linear progress and certainty in the perennial might and morality of the British empire. Observers, like Angas, now used the scientific discourse of racial supremacy. Charles Darwin, for his part, had been perplexed by the social devastation he had witnessed in Australia and elsewhere. Social causes such as the impact of disease were obvious, but there was also a 'mysterious agency generally at work' for 'wherever the European has trod, death seems to pursue the aboriginal'.[48] Much as Darwin resisted its application to humanity, his theory of evolution would come to rationalise the 'inevitability' of racial decline and extinction.

Aboriginal people did not die out. Indeed, they continued to occupy the harbour – refugees for the most part from the farmlands of the south coast and elsewhere. In the late 1870s they camped at Circular Quay, where their presence confronted busy commuters, and the quieter waterfront at Berrys Bay across the harbour. For one local resident the gathering prompted empathetic thoughts of dispossession and restitution. Education advocate and future Federation campaigner Edward Dowling wrote to the *Sydney Morning Herald* in 1878: 'Considering the vast territory which has been wrested from these poor people without compensation, I take it would be a graceful act to allow them the privilege of pointing to one of these small islands at the entrance of the metropolis as still their own'.[49] Dowling had in mind Goat Island, Bennelong's erstwhile Me-Mel. But by then the little island was housing explosives for the colony's defence. Aboriginal people around the harbour were, instead, relocated to a reserve at La Perouse on the far southern edge of the metropolis.[50] They were literally exiled to Botany Bay.

[FIVE]

FORESHORE
DEFENDERS

'WHAT A
MAGNIFICENT
PICTURE ...'

Summer on the mid-19th century harbour was a time of bright light, passing smells and varied sounds. Darling Harbour and Sydney Cove were all bustle. The sun's heat made the moored whalers even more pungent. The occasional whiff of coal smoke which drifted over the water with each passing ferry and coastal steamer became more frequent as the century progressed. For many years these boats were powered by paddles rather than propellers, and so the sound of splashing water accompanied arrivals and departures. Down the harbour the steam whistle punctuated the drone of cicadas and mixed with the screech of parrots and the crack of whip birds. Forest and scrub were still prominent around the water on both shores all the way to the cove and beyond. At the water's edge the scent of eucalypt mixed with salt spray. Closer to the Heads the spray accompanied the thumping of waves.

The pre-eminent poet of the Australian forest, Henry Kendall, wrote as fondly of the interplay of water and foreshore in the 'lordly harbour' as he did the beauty of 'the bush':

> ... the days when limpid waters glass
> December's sunny hair and forest face,
> A roaring down by immemorial caves,
> A thunder in the everlasting hills.[1]

There were places where the moist smell of moss and ferns and the sparkle of small waterfalls could still be enjoyed. The area around Neutral Bay on the north side was one. Darling Point on the opposite shore was another. English writer Frank Fowler visited the 'Dripping Rocks' there in the mid-1850s: 'It is so pleasant to stand under their overhanging ledges, and see the bright water falling just in front of you – sparkling in the sun, like a curtain of crystals.'[2]

The summer harbour was a time and place to mark history. Since the late 1820s Phillip's arrival had been commemorated on 26 January with 'Anniversary Day' regattas. In the 1840s these were a series of egalitarian races that reflected, to some extent, the diversity of harbour life. Licensed watermen pulled skiffs, working men manoeuvred their whaleboats and gentlemen sailed their 'first class' racing yachts from the Darling Harbour Gas Works around Shark Island and Sow and Pigs Reef to Manly Cove and back. Their womenfolk presumably watched and waved. Geometric planes of white sailcloth contrasted sharply against water made blue by the sky above.

Harbour winters, by contrast, could be very grey. The morning fogs were thick and the water reflected slate-coloured clouds just as well as it did an azure sky. At Sydney Cove this gloom was deepened by the expanse of mud that spread out from the mouth of the Tank Stream. The place had been silting up for years as a result of tree clearing, building and pollution. A bar of sand and mud had formed around the intransigent remains of the brigantine *Ann Jameson*, which had exploded at anchor in 1834 after its cargo of gunpowder ignited.

110

Work had begun on deepening the cove in 1843 when a steam dredge called the *Hercules* began digging up the sludge on the eastern side. That vessel had been built with local expertise, around the corner at Pyrmont. The *Ann Jameson* was finally cleared away with the help of an imported English diving bell. A stone wall was constructed along the east side, around to the south. Where necessary the foreshore would be 'scarped', or simply cut away, to create a deep anchorage. As early as 1825 Governor Thomas Brisbane admitted that his underutilised foreshore presented 'a pleasing prospect to the Eye' which could no longer be countenanced in light of the overcrowded facilities.[3] The suggested release of the Domain waterfront to fund the new Government House was eventually acted upon and by the early 1840s Blore's edifice stood behind, adding to the facelift. It was joined by the handsome Customs House designed by Mortimer Lewis on the improved southern waterfront. Thomas Mort's woolstore was completed by 1850. Mort had pioneered specialist wool auctioning in Sydney and was the most significant dealer in the city. His premises symbolised the importance of the fleece and they grew to resemble a palace as the tonnage of fleeces exported increased.[4]

The new waterfront was first called Semi-Circular Quay and then, as the shaping continued, simply Circular Quay. It matched the impressive sandstone buildings behind and created a distinctive sense of place: 'docks built of hewn stone, are the first objects that attract the observation of the stranger ... Stone is the most prevalent material', remarked the writer William Shaw in 1854.[5]

When the eastern and southern sections of Semi-Circular Quay were complete by the mid-1840s there was little left of the original topography of the shoreline. The west side was still silty, with rocks and little beaches between the wharves. This was where George Bass's whaleboat had ended up. The pale clay used in Josiah Wedgwood's medallions was undoubtedly darker by now. This shore too would be duly covered over. The original Hospital Wharf, where the dying of the Second Fleet had been lifted ashore, was pulled down around 1854. It had since been renamed King's Wharf and then Queen's Wharf with

John Carmichael's 1833 engraving shows the dual use of the site as a port facility and pleasurable lookout. The station communicated by line of sight then by telegraph with South Head. The flags here are probably reporting the arrival of a colonial brig from China via Van Diemen's Land. *Sydney Cove from Fort Phillip*, 1838. John Carmichael, engraver.

Beat Knoblauch Collection, Historic Houses Trust of NSW

the ascension of Victoria in 1837, but despite its regal nomenclature it was still a convict relic. A long quay that replaced it ran from the old Tank Stream to Campbells Cove.[6]

Much of the dredge's good work was undone with the connection of the city's first sewer pipes the following decade. The outfall at Bennelong Point filled Sydney Cove with filth and sediment. The dredge *Hercules* worked on. It had been aptly christened, for clearing the cove was akin to the task of cleansing the manure-filled stables that had confronted its mythological namesake. The job took a heavy toll on the dredge's master Thomas Cronin, who lived aboard the vessel with his family. His son died of an unnamed disease which doctors associated with the effluvia that swirled around the dredge. More probably the cause was dirty water. After the boy's death, the Cronins abandoned ship to live ashore.[7]

Above the quay, atop the Rocks on Flagstaff Hill, the government built a fine sandstone observatory with its own transit telescope to accurately calculate local time. From 1858 the eyes of the ships' captains were trained on its time-ball tower at one o'clock so they might set the chronometers that would allow them to determine longitude and minimise the threat of wreck on an unexpected shoal or coast. Night-time observations were soon hampered, however, by light pollution from the gaslit streets around. At the signal station nearby, observation had been a daytime activity. The signal master poked a hand-held telescope through a porthole in his cottage window in order to decipher the shipping news from the Heads. Optical signalling worked best on clear days, and there could be no news after dark until an electric telegraph was installed in 1858. The hill station had communicated with South Head since 1810. Its stock of flags once contained pennants that relayed news as specific as the arrival of female convicts from Ireland. By the 1840s the widely understood combination of flags and telegraph arms generated anticipation of reunion, European news, English fashion and opportunity. With each new arrival, butcher's clerks ran down to waiting watermen in a race to secure contracts to provision the vessels:

> Jupiter of old shook the Heavens by a nod: our signal master has but to hoist a square blue flag with a pointed red one beneath, together with a black ball on the southern yard-arm, and the great city is immediately in a commotion. The cry of 'the Packet's in' 'a ship from London' runs from mouth to mouth with amazing rapidity.[8]

Administratively, Flagstaff Hill was one of the most important sites in the harbour. Yet the breathtaking view was available to all. One contemporary account described the 'neatly dressed children ... sitting or wandering about totally regardless of the signal-master'. The democratically inclined journal *Heads of the People*, which provided profiles on prominent port identities such as the signal master, the steamboat captain and the customs collector, urged townsfolk to see for themselves 'what a magnificent picture does the harbour present.'[9] High on the hill, it was easy to overlook the mess immediately below.

'Population and wealth will flow in upon us ...'

The second Monday in June 1849 was as grey a day as any. There was no view of the South Head signals in that weather. Standing at the Queen's Wharf, one might have heard the intermittent cheers of the five thousand people – more than one-tenth of the city's population – who had gathered by midday on the new quay for the 'Great Protest meeting' to oppose the return of convicts to Sydney.[10] Having ended transportation to the mainland in 1840, the Colonial Office had decided to start it up again in order to take the pressure off British prisons, which were again overcrowded. The people they wanted to be rid of had served some time in goal. The remainder of their sentence would be spent in what was called 'exile', labouring in New South Wales. And the colony would benefit from the 'free' labour. The scheme's advocate, the British foreign secretary Earl Grey, had a point: the new quay had been built by convicts.

A committee headed by WC Wentworth agreed with the idea. Some other landowners also thought the return of the servant class would be a good thing. But a great many others were horrified and, on the wet June Monday, they met to confront the first of the anticipated new wave of convict ships, the *Hashemy*. The radical *People's Advocate* had been urging the people to act for weeks. Now even the wind complied with the popular mood: the bitter sou'wester blew straight back up the harbour's south arm, making progress for any inbound sailing ship difficult, if not impossible. But the *Hashemy* had already arrived and it was lying at anchor in the cove.

The waterfront and nearby Macquarie Place and Barrack Square were favourite places for popular politicking in mid-19th century Sydney. Speakers stood on a bullock dray parked under the oak trees growing along Bridge Street, which crossed the stream close to the cove.[11] Anti-transportation meetings had already been held in one of the city's theatres and up the river at the Homebush racecourse, ironically enough on a former Wentworth family estate. But for the 'Great Protest meeting', the new quay had particular practical and symbolic significance. Renewed transportation ran counter to the wish for ongoing free immigration, free labour and greater commerce – all things invited by the new harbour facilities. From the quay the protestors could see the thing that threatened to turn the clock back and recreate the penal colony. The *Sydney Morning Herald* described the occasion as if it were a scene from a Gothic novel: 'hitherto they had seen its odious features limned in official despatches: now they saw its solid substance in the shape of a convict ship floating upon their harbour ... There the monster lay; but they met it as British freeman should.'[12] And Government House, with its pro-transportation resident, was just up on the rise. On this occasion that 'palace' was less a symbol of a rising colony than one of an oppressive home rule. Governor Charles Fitzroy was so concerned at the mood of the crowd that he doubled the guard on the gate.

The *Herald* treated the matter as if it were an invasion and urged 'every man be at his post!'[13] Among the prominent defenders present was Robert Campbell Jr who, like his merchant father, had opposed transportation since the 1830s. Another was the mercurial barrister and politician Robert Lowe, who had seen which way the political winds were blowing and set his course accordingly.[14] Now he roused the crowd with images of the waterway 'again polluted with the presence of that floating hell – the convict ship'. Instead of boatloads of merchandise and free immigrants, they had been delivered a 'cargo of crime'. Lowe was denying history as much as he was trying to change it. The passengers of the *Hashemy* were condemned as 'the moral filth of Great Britain', despite the penal origins of many in the crowd.[15] But Lowe was also tapping into a possessive sentiment linked to a rising democratic instinct and sense of colonial identity: Port Jackson was becoming the people's harbour.

At a second meeting the following Monday, anti-transportation merged into calls for representative government, the censure of the governor and the dismissal of the reviled Earl Grey. The mention of William Charles Wentworth's name had already prompted booing from the crowd. Yet despite the hostility, few of these people were revolutionaries. They saw themselves as 'British freemen' with ancient rights to uphold. They were, in the words of the democrat Henry Parkes, 'free and loyal subjects of Her Most Gracious Majesty', who rightfully opposed the 'landing again of British convicts' while demanding 'self government'.[16] They achieved both.

In 1853 transportation was officially ended and the colony was granted self-representation, pending the passage of a constitution. The following year the anti-democratic Wentworth left the 'spacious harbour' for England to champion an hereditary upper house. He had achieved the goal of colonial government, but his preference for a local equivalent of a House of Lords jarred with the popular mood. Wentworth still supported the shipowners, whose enterprise filled his harbour with masts and took the produce of the inland back to the mills of Britain, but he despised the multiplying merchants who contributed nothing, as he saw it, to the generation of wealth. Former shopkeeper and customs agent Henry Parkes – one of the free immigrants of the 1830s – won the by-election for Wentworth's vacant Sydney seat in 1854. Two years later the new colonial parliament was convened with its nominated council and elected assembly. Wentworth saw the harbour briefly once more in the early 1860s but died back in Dorset in 1872. His body was returned to Port Jackson with the marble sarcophagus within which he was interred in a mausoleum overlooking the cove at Vaucluse.[17]

News of the final termination of transportation and approval of self-government arrived at the quay by international mail steamer in April and May 1853.[18] Steam power had nearly halved the time taken to travel between Britain and its colony – from as long as 130 days down to 70. Establishing this service had been another drawn-out concession from a reluctant Colonial Office and so the delivery, in itself, further suggested a new relationship between colony and 'home'. Accordingly, a gala ball and supper was held at the still-incomplete Greek Revival sandstone Australian Museum to celebrate the arrival of the 'First Royal Mail Steam Ship from Great Britain' in August 1852.[19] The queen was toasted and guests danced the 'Chusan waltz' in honour of the triple-masted, single-funnelled screw steamer that had brought the mail on the last leg from Singapore.[20] The immediate impact of the long-distance steamers was short lived. The British screw and paddle steamers were recalled for military use during the Crimean War from 1854 to 1856.[21] In any case, the heaving engines of the steamers were inefficient, allowing the sleek, wind-powered clippers to remain competitive for years after that: they held their own against steam, carrying wool and passengers, until the 1890s. There were still forests of masts at the quay and Darling Harbour into the 1900s.

Parkes and others were just as optimistic about the political and social changes heralded by the discovery of gold in New South Wales in 1851. Indeed, colonial gold had influenced the decision by the Home Office to finally allow the long-delayed trial of 'steam communication' between Britain and Australia. Watery metaphors abounded as the *Herald* anticipated the effect of the technology on Sydney and its harbour: 'Population and wealth will flow in upon us in copious, rapid, and continuous streams. Port Jackson will ere be one of the most, crowded, bustling harbours in the world, and Sydney take her place amongst the richest and most flourishing of cities.'[22]

The newspaper was mostly right. The value of gold exports eclipsed that of wool – but just for a decade. In that time, however, the population of greater Sydney grew to over ninety-five thousand, and the relatively compact city, where most people could still walk to the water, expanded from over forty-four thousand in 1851 to more than sixty thousand in 1861.[23] The introduction of steam power followed the end of the restrictive navigation laws in 1849, which opened the colonial trade to ships from outside the British empire. William Shaw described the scene at the quay:

A Singapore trader, manned by Malays, is discharging tea
chests and sugar bags. A clumsy old liner from Liverpool is
unloading wet and dry goods, for odd shaped packing cases,
and barrels of Dunbar's porter, are piled alongside it. The
deck of an adjoining vessel is thronged with emigrants; they
are grouped around colonists, who are giving unvarnished
accounts of the country. The cracking of whips announces the
advent of bullock-drays piled with wool-bags' bales pressed on
quay ...[24]

Gold blew away the lingering effects of the depression of the 1840s and
set the basis for metropolitan growth. It also inflated living costs and
incomes which, in turn, enlarged the number of men eligible to vote,
eligibility determined by the value of their property or the amount of
rent they paid: the £10 franchise. So in Sydney almost all men had the
vote. The precious metal expanded the electorate and levelled it. In
doing so it consolidated the popularity of such men as Henry Parkes.[25]

There was a downside. The lure of gold exacerbated congestion
and social dislocation in the city, particularly in the already densely
settled foreshores around Sydney Cove, the Rocks, Darling Harbour
and Woolloomooloo. The young English gold assayer and social
theorist William Stanley Jevons conducted a private survey of the
city in the mid-1850s. He ranked the Rocks below 'the worst parts' of
London and Liverpool: 'nowhere have I seen such a retreat for filth
and vice'.[26] Henry Parkes was also concerned. He commuted to his job
in the Legislative Council by steam ferry from bucolic Kissing Point
to busy Darling Harbour, where he was confronted by all the sights,
sounds and smells of the working waterfront. In 1859 Parkes chaired
an inquiry into the condition of working people in the metropolis and
the findings confirmed his fears. It echoed the commissions that had
followed the outbreak of cholera around the river Thames and the
language recalled the exposés of the English social reformer Henry
Mayhew. There was a 'darkening mass of moral and physical disease'
in the harbour city, declared Parkes, akin to the worst parts of the 'old

world'. Families were abandoned by men leaving for the goldfields. Children roamed the streets, lanes and wharves of the waterfront precincts. Inadequate drainage left cesspools throughout. The problem was particularly bad where waterfront reclamations at Darling Harbour had raised the foreshore, preventing run-off: the foreshore there now bristled with wharves, and the natural curve and decline of the original waterfront was lost beneath the dozens of piers that pointed west. 'The smell on a close morning is almost overpowering in this locality,' reported one alderman. The presence of slaughterhouses in the area added to the stink and filth. In the 1860s, before Louis Pasteur and Joseph Lister had identified the link between germs and disease, foul-smelling 'miasmic' air was itself thought to be the cause of contagion. One witness concluded that it was only the sea breeze that had prevented the spread of epidemics.[27]

Council rate collector Joseph Clayton, who was asked to comment upon the conditions in which Chinese immigrants lived in the Rocks, reported that as many as 25 were living in a single Cambridge Street house. At a building owned by the Underwood family there were more. It is not clear from the evidence whether they were gathered there together socially or residentially. In any case, it was the cooking odours that Clayton most objected to: 'The smell is very offensive ... they told me it was some of their Chinese fish ...'[28] The committee made no recommendations with regard to the Asians, but their presence was clearly regarded as an unwelcome side effect of the gold rush. Although there were considerably less than two hundred residing in the city, mainly in the Rocks area, as many as ten thousand Chinese men had passed through the port on their way to the diggings. Having stopped the convicts, colonists turned their attention to these arrivals. In 1861 an *Immigration Restriction Act* was passed, limiting incoming vessels to one Chinese passenger per 10 tons of shipping.[29] In 1888, when another unwelcome ship called the *Afghan* arrived in the harbour carrying some two hundred Chinese passengers, Henry Parkes bowed to a xenophobic and riotous constituency and raised the tonnage restriction to 300 tons.[30] The port proved a most effective place to stem the tide of the unwanted.

There was a note of optimism in the 1859 report. The working classes were, the Legislative Assembly was assured, essentially moral people living in unpleasant environments. Parkes's committee suggested, therefore, that 'good government' should strive to provide 'human happiness' for 'all members of society'. This democratic sentiment, of course, extended to Europeans only. Encouraging settlement on 'public lands' in the interior was one part of the solution. But for those in the port city, more salt- and freshwater baths would improve personal cleanliness. More important was the construction of well-ventilated and adequately sized model workers' cottages.[31] It was one of the earliest arguments for remedial town planning in the colony. The entrepreneur Thomas Mort had just begun experimenting with the provision of housing for his waterside workforce while they built the huge Waterview Dock at Balmain to service new steamships such as the *Chusan*. But that was relatively cheap empty land. Fixing the unplanned clutter around the now-expensive foreshore of Darling Harbour and Sydney Cove was another matter. It would take 40 years of hand wringing and the arrival of the bubonic plague in 1901 before model housing was provided there for the waterside workers of Port Jackson.

The committee also recommended the establishment of a nautical school as a means of 'reclaiming' the 'vagrant' boys of the waterfronts – they had found children 'floating about the streets and lanes like fish in a pond' and, indeed, swimming naked around the wharves.[32] Such a school might also satisfy 'a growing want in our maritime trade'. The Rocks was home to many sailors, but captains had difficulty procuring local crews while in Port Jackson, especially when the possibility of finding gold increased the number of desertions. And those employed on the water divided their time between seafaring and working on harbour craft or the wharves. They did not 'follow the sea constantly', as one captain lamented.[33]

Parkes had been pushing for the establishment of a school that would turn poor boys into productive sailors since taking up his Legislative Council seat in 1854. He remained hopeful despite the reluctance of his peers – country gentlemen in the main who were less concerned with the problems of the urban poor. By 1866 Parkes was colonial secretary, there was a democratically elected lower house and he had the power to enforce the idea. An old ocean-going paddle steamer – the wheels of which had long since been removed to maximise the economy of sail – was bought from Robert Towns, a whaler, merchant and the Millers Point wharf owner. The refitted *Vernon* housed 113 boys and was moored in Farm Cove within sight of Government House. In 1871 it was taken to Cockatoo Island, where the youngest of the would-be sailors – boys of three to seven years of age – were accommodated on shore at the Industrial School for Girls established at the same time. Their older compatriots clambered up and down the *Vernon's* rigging in well-reported public performances intended to reassure the respectable that discipline and seamanship were being instilled in the city's wayward youth.

By 1891 the *Vernon* was rotting away and was replaced by a Scottish-built metal-and-timber clipper ship, the *Sobraon* – once one of the fastest and most luxurious windjammers to carry passengers from Britain to Sydney. By the turn of the new century destitute boys were being rounded up for incarceration on the hulk from as far away as Cootamundra in the west of New South Wales. They symbolically cast the material reminders of their former lives into the harbour before taking up berths in their floating reformatory.[34] There they learned to read and write. They were also taught to swim. Young Barney Kieran, son of a Sydney seaman and wharf worker, left the *Sobraon* to become an Australian champion in the water. Few, however, chose to 'follow the sea'.

The 'defence of Port Jackson ought not to be denied'

It had taken the colonists some time to find a use for Cockatoo, which had been known to the harbour clans as Wa-rea-mah. It is the largest of the harbour islands and emerges from the water where the harbour meets its estuaries. Although its peaks were progressively sheared off, the island's area actually grew by half again as a result of the reclamations and work carried out through the 19th and 20th centuries. There were two other smaller outcrops nearby and the colonists thought that the group looked like a hen with its chickens – and they referred to them as such. By the 1830s the noisy flocks of parrots that frequented the place prompted the name Cockatoo. Islands are always good for exiles and in 1839 convicts who had been employed in constructing powder magazines on Goat Island were transferred to Cockatoo to start building facilities for prisoners from another water-bound place of exile – overcrowded Norfolk Island. They also cut two huge bottle-shaped silos into the rock as emergency stores for grain. A wharf was built and some of the quarried stone was used for a sea wall at Circular Quay. They were among the best building blocks in Sydney.[35]

The convicts stayed and the island became a high-security prison from which there was only one known escapee: the bushranger Frederick Ward. In 1863 the legendary 'Thunderbolt', as he became known, braved the sharks, swam to Balmain and made his way up to New England on the northern tablelands, where he was shot dead seven years later. The regime Ward fled was brutal. Committees of inquiry in 1858 and 1861 revealed levels of overcrowding, poor food

This photograph by Charles Bayliss shows two unidentified ships in the Fitzroy Dock around 1880. It shows the use made of sandstone in engineering. The dock was completed in the 1850s, a contemporary of the sandstone improvements of Circular Quay. The size of the facility is evident from the two humans on the right.
National Library of Australia PIC P743/28

and ill-treatment that shocked those who heard or read the evidence. The convicts were eventually removed and their facilities given over to the 'reform' of destitute girls and the boys of the nautical school. If convict associations were unpopular in the 1840s, they were an embarrassment in the 1870s. In order to remove the stigma, the island was renamed Biloela, a north Queensland Aboriginal name for the screeching parrots. The semiotic sleight of hand was not very successful and the place remained Cockatoo in the minds of many.

The outcast boys and girls shared their island home with the navy. The harbour's malleable bedrock again lent itself to the task of colonial improvement as convicts set to work cutting a dry dock out of the living stone. Generations of Aboriginal people had lived under ledges created by wind and water. They had given their stone places meaning with ochre and engraved images and occasionally they fashioned small wells. Europeans simply cut the harbour stone as they saw fit – for shelter, defence, storage, commerce and beauty. Headlands were sheered away to provide ballast to counteract the buoyancy of underfilled ships. At Cockatoo gunpowder was used to smash the cliffs on the southeast shore of the island. The Fitzroy Dock, begun in 1851, was not completed until 1857.[36] Thomas Mort's paid workforce took just one year to finish his larger facility in 1855 across at Waterview Bay. That project was almost entirely funded by Mort, who had made a fortune from auctioning goods and property, investing in gold mines and brokering wool. Well over half the fleeces that came through Sydney were handled by his company. The completion of these two docks, in addition to the existing Australian Steam Navigation Company slip in Darling Harbour, vastly improved the maritime facilities available at Port Jackson. Where once wooden hulls were careened – scraped and cleaned – by winching a ship onto its side on one of the harbour's beaches, these new docks allowed the huge composite-and-iron hulls of ocean-going vessels to remain upright in a dock that could be emptied or flooded via a caisson gate. Mort's Dock serviced commercial needs. Cockatoo Island was given over primarily to the needs of the Royal Navy. The larger Sutherland Dock was completed on the other side of the island in 1890.

In the 1840s only two British corvettes were based in the harbour and its fortifications inspired confidence in no one. It was hoped that the provision of the Fitzroy Dock would foster the presence of Britannia's fleet. For as colonial democrats were considering greater autonomy from Her Majesty's government through self-representation, the governor and others were pressing for more protection. Sir George Gipps had suggested the facility as a 'naval establishment' to the colonial secretary in 1845 when a squadron of French Navy steamers was cruising the Pacific and the Americans were extending their westward reach with a fleet of ten windjammers. Six years earlier, in 1839, two uninvited American warships had simply sailed up to Sydney Cove under cover of darkness, unseen by the South Head station or anyone else. By then charts of the harbour were readily available to mariners. Armed with these and keen to make use of a good wind, the Americans set protocol aside and entered without warning or a pilot. Captain Hudson of the sloop-of-war *Peacock* recalled: 'When the good people of Sydney looked abroad in the morning, they were much astonished to see men o' war lying among their shipping.'[37]

Ships of the Royal Navy had anchored in Port Jackson many times since colonisation but the harbour was not a naval base. From 1821 a warship visited annually from the East India station, which defended British interests from the Persian Gulf to Australia. Colonial wars against the New Zealand Māori changed this, and from 1848 the navy patrolled the Pacific from the harbour with a view to giving 'the natives an impression of the power and friendly disposition of the British nation'.[38] The Australia station of the Royal Navy was finally established in 1859 and Garden Island, where Bungaree had drawn his last breath, was handed over to the British Admiralty.

It was difficult enough attracting warships to the harbour despite an imperial strategy that relied upon the reach of the Royal Navy. Extracting funds from the home government for the improvement of fortifications was even harder. The task had confounded colonial governors since the beginning of the harbour settlement: an open-air, waterside prison hardly justified the expense of defence. The successful conclusion of the Napoleonic Wars in 1815 and the consequent reduction of the French threat further reduced the rationale for spending. The Colonial Office's disapproval of Lachlan Macquarie's love for neo-Gothic and classical structures prompted a report on the colony's defence needs from Major James Taylor. The place was not, he thought, worth attacking.[39]

In 1835 there was some concession to local concerns when Captain George Barney from the Royal Engineers was duly despatched to take up a post as engineer officer.[40] He brought with him his family and an expertise in defensive engineering gained from imperial service in the Peninsular Wars against Napoleon and in the West Indies. The captain was promptly given civil duties on top of his military role and soon developed an affinity with the local stone. Before he built Fort Denison, Barney advised on the construction of the Semi-Circular Quay and the initial excavation of the Argyle Cut, the small canyon that would eventually join Sydney Cove to Darling Harbour. He supervised the excavation of the Cockatoo Island silos and produced a plan for a new panopticon-type gaol that would have delighted Jeremy Bentham. By the time of his death in 1862 Barney had influenced the workings and look of the harbour as much as any person.

And like so many others who administered, shaped or profited from the waterway, he chose a home with pleasing aspects from which to contemplate it. Barney owned two fine stone bungalows overlooking the water on the north shore. The grounds of the Priory, next to the property of his friend Conrad Martens, extended down towards the water at Berrys Bay. Wotonga sat right above the Kirribilli headland and the defensive battery Barney had had built there in 1856. The military engineer could view all the defensive works for which he had responsibility from the vantage of the verandah.[41] The house was bought by the colonial government and then transferred to the Crown in 1885 for the use of the commanders of the Australia station. Admiralty House, as it was known, was greatly enlarged and after Federation became the residence for governors-general and one of the enduring landmarks of the harbour.

Barney had quickly concluded that the harbour defences were 'in a very dilapidated state'. In 1840 he set two hundred convicts to work preparing a gun emplacement at Bradleys Head and cutting down the pyramid-shaped Pinchgut so that it might accommodate a major fort. The convicts were among the last prisoners transported to the colony and were housed in wheeled wooden boxes located at the worksites. Barney anticipated Colonial Office approval for these works, which seemed like an obvious necessity. When funding for the work was refused, the captain and a supportive governor proceeded anyway. Convicts may have been slow but they were cheaper than wage labour. By 1842 Pinchgut had been levelled to the high-water mark. Some of this stone was used for Semi-Circular Quay. As winter loomed, the convicts completed the job half-naked, their clothing worn away by the work.[42]

The concoction of headlands, bays and islands that delighted artists also presented strategists with an array of potential defensive positions from which to confound an enemy. However, there was disagreement over whether it was best to stop an invasion at the Heads or to defend the port town itself. Barney favoured the latter and proposed a fort on Pinchgut and improvements to the old Dawes Point battery and Fort Macquarie. By way of forward defence, there were guns at Bradleys Head and a fort to be built on the Sow and Pigs Reef that divided the main harbour into east and west channels. That shoal had earlier accommodated the harbour's first navigation beacon, derisively referred to as a 'tar barrel on a mop-stick', but some felt a lighthouse should have been erected there.[43] Barney suggested instead a circular Martello tower of the type that already dotted the east and south coasts of England. Barney's replacement as commanding royal engineer, Lieutenant Colonel James Gordon, who took over in 1843, believed instead in fortifying the Middle, South and Georges heads. He retained the idea of fortifying the reef and thought that, since Pinchgut had already been levelled, a Martello tower would work for that site. But the strategic shift and the depression that overtook the colony meant the island remained a flattened rock, with a few cannons behind a stone parapet, for another decade and a half.

The people of Sydney Harbour were not indifferent to defence issues and the press frequently aired schemes and responses to them. But regardless of one's literacy, the destruction of Pinchgut was a very obvious public work for all to see and comment upon. The utilitarian attitude towards the outcrop was not universally condoned. The excavation, and the apparent dithering that followed, incensed the radical democrat and republican preacher John Dunmore Lang: 'This natural ornament of the harbour ... which no art could have equalled, this remarkable work of God, which had stood, like a sentinel looking over the harbour for thousands of years, has been destroyed by the folly of man ...' His was surely one of the earliest protests against the despoliation of the harbour: a 'romantic islet ... replaced by the unsightliness of an abandoned quarry', lamented Lang. But just as significant was the polemical association of the 'vandalism' with the lack of popular representation. The harbour was 'perfectly defenceless', Lang agreed, but the episode demonstrated that the greater danger came from an 'incapable and irresponsible government' that wasted public resources without consultation.[44] It was another argument for democratic reform. Lang was still fuming 20 years later.

The British government, for its part, was as uninterested as ever. In August 1847 Governor Fitzroy had conveyed the concerns of 'gentlemen connected with the commercial interests of Sydney' regarding the 'defenceless' state of the harbour to the intransigent Earl Grey who, it was pointed out, had recently approved improvements to harbour defences in Canada. Their anxiety was exacerbated by the land wars in New Zealand, which had drawn British troops away from Sydney to fight the tattooed warriors across the sea. The 'defence of Port Jackson ought not to be denied', suggested the governor. A petition from Sydney aldermen followed in November. It emphasised the imperial government's duty to protect its colonies or provide the means of protection. The colonial secretary responded with a suggestion of his own: the colony was now wealthy enough to pay for its own forts, even if it was not ready for self-representation. The 'despot' Grey was disliked as much by nervous merchants as he was by colonial democrats.[45]

From 1851 gold increased the funds available in local coffers for defence while elevating the perceived worth of the colony. Britain's war with Russia, forecast in early 1854, tipped the balance. Approval for defence improvements came the following year. George Barney was returned to orchestrate the work and a new governor, Sir William Denison, brought his military experience and opinions to bear. He concluded that 'those works which bear upon, or protect in any way, the anchorage in front of the town should be completed first'.[46] Fortifying the Heads could wait. The Martello fort that bore the governor's name was finally completed in 1857. Having levelled the island and disposed of the rubble more than a decade earlier, stone for the fort itself had to be cut from the cliff at Kurraba Point on the north side. The guns were installed by the following year, accompanied by batteries at Kirribilli and Mrs Macquarie's Chair at the end of the Domain parkland and improvements to the existing Fort Macquarie and Dawes Point. This bristling inner ring of cannons shielded the commercial heart of the harbour with its new quays, Observatory and Customs House. The entrance was less protected. By then, however, the brief but bloody Crimean War half a world away was over.

New ballistic technology had made these fortifications redundant almost as soon as they were completed. Kirribilli, Fort Macquarie and Mrs Macquarie's Chair were soon decommissioned and most of the guns at Dawes Point removed. Fort Denison, on erstwhile Pinchgut, became a harbour landmark with its own aesthetic associations – as well as a place to drill volunteers, mount navigation lights and measure the tide. Extensive areas of land at Georges and Middle heads were resumed in 1861 for defence purposes. In 1870 yet another review of defences confirmed a shift in emphasis again towards the east. It followed the final departure of British troops from the colony. By the middle of that decade colonial soldiers manned 41 guns trained on the harbour at Inner South Head on the southern side, and Bradleys, Middle and Georges heads on the north shore. A track, the Military Road, had been cut through the scrub to supply these establishments with ordnance. The enormous gun barrels were encased in timber and rolled along beams until they reached the emplacements. Military technology had also brought to the world torpedoes and electrically fired mines. A station for operating the latter was built at Chowder Bay, where once American whalers had anchored and the crews reputedly made soup from the local shellfish.

'[H]ateful, and hated Waves of the Sea!'

Death and destruction had, in fact, been visited upon the harbour even before Fort Denison was finished – not with Russian guns but by the sea itself. The immigrant ship *Dunbar* was dashed to pieces on a stormy winter's night in August 1857, when its captain mistook an indent in the cliffs just before South Head for the port's entrance. Without power of its own, the *Dunbar* was broken by wind and waves and all but one of the 122 people aboard were killed. It had been a beautiful ship, built with the best skills and materials the empire could provide: British oak and Indian teak assembled by shipwrights from Sunderland. The *Dunbar* took over 16 months to complete and cost a substantial £30 000. But such was the gold-fuelled demand for immigrant ships in the 1850s that its owner and namesake, Duncan Dunbar, thought the outlay would return a profit. After being pressed into Crimean War service in 1854, the *Dunbar* began its Australian runs. The first to Port Jackson in 1856 was successful. The second was not.

The reality of the disaster unfolded slowly. The terrible weather had meant that the optical signals at South Head were useless. A horse and messenger were despatched from the station there after the wreck was discovered on the morning of 21 August. News did not reach the harbourmaster Robert Pockley until 10.30 am and then he had to travel 'by land' back to South Head to assess the situation for himself, 'the weather being too thick and violent to communicate by boat or telegraph'.[47] The identity of the ship was a mystery. Navigation had improved greatly since the days of Cook and Phillip, but exact arrival details remained unpredictable before the introduction of ship-to-shore wireless communication in the 1900s. That the doomed vessel was the *Dunbar* was gradually confirmed by inscriptions on the first bits of debris to be found – a mailbag and a cask of tripe.

Thousands rushed out to the Heads to watch the sea pound the remains of the ship and its passengers for themselves. Body parts, dead animals and cargo were washing up in the harbour for more than a week. The floating carcass of a cow, 'red with white spots', was seen being circled by sharks near Georges Beach, where the naked body of a little boy had been recovered.[48] There had not been so many corpses around the waterway since smallpox devastated the harbour clans and the tragic cargo of the Second Fleet had been thrown overboard. Much of the human and material debris went up Middle Harbour and around to Watsons Bay. The proprietor of the Pier Hotel at Manly recalled fighting with a shark over the body of one man:

> I think this dreadful disaster, filling the sea around here with more than a hundred corpses, has attracted every shark in the Pacific Ocean. This one was a huge monster and he was determined not let go of his victim. I tried to take the poor man away from the shark, but the shark won and disappeared with it into the deep water.[49]

It fell to Robert Pockley to steam around the harbour in a Manly ferry called the *Black Swan* and haul the awful mess out of the water. People gathered at the quay awaiting his return. Some were morbid onlookers, others were desperately trying to locate loved ones. The *Sydney Morning Herald* printed a special supplement with news of the disaster and a passenger list in their Saturday edition. The names of the deceased began appearing the following week. Unidentified remains were buried in a mass grave at Newtown and thousands lined the streets as the coffins went past. Sentiment, however, was soon joined by self-interest and people began picking over the wreckage and carting off reusable metal and timber before any inquest could be convened.

The destruction of the *Dunbar* shook Sydney to its core. The tragedy had added impact for, alongside the cabin loads of strangers, there were many local people returning home. Henry Kendall expressed both the sense of loss and the fear of the sea evoked by the wreck. He lived near the *Dunbar* tomb in Newtown and knew the ocean firsthand from his days as a cabin boy on a whale hunter. The poem 'Drowned at Sea' was printed in 1862. It included the words:

> Oh, the sorrow of the morrow!
> – lamentations near and far! –
> Oh, the sobs for dear dead sisters perished in the lost Dunbar!
> –
>
> Ye ruthless, unsated,
> And hateful, and hated
> Waves of the Sea! ...[50]

The *Sydney Morning Herald* also vividly conveyed the collective horror and disbelief that followed the happy expectation of homecoming:

> Instead of the warm and loving welcome, come tidings of a terrible catastrophe and then the cold, mutilated half-recognisable forms of those who will never cheer the social circle anymore ... Wrecks are frequent with flimsy ships near bad harbours and with reckless or incompetent commanders. But here was a vessel built as strongly as teak timber and honest English shipwrighting could make her entering one of the finest harbours in the world ...[51]

The *Herald*'s tone of incomprehension was telling. The ever-present reality of shipwreck had never intruded so completely upon Port Jackson. The emotion was compounded in October when, despite being anchored and tended by pilots, the *Catherine Adamson* was pushed onto Inner North Head by the swell, killing another 21 people. The government could not fail to respond.

An electric telegraph was installed in January 1858 connecting the South Head signal station with its counterpart above Sydney Cove to provide almost instantaneous communication in any kind of weather.[52] The Hornby Lighthouse, near Macquarie's tower, was completed within a year. Henry Kendall likened the new constant beam to a 'mighty fallen star' burning 'through the darkness like a splendid ring of Tenfold light'.[53] For Kendall, the *Dunbar* wreck and the consequent construction of the Hornby Light, atop the 'rampart' like cliffs, accentuated the sense of the harbour as a sanctuary from the 'hateful sea'. It was as 'calm and lucid as an English lake' – much like Conrad Martens' beloved waterway. The tragedy of the *Dunbar* was that it did not quite reach the haven.

'[T]o develop the physical powers and courage of the people'

Robert Pockley was not an artist or a poet, but few people understood the different moods and identities of the waterway better than its harbour-master. He had been at sea with his father since he was nine. At 19 the Englishman sailed into Port Jackson on a brig from New Zealand. He spent a decade in a windjammer called the *Emma* racing steamers to and from the harbour as part of the coast trade, before settling down as the harbourmaster in a St Leonards villa with water views, not far from Conrad Martens and George Barney. Pockley chose the site because he had used the tall tree that grew there as a beacon as he negotiated the waterway in foggy weather.[54] Having done his morbid duty assembling the human remains from the *Dunbar*, he drafted *Sailing Directions for the Harbour of Port Jackson*, an updating of John Hunter's original instructions written to complement the erection of the Hornby Lighthouse. Pockley did not mention the tall tree at St Leonards, but he did point out other visual cues for safe harbour navigation not present when Hunter surveyed the harbour in 1788. These were the lighthouses, the Macleay family mansion above Elizabeth Bay and the spire of Greenway's St James Church. The red light on the new Fort Denison was 'intended for the more especial purposes of guiding Steamers and Coasters'. Foreign ships, he continued, were 'forbidden by the Port Regulations to pass this light until boarded by the Health Officer and other Authorities'.[55]

That year Pockley bought John Lamb's wharf in the busy bay below the Observatory and conducted a private shipping business from the city. Port-bound, the captain sailed whenever he could in a 10-ton pleasure yacht called *Mazeppa*. With several others, he formed the Australian Yacht Squadron in 1862 to race for fun and honour on the harbour's 'limpid' waters. It became the Royal Sydney Yacht Squadron soon after. Among the foundation members was the boatbuilder, businessman and property developer Richard Harnett, who had bought Archibald Mosman's land with the view to residential subdivision.[56] Ten years after the *Black Swan* combed the northern shores for the dead of the *Dunbar*, the enterprising Harnett chartered the same steamer to take picnickers to the pleasure grounds he had opened on the northern foreshore. In the same year as the Hornby Light went up and Denison got its guns, he had designed one of the most innovative racing vessels of the age, the poignantly named *Australian*. Harnett had eschewed the lines of the English- and American-style yachts then sailing in the Anniversary Day regattas. Instead he drew inspiration for his symmetrical hull from a streamlined mackerel he had pulled from the water at Woolloomooloo.[57]

Ownership of a yacht was a mark of a harbour gentleman – much like residence in a waterside villa. The first such vessel in Port Jackson probably belonged to Robert Campbell, the merchant from Sydney Cove.[58] Also there at the beginning of the squadron was James Milson Jr. He had been given a first-class vessel by his father, James Milson, himself a pioneer of harbour racing. The Milsons possessed yachts and several large properties around Kirribilli and Lavender Bay. The elder James was perhaps the first European to live permanently on the Gamaragal land, supplying visiting ships with the meat and vegetables. He was forced to contest his land title with Robert Campbell after records were destroyed in one of the many bushfires that swept the overgrown north shore forest. So, in an irony of dispossession, a grant of 140 hectares could not be proven. Campbell won but the Milsons held on to some land, including 20 hectares above a bay with a freshwater spring that the Gamaragal had called Gooweebahree. Europeans acknowledged it as Quiberee. The meaning and identity of harbour places were in a constant state of flux through the 1800s as possession and use shifted. Later, when convicts were imprisoned on a ship offshore, this cove became Hulk Bay and then Lavender Bay after the man who supervised the prisoners and built his small home there. The Milson family home which sat above this bay was called Brisbane House in honour of the governor – Thomas Brisbane – who promised Milson his 140 hectares.

James Jr and his brother John lived in fine homes overlooking another creek-fed cove to the east. John called his house Wia Wia, an echo of the Gamaragal name for the place. Like Campbell, he was a merchant and a grazier. He was also a practical man, and next to Wia Wia he had an abattoir reputedly erected from timber washed up from the *Dunbar*. For a while the recycled structure gave the cove a new, no less evocative, name: Slaughterhouse Bay.

While Pockley, Harnett and the Milsons were enjoying the salt spray aboard their racing yachts, others were immersing themselves in the harbour itself. The therapeutic benefits of the sea had been appreciated by Europeans for a hundred years. The English went to Brighton, the French to Nice – to bathe and be rejuvenated by sea air. Some even drank the salty liquid in the hope of curing jaundice and other ailments. The physical stimulation was enhanced by the underlying sense of danger and awe generated by the Sublime vastness, power and coldness of the sea. With temperate waters and no waves, the main threat in Sydney's saltwater came from the ever-present sharks. Fifty years earlier, Governor King had warned convicts of these 'voracious' fish and forbade them from bathing in Sydney Cove – presumably for fear of attracting the monsters to the bay. Nonetheless, bathing, often nude, was very popular. So much so that Macquarie had again forbade the practice at the government wharf and dockyard, this time in the interest of decency.[59] But the governor could recognise a good beach himself. In 1821 he had noted that the pilot's station at Watsons Bay was 'admirably well calculated for sea bathing, there being a very fine smooth sandy beach below the House for that purpose'.[60] In 1828 Ralph Darling's castellated bathhouse provided more accessible privacy for the governor's vivification. By then a fondness and aptitude for swimming was being recognised as a defining characteristic of a distinct colonial 'type'. Local boys seemed oblivious to the dangers of sharks and many of the girls of the port could 'swim and dive like waterhens'.[61] There were baths in Darling Harbour in the 1820s and, in the 1830s, swimming enclosures had opened for men and women in Woolloomooloo Bay. The men's baths used the hull of an obsolete American-built paddle steamer called the *Ben Bolt* and took its name from the same.

By the 1860s children were swimming around the wharves of Darling Harbour without supervision and also, it seems, from the beach at the bottom of the Brisbane House garden across the harbour. That small spot was known colloquially as 'the reserve'. James Milson disapproved of the bathers while coveting the waterfront and he applied to acquire the foreshore and the land down to the low-water mark. The attempt prompted the local member for the Legislative Assembly, William Tunks, to mobilise his constituents and oppose the application on the grounds that so much of the waterfront to the west and east had already been alienated from the public. Tunks was developing a passion for defending public lands around the harbour. When Milson's application was approved, Tunks took it before a parliamentary committee and ensured he was the chairman.

The value of controlling foreshore land had dawned on colonial authorities rather late. Had Milson confirmed his 20 hectares before 1828 the waterfront would have been his. For the first 30 years of colonisation there was, apparently, plenty of foreshore. The land between Rose Bay and Watsons Bay, where Vaucluse would

The north shore around Kirribilli was another exclusive enclave in the late 19th century. This photograph shows the private bathing enclosure at the bottom of the garden of the villa 'Wyreepi', the home of the representative for North Sydney in the new Federal parliament, Dugald Thomson. The house, now called 'Sunnyside', still stands but without the enclosure.

North Sydney Heritage Centre, Stanton Library

subsequently be built, was alienated from 1793. The first 32-hectare parcel was granted to one of the New South Wales Corp monopolists, Quartermaster Thomas Laycock. Large tracts of the river-front had been given away in the 1790s to officials, former soldiers and deserving convicts such as James Wilshire. The surgeons John White, John Harris and William Balmain received acreage closer to Sydney Cove. Balmain's land was sparsely settled even as Thomas Mort was building his dock there in the 1850s. Property in Darling Harbour and Pyrmont had changed hands several times by 1800. The land around Kirribilli contested by Campbell and Milson had originally been granted while the Gamaragal clan was still in occupation. The waterman Billy Blue got 28 hectares to the west in 1817. In that year John Piper acquired his 285 hectares to the east, having already secured the Point Piper estate opposite.

It was not until 1825 that Governor Brisbane was instructed to consider the importance of reserving public ownership of land near, among other places, 'navigable streams or the sea Coast, which may be convenient at some future time to appropriate Quays and Landing Places'.[62] In 1828 Darling decreed that 100 feet (30 metres) be reserved above high water around 'the Sea Coast, Creeks, Harbours and Inlets' on all Crown land still unalienated.[63] But by then much of the foreshore land around the harbour had been sold or simply given away.

By the 1860s the government was clawing back some of this foreshore. Land at Middle Head and Georges Head was resumed for defence. In 1866 the democrat Tunks was more concerned about public access and recreation. There was the Domain enclosure and a 'warm and cold seabathing establishment' at the popular resort of Manly Cove – near the spot where man and shark had fought for possession of the *Dunbar* corpse – but little else in 'ninety-five miles [150 kilometres] of water frontage'. Tunks was as tenacious as he was dismissive of the evidence that suggested that Lavender Bay was in fact not well suited to bathing. His committee duly recommended that 'facilities should be afforded for public recreation and cleanliness especially among the working classes; and that places for sea-water bathing are desirable, as affording a healthful and invigorating recreation, and calculated to administer to the comfort, as well as to develop the physical powers and courage of the people', and that the contested site at Lavender Bay 'be permanently reserved as a place of public recreation and as a site for public baths'.[64]

By the early 1900s there were baths at Lavender Bay, Pyrmont, Balmain and more up the river. 'Professor' Fred Cavill operated enclosures at Farm Cove and Woolloomooloo. He had leased baths below the Milson property since the 1880s to instruct Sydneysiders in the 'noble art' – for they were, after all, 'constantly on the waters of the Harbour'.[65] It was there, reputedly, that his son Dick developed the Australian crawl, the overarm style that revolutionised competitive swimming around the world. It was at Lavender Bay also that the young Barney Kieran, the graduate from Henry Parkes' nautical school, broke the world record for a 440-yard (400-metre) swim in 1905. Kieran travelled to Britain to compete that year, where he bettered more records and was declared, by an astonished onlooker, to be 'a fish, not a man'.[66]

Kieran was not the first 'colonial' champion to emerge from the people's harbour. The rower Edward Trickett had a local pedigree to rival Kieran, having grown up beside the Parramatta River and married the daughter of the South Head lighthouse keeper. In 1876 he became 'the champion sculler of the world' after defeating the Englishman James Sadler on the river Thames. The following year 'the harbour was dotted with every imaginable species of craft' as Sydney's traditional Anniversary Day regatta celebrated both imperial foundations and Trickett's achievement on the water.[67] The presentation of a public purse of '900 sovereigns' made the sentiment all the more tangible. The water and the quay was crowded again in 1887 with well-wishers trying to glimpse and touch the muscular sculler William Beach when he returned from another successful colonial assault upon the British. The *Illustrated Sydney News* described the 'magnificent affair' in a manner that was both biblical and almost profane: 'To see Beach, to touch him, to rub shoulders with him, was an enviable joy, while to walk in his footsteps around the town was the consummation of all earthly joy.'[68]

The adulation accorded Trickett and Beach reflected the incipient sense of nationalism in the colony, an identity increasingly separate from the imperial centre that immigrant and local-born still called 'home'. Four years after Federation, the world champion Kieran was one of Australia's first truly national heroes. He soon became one of its first tragic heroes. Kieran died of appendicitis within weeks of returning to the harbour city – at the age of 19. The inscription on his grave echoed the intent behind William Tunks's campaign for public bathing at the bay where Kieran broke his first record: 'He won his laurels by courage, self-denial and patient effort.'[69]

SIX

A HARBOUR OF WONDER, A HARBOUR OF FILTH

'BETWEEN UTILITARIAN AND AESTHETIC'

Like Lavender Bay, Robertsons Point had been Gamaragal land. Descendants of the clan may still have been walking the area with Bungaree's people in the 1820s when the peninsula was 'granted' to the government's superintendant of clocks, John Robertson, by Governor Brisbane. What the Crown took from the clans it passed on with corresponding alacrity to worthy colonists. But Europeans still remembered that first possession and its original name Wulworra-jeung. James Robertson's grant exemplified again the ease with which foreshore was alienated before its worth for commercial and strategic uses was officially acknowledged in 1828. It also highlighted the imprecise system of land title that Brisbane had inherited from his predecessor, Lachlan Macquarie. Brisbane's promises and 'tickets of occupancy' continued to leave a legacy of dispute. And so James Milson Jr's purchase of Robertson's land in the mid-1850s locked the family into a second dispute with the government over ownership of the harbour foreshore.

This long finger of lightly timbered land had 2 kilometres of waterfront with magnificent views of the harbour and huge potential for wharfage. In 1877 Milson asked that any public claim to the foreshore be revoked and he be allowed to acquire it. Despite having been denied this very request at Lavender Bay, Milson was hopeful because others had been successful in purchasing absolute waterfront after 1828. The appeal was promptly rejected on the grounds of public interest. Some in government thought that this interest would be best served by retaining the land for recreation, while others thought its development as a publicly owned coal and rail terminus would benefit all the colony. Milson responded with an offer to swap one tidy piece of potential parkland at the end of the point for the rest of the commercially valuable foreshore, and he formed a syndicate with real estate agents to press the matter further. The compromise was accepted by Henry Parkes, who felt it satisfied all public needs, and the local East St Leonards Council, who were concerned about losing the entire foreshore for the public if the offer were refused.

But in the 1880s tolerance to disposing of public waterfront was waning and this time the parliamentary opposition objected. The arguments against the sale echoed Tunks's claim for Lavender Bay but they also invoked the concept of 'heritage'. The suggestion was that democratic government was the custodian of the natural, and occasionally the built, environment – and that land was an asset to be preserved and bequeathed to future generations as a 'birthright'. In the minds of many Sydneysiders in the 1880s there were few more 'magnificent' examples of such heritage as the harbour and its foreshore.[1]

When the transfer stalled, Milson's group began referring to the 'alleged' reservation of 100 feet (30 metres). They started clearing the land as if ownership had been secured and then advertised it for sale. Milson argued that because the Robertson grant dated from 1825, it predated the existence of foreshore reservation. The government maintained it was not officially recognised until 1833, five years after Crown rights to the foreshore were reserved. Consequently, a writ for trespass was issued and contested in the Supreme Court in 1891. There the syndicate changed tack. Leaving aside the existence of the 100-foot reservation, Milson's counsel referred to the principle of *nullius tempus*, which held that continuous and uncontested private occupancy of the whole point for at least 60 years had entitled his clients to ownership of the waterfront, regardless of any official reservation.

The problem for Milson, however, was the absence of 'a documentary title to the land'. And so the court heard oral testimony from locals, former residents and others who recalled visiting the place over the decades. These people spoke of the structural evidence of European use and possession of the foreshore. Their recollections described a sequence of changes typical of many places that dotted the foreshore through the 1800s.

The 82-year old Brent Rodd remembered the place in the late 1820s with 'fowls' running around, a four-room stone hut, a path 'down to the rocks and to the waterside' and 'a fence which went across from rocks to rocks'. Then, or later, another fence stretched across the back of the point from cove to cove to enclose the site. In the absence of roads and bridges, there was a jetty for mooring the rowing boat or dinghy that provided access to the town. This was a simple structure made by piling rocks in line out into the water. A subsequent occupant in the 1840s built a smelting works on the waterfront. By then the wharf had become something more substantial, with the rocks 'carefully put there'. A decade later the smelter was gone and there was a pleasure ground with an entry fee. The place acquired the name Cremorne after the public gardens in London. That enterprise was short-lived but the name remained and the use of the site for polite picnicking was revived in the 1880s. Cremorne became one of several recreation grounds along the northeast shore of the harbour accessed by chartered ferries.[2]

The onus, however, was on Milson and his partners to prove continuous occupation and apparently there were too many gaps in the timeline as it was collectively recalled. The jury found against the syndicate within minutes of the judge's summation. Milson appealed to the Privy Council in London but lost in 1895. The verdict saved the Cremorne foreshore for the Crown but did not ensure its preservation as a beauty spot. Working waterfronts were in the public interest, even more than beauty spots.

One possible future for Cremorne Point was being starkly laid out back at Lavender Bay. There the government resumed half the waterfront, from Milsons Point around to the little bathing enclosure that Tunks had secured for recreation at the tidal mouth of a creek. The public interest this time was transport and port development – specifically the completion of a huge loop railway linking the northern foreshore to the city via Hornsby. In the absence of the technology and funds necessary for a direct bridge or tunnel harbour crossing, this was an unlikely compromise. But it was hoped that the line would also open the foreshore to the west around Balls Head and Berrys Bay and to the east all the way to Cremorne Point, with deep-water wharf development mirroring the now-crowded Darling Harbour and Pyrmont on the opposite shore.[3]

The Lavender Bay resumption certainly returned that foreshore to public ownership. It also destroyed a small piece of waterfront with intimate economic and social connections to the harbour, developed over 50 years of subdivision and leases. By the early 1890s stone and timber cottages, hand-built rock wharves and boatsheds lined that part of the bay. Like the original cottages at the Rocks, most of these dwellings faced the water. The boatbuilder Henry Younger lived on steep, dusty Fish Street which ran straight down the hill to the water. George Alderton had his lime kilns near the water's edge there, fed by shells brought down from Broken Bay. His house overlooked the water in adjoining Glen Street, alongside the homes of two master mariners.

By 1893, when the rail line was complete, all the waterfront structures and several up the hill had been demolished and the stony escarpment cut away. The shore was 'reclaimed' from the harbour, flattened for the rail line and filled with the spoil. The resulting steep rubble slope at the waterline prevented access to and from the harbour except at the ferry wharf at the head of Lavender Bay. A brick viaduct had been built there to take trains from the new station at Milsons Point around to a tunnel dug under the western headland. The structure visually severed the waterfront from the shrubby and rock escarpment behind. People now accessed the foreshore through the viaduct arches. Completed in the midst of a depression, the railway did not fulfil its purpose of stimulating the development of the western headlands. In any case, the topography was not conducive to building trunk lines. The eastern extension of the rail line to Cremorne Point was never begun.

In the meantime, a government diamond drill had been boring into the spine along Cremorne Point to test for coal. The possibility that the north and south coast deposits were part of a great seam that ran under the harbour had been suggested back in 1847 by the Reverend WB Clarke, one of the leading geologists of the colony and part of the harbour-minded clique of north shore gentlemen that included Conrad Martens and George Barney.[4] The 1891 bore turned up poor samples, but others nearby had promising results. Three years later Sydney Harbour Collieries Ltd applied for a mining lease at Bradleys Head, just to the east. The newly formed local council at Mosman objected on grounds of aesthetics and amenity. A coal mine on the harbour there would 'deface' an area they had already decided would be a desirable residential locality rather than a commercial or industrial precinct.

When Milson lost his case in the Privy Council in 1895, the colliery sought to lease the public foreshore at Cremorne. The main protagonist in this second battle for Cremorne Point was Edward M Clark, who had taken up the mantle of William Tunks as both the local member of parliament and the area's foremost defender of public land. Clark opposed the mine on the grounds of public access and interest rather than aesthetics. He reminded his colleagues that the government had just fought to save the land for the public and now the Department of Mines was considering a lease that could potentially lock up the site for 40 years.[5] The company's application to lease public land cheaply rather than buy freehold property at market prices was, he maintained, an attempt to minimise costs at the public expense.

A new colonial government headed by George Reid concurred with Clark's claims for Cremorne, but promptly granted the company a lease to the waterfront at Bradleys Head for less than a pound a year. The applications had been publicised in the *Government Gazette* and obscure postings in government offices where there was little likelihood of public scrutiny. An exasperated Clark drove home the issue of transparency. The public had a right to know how their land was being managed: 'Every publicity should be given to any application which is made to the Mines or any other department.'[6] Clark succeeded in initiating a parliamentary and public debate on the matter. The discussion was broadened and ranged over matters of despoliation, the rights and wrongs of privatising public lands and the social and economic benefits that might flow from revenue and jobs – a point of some relevance in the context of the depression. In October 1895 the matter ended up in the Land Appeal Court, which found against the company. The court considered the government's role as trustee of public lands, argued that Sydney Harbour Collieries' intent to lease public land at minimal cost was exploitative and, most significantly, concluded that: 'No consideration in the nature of rent could afford any compensation or consolation for the disfigurement of the harbour,' which it described as the 'people's inheritance'.[7] As a result, the Reid government refused the wharfage lease upon which the venture was dependent and the project was terminated. The defeat of the mining proposal was the first time that claims for beauty trumped demands for development in the harbour.

The court's assessment of the waterway as 'one of nature's choicest masterpieces' had widespread resonance. Popular pride in the place had been welling for many years. The English novelist and travel writer Anthony Trollope was just one of many visitors to remark upon its local significance: 'the people of Sydney are by no means indifferent to the beauty of their harbour, and claim for it the admiration of strangers with something of the language, but not with the audacity of Americans'.[8]

It was clear, however, that the court's description was selectively applied to areas largely undeveloped and far removed from the commercial heart of the port. By the 1890s this was essentially the eastern harbour, where vast tracts of reserved defence lands, high headlands and the absence of a fixed crossing by way of bridge or tunnel had forestalled development and preserved a sense of the natural waterway that had entranced the first colonists and now gave Sydney its 'pride of place amongst the capitals'. Lavender Bay's waterfront, with its mix of small-scale cottages, boatsheds and wharves, did have aesthetic interest as an example of what might be called the cultural picturesque. The artist WC Fitler represented it in an engraving published in the 1886 *Picturesque Atlas of Australasia*. Photographer Nicholas Caire included it in his set of Sydney views in the mid-1870s. But such places did not yet warrant preservation. Even less of a 'masterpiece' was the waterfront at Balmain, near Mort's slipway and adjacent to Cockatoo Island. There, in one of the area's few pieces of public parkland, Sydney Harbour Collieries finally secured its right to tap the harbour's rich coal seam. And the company got its lease with the overwhelming endorsement of the local council and ratepayers, who thought development and jobs far outweighed the preservation of what little natural waterfront survived.

In early 1896 – a few days after the residents and representatives of Balmain formally endorsed the colliery – passengers on a passing ferry contemplated the abandoned mine site at Bradleys Head. One dismissed it as 'a little battleground between utilitarian and aesthetic members of the Legislative Assembly'. Another rose furiously to denounce the 'aesthetes' who had sunk the proposal: 'What is more disfiguring to the harbour than a coal-mine is the hundred, if not thousand, of our fellow-creatures who are living in caves, or holes, in gunyahs or humpies, on the shores of our harbour, with empty stomachs, or only what they can procure by charity.'[9]

The simple dichotomy between 'utilitarian and aesthetic' camps did not do justice to the basic principle of accountability championed by Edward Clark MLA, but clearly the issue of the public interest and development on the harbour had not been entirely settled in the public mind.

'[A]n artist's city'

The depression of the early 1890s took a harsh toll on the fortunes of working people, and the unemployed and homeless who were living rough around the harbour. The homeless population of the Domain hovered around two hundred even in good times. Sandstone rock ledges down near Mrs Macquarie's Point afforded some shelter and the panoramic views might have given solace to the dejected, at least in the warmer months. There were other places where cabins were erected and tents pitched to avoid unaffordable rents. Some of these, on the north side, had begun more as weekend retreats than abodes of last resort. Livingston Hopkins, the *Bulletin's* pen-and-ink artist, rented 20 hectares at Edwards Beach in Middle Harbour in the 1880s and set up a series of tents, which accommodated artistic friends interested in the new practice of *plein air,* or outdoor, painting and enjoying the casual recreations afforded by seclusion on the foreshore – fishing, swimming and drinking.

Another site was pegged out south of Hopkins's camp on the shore of the main harbour in Little Sirius Cove, one headland removed from Archibald Mosman's old bay. The land around there had been subdivided and sold off by yachtsman and entrepreneur Richard Harnett in the 1880s. Much of the eastern foreshore of Little Sirius Cove, however, had been resumed for military purposes in 1872. It was still undisturbed and lined with endemic woodland – trees such as the bangalay, with its rough bark and small white summer flowers, and the smooth-barked angophora. Banksias and smaller trees leaned out over rocks along the water. The contested Cremorne peninsula could be seen poking out on the other side of Mosman Bay. The Curlew Camp, as it came to be called, had been established by 1890 as a retreat by the department-store owner Reuben Brasch. It would later become home to impecunious artists such as illustrator and painter AH Fullwood, who lost his savings when the banks collapsed in 1893, and Tom Roberts, who was grateful to pay a modest '7 or 8 shillings per week' to live there after the crash.[10] But in 1890 the economic storm was only beginning to blow and the place was somewhere to enjoy the harbour and paint in the *plein air.*

Roberts had become familiar with the area in the late 1880s. In 1891 he took his friend and fellow Victorian Arthur Streeton there shortly after they arrived together by steamer from Melbourne. Both artists had practised painting out in the open at the 'bush' camps around Heidelberg on the rural outskirts of Melbourne in 1888, but the *plein air* of the harbour had a special appeal for Streeton. Describing his entry through the Heads to a Melbourne friend, he borrowed a line from the poet Adam Lindsay Gordon and wrote of the exhilarating effect of 'Gods glorious oxygen'. Soon after, he was pulling 'through the lazy green water' of Mosman Bay with Roberts to lunch in the shade with 'eggs, meat, cheers & 2 big bottles of claret grown in Australia'. There the perfume of 'orchids & the purple glory of sarsaparilla' filled the 'Warm balmy air'. It was, for him, 'A Land of passion-fruit and poetry'.[11]

Streeton's passion for the harbour was not confined to secluded patches of foreshore. The quay, he enthused in 1891, was filled with steamers behind which towered the port's institutional landmarks, the '[Hotel] Metropole Customs & Morts'. Sydney was 'an artist's city' because the commercial harbour engaged the artist's senses as much as the natural waterway: 'Little steamers puffing hard & skipping over the blue water clouds of smoke, next the steamers whistle & flute in different keys & over all the bright harmony the warm palpitating sky of the Sunny South.'[12] He would paint the quay in 1892 and 1893 in three oils that depicted an intensely urban waterway in which the only natural features – sky and water – blended effortlessly with steamers, smoke, wharves and buildings. Streeton compared the scene sometimes with Venice, sometimes with the Orient.

Arthur Streeton had come to Sydney in 1890, pushed by the economic gloom already enveloping the southern colony and pulled by the purchase of one of his 'pastoral' paintings by the Art Gallery of New South Wales. He painted the sea and beach at Coogee and then the harbour from Lavender Bay, where his friend the photographer Walter Barnett lived.[13] Sitting at McMahons Point, he sketched and possibly completed two paintings looking across the Bay to Milsons Point. *McMahon's Point Ferry* and *From McMahon's Point – Fare One Penny* were vertical canvases dominated by the expanse of calm blue water in the mid-ground. Streeton's painted bay looked far wider than the real thing. The blue there had its counterpart in the big sky of 'the bush', depicted earlier that year at Heidelberg in the painting *The Selector's Hut (Whelan on the Log)*. That image of a 'settler' sitting astride a giant tree he had felled with an axe was one of Streeton's most emphatic evocations of the pioneering spirit that was becoming central to the Australian sense of self. The clear blue sky and the associated glare presented the bush as a place of light, heat and hard work. By contrast, the harbour with its 'little steamers', seagulls and waterside houses was reassuringly picturesque and apparently devoid of labour. 'Hundreds and hundreds of yachts are coursing over the purple sea (it is as wine)', he wrote later in 1891. 'Ferryboats puff and paddle along crowded with pleasure-loving folk ...'[14]

Streeton was happy to record commercial bustle and the grandeur of steamers from a distance, but he never depicted waterfront workers as he did the 'pioneer' in *The Selector's Hut*. There was little interest at all in the work on the wharves of Darling Harbour or the boatyards of Pyrmont, Balmain or Berrys Bay. McMahons Point was as far west as he seems to have roamed in search of views. However, harbour paintings such as *From McMahon's Point – Fare One Penny* do engage with the routine intimacy between Sydney people and their harbour. The stone villa in the foreground had been built with its back to the land and its front to the bay, sharing the outlook of the painting. Ferries take passengers about their business from point to point. Another group chooses its own way in a small rowing boat.

In a letter to Roberts at this time, Streeton likened the great heaving expanse of the ocean with the terror and attraction of 'death and sleep'.[15] But, like Martens and Kendall, his harbour was a sanctuary. The point was made almost metaphorically in paint with the inclusion in *From McMahon's Point – Fare One Penny* of a small boy in sailor's outfit contemplating the view with toy yacht in hand. The boy and his boat were real enough – Streeton met him at the point – but their placement in the painting may have been more imaginary. Beyond the bay is the eastern shoreline, already slated for destruction when the paintings were being composed. Streeton shows the escarpment as a mix of nature's green, with buildings and wharves in blocks of brown. Descending brushstrokes suggest fence lines and tracks – distant impressions of a settlement relating to its harbour. He gave these features greater emphasis in a small horizontal painting on a board with dimensions similar to the 'cigar box' works displayed in the groundbreaking *9 by 5 Impression Exhibition* in Melbourne in 1889.

The two larger paintings from McMahons Point were entered in the Art Society of New South Wales exhibition in September 1890, along with eight others. Critics disliked their 'smudginess' and 'splotchiness' – just as they had dismissed the impressionist works in the Melbourne exhibition. The show was not a financial success for Streeton, but he did sell *McMahons Point Ferry*. Indeed, it was the only work he sold.[16]

The waterway Streeton painted from McMahons Point, and described in his exuberant letters, was a democratic place. There was much in this impression, for the harbour provided sustenance in the manner of a town common and recreation like a public park. Its bounty of fish was free for anyone able to harvest it. No licences were needed to cast a line or net if one wanted to catch a snapper or rock cod for sport or food. Oysters were commonly chipped from the foreshore rocks during picnic outings. Sydney's working boatmen had raced in the Anniversary Day regattas since the 1840s. The amateur Sydney Rowing Club shared East Circular Quay with the woolstores, clipper ships and overseas steamers from 1870 to 1888, when the needs of commerce pushed the rowers permanently up the harbour to Henley. They also shared Sydney Cove for a time with the Sydney Amateur Sailing Club, originally formed in 1872 by amateur and professional fishermen who wanted to race their open boats. The sailing boats that thrilled Streeton as they coursed 'over the purple sea' might also have been crewed by working-class men from Woolloomooloo, Balmain, Pyrmont and Lavender Bay. The Sydney Flying Squadron Yacht Club was formed in 1891 to challenge the dominance of the exclusive Royal Yacht Squadron and champion the inclusion of different classes in competition. The 1890s became the decade of the racing skiffs – 24-, 20- and 18-footers whose enormous expanses of billowing sails carried shallow hulls at breakneck speeds across the water.[17]

People had milled around the signal station on Flagstaff Hill enjoying the views there since the 1830s. Now all along the waterfront fine weather prompted picnic parties to head out for the dance halls, lawns and promenades of the pleasure grounds of Cremorne, Clontarf and Manly Cove. Their respectable enjoyment was occasionally disrupted by ferry loads of city roughs intent on claiming a piece of foreshore for themselves, albeit temporarily. For all the privatisation of the foreshore, Sydney people routinely lined every available headland and point to watch the harbour's frequent civic spectacles – sporting contests, momentous arrivals and tumultuous departures. Five years before Streeton sat at McMahons Point to take in the everyday happenings of the waterway, an estimated quarter of a million locals and a hundred thousand 'country folk' came to the harbour to watch the departure of colonial troops for the war in the Sudan: 'the Tarpeian Way was literally swarming ... Dawes Point had more occupants than were ever seen at a Regatta, and across the water, Milson's and Kirribilli Point seemed to have afforded temporary accommodation for all the inhabitants of the North Shore'.[18]

Streeton went back to Melbourne shortly after selling his McMahons Point painting but he returned to the harbour repeatedly over the following six years. He lived with Roberts at Curlew Camp in 1892 and again, with interludes elsewhere, from 1893 to 1896. The artist crouched low among the rocks of Little Sirius Cove, looked out at the quay from office vantage points and tramped across the northern headlands in the footsteps of Conrad Martens to capture vistas and the play of light upon the water and land. To best convey this he experimented with narrow slice-like views: the horizontal sometimes painted on long drapers' board emphasising the breadth of the harbour, the vertical engaging the viewer in an intimate, almost abstracted, interaction with details of light, water and foreshore. Streeton's harbour, like that of Martens, was never an entirely natural place – culture was always present in the form of a yacht, rowboat, distant houses or the plume of a steamer's smoke. It was a welcome presence rather than an intrusion, for these were landscapes that explicitly drew their significance, meaning and fascination from their relationship with people. The harbour was, for the artist, spirit, life and movement.

However, when civilisation in the form of the coal mines and collier wharves threatened to intrude too closely on this sanctuary, Streeton added his voice to the chorus of protest in the form of a letter to the press. The drilling and ensuing controversies at Cremorne Point and Bradleys Head had been underway throughout Streeton's residencies at Curlew and the artist could hardly have been oblivious to them. The date of his literary protest is unclear but he recalled its tenor years later:

> It pointed out that all the loveliness of the harbour just inside the Heads was likely to become obliterated by a mass of coaling hulks and machinery. This letter was referred to as 'Streeton's Shriek'. But other protests followed, people woke up, and the infamous project came to an end.[19]

While the influence of the artist's letter upon the public debate is unclear, his feeling for the threatened peninsula was emphatically expressed in the painting *Cremorne Pastoral*. It was the largest of his harbour works to that time and was the outstanding success of the 1895 Art Society of New South Wales exhibition. He completed the canvas and then sold it to the Art Gallery of New South Wales as the coal-mining controversy was reaching its conclusion. *Cremorne Pastoral* shows an elevated gentle green slope with a small stand of trees and the deep blue of the harbour behind. There are no people or boats visible, but Streeton could not bring himself to completely expunge the signs of civilisation – houses on the southern shore peep through the branches and between the trees. Still, it is clear that this is a place of special beauty, a modern arcadia by the water. Apparently anticipating approval of the mine, the *Australasian Star* characterised the painting as a historical document, 'a fair representation of the place as it existed before the invasion of the colliers'.[20]

Years later, Streeton would be recognised mainly for his Heidelberg works. These, in turn, came to be considered as pivotal interpretations of the 'the bush' and the people who were shaping the landscape of the interior. But his output in Sydney was so prolific and fresh in the 1890s that the *Bulletin* called him the 'discoverer of Sydney Harbour'.[21] Between 1907 and 1927 Streeton completed another 145 pictures of the place. By then the artist was being driven by the demands of the art market as much as his love of the waterway. He remarked upon the parochialism of the 'Sydneyites' to Tom Roberts after a successful show in 1907: 'they only bought the few panels I painted here … They only want their harbour.'[22]

The art-buying public was just a fraction of the city's population. The majority of people in the late 1800s or early 20th century would not have seen a Streeton painting in a gallery or a residence. However, his celebration of the vitality of the harbour, its leisure and commerce, natural beauty and sense of place, had a counterpart in the mass-market images already appearing in journals, illustrated newspapers and on thousands of inexpensive postcards. These pictures, the means by which most people experienced art, filled domestic scrapbooks and adorned the walls of the most modest dwelling. Streeton's themes were anticipated in the remarkable aerial views and panoramas that emerged from Sydney's International Exhibition in 1879 and then the centenary of colonisation in 1888. One hundred years after Phillip sailed into the unexpected harbour, the *Illustrated Sydney News* chose to educate its readers in the history of the waterway with a ten-part illustrated series, 'Sydney: Its Harbour and Bays' by the Reverend Canon Wilson. It was the most detailed account of the waterway's social history, geography and contemporary character produced to that date, replete with picturesque engravings of forts, yachts, coves and lighthouses.

The *Picturesque Atlas of Australasia* probably did more than any other single publication to bring quality illustration to the people.

Some fifty thousand subscribers received their monthly instalments between 1886 and 1888.[23] The *Picturesque Atlas* included some of the best engraved images yet published in the colony. Three of its staff artists, Frederick Schell, WT Smedley and WC Fitler, were recruited from North America and the publication also employed some of the finest colonial artists working commercially. Among them were Tom Roberts, AH Fullwood and Julian Ashton, all of whom socialised with Arthur Streeton at the Curlew Camp.

The subject matter of this and other illustrated publications was dominated by rural rather than urban scenes. As one contemporary observer noted, next to the dramatic subjects, Australians loved 'horses, cows or sheep' in their pictures.[24] The *Picturesque Atlas* also included a great many city views. Most were of grand buildings and boulevards but some, such as Fitler's engraving of Sydney's Haymarket area, captured the intensity of the urban crowd. The harbour, not surprisingly, was well represented. Fitler and Schell executed many of these pictures, including a scene of the boatsheds at Lavender Bay and a very Venetian rendering of waterside villas at Elizabeth Bay and Darling Point. Ashton pictured Fort Macquarie with discoloured stonework and shell-encrusted foundations, which spoke of an 'ancient' lineage and would have delighted its originator and namesake. Ashton's *Shipping, Circular Quay* showed tall-masted ships being loaded and unloaded on the east side of the quay. The image was probably copied from a glass-plate photograph and it accompanied a brief mention of 'the strong-pulsed life and bustling activity' at the cove.[25]

Yet the lumpers in Ashton's picture were hardly bigger than ants. There was no place for character studies of wharf workers, sailors, fishermen in the *Picturesque Atlas*, no portside equivalent of Ashton's rangy *Boundary Rider*, who appeared in volume 3, or the axeman of Streeton's *The Selector's Hut*. The situation was different 40 years earlier, when one of the earliest illustrated newspapers had shown a one-legged mariner looking out at the harbour through a waterfront window. It accompanied a poem called 'The Retired Seaman', a nostalgic romance of the sea. But that was in 1847, when memories of a Port Jackson whaling fleet were still fresh and the gold rush and Selection Acts (which made land for grazing and cropping available to those with limited means) had yet to tempt the adventurous to the interior. In 1896 one Royal Navy officer from the harbour's Australian station could generalise that the 'Australian-born does not appear to take readily to a seafaring life as a profession'.[26]

By then there was a consensus emerging among writers and artists that the national type was being forged in the continent's interior rather than on its rim. Charles Darwin, it seems, had miscalculated the commercial potential of the open lands. In popular artworks, as in Streeton's paintings, 'the bush' was well on the way to becoming the emblematic Australian landscape fostering a unique national spirit – even before the fact of nation existed. The reasons are complex. They range from the dramatic appeal of continental conquest to the undeniable economic importance of wool as an export commodity. There was the influence of French realism – with its emphasis on rural labour – upon Australia's urban-based artists, who looked with romantic fascination at the 'real' work undertaken in the forests and paddocks beyond city and suburban streets. There was also the generic representativeness of 'the bush' for colonies beginning to consider their common destiny and identity in a federation. Sydney's harbour, however much it was celebrated, was still a particular place suggestive of nowhere but itself.

One result of this was an absence of narratives relating to the harbour, stories of the people who lived and worked around the waterway. Paintings such as *The Selector's Hut* implied stories merely by focusing on the individual. Aerial views, vistas, glimpses and panoramas of the harbour conveyed the impression of a sense of place but without its detail. Nor were stories from the port any more apparent in literature. Most of the writing was picturesque or travel based. For the Scottish writer James Inglis, the very beauty of the place erased the drama of its history: 'The wrecked hopes, the bad passions … failures, cruelties, crimes, all fade away in the presence of the majestic beauty with which bountiful nature has surrounded the city.'[27] Sydney's harbour was internationally famous for its scenery. Anthony Trollope had done much to promote this with a relatively brief but powerful evocation of the place: 'I despair of being able to convey to any reader my own idea of the beauty of Sydney harbour. I have seen nothing equal to it in the way of land-locked sea scenery.'[28] Where Trollope despaired, the Australian writer Francis Myers persevered and described the waterway at night and at dawn in some of the best prose ever written about the place: 'the water is still then, and all the hills are vested in a luminous grey, actually melting, fancy might say, in the crucible of dawn, phantom shapes they seem wrapped in the shrouds of mist'.[29]

The writer and poet EJ Brady was an exception, perhaps because he worked on the wharves, witnessed the labour and empathised with the people there. He had grown up in sheep country west of the Blue Mountains and by 1890 was working as a timekeeper, clocking labourers for the rural agents Dalgety and Company at Millers Point. Brady developed a love for the sea and for the people who worked on and by the harbour: 'it was the golden portal through which I peeped one morning and saw for a brief moment wide mysterious domains of Glory and Romance spreading out and away across the whole world'.[30] But the timekeeper was sacked after he refused to sign up as a special constable during the violent and divisive maritime strike that year. He then became involved with organised labour and edited the newspaper of the Australian Electoral League, the *Australian Workman*. Where others wrote of droving and farming, Brady wrote numerous poems about the sea and port life for the *Bulletin* during the 1890s. One of them, 'Laying on the Screw', made explicit the relationship between the interior and the harbour, and the unacknowledged role of the waterside worker in pressing and handling the hated 'staple' wool:

> You can dunnage casks o' tallow; you can
>   handle hides an' horn;
> You can carry frozen mutton; you can lumber
>   sacks o' corn;

> But the queerest kind o' cargo that you've got to
> haul and pull
> Is Australia's 'staple product' – is her God-
> abandoned wool.
> For it's greasy an' it's stinkin', an' them awkward
> ugly bales
> Must be jammed as close as herrings in a ship afore
> she sails ...[31]

Brady's friend Henry Lawson also knew the bush and the city – and something of the sea. His father was a sailor from Norway who had deserted ship to dig for gold in Victoria. Henry was brought up on an unproductive selection in western New South Wales. His mother Louisa left the land and her husband and in 1883 moved to Sydney, where young Henry joined her and began a literary life. In 1888 he wrote his searing poetic critique of urban poverty and alienation, 'Faces in the Street'. That year also he invoked the hardship on the land in the poem 'Andy's Gone with Cattle'. The 1896 collection of short stories, *While the Billy Boils*, confirmed his reputation as a chronicler of the bush.

But Lawson had spent much of the intervening years living near the harbour. He was as familiar with the cheap boarding houses and wharves of Dawes Point as he was the barren selections of the western plains. Lawson based few of his stories and poems explicitly around the waterway in these years, and those he did were rather bleak. But the harbour clearly had an exhilarating effect on him and he described his emotional connection to the place upon returning from New Zealand in 1898. As his ship entered the Heads, the bush poet admitted that '... in loneliness and hardship – and with just a touch of pride – / Has my heart been taught to whisper "You belong to Sydney-Side".' He proceeded to describe the bays, places, sounds and scenes of the waterway:

And the sunny water frothing round the liners black and red,
And the coastal schooners working by the loom of Bradley's
   Head;
And the whistles and the sirens that re-echo far and wide –
All the life and light and beauty that belong to Sydney-side …[32]

Lawson had lived at McMahon's Point in the early 1890s, near the spot Arthur Streeton chose for his *plein air* painting, and was reputedly a regular visitor to the slate-roofed villa shown in *From McMahon's Point – Fare One Penny*.[33] Ten years later, as he battled alcoholism and the breakdown of his marriage, Lawson returned to the area and wrote of the communities, individuals and places there. The fondness exhibited in this small body of prose and poetry about 'harbour people' differs markedly from the alienated urbanism of his earlier writing. His work from this period contains some of the most intimate impressions of the waterway and its people ever written. Lawson described the 'democratic' horse ferry that ran from Blues Point to Dawes Point on which 'the cart of Bill the Bottlo' jostled with the 'sulky of his boss'.[34] Near the ferry wharf he watched children loading billy carts with the waterborne mess washed up nearby: 'butter boxes, fruit cases, occasional bottles etc from ocean-going craft'.[35]

Where others went to Manly to engage with nature, Lawson found beauty at Lavender Bay despite the railway. There, above the 'dusky blue', he watched 'the toy trains run' and 'fairy lighted ferry boats' glide across the water. In 1914 at Kerosene Bay – so-named because of an earlier industrial venture – he pondered German ships interned where once 'British lumpers worked till tired / With Yacob and with Hans'. He asked, 'How can the Harbour be so blue, the Harbour sky so fair?' when the world was at war. At Balls Head Lawson marvelled that such 'wild Australian bush' could be found in 'the heart of Sydney'.[36]

That piece of foreshore had survived the hopes for development that accompanied the railway to Milsons Point. However, in 1918, it was finally to get its coal-loading bunker and wharf – a modern

complex of gantry cranes and hoppers. Lawson was outraged and he echoed 'Streeton's Shriek' with a poem called 'The Sacrifice of Balls Head'. But where the painter's beauty lay to the east, the poet cried out for the rights of 'harbour people' in the waterway's grimy west to keep a little piece of nature:

> They're taking it, the shipping
>   push,
> As all the rest must go –
> The only spot of cliff and bush
> That the harbour people know.
> That spirit of the past is dead,
> North Sydney has no soul –
> The State is cutting down Ball's
>   Head
> To make a wharf for coal ...[37]

Lawson was a bit too pessimistic. The loader went ahead but in 1926, just four years after the death of the poet, the remainder of Balls Head was preserved as a public park.

'In the harbour I think the water is poisoned'

Port development at the western end of Port Jackson had increased markedly since the middle of the 19th century. The water across which the heroic rowers Trickett and Beach had skimmed was frequently a filthy mix of run-off and waste from sewer pipes, ships and the waterfront

---

Julian Ashton's image of the bustling waterfront of the western side of Circular Quay appeared in the *Picturesque Atlas of Australasia* in 1886. Mort's woolstore and the smaller Customs House are visible through the rigging.

Powerhouse Museum, Sydney

---

industry that lined the coves. William Tunks had known this even while he championed recreational access to the harbour back in 1866. That year he was one of 33 witnesses who gave evidence to the Commission into the Condition of the Harbour of Port Jackson. Huge amounts of refuse, sand and silt from the streets were washing down drains and straight out into the harbour at outfalls in Woolloomooloo Bay, Bennelong Point, the Tank Stream, Darling Harbour and Blackwattle Swamp. Wharf owner and former city mayor William Speer reported that the 'shoaling' in Darling Harbour had occurred at a rate of 1 metre in three years. There was suspicion that the Australian Gas Light Company intentionally dumped coal ash and rubbish to reclaim foreshore property from the harbour. At some parts of east Darling Harbour, where vessels of up to 800 tons once berthed, there was dry land.[38]

The situation was similar in Sydney Cove. There a sewer pipe ran from the city along to the end of Bennelong Point, where it disgorged faeces, food scraps, mud and sand into a cove already filling up with years of run-off from the degraded Tank Stream. The heavy particles sank while the organic material floated and washed back and forth with the tide, sometimes ending up in waterfront cellars. In the hot months of summer decomposition quickened so that the smell from the harbour enveloped large parts of the town and raised concerns of contagion. At Woolloomooloo Bay the pollution was so bad that former mayor George Thornton thought locals would soon be deprived of the 'wholesome luxury of seabathing'.[39]

The danger of polluting watercourses was not a recent revelation. The *Police Offences Act* of 1833, for instance, forbade people from throwing dead animals into the harbour and disposing 'any filth or rubbish' into water courses.[40] Tunks and those inquiring into the condition of the harbour were therefore bewildered by the scheme that had been implemented little more than a decade earlier: 'In getting rid of the street matter in the cheapest manner, they have found a convenient receptacle in the harbour and have, as it were, converted it into a large cesspit, thus doing enormous injury to that which is the most valuable possession of the citizens.'[41]

Henry Lawson's 'harbour people' with a shark that was caught in Berrys Bay in 1922. The successful fisherman was probably Sidney Barnett who is standing next to the fish smoking a pipe. Barnett regularly hooked sharks off Blues Point. His was a renowned harbour boat-building family.

North Sydney Heritage Centre, Stanton Library

The decision had been based, in part, upon the hope that the tide would simply carry the mess away. But it was also mired in the conflicts and expediencies that followed the colony's first experiment with democracy – the election of a city council. In 1842, a year before elected 'gentlemen' first took up their positions next to the appointees of the Legislative Council and a full 12 years before the democrat Henry Parkes won WC Wentworth's old seat, Sydney men voted for their mayor and aldermen. Governor George Gipps had been happy to defray the expense of delivering services to the people, just as the Colonial Office was offloading costs onto his administration. The elevation of Sydney to the status of city, with its own city corporation, was the perfect way to do this. But Gipps was less than pleased with the people's choices – a bevy of self-made city men that included three butchers, two tanners and a warehouseman. The corporation men stood in contrast to the gentlemen elected to the Legislative Council the following year. There ensued a class-based hostility between the two levels of government, which undermined the corporation's standing and exacerbated difficulties arising from inadequate power to regulate and poor funding.

Ultimately, the problems of managing development and improving sanitation in the port city defeated the corporation. By 1851 only the wealthiest households were connected to piped water. Few had flushing toilets – and these just emptied into cesspits for there were still no underground sewers. Heavy rain caused overflows and the muck ran into the open drains that washed down the streets. The corporation was dismissed by an antagonistic and impatient legislature in 1853 and three commissioners were appointed to implement improvements to water, sewage and other services.

The following year the legislators sought advice on the construction of a sewage and water system. The surveyor-general Sir Thomas Mitchell was one of those they consulted. He was very familiar with the beauty and topography of Port Jackson, having completed a survey of the harbour in 1829 and built his neo-Gothic home Carthona on the water's edge at Darling Point between Vaucluse and Government House. It seemed obvious to Mitchell, however, that any system of subterranean pipes would have to discharge into the Tank Stream and then into the harbour, simply mirroring the function of the river Thames as the 'grand sewer of London'.[42] But he was aware of the desirability of minimising the amount of solid waste in the waterway, and so recommended the separation of lumps from liquid in a series of brick cesspools positioned along the pipes to collect 'faecal matter' for disposal on infertile wasteland. The excrement represented an opportunity because each person's annual discharge was, he suggested, enough to grow '800 lbs [363 kilograms] of wheat, rye or oats'. To 'throw it into the harbour is to lose the benefit which might be derived from its use, and to do damage to a good harbour'.[43]

The legislators reviewing the options were less interested in recycling. They simply wanted to 'to carry the filth of the city out to the sea as speedily as possible'.[44] As a result, nothing was done to stem the flow of sewage into the waterway. Ironically enough, the first section was complete just before London experienced its 'great stink' – the hot summer of 1858 in which the smell of sewage in the Thames became so overpowering that plans began for a new system of pipes extending down the river's estuary.

In the short term the 1866 select committee recommended better waste traps near the outlets and a longer outfall pipe at Bennelong Point. The commissioners signalled the need for a complete rerouting of the pipes away from the harbour, along the lines of the new Thames estuary outfall. It was a project well beyond the means of the reinstated city corporation. The harbour continued to receive the bulk of the town's excrement and storm water until the colonial government funded the completion of an ocean outfall off Bondi in 1889. A young EJ Brady was one of those who worked on that immense project, although he might have wondered at its effectiveness while he was monitoring labourers at Dalgety's wharf just around from Darling Harbour in 1890. Toilets there were emptying and oozing into the waterway well into the 1900s.

Sewage was compounded by industrial pollution, much of which was generated to the west of the town. The complex series of coves adjoining Darling Harbour – Pyrmont Cove, Blackwattle Bay, Rozelle Bay, White Bay, Johnstones Bay and Waterview Bay – were ideal sites for small- and large-scale waterfront industry because of their proximity to the big wharves and the city. Boat-building attracted timber yards, coal depots and iron works. The City Iron Works sat directly on the water's edge at Pyrmont from 1867. Elliott Brothers established a chemical factory at Iron Cove the previous year.

From 1878 steamers delivered cane from Queensland and the Pacific to the huge Colonial Sugar Refinery at Pyrmont.

The public abattoir that opened on Glebe Island in 1860 was the biggest polluter of water and air in the city.[45] It had been built by the colonial government on the bulb of land that separated Rozelle Bay from White Bay in an attempt to replace the dozens of unregulated fellmongers whose slaughter yards sluiced into the various coves west from Darling Harbour. Blackwattle Creek, for instance, provided one local woman with a regular supply of offal for her piggery.[46] Glebe Island was far enough away from anywhere that the smells would dissipate before bothering householders.

But not only did the meatworks fail to end the practice of backyard disposal of blood and offal down drains and sewers, it compounded the problem with its own flood of effluent. The slaughter yards catered for an insatiable appetite for red meat by processing sheep and cattle on an unprecedented industrial scale. 'All eat meat to an incredible extent,' wrote the incredulous English observer Richard Twopeny in the early 1880s.[47] The killing went on through the night by the light of 'slush lamps', fuelled by the fat of dead animals. More than 153 000 animals were killed there in 1865. This had jumped to 1 270 655 in 1897.[48] Tides, winds and wakes distributed animal fluids around the nearby coves. In 1879 a series of newspaper exposés led to the first parliamentary commission that confirmed the worst aspects of the meatworks' operations. Little was done and in 1888 the *Illustrated Sydney News* could still describe the 'thick discoloured tide and pestiferous slime clinging to everything at low water'.[49] As late as 1902 Blackwattle Bay was being coloured 'blood red'.[50] The problems of the government abattoir were finally shifted back up the harbour to Homebush in 1916.

The impact of the meatworks was greatest in the west but its presence was felt along the length of the harbour. Most of the unwanted guts were carried along the waterway by punt, four to five times a week, and dumped by hand outside the Heads. The stuff kept coming back with the swell, however, and offal from the Glebe Island abattoir could be found as far away as Manly Cove. One result of this was an increase in the already prolific shark population of the harbour. There were now so many of the monsters that, according to one fisherman, trawling was nearly impossible.[51] In 1888 the *Illustrated Sydney News* linked the prevalence of sharks directly to the meatworks at Glebe Island, noting 'never within the remembrance of harbour folk were these pests so numerous and so savage'.[52] One specimen caught in Woolloomooloo Bay was filled with 'sheep's heads and bullock's bones'. The concern was real and widespread but there also developed a form of popular currency in shark tales and an obverse pride in their prevalence. The *News*, for instance, made light of the threat to locals with a cartoon of a swimmer sporting spiked metal bathing trunks. It reported that a waistcoat and watch had been retrieved from one animal, with the observation that these had apparently 'resisted the digestive processes' that had dissolved the remains of their owner.[53]

Leatherjackets, too, thrived on viscera. They were only slightly less reviled than their larger brethren – in part because they fouled fishing lines but also because local folklore associated their first massed appearance with the wreck of the *Catherine Adamson* in 1857. Then they had reputedly 'flocked into the harbour to prey on the drowned crew and passengers'.[54] Leatherjackets, in fact, were endemic – drawings of the fish were published in the journals of Governor Phillip and Surgeon White – and the offal from the abattoir had apparently increased their population to plague proportions. The much-loved snapper, conversely, was spoiled by exposure to the discards from Glebe Island. Fishermen noted that fish caught outside the Heads with 'the offal of cattle in them' tended to swim sluggishly and smell badly when cleaned and gutted. The 'stink' of an engorged snapper was so 'dreadful' that the flesh was rendered inedible.[55]

Sharks and leatherjackets may have been flourishing but many other species were not. The harbour's fish stocks had been variable and confounding since European occupation. Colonists were now beginning to question the impact of humans upon the ecology of the waterway. There had been no regulation of fishing prior to 1865 when the *Act to Protect the Fisheries of New South Wales* was passed with the intent of establishing sustainable netting practices. This legislation narrowly predated the *Game Protection Act* of 1866, sometimes regarded as the first law protecting fauna in New South Wales.[56] The *1865 Act* certainly represented the first formal attempt to manage the ecology of the harbour and other waterways. It did so by dividing the year into two seasons, winter and summer, and limiting the size of the net mesh used in these periods. It had been 77 years since the first seine net had been cast in the harbour and by now some were beginning to understand that catching small 'fry' in narrow mesh during the barren 'winter' months – April to August – seriously depleted future stocks. Consequently, the legal winter width of the mesh in the main length of the net (the bunt) was set at 1¼ inches (3.2 cm). In summer, from September to March, it was 2 inches (5.8 cm). No fixed nets were permitted within 1 mile (1.6 kilometres) of a shore or river mouth, which effectively banned these permanent traps from the harbour. The use of lime to 'intoxicate' fish was also forbidden.[57]

A decade later fishing expert Edward Smith Hill warned that popular and professional practice had still not adapted to the 'feast or famine' ecology of the harbour: 'we kill and destroy without reference to numbers, or to the mischief we are doing'.[58] By 1880 the health of the waterway had deteriorated markedly. That year a royal commission was convened 'to Inquire into and report upon the Actual State of the Fisheries of the Colony'. It was prompted most immediately by concern over the health of the fishery. But there had been longer term official frustration at the difficulty of establishing profitable large-scale fishing in and around Sydney. In 1871 the public servant and trustee of the Australian Museum, Alexander Oliver, had described it as 'a postponed industry'. It bothered him that there was nothing in Sydney to approximate the fish markets at Billingsgate in London. While exports of agricultural produce were increasing, there was neither the 'skilled experience' nor the 'capital' to stimulate the local fishing industry:

the writer may be excused for venturing to express a hope that
the time is not far distance when Sydney and other sea-port
towns of New South Wales may be in the possession, each of
its little fleet of fishing smacks – propelled by steam or sails,
and manned by an industrious and intrepid body of men,
associated together on a system of regulated co-operation.[59]

The 1880 inquiry was headed by the colony's most eminent gentleman–
naturalist, William Macleay, a member of the Legislative Council
and fellow of the Linnean Society. Macleay had inherited the domed
mansion at Elizabeth Bay that Robert Pockley thought such a useful
navigational landmark. With the house came a huge natural history
collection that soon grew larger with Macleay's extraordinary zeal
for collecting. Elizabeth Bay House was an ideal place from which
to explore the marine life of the harbour. Macleay combed the beach
below his home for specimens and chugged around the waterway in
a small steamboat, dredging for shells and netting fish.[60] He visited
the early morning auctions at the municipal fish market at nearby
Woolloomooloo in the hope of finding something unusual. Before
the street hawkers and fishmongers gathered their daily stock, the fish
were simply laid out on the concrete floor there, grouped together in
chalk-drawn areas that identified the catch with the fisherman.

Macleay was one of a number of scientists and gentlemen–
naturalists who had become interested in the biology of the waterway
in the 1870s. The group included the president of the Linnean Society
Reverend Julian Edmund Tenison-Woods, curator at the Australian
Museum EP Ramsay, ichthyologist James Douglas Ogilby, naturalist
Thomas Whitelegge, the conchologist John William Brazier, and
H Atchison Haswell whose interest was marine crustaceans. These
men built upon work undertaken by the diplomat and naturalist
Comte de Castlenau who completed a 'Catalogue of the Fishes of Port
Jackson' in the late 1870s. Macleay also worked closely with the visiting
Russian biologist Nicolai Miklouho-Maclay to establish a marine
biology station at Camp Cove near the pilot's station at Watsons Bay.

That turned out to be a relatively short-lived venture but the year in which the royal commission was called was a productive one for the group.[61] Macleay wrote up his discovery of 'two hitherto undescribed Sydney fishes' and published parts of his own 'descriptive catalogue of Australian fishes'. Ramsay described 'a rare species of Perch' from Port Jackson, while Brazier published notes on new molluscs from the harbour.[62]

Macleay was joined on the commission by Ramsay and several public servants (including Alexander Oliver), politicians and lawyers. Francis Hixson was also there. He knew the harbour intimately as the president of the Marine Board, which regulated the lighthouses and operations of the waterway. The commissioners drew upon the published science and they also took evidence from the fishermen themselves. In the absence of artistic and literary representations, the report of the 1880 'fish inquiry' contained the most comprehensive insights into the working lives of these 'harbour people' yet recorded. In turn, the picture these men painted with their evidence was of a harbour in crisis.

At this time the fishing fleet of Port Jackson numbered some 27 net boats and another eight that used hooks and line. They were small craft, each crewed by up to four men. Most worked the shoals outside the Heads, all the way down to Botany Bay and Port Hacking in the south and Broken Bay in the north. This is what would be called the 'home fishery' – Port Jackson was the home port and was still being fished. Samuel Congdon had trawled the harbour for 17 years. He caught whiting and trumpeter around the eastern beaches in March and April but had noticed a great 'falling off' of numbers. Congdon blamed the sewage for deterring the fish from coming in too far. 'In the harbour I think the water is poisoned' was his straightforward observation.[63] Thomas Mulhall was born in Sydney and had been a fishermen. He was now a boatman who still took an interest in the fish business. He noticed the decline in morwong: 'they used to be very thick here one time, you could load a boat here, but now there are none'. Black rock cod were 'scarce' and mackerel had disappeared.

Mulhall thought that the noise of so many paddle-wheel steamers had scared them away. The snapper was more elusive than it had been 30 years earlier. He initially put their decline down to the high use of bream lines and hooks, which broke and 'damaged' the fish. Mulhall also blamed 'the continual race of steamers' for 'injuring' the fish around the coast, although it was not clear how this damage took place. Upon prompting, he agreed that the netting of red bream – the young snapper – had contributed to the decline in snapper numbers.[64]

James Nowland thought that the fish had changed their habits to avoid the seine nets. They stayed near the rocks, whereas before they swam in the channels. The fishermen, however, were apparently following them there, setting mesh nets around the headlands.[65] Nowland noticed a decline in black fish stocks: they were 'almost gone'. He knew enough of their feeding habits to link the decline to the destruction of staple seaweed beds caused by the dumping of coal 'ash' from steamers. Charles Hasty spoke of a recent killing of jewfish in Johnstones Bay and attributed that to chemical 'poison'.

James Goond was a river fisherman. He spoke with the passion and certainty of someone who had observed and considered the ecology and communities of the waterway over many years. He too noticed a change in habits of the fish: the trumpeter and whiting used to school 'but they have been hunted about that they have forgotten to shoal – they are almost exterminated'. He had once caught saltwater herring by the 'bushel' in Darling Harbour 'but not since the place has been filled in'. 'I am sure', he continued, 'that the heads of the bays being reclaimed does away with the proper breeding grounds of the fish. I am certain that the fish deposit spawn in shallow water.' He may have been thinking of Blackwattle Bay, which had been reclaimed for parkland by Henry Parkes's government. The tidal flat at Farm Cove had been filled from 1867 to enlarge and improve the Botanic Gardens. Fish spawn was continuously disturbed and broken up with the wash from each paddle steamer.

Like many of the other fishermen, Goond was critical of the use of narrow-mesh nets. The 1865 law had been poorly enforced and the use of fine prawn nets for fish was still prevalent. 'That little net is destroying and ruining the harbour,' he declared. But Goond's evidence suggested that the harbour and its estuary were being fished by far more people than just commercial fishermen. Among this wider group there was apparently little regard for the impact of overfishing or catching 'fry'. A local economy had developed around the Balmain waterfront, for instance, where people hauled the fish ashore to 'sell them around a penny a dozen'. Small fish were not returned to the water but rather used as manure or fed to pigs. In such close-knit communities, the affiliations of locality were often more powerful than any respect for the law: 'They know you do not like to be an informer,' admitted the frustrated Goond.[66]

Fish was far more expensive than the red meat being carted out of Glebe Island. And it was often much less appetising after making its way in a hawker's barrow from the Woolloomooloo markets all the way to Balmain or beyond. Oyster inspector William John Langham told the commission that 'fish as a rule are a luxury in Sydney – only certain persons can afford them'. Not surprisingly, many of those who could afford them ate their fish at breakfast when it was freshest. It was probably not the case, however, that 'the inhabitants of Sydney are not a fish-eating people' – something suggested by the witness Congdon.[67] They may not have been buying their snapper and bream from the markets, but a great many were harvesting the harbour for themselves. Philip Cohen of the Nimrod Fishing Club spoke of 'the hundreds of boats that are out in the day' catching 'enormous quantities of red bream'. Added to this flotilla of casual fishing craft were the young boys who gathered 'off every point and every locality inside the harbour'. Again it was the red bream – immature snapper – that were taken, 'in thousands and tens of thousands'. As a result of the destruction of 'the young fish in the harbour', the Heads were '[a]bsolutely bare'.[68]

The commissioners agreed that local fish stocks had been devastated. They reported to parliament that 'Port Jackson, although at one time, and not very many years ago, holding a very high rank among our fishing-grounds for all kinds of the best net fish, is now scarcely deserving as being regarded as a source of supply at all.'[69] Fish numbers had fluctuated at the very beginning of the colony when there were around three thousand Aboriginal and European people living around the harbour. Variations notwithstanding, fish were a finite resource. The population around the port city, however, just kept growing. By 1881 there were some 77 144 people living in metropolitan districts with harbour and lower estuary foreshore.[70] The impact of population growth was undoubtedly compounded by unrestricted fishing and the use of small-mesh nets. Some consciously flouted the law to do this, using prawn nets or inserting fine-mesh 'beakie bunts' within their legal nets.

James Goond's concern for the broader good was exceptional. His use of a large-mesh net and his desire to preserve the immature fish must have reduced his take. Most, if not all, of the others who were pulling the shoals from the water simply aimed to maximise their individual share of the harvest – and their reasons were not necessarily malicious or thoughtless. There was a deep-rooted and wide-spread belief in 'the public right to fish' – one that extended back in English law to the 13th century. Fish belonged to no one until they were caught.[71] Commercial fishermen sought to maintain what was probably a modest livelihood. Those residents who overfished the coves around Balmain were supplementing incomes and putting fresh fish on local tables when market stocks were unaffordable. Others fished simply for the fun. James Goond and other fishermen could easily identify the impact of these practices yet, because the harbour's bounty was free or common property, there was little regard for the collective impact. The consequent pressure on the finite resources of the aquatic common was immense.[72]

However, regulation was directed at commercial fishermen rather than the broader group of users. Boats and fishermen 'catching for sale' were now to be licensed whereas others were able to fish for free. A further set of complex regulations, again varying the mesh width and size of seine nets, was introduced. These were to be enforced by a new group of fishing inspectors under the direction of five fishing commissioners. Minimum catch sizes were also introduced: 16 ounces (450 grams) for a snapper, 8 for a flathead and 4 for a whiting.[73] But because this was usually policed at the fish markets it caused little impact upon non-commercial fishers. And while the commissioners had listened intently to the evidence about netting, they largely dismissed the fishermen's concerns about the broader systemic problems such as sewage, shipping and foreshore development. Consequently, they made no recommendations with regard to the pollution of the harbour, the ever-increasing growth in boat traffic and the destruction of breeding grounds through foreshore reclamation.

The new regulations were zealously enforced and nets were regularly seized. A decade later, the chief inspector of the fisheries Lindsay George Thompson acknowledged the hostility that had developed between fishermen and inspectors, with the former accusing the latter of 'harsh and tyrannical action'. There was the strong implication in his account that these were local communities, or at least families, doing battle with a bureaucracy. His inspectors had not only to contend with 'ever-watchful offenders' but 'their folk' as well. Significantly, Thompson characterised the conflict as a clash of rights and interests: those of a group competing with those of the majority. The fishermen 'had hitherto considered the finny tribes in our harbours and rivers their legitimate and indeed absolute property', he suggested, with the corresponding implication that the harbour and other waterways belonged more broadly to the public. It was 'self interest and convenience' that had stopped the fishermen from 'caring for, or even apprehending, the inevitable consequences which would follow the attempt to supply an ever-increasing population with fish under conditions so extravagant and so wasteful'.[74] At stake again was a definition of the government's duties to protect what Thompson called 'the public estate' – what, in the debate over Cremorne, had been called 'the people's heritage'.

The regime enforced by the fishing commissioners was heavily criticised in a subsequent inquiry, and concern was expressed over the 'hardship, bordering on destitution' that had resulted from the net confiscations.[75] However, regulation had become a fact of life for the fishermen of the aquatic common. And yet for some like EJ Brady, who looked wistfully out at the waterway from its busy city, the fishing lifestyle still retained the image of unfettered charm: 'Their free and simple lives are far more interesting and perhaps happier than the lives of many among the half-million residents who move and have their beings by the shores of this wonderful harbour.'[76]

SEVEN

BIG PLANS AND A BRIDGE

'A REFLECTED GLORY ...'

Not long after the chief inspector of fisheries had castigated the fishermen for their selfishness, a young barrister and future public servant and parliamentarian, AB Piddington, notionally extended collective ownership of the harbour to the citizens of Melbourne, Adelaide, Brisbane and beyond: 'We in Sydney are the trustees for all Australia and of all time of that national heritage of beauty which gives to us our pride of place amongst the capitals of this continent and endows these with a reflected glory amongst the people of all nations who visit us.'[1] It was a somewhat premature declaration of national relevance, for the colonies would not federate until 1 January 1901. But it spoke of the sentiment with which many in Sydney, at least, were regarding the place and anticipated its unequivocal significance a century later.

The creation of the Australian commonwealth was a culmination of the movement for self-representation that had found early expression on that wintry day at Circular Quay in 1849 when, in the course of turning away the convict ship *Hashemy*, the crowd frightened the governor, cursed the name Wentworth and demanded a colonial constitution. The young agitator Henry Parkes had done well since then, becoming a most respectful servant of the queen, a knight and a leader of the federation movement before his death in 1896. The 'crimson thread of kinship' that Parkes saw connecting the colonies also linked Australia to Britain. The shift from colonies to Commonwealth in 1901 was then a far more respectful affair on all sides and the goodwill erased the bitterness of that earlier time. 'Shall Wentworth, Parkes and all the patriots train / Forgotten in the triumph hour remain', asked one versifier, who was clearly determined that they would not.[2]

The waterway's role in the consummation of nationhood was also more festive than it had been 50 years earlier. The Commonwealth's first governor-general, Lord Hopetoun, arrived at Farm Cove and was welcomed in an ornate, albeit temporary, pavilion before making his way to the huge suburban park where he would sign his oath of office. As many as 70 ships lay at anchor festooned with flags and bunting. Good use was made of the 'reflected glory' that evening when the vessels were strung with illuminations, fireworks were released and the lights sparkled on the water. The following day the Fitzroy Dock at Cockatoo Island was turned over to competitive swimming. Filled with harbour water, it became a giant lap pool and spectators gathered on the graving steps to watch schoolboys compete. Barney Kieran was among them, although he was yet to make his mark.

The city streets were spanned by classically inspired triumphal arches designed by the government architect so as to lay out an iconography of nationhood. Coal, wool and wheat were represented, but maritime commerce was not – another indication perhaps of the primacy of the interior in the public imagination. It was left to the city's shipping interests to fund and mount a suitably nautical display to 'show the importance of Sydney as a maritime port'. The flags of shipping lines and trading firms were draped from the Exchange Building alongside the words 'A United Empire', 'Ships, Colonies, Commerce' and 'Freedom, Civilisation, Peace'. A mast on top of the building carried the message 'Welcome to Australia', spelt out in Marrayat signal flags for the benefit of those who knew the code.[3]

Federation meant that three tiers of government – commonwealth, state and municipal – now had an interest in the harbour. The defence lands were transferred from New South Wales to the Commonwealth. Cockatoo Island, with its naval dockyard, was handed over for a fee in 1913. The militarily redundant Fort Denison and Fort Macquarie remained with the new State government. Basic services in suburbs and residential precincts around the water were the responsibility of local councils. But the transitions were not always simple or amicable. The State refused to relinquish its claim to ownership of Garden Island when the Royal Navy left in 1913 and it fought the case against the Commonwealth through the courts until it won in the 1930s. State ownership was only relinquished in wartime 1944. Similarly, when the Royal Navy vacated Admiralty House in 1913 the Commonwealth assumed control in the short term but was forced to lease the property after New South Wales took the case to the Privy Council and won. From 1927 the Crown's Australian representative resided at the nation's new capital Canberra, but a vice-regal residence in Sydney was still needed. Its ownership confirmed, the State government leased, then granted, the grand home to the Commonwealth on the understanding that no one but the governor-general use it.[4] The neighbouring Gothic villa, Kirribilli House, had been bought by the Commonwealth in 1919 to accommodate the governor's servants. In 1954 that property became the Sydney residence for the prime minister.

There was some acrimony also over the quarantine station at North Head. It was one of the oldest of the harbour's institutions.[5] In the days of seaborne migration, ports were more vulnerable to disease than they were naval attack. Sydney had never been bombarded, but numerous ships had bought smallpox, cholera, typhus and influenza to the harbour throughout the 1800s. The quarantine buildings had gone up in 1837, but the place had been set aside nine years earlier as somewhere to keep vessels flying the yellow flag of contagion as far away as possible from the town. When George French Angas came across its burial ground on one of his rambles in the 1850s, he wrote: 'I have seen no spot where the dead repose which is more melancholy or more exquisitely picturesque than this lonely burial-place in the wilderness, where the howling of the storm, and muffled beat of the surge sound a requiem to the dead.'[6]

The State's reluctance to hand over the quarantine station was not based upon sentiment or history but rather raw experience and the desire to maintain control over a vital port facility. For bubonic plague had arrived in Sydney's harbour just 12 months before the new governor-general stepped ashore, and the station had been central to the containment strategy. A Darling Harbour wharf carter called Arthur Payne became the first official victim. He was diagnosed on 19 January 1900 and five days later taken to the quarantine station alongside three women and two children with whom he had close contact. That day medical officers went to his home in Ferry Street, Millers Point, to fumigate.

All was quiet for a month until a sailmaker named Thomas Dudley began showing symptoms. He lived in a loft on Sussex Street near the Huddart, Parker and Company's wharf in east Darling Harbour. Dozens of dead rats had been turning up near there in the weeks preceding Dudley's infection and the sailmaker had been pulling the animals from his toilet in the days before falling ill and becoming the first fatality. A mass rat kill often precedes plague epidemics in human populations since the rats are, themselves, infected and killed by the fleas they host. In Sydney the fleas had been brought ashore by ships' rats. In the absence of barriers, the rodents simply scampered down the thick mooring ropes connecting ship to shore. The diseased parasites they carried spread to the rats already infesting produce stores and the rubble sea walls beneath the many timber wharves that gave the waterfront the profile of a broken comb in the maps of the day. The small brown carcases littering the ground near Huddart's had been a sign of what was to come.

The disease flourished in the warm, wet Sydney autumn. It was at its most virulent in the waterside precincts facing Darling Harbour, where the living conditions had hardly improved since Henry Parkes chaired his inquiry in 1859. From there, the contagion followed the transport routes that radiated out from the port. Ferries probably took it across the water to North Sydney and Manly, where there were clusters of infections around the waterfront. Further cases fanned out along the suburban tramlines to the west and south. Coastal steamers would have taken the disease north to Brisbane. Of the 303 recorded cases in Sydney, 128 were city residents. Victims and contacts were taken to Woolloomooloo Bay and transported by 'green-painted' launches, sometimes called 'death boats', to the quarantine station. Those infected were isolated from contacts and the bodies of the dead were buried with shovel loads of quicklime to speed up their dissolution. By the end of the year 1746 people had been quarantined at the station.[7]

The official and popular reactions to the plague were dramatic. Many people chose to stay away, or get away, from the harbour so that the city streets were noticeably quieter. Real estate agents fielded more inquiries for suburban properties than usual. The panic also fanned the latent hostility towards those not bound by 'the crimson thread of kinship'. The *Bulletin* attacked Italian fruiterers for their supposed unhygienic practices. But it was the Chinese community – many of whom lived adjacent to the harbour in the Rocks – who bore the brunt of the xenophobia. In their case, the reaction had a history that went back to the gold rush. Restrictions on Chinese immigration imposed in 1861 had been reviewed and made more draconian in the 1880s and 1890s.[8] Many Sydneysiders would have recalled the violence that erupted in 1878 when the Australian Steam Navigation Company's employment of Chinese sailors prompted a seamen's strike and Asian businesses were attacked in the Rocks. And in 1881 the Chinese had been set upon in various places around Sydney during the outbreak of smallpox. That the plague of 1900 may have originated in Hong

Kong did not help their cause. The New South Wales government's chief medical officer Ashburton Thompson gave the discrimination a 'scientific' grounding when he suggested that Chinese were at a higher risk of infection because they did not eat the quantities of red meat that filled the white Australian diet. Consequently, the Chinese people deemed to be infectious were doubly quarantined. Having been transported to the station, they were isolated in tents from the other inmates.[9]

There was little love lost between the predominantly Anglo-Celtic residents of Millers Point and the Chinese at the Rocks. The people of the point regarded themselves as a respectable white working-class enclave and many shared the prejudices of the wider community. Their homes were modest but generally not as crowded and dirty as those in the Rocks or farther south behind Darling Harbour where the sailmaker Dudley had become sick. Nonetheless, those in Millers Point were subjected to the same intrusive regime of cleansing and isolation as residents in the Rocks and Darling Harbour. Houses were lime-washed inside and out. One family had their bathroom removed on the back of a cart. The entire waterfront from Millers Point down to south Sydney, where another larger Chinese community had established itself, was quarantined so that the residents were 'cooped up like fowls in a crate'.[10]

The responsibility for cleansing fell mostly to the city council. It was a great purge that sometimes engaged the labour of residents, who themselves had lost work on the inactive waterfront. Nearly 28 500 tons of sweepings and rubbish were barged out past the Heads and dumped.[11] More than 108 000 rats were killed by catchers motivated by a bounty of sixpence a head. But it was the colonial government that initiated the most far-reaching response: the quarantining of streets, the wharf closures and then the wholesale resumption of private property. There was a sense of inexorability about the process. The cordoning of precincts had begun immediately after Thomas Dudley's infection was discovered. Moves to formally acquire the land started with a parliamentary petition in March and the implementation of the *Lands for Public Purposes Acquisition Act* two months later. The first land resumed was a strip of foreshore running from the head of Darling Harbour up its east side, around Millers Point to Dawes Point and back from the water about 300 metres. A similar section on the west side of Circular Quay had been resumed a decade earlier. The whole of the Rocks in between these waterfronts was also bought. It was the most expensive public reclamation of land around the harbour since the privatisation of the foreshore had begun in the 1790s.

The Sydney Harbour Trust was established to manage the public waterfront and it began its work in February 1901: under the new federation, the new trust reported to a new State government. Four months later it assumed responsibility for the Rocks.[12] The existing city council – which had long wished for the power to take over and reconstruct those parts of the city it considered substandard and dysfunctional – was left out of the equation. Having been blamed for permitting the conditions that allowed the plague to spread, it was now sidestepped by the new arrangement. There was, as a result, little love lost between State and city government – but then that had been the case since the first city council was elected in 1842.

The antagonism was further fuelled by suspicions that the government purchase had less to do with plague mitigation than with long-awaited port improvements and the perennially debated need for a fixed harbour crossing. Government calls for competitive designs for a bridge had preceded the first diagnosed case of plague infection by 16 days in January 1900. When demolition followed resumption in the trust's new precincts, there was little immediate attempt to rehouse those displaced – because the land at the Rocks and Millers Point would

---

Harold Cazneaux was Sydney's pre-eminent artistic photographer.
His image *The Ship's Cat* was a rare character study of the working harbour.
It was taken around 1912, probably at Darling Harbour.
Courtesy of the Cazneaux Family, National Library of Australia, NLA PIC AN 2381209

" The Ship's Cat "

probably be needed for the approaches of any bridge to either Milsons Point or Blues Point on the opposite shore. And despite occasional return visitations of plague, there was no attempt to build rat-proof walls near the waterfront until 1907. By then another 63 people had died of the disease.[13]

'I do not think land should be more valuable than human life'

Joseph Conrad loved the vitality and centrality of Sydney Cove. The mariner and writer had sailed down from Bangkok in a ship full of teak in 1888 and recalled several visits to Sydney's quay in his memoir *Mirror of the Sea*: 'from the heart of the fair city, down the vista of important streets, could be seen the wool-clippers lying at Circular Quay – no walled prison-house of a dock that, but the integral part of one of the finest, most beautiful, vast, and safe bays the sun ever shone upon.'[14]

But few of the locals thought so highly of the facilities or their administration. The uncoordinated wharf development was no longer adequate for the ever-growing flow of people and goods, or the size of the ships that transported them. Shipping arrivals in the port more than doubled in the 40 years before the plague rats came ashore, and the aggregate tonnage of these vessels increased at least nine-fold.[15] When Norman Selfe arrived from England as a boy in 1855 there were still ship's timbers stuck in the mud at Sydney Cove. He watched the traffic grow and, as one of the city's foremost marine engineers in the 1870s and 1880s, strengthened and lengthened private wharves at Millers Point and Darling Harbour. At Parbury's wharf he used 36.5-metre piles, each made from the butted trunks of two Australian ironbark trees driven down into 15 metres of clay. Nonetheless, in 1908 Selfe admitted that these jetties were no longer adequate for the 'modern monsters' then arriving. Indeed, the whole waterway now appeared 'circumscribed' by the size of the steamers.[16]

The iconography of national identity might have favoured the bush but, by then, Sydney was the uncontested centre of the colony's export and import trade, and the government-built rail network spread out like a tattered web from the harbour to towns and farms in the north, south and west. Many in the regions resented the centralisation of commerce and the apparent neglect of outports and alternative centres. Sydney-based steamer companies transported goods and people to and from the outports up and down the coasts. The wool, grain, meat and sugar not consumed in the metropolis were reloaded in Darling Harbour for markets overseas, and manufactured goods from Britain, Europe and the United States arrived for unloading and despatch near and far. That anything from tinned Yarmouth herrings to German-made violin strings could be bought in the emporiums of George Street was perhaps not surprising. That they could be found in an isolated country store, surrounded by sheep and forests of ring-barked eucalypts, was remarkable.[17] Sydney's harbour was the conduit through which New South Wales engaged the world, commercially and culturally. Its safe deep-water anchorage was 'unrivalled' by the outports where shifting sands and open bays made navigation difficult. The heavily dredged Newcastle Harbour was good and the 'magnificent sheet of water' at Twofold Bay to the south promising. Others, however, were barely 'snatched ... from the sea'.[18]

Well before the creation of the Sydney Harbour Trust, efforts were made to bring wharfage facilities into line with the waterway's natural advantages. In the early 1880s Henry Parkes's government was resuming land on the western side of Darling Harbour to extend the railhead established there in the 1850s. Darling Island, now a knob of land connected to the shore by a causeway, was purchased in 1889 to develop a grain-handling facility. The wharves of Sydney Cove around Campbells Cove, where the young merchant from Calcutta had built the harbour's first private facility back in 1800, were bought in the same period.[19]

The arrival of plague was undoubtedly the catalyst for extending public control over a working waterfront that was now widely regarded as a 'national asset'.[20] Norman Selfe, for one, applauded the end of private ownership and the reconstruction undertaken by the trust, even though it undermined his own contract business. Much of the responsibility for managing this asset was handed to two Irish-born engineers: Robert Hickson, the president of the trust, and Henry Deane Walsh, his engineer-in-chief. Walsh had already supervised the dredging of Newcastle Harbour. In Sydney he began by examining the timbers of the old wharves as they were pulled apart. He was impressed by the durability of the ironbark and turpentine, although he suspected this might have been enhanced by the sewage-filled water, which deterred marine borer almost as much as the timbers' own essential oils.[21] Walsh's new wharves would also be built of Australian hardwood – some of it recycled, most of it shipped from native forests that still covered hinterlands to the north and south of the state. The old jetties were replaced by a series of uniformly enclosed double-decked 'finger wharves'. Over the course of a decade and a half Sydney's central waterfront was transformed into a modern port.

They were masterful unions of form and function. The new No. 4 jetty at east Darling Harbour was 150 metres long and 30 metres across and built to handle overseas cargo. It was nearly complete by 1913 and joined two other similar wharves at the northern end. The top floors of these jetties abutted a concrete roadway built above a new access road, itself progressively cut out of the rock from 1909 to 1921. In the bay between Millers Point and Dawes Point, named after Walsh as the work neared completion, the cargo wharves were up to 40 metres wide and fitted with wool-pressing and -handling machinery. The No. 1 wharf here was designed for both passenger and cargo use. Its ground- and top-floor balconies, included to shelter those greeting and farewelling loved ones, differentiated it from the other wharves. The new finger wharf at Woolloomooloo Bay extended 365 metres out into the harbour – far enough to fit two berths on each side for overseas steamers.

Modern facilities demanded new technologies and materials. While tons of forest timber were cut for the piles, decking and superstructure, the wharves were among the first structures in Australia to use the lightweight, fire-resistant asbestos sheeting that would become widely known throughout the suburbs as 'fibro'. Norman Selfe had pioneered concrete in his earlier private wharves and Walsh now employed it in a variety of ways. The turpentine-and-ironbark piles of the Woolloomooloo wharf were encased in huge precast cylinders. Smooth reinforced concrete made ideal rat-proof sea walls behind the wharves.[22] At Jones Bay beside Darling Island Walsh built a 'concrete quay' that Selfe described as the 'finest' in the harbour.

The trust did turn its attention to rehousing displaced families and waterside workers around the Rocks and Millers Point – but only after cajoling from the city council. It erected rows of dark brick dwellings with wooden verandahs that matched the No. 1 pier at Walsh Bay. Other homes were made entirely of brick in a functional style that anticipated modernist design. Fifty years after Henry Parkes had recommended 'the improvement of dwellings for the working classes' around the waterfront,[23] these were among the first examples of model housing erected in Australia: clean and relatively spacious, with corner shops included in the terraced rows to make shopping and neighbourly interaction easier. The trouble was that there were too few of them. Hundreds of homes had already been knocked down when the trust reported in 1909 that 34 new houses had been completed. And as the homes came down, the population had gone up because more people came to the waterfront to work on demolition and construction. The reluctance to replace dwellings reflected the priority given 'accommodation for shipping' over homes for people. By way of explanation, Hickson invoked the interests of the majority: 'housing had to be sacrificed ... for the general good of the community'. But others disagreed. 'I do not think land should be more valuable than human life,' suggested the unionist Catherine Dwyer.[24]

The resumptions, demolition and consequent housing shortage impacted particularly severely upon a community that was tied to the waterfront. In the first decades of the century, coal-lumpers worked night shifts as often as they laboured in the day. Lumping took place

out in the harbour – 'the stream' – and involved the precarious transfer
of fuel from the holds of colliers to cargo and passenger steamers.
Wharf workers, who heaved cargo to and from coastal and overseas
vessels, were at the mercy of the 'shipping news'. Work was intense
when the vessels finally docked but the wait before the 'pick-up' could
be long and uncertain if a ship was delayed. Don Peel began working
on the Sydney wharves around 1916. He recalled the system in 1952,
after it had been abolished and his generation had come to be revered
in his union as 'pioneers' of the waterfront:

> The pick-up was at the wharf gate; if you missed one job
> you went to another, often to get knocked back there. Pick-
> ups were sometimes in the rain so you often got sick ... then
> perhaps there'd be no job at all. Maybe after waiting around
> all day and part of the night, we'd get a job to work through
> for 24 hours.[25]

The pick-up operated along the new access road that the trust cut
from the rock behind the Darling Harbour wharves to connect Sussex
Street to Dawes Point and Circular Quay. The trust christened the
thoroughfare Hickson Road in honour of its first president. The wharf
workers, who sometimes subsisted on one meal a day, knew it as 'The
Hungry Mile'. Long tram trips to far-flung dormitory suburbs were a
poor option for these people. If you got a house at the point you stayed
'for the rest of your life'.[26]

'[A] pond in a privately owned and guarded paddock'

The establishment of the Sydney Harbour Trust coincided with a
wide-ranging zeal for urban reform aimed at undoing past mistakes
and the unplanned development that had allowed the town to 'grow

like topsy'. In some cases this meant applying the most basic tenets of utilitarianism. Fort Macquarie, which had distinguished Bennelong Point since 1817, was demolished in 1901 and replaced with a tram depot. The State government disingenuously suggested that the castellated façade surrounding the enormous shed would elevate the structure to 'an order of architecture ... [corresponding] with that of the fort ... as well as that of Government House'. Others were not convinced. 'Useful and even necessary such dismal places may be, but beautiful and conducive to the enjoyment of the people they certainly are not,' was the view of one correspondent.[27]

The design competitions for a harbour crossing in 1900 and 1903 were more thoughtful. Norman Selfe entered both and won the approval of the government's committee in the second with a design that accommodated trams, trains, pedestrians and horse traffic along a cantilevered span stretching from McMahons Point to Dawes Point. To span the beautiful harbour with a bridge horrified some. Planning expert John Sulman recommended a tunnel to avoid interference with navigation, minimise cost and preserve the beauty of the waterway. There were schemes to completely remodel the Rocks – long hated and feared by the middle classes for its unplanned mess of cottages and lanes and the gangs that inhabited them. The desire to erase this link with convictism was most starkly expressed in a plan drawn up in July 1900 showing a precinct flattened and totally rebuilt with avenues and enormous city blocks in the manner of Baron Haussmann's 19th-century remodelling of Paris.

The most ambitious manifestation of the urge to establish order and institute modern planning ideals came in 1909 with the Royal Commission into the Improvement of the City of Sydney and its Suburbs, whose board of commissioners included Norman Selfe and Robert Hickson. It was an extraordinary inquiry that ranged across proposals both realisable and improbable. Many of its recommendations, however, had long-term ramifications for the development of the harbour and its foreshores. High on the list of reforms were communication and transport around the waterway: the hilly topography that made Sydney's deep-water harbour such an enviable anchorage also complicated access to and from the water. The streets were clogged with exhausted horses pulling wagons of wool between warehouses and the holds of waiting ships. Many of the problems stemmed back to 'the mistakes of the early rulers and residents', but in an age of heroic engineering there was great confidence in the remedial potential of tunnels, bridges, railways and resumption. The city should have an underground train loop, it was argued, heading from Central Station down to Circular Quay and back. The lines would branch off in underwater tunnels to Balmain on the west side and North Sydney on the east. A tunnel should also link Woolloomooloo with the city. A widened north George Street would integrate the Rocks into the 'business centre' of the city – with the implication that more houses would go. One-third of Darling Harbour should be filled in to allow a high-level gently graded bridge connecting the city with the shipping precinct of Pyrmont.

The commissioners embraced the two dominant strains of thought in town planning at the time: the City Beautiful and the Garden City. The first emphasised the power of architecture through the use of beaux-arts inspired classicism, Parisian-style boulevards and grand symmetrical civic spaces. The 'principal water-front' at Circular Quay was among the most important of these and it should, therefore, be a showcase of significant architecture.

John Sulman suggested the remodelling of the already grandiose woolstore that Thomas Mort had built and the relocation of the neighbouring Customs House in order to better balance its commercial counterpart. That the latter had recently been enlarged and embellished at considerable public expense mattered less than the creation of symmetrical plaza. The plan would also sweep away the bulky Arts and Crafts-style ferry terminals built by the trust just six years earlier. The waterfront railway line and station – that all agreed were essential – would be placed underground. However, although Sulman's Circular Quay was to be an open space, a line of ferry terminals blocked the views down to the water that had earlier enchanted Joseph Conrad. Remarkably enough, few others thought this fundamental feature of the place was worth preserving and most of the commissioners favoured an overhead railway line that also cut the foreshore off from the harbour. A dissenting Robert Hickson was appalled. It would be 'a great eyesore' that would 'shut out the view of the Cove and the North Sydney heights from the Quay'.[28]

City Beautiful aesthetics drew inspiration from Europe and North America, where the 'White City' of the 1893 Columbian Exposition in Chicago had led a revival in classically inspired urban reform. The notion of a Garden City, conversely, was very English. It embraced the reformative power of nature and emphasised access to green spaces in residential 'garden suburbs', parks and pleasant foreshores. The commissioners conceded the need for accommodating wharf workers near the waterfront – as the trust was just beginning to do – but agreed that most people should live in low-density suburbs spreading away from the city. They also acknowledged that 'the charm of the city' lay 'in its harbour and the picturesque heights surrounding it' and therefore stressed the need to control residential development around the foreshores along 'artistic' lines.

While some viewed the commercial potential of the lower harbour with anticipation, Hickson, Selfe and their fellows preferred some degree of separation – essentially a picturesque east and a working west, with the dividing line around Woolloomooloo.[29] It was a 'natural trend' that had already begun to emerge because, despite proposals to mine coal and harbour ships at the beautiful crescent sweep of Rose Bay, the waterfront from there to Potts Point had retained the air of residential exclusivity established 80 years earlier by Captain Piper. Newer mansions competed with established villas such as Elizabeth Bay House for views and prominence. At Toft Monks, opposite Macleay's house, terraced gardens and a large glasshouse cascaded down the headland to an ornate boatshed on the foreshore. Tiny Watsons Bay remained a distant, picturesque village of fishermen, lighthouse keepers and harbour pilots. Bradleys Head and Cremorne had been 'saved' from the colliers. Mosman had long cast off its associations with whaling and was now 'one of Sydney's most picturesque and beautiful

This somewhat fanciful illustration of Toft Monks at Elizabeth Bay appeared in the journal *Art and Architecture* in 1906 to suggest what could be done to better relate homes to their harbour so that Sydney 'might rival Italy'. Note the Venetian gondola. The suburbs along the harbour's southeastern shore had been desirable since the days of John Piper and WC Wentworth.

Fisher Library, University of Sydney

marine Suburbs'. By way of contrast, Norman Selfe thought Balmain could be Sydney's equivalent of New Jersey and the foreshore around Henry Lawson's beloved Balls Head might be another Brooklyn 'with miles of magnificent water frontage admirably adapted for quays and wharves, that can be brought into direct communication with the city once the two shores are connected by a Bridge'.[30] The foreshores on the north shore were already busy with numerous small boat-building yards in Lavender Bay and Berrys Bay, and a sprawling timberyard beside Blues Point where the sawn timber of foreign and native forests was piled before feeding the spread of the city's suburbs.

Finally, the commissioners stressed the need to put an end to the privatisation of the foreshore 'on the headlands or along the bays of the harbour'. In this they were influenced by William Albert Notting, a yachting enthusiast and secretary of the newly established Harbour Foreshores Vigilance Committee, who had emerged to take up the mantle of William Tunks and Edward Clark. Reading a prepared statement before the commission, Notting declared memorably that 'Sydney Harbour has now become a pond in a privately owned and guarded paddock'.[31] Notting's committee had been formed in 1905 in response to the subdivision of land around Vaucluse. The coincidental drowning of seven members of a boating party, who had been driven off the private beach at the Wentworth estate while seeking shelter from fierce southerly winds, added the weight of outrage to their cause. Public safety and amenity were only part of Notting's case before the commission. Public foreshores, he added, would 'foster the love of the sea in the rising generations, and thus help to develop an aquatic race of hardy coast defenders – men who will be more ready, if needs be for crews for our Australian navy'. That was a blatant and somewhat thin appeal to national interest in the wake of the departure of the British fleet from the Pacific and the rise of Japanese naval power, but his appeal to call to defend 'a royal heritage' against 'private monopoly' tapped into a growing mood for resumption. By reclaiming public control over foreshore development, the city's 'natural harbour portico' would be preserved.

In fact, as Notting was giving his evidence in November 1908, the State government was preparing to gazette a large parcel of former defence land on Bradleys Head, from Taylors Bay to Little Sirius Cove, where the Curlew Camp was in the final throws of life as an artists' colony. Four years later, in 1912, part of this park was dedicated as a zoological garden: Taronga Park Zoo. But Notting's insistence was more directly rewarded after the election of the State's first Labor government in 1910. Some £150 000 were spent on the wholesale resumption of waterfront land around North Head and Vaucluse. The enthusiastic response of the mainstream press reiterated Piddington's earlier remarks: 'The harbour ... [should be] the unrivalled recreation ground for the country at large.'[32]

Notting must have been especially pleased with the State's acquisition of Vaucluse House and 9 hectares of WC Wentworth's old estate surrounding it. Vaucluse Park was resumed in 1910 and, after the construction of a public wharf, the beach became a 'recreation ground' for thousands – although no one was permitted to wander about 'unclad or in a bathing costume'.[33] Another parcel of resumed land and beachfront nearby, which had also been part of the original Wentworth purchase, was named Nielsen Park in honour of the minister of lands, Niels Nielsen, who had orchestrated the foreshore reclamation. The emphasis in the first years at Vaucluse was upon public use of the beach and park. Gradually, however, the history of Wentworth's estate assumed more importance and the trustees of Vaucluse Park began gathering a collection of 'Records and Relics' with a view to opening the property as a museum. In 1916 they added towers and battlements to the façade that faced the harbour – completing work it was assumed Wentworth had intended before the onset of the 1840s depression. From 1918 Wentworth's birthday was publicly celebrated annually and schoolchildren invited to write essays about his life and times. The house was restored through the 1920s and filled with period furnishings depicting, in a generic and nostalgic way, the genteel lifestyle of colonial times. Little mention was made of Wentworth's ambivalent relationship with his fellow colonists – rich and poor alike.[34] The historical irony of creating a 'people's park' around an intimate cove originally acquired as the family seat for a 'natural aristocrat' might have been lost as well.

'What a landmark!'

Sydney's population more than doubled between 1901 and the early 1920s when the city accommodated over a million residents. Vaucluse was only one of many 19th-century waterfront properties being subdivided. In 1899 the Woollahra House estate, the land that had surrounded Henrietta Villa in the 1820s, was partitioned for a second time. With each division, the foreshore became more expensive and more intensely settled. Grand mansions gave way to Edwardian villas and these were often followed by blocks of flats – particularly in harbourside suburbs to the east of the city and on the north shore, where water views and proximity to the harbour and beaches added a premium to real estate.[35] In the 1920s the famous gardens of Elizabeth Bay House, some 22 hectares of land, were subdivided and rebuilt with apartment blocks, such as the 'flatiron'-shaped eight-storey Meudon, which made maximum use of its triangular block.[36] The bayside flat of writer and poet Kenneth Slessor was so close to the water that he could lower a bucket from his verandah to the Italian fishermen below, who would fill it with fresh catch.[37]

Elizabeth Bay was within walking distance of the city, but the spreading development was only possible because of the fleets of steam ferries that now plied the waterway. Many of the larger craft were double-ended to avoid time-consuming turnarounds. Norman Selfe had designed Australia's first such screw steamer back in 1879. By the early 1900s appropriately christened double-enders such as the *Vaucluse, Greycliffe* and *Woollahra* serviced the far-eastern suburbs among the crush of northern- and western-bound ferries that slipped in and out of Circular Quay in peak hour. The artist Lloyd Rees regularly got aboard for the north shore in search of views of the harbour he had fallen in love with as a new arrival from Queensland – he was especially excited to find 'the exact location' of Streeton's *Cremorne Pastoral*. Rees painted a word picture of the quay in winter to rival his artworks: 'when in the dusk the ferries would fan out from

Sydney Cove like slow-moving clusters of golden rockets and spangle their lights across the velvet waters'.[38]

The largest vessels serviced the Manly run for the Port Jackson and Manly Steamship Company. Some passengers were commuters, but many were day-trippers eager to test the company's motto for the harbour and seaside resort: 'Seven miles from Sydney, a thousand miles from care.' The boats even had bands playing on the weekends. At 67 metres long, the *Brighton* was the biggest paddle-steamer to have travelled the waterway. It was the work of Scottish shipwrights and was nearly lost at sea as it journeyed out under its own steam and auxiliary sail power. Having run out of coal on the final leg, the crew threw cabin doors into the furnace to get the vessel through the Heads in 1883. The 52-metre *Kuring-gai* had only to slip out of Mort's Dock in Balmain in 1901. Its design by the renowned Sydney-based marine architect Walter Reeks served as the template for generations of future Manly ferries.[39]

The large barrel-roofed ferry and tram terminal and shopping arcade built at Milsons Point in the mid-1880s had become as much a harbour landmark as Fort Macquarie. The service the Milson family had pioneered on that site in 1861 was, in 1899, Sydney Ferries Ltd, a large transport company of 18 vessels which ran to Neutral Bay and Mosman. The company had a tradition of naming vessels after Aboriginal people and clans. The names, if not the memory, of Bungaree, Bennelong and Barangaroo were kept alive on three of the vehicular ferries that carried horse carts and then motor vehicles across the water. By 1920 Sydney Ferries Ltd had absorbed the services to Balmain, the Parramatta River and the eastern suburbs: in 1927 its vessels handled 27 million passenger journeys around the waterway annually.[40]

Waterfront communities were linked by the harbour, as they had always been. A casual local traffic still wended its way back and forth despite the web of ferry wakes. DH Lawrence evoked this relationship of boats, people and water in his 1925 novel *Kangaroo* when he described a 'huge, restless, modern Sydney, whose million inhabitants

CIRCULAR QUAY.
1254. Kerry. Sydney.

This Charles Kerry photograph shows Circular Quay around 1900.
It shows a city intimately joined to its harbour with ferry wharves,
Mort's woolstore and Customs House. Sixty years later this connection
was severed by the Cahill Expressway.
Tyrrell Collection, Powerhouse Museum

seem to slip like fishes from one side of the harbour to the other'.[41]
As a boy Bill Barnett had a regular job rowing one of the old men of
Berrys Bay to the south side for Sunday card games and long bouts
of drinking: 'he used to get me to row him over to Darling Street,
Balmain every Sunday morning … it was all right going over … [but] I
used to have to get him out when we got home'. Not long after Barnett
got a boat-building apprenticeship in Lavender Bay and became one of
best builders of wooden boats on the harbour.[42]

But it was regular ferry services that underpinned the transformation of the lower north shore. Henry Lawson, for one, was not
happy with the 'shifting' of his 'old North Sydney' and the 'brand

197

new crowds' that now thronged 'the brand new streets'. Mosman's suburbanisation was rapid too. The Queen Anne-style bungalow and villa had become the dominant architectural style there. In the early 1900s Lawson referred to Mosman's 'red-tiled roofs of comfort' amidst 'gardens and lawns of taste'.[43] He may have been irked by the smugness of the residents, but Lawson was not obviously critical of the suburbs themselves. For Lawrence, conversely, the overall effect seemed to be profoundly depressing. He described the 'low wooded tableland reddened by suburbs' around the harbour as 'dark-looking and monotonous and sad'.[44] The ubiquitous terracotta tiles came to represent the despoliation of the foreshores that the 1909 royal commission had cautioned against. Twenty years later the 'red roofs' of 'modern Mosman' were being described in terms of a 'desolate monotony' covering 'once lovely hills'.

For that writer, the one bright spot on the northern foreshore was Castlecrag, where the architect Walter Burley Griffin was a 'modern Canute holding back the advancing tide of ugliness'.[45] Castlecrag was built on an escarpment overlooking Middle Harbour from 1923 with 'No fences, no boundaries, no red roofs to spoil the Australian land-scape.' The model suburb that Griffin designed with his wife and partner Marion Mahoney Griffin was a small, short-lived but none-theless significant experiment in integrating a subdivision sympa-thetically into the environment and imbuing that with a communal sensibility: 'I want Castlecrag to be built so that each individual can feel the whole landscape is his.'[46] The ridge top there had been severely degraded through logging but replanting was part of the Griffins' intent, and angophoras, boronias and other endemic plant types survived on the slopes. Most of the first houses were made of local stone or sand-covered concrete blocks. They had flat roofs so as not to block the water views of others. Castlecrag's strict covenants were aimed at exclusivity, but within the 'community' there was an emphasis on common purpose. Pathways led down to a waterfront reserve, which was communally owned and cared for by the residents.[47]

Arthur Streeton was also bothered by the clamour for waterside living. He had spent many years in Europe after leaving the Curlew Camp. From the 1920s he visited Sydney from his home in Victoria. In 1931 he described his cherished Cremorne peninsula as 'a place which is now almost denuded of trees, and where bungalows and some rather hideous piles of flat dwellings rise up in their place'.[48] Streeton had painted it as such in 1926 in an oil called *Cremorne* but probably found solace when he turned around and painted the reverse view to the east. *Evening, Sirius Cove, Athol Bay*, completed that same year, presented a harbour seemingly unchanged since the heyday of the Curlew Camp. The illusion was only possible because the darkening green headlands of Little Sirius Point and Bradleys Head had been resumed for defence and then preserved for the public two decades earlier.

Painter and printmaker Margaret Preston had fewer qualms about the tiled foreshores. The daughter of a marine engineer, she had moved to Mosman in 1920 with her new husband, a company director whose salary allowed her the time to perfect her art. Preston quickly became one of the most influential and popular artists of her generation, with work reproduced in the new colour-printed magazines unavailable when Streeton, Roberts and others were painting in the 1890s. Preston shared Streeton's fascination with harbour glimpses through trees, and his openness to depicting a waterway of both steamers and secluded coves. But where he captured light, she took a modernist's interest in colour and form: she 'put Sydney's urban environment through a Japanese sieve'.[49] And so in her woodblock prints of Mosman Bay, Balmoral and the Heads, Sydney's rooftops become little red triangles and parallelograms startlingly contrasted with muted swirls of rock, leaf and water.

There was a largely ineffective attempt to empower local councils to control the 'height, materials, stability and design' around the foreshores in 1927.[50] The resulting development, in any case, provided modernists such as Preston, Muriel Cornish, Grace Cossington Smith and Roland Wakelin with landscapes of planes and curves and repeating patterns. All were in abundance when the 'grand arch' of

In 1931, Harold Cazneaux juxtaposed the ropes and bow of the
Chilean square rigger, *General Baquedano* with the arch of the nearly
completed Sydney Harbour Bridge to create *A Study in Curves* and
compare the past and future harbour.

Courtesy of the Cazneaux Family, National Library of Australia, NLA PIC AN 2381159

the Sydney Harbour Bridge finally began emerging from each shore
in the late 1920s. Artists and photographers relished the opportunities
presented by modern engineering. Cossington Smith painted two
studies, *The Curve of the Bridge* and *The Bridge in Curve*. In *A Study
in Curves,* photographer Harold Cazneaux balanced the arch with the
figurehead and bowed mooring ropes of one of the last clipper ships
in the harbour – a study in temporal as much as formal juxtaposition.
The ferry would in turn be displaced by the traffic across the Bridge.

If the ever-increasing size of the overseas steamers had 'circumscribed' the scale of the harbour, then the construction of the Sydney
Harbour Bridge utterly transformed the waterway and stamped the
mark of humanity upon it. It gave the harbour a skyline and, in doing

so, created a visual icon that instantly symbolised the waterway. The arch then entrenched the waterway as a place of undeniable national significance: Sydney's harbour and its bridge came to represent Australia as much as flocks of sheep. That the completion of this visual shorthand coincided with a new era of graphic promotion, that so relied upon a single potent image, enhanced the iconographic status of the place even more.

There had been other harbour bridges but these crossed the waterway at its periphery: to Glebe Island abattoir in 1862, across Iron Cove in 1881 and at Pyrmont, where a swing bridge in 1902 replaced a fixed crossing built in 1858. The new Bridge leaped the harbour in a single bound. The visual impact was most apparent in its first three decades when the structure dwarfed the buildings around it. It could be seen from South Head and, though occasionally hidden from the view of approaching vessels by headlands, its ultimate emergence added to the sensation of unfolding surprise that had captivated the first Europeans. The almost set-piece experience of arrival was related in florid prose by the local writer and poet William Beard:

> Slowly, as the ship rode further into the Harbour, all the beauty of Sydney foreshores was revealed to our friends ... the red-tiled roofs stood out, making a contrast with a livid green of the lawns ... Ralph drank in the beauty around him with wonder and admiration, whilst Clair Rathmore rattled on with her description with an obvious relish.
>
> 'Look over to the left now Ralph!' she exclaimed. 'You will see Vaucluse stretching from the Harbour to the ocean. See the lovely homes in tiers rising from the Harbour front. Vaucluse House is situated among the trees not far behind the shore ... Behind that again you can see the huge and luxurious flats and comfortable homes of Bellevue Hill ...'
>
> Suddenly, Ralph interrupted her with an exclamation, 'Oh look, Mrs Rathmore, I can see the Bridge! Isn't it huge? What a landmark! No wonder you are all so proud of it.'[51]

For the young postwar British migrant John Jordan, who really did arrive, the Sydney Harbour Bridge 'was the signature of Australia'.[52]

The official consensus to build a bridge rather than dig a tunnel had been arrived at in 1912 after the engineer JJC Bradfield convinced the politicians that it was possible to construct a single span which would not block shipping with additional pylons rising up mid-stream. The structure was to be an integral part of the residential decentralisation that social reformers found so compelling. When the Sydney Harbour Bridge Bill was finally introduced in 1916, garden suburb enthusiast and legislative councillor JD Fitzgerald anticipated the housing of 'happy and healthy people' in spacious subdivisions carved from orchards and bushland on the upper north shore.[53] But the exigencies of World War I delayed the final legislative approval until 1922. Soon after, Bradfield's preference shifted from cantilever designs, in which trusses draped down from pylons like lacework, to an arch bridge that rose up above the harbour like a rising sun. The latter had definite engineering and cost benefits and the geology of the sandstone foreshores at Milsons Point and Dawes Point made it viable. An arch was also, in Bradfield's view, the 'most handsome' alternative.[54]

The long-delayed Bridge came towards the end of a spectacular era of bridge building, which saw the brick suspension Brooklyn Bridge completed in 1883, the immense girdered bulk of the Forth Bridge at Edinburgh clear 520 metres across the Firth of Forth in 1890 and the elegant cantilevered Queensboro Bridge span the East River in New York in 1909. When it was opened in March 1932, Sydney's Bridge was 60 centimetres shorter than the one at Kill Van Kull, a similarly designed arch connecting New Jersey and Staten Island. But it was wider and heavier than that one, or any other in the world. And Sydney's Bridge was far more attractive, due in large part to the decorative pylons which distinguished it from its American counterpart. They displayed a form of 'stripped down' classicism that hinted at the monumental antecedents of the ancients without engaging in anachronistic embellishment. And so, whereas the earlier spans all had the air of Victorian or Edwardian engineering about them, Sydney's single leaping arch suggested machine-age progress.

During its construction, pictures of men and metal were as irresistible to image-makers as patterns of steel. The photographer Henri Mallard captured Sydney's bridge-workers as modernity's heroes far more unequivocally than the contemporary American Lewis Hine presented his working-class machinists and skyscraper constructors. The celebration of labourers was carried on into the documentary images created by the government photographers, the amateur enthusiast Reverend Frank Cash and artists such as Jessie Traill and Robert Emerson Curtis. Bridge workers were the objects of public adulation in a way that wharf workers and sailors simply were not. For a period they presented an industrialised alternative in mythic typology to the pioneering stockmen.

The joining of the arches in 1930 was anticipated and watched by most of harbourside Sydney. The exuberance belied a profound sense of displacement and loss that followed resumptions on the northern and southern shores. Henry Lawson had died just weeks before the *Sydney Harbour Bridge Act* was passed so would never know that the changes he witnessed in the early 1900s were minor compared with the 'shifting' that occurred to build the Bridge's approaches and new railway lines. Some five hundred buildings were knocked down around North Sydney and Milsons Point. These included the once-crowded Milsons Point ferry arcade and two of the oldest Milson family properties, Grantham and Brisbane House above Lavender Bay. Memories of 'the old Milson's Point ferry wharf' and a passenger falling into the water formed one of Lloyd Rees's enduring 'Harbour Impressions': 'I join the slow-moving mass inching ashore – there are no gang-planks – at Milson's Point. Suddenly there is a gap in the queue, a splash, some confusions and cries; then a ring of tense faces ... gazing into the strip of deep water, inky in its winter gloom.'[55]

That the destruction also impacted upon a strong local sense of place was obvious to contemporary commentators: 'Some residents are lamenting the changes,' noted one paper. 'They say that North Sydney will have entirely lost its familiar appearance by the time the bridge is built. But progress knows no sentiment.'[56] The resumptions also prompted wistful firsthand recollections of good times past when ferries delivered day-trippers to Neutral Bay and 'a day's sport' could be had shooting possums, wallabies and parrots around undeveloped foreshores. On the south side, the 1823 Scots Church that JD Lang had had built behind the Rocks was demolished and replaced with the larger structure that might have mollified the outspoken Reverend's sense of justice, if not heritage. The old Dawes Point battery – 'another pregnant souvenir of bygone times' – was destroyed as well.[57]

Built heritage was one casualty, but many also lost livelihoods and homes. For although property owners were compensated, leaseholders and casual renters – the majority of those affected – were not. Those who lived in the path of the southern approaches at the Rocks and Millers Point confronted upheaval greater than that which had followed the plague resumptions and wharf reconstruction two decades earlier. Many posted desperate but polite, and ultimately ineffectual, letters outlining their plight to government bureaucrats. When the widow and mother Mrs Pitcairn faced eviction from Alfred Street in North Sydney she wrote: 'through the Bridge, everything is taken from us ... we have no man to help – woe to the women – who have to fight the battle of life alone ...'[58]

Bradfield anticipated great works of urban renewal in the wake of the Bridge: civic spaces similar to those imagined by the 1909 Royal Commission on the Improvement of Sydney. A huge Italianate landscaped walkway was proposed for the site of the great saw-toothed steel fabrication shops on Lavender Bay. It would be a 'most picturesque spot ... for residents during long summer evenings'.[59] Bradfield was no doubt right, for the waterfront around from Milsons Point had been an unsightly mess since the railway took away the cottages and natural rock in 1893. But like most other Bridge-related schemes, this one was not realised. Instead, the vacant and vast workshop site accommodated an amusement park – Luna Park – which had been transported from Glenelg in South Australia in the wake of local opposition to its apparently disruptive presence there. The Town Planning Association of New South Wales was appalled at the decision. 'A Luna Park at Lavender Bay', it argued, would 'despoil the foreshore ... and lower the dignity of the city.' For its part, North Sydney Council was determined to attract work and business to an area still reeling from the Bridge resumptions and the economic depression that followed soon after. Alderman Hardy retorted with some justification, 'I haven't seen any natural beauty in Lavender Bay during the past 35 years.'[60] Luna Park was joined the following year, 1936, by an in-ground 'Olympic Pool', which continued the tradition of competitive national swimming at the bay. When Australians raced there against the British, Canadians and others during the 1938 Empire Games, they were swimming in harbour water that was now pumped and filtered with the latest technology. Humour was as commonplace at the local council as refuse was in the waterway. As the new pool opened, Alderman Faulkner joked that 'the man who has drowned his cat in the Harbour can bathe here in the certainty that the corpse will not confront him'.[61]

The park and pool owed their existence to the Bridge, and the three sites together formed a curious ensemble that ran from the ridiculous to the sublime. In doing so, they encapsulated key elements of national self-identity. Luna Park epitomised the irreverence many considered quintessentially Australian, the pool was a crucible for the country's vaunted sporting prowess and physicality, and the Bridge was the fulfilment of the prophecy of progress and conquest apparently laid down by Erasmus Darwin at the commencement of colonisation.

Eleanor Dark's 1938 novel *Waterway* expressed this last sentiment with both equivocation and resignation. She had her central character Oliver Denning imagining a pre-European harbour as he looked back from Watsons Bay in the pre-dawn: Fort Denison became Mattewaya again. With the dawn came 'red roofs' and finally the 'great ghostly arc of the bridge'. Denning's moment of 'wilful mysticism' evaporated with the sunrise and he was 'well pleased' that it had.[62]

Dark's novel coincided with the 150th anniversary of colonisation, during which the 'great arch' formed an unambiguous backdrop to many of the images and motifs. At night 'its every feature' was 'picked over' by searchlights from visiting warships anchored below. But there was one sesquicentenary event in which the Bridge and other signs of 'civilisation' were carefully avoided for another moment of creative anachronism, if not 'wilful mysticism' – the re-enactment of the landing of Governor Arthur Phillip on 26 January. It was no longer possible, of course, to stage this at Sydney Cove for there was no natural foreshore left there. The Botanic Gardens at neighbouring Farm Cove, however, were ideal and 'a specially constructed sand spit' was built over the sandstone sea wall and the land behind planted temporarily with ferns and grass trees. Longboats carried a costumed crew from 'an exact replica' of the *Supply,* which had been built from the recycled hull of the old lightship *Bramble* that used to warn arriving vessels off the Sow and Pigs Reef near the Heads. The *Sydney Mail* thought the 'scene was made remarkably natural by the appearance of natives and by the bush plants and tree-ferns placed there specially for the occasion'.[63]

There had, in fact, been no attempt at authenticity when it came to representing Aboriginal Australians. The actors in this instance were transported from western New South Wales to perform a 'corroborree' as Phillip arrived. The press-ganged men wore sports shorts overlaid with leaves. And they had spent the previous evening locked in police stables to prevent their interaction with political activists. Sydney's Aboriginal organisations had refused to participate in the event, fully aware of its symbolism. Instead, they labelled it a 'Day of Mourning' and held a conference to protest the seizure of their country and demand full citizenship and social equality. Down at the cove the Gadigal had called Woggan-ma-gule, the dragooned Aboriginal men were observed to be nervous and hesitant, but the *Sydney Mail* thought they had 'put up quite a good show' anyway.[64]

EIGHT

WORKERS AND WARRIORS

'A LAST LOOK AT SYDNEY'

The Bridge was always going to be seen as the realisation of Erasmus Darwin's poetic prophecy of a 'proud arch, Colossus-like' spanning the harbour. But early in its development, JCC Bradfield hoped that the span might also make a fitting memorial to the more than 300 000 men who served during the recent awful Great War. Friezes depicting Anzacs were planned for the approaches. The arch was thought to be an ideal evocation of the rising sun badge that had pinned the slouch hats of the soldiers. Those men had started steaming out of the harbour as early as August 1914 to fight Germans close to home in New Guinea. Thousands more followed in December. There were so many that the city's transport system was dragooned into service. Men were trammed to Circular Quay, where passenger ferries took them out to the waiting transports – converted passenger steamers. They left from the Man of War Steps, next to the turreted tram depot where watermen's skiffs still bobbed about. Archie Barwick of the 1st Battalion recounted the procedure in his war diary on 18 October 1914: 'as each company passed through the barrier, they were checked, + marched straight off to the ferryboat, + they lost no time getting us over to the A19 (Afric)'. The departure of the *Afric* and other troop ships was not advertised, but details were 'leaked' and crowds lined the foreshore to send the men off. It was a week before Christmas and the surface of the water was pockmarked by drops of summer rain:

> as we passed down the harbour we could hear the cheers floating across the water to us + all the boats in the harbour set their sirens going for all they were worth, we could see the people still waving as we disappeared round the heads, everyone was straining to get a last look at Sydney.[1]

The *Suffolk* left the same day carrying a thousand or so men in the 2nd Battalion. The larger liner *Euripides*, requisitioned from the Aberdeen White Star Company, followed two days later with two to three thousand more men from the 3rd and 4th battalions. The departures were repeated the following February as newly raised reinforcements were sent across the sea. And so it went on.

The image of soldiers heading to war on passenger ferries underlined the extent to which this was a civilian army of volunteers drawn from the coast and the countryside. Barwick was a 24-year-old farmer from Surveyor's Creek, way up north in the New England district of New South Wales. It might have been his first experience of 'boating' on Sydney's famous harbour. There were a few shearers and stockmen among the ranks of these first Anzacs; in a developing national mythology these men's exceptional fighting skills were equated with a life spent battling the elements in the bush. But most of the 1st Battalion came from Sydney, and many of them from around the harbour. They had made the decision to join up within a week or two of war being declared. Barwick's commanding officers, Lieutenant

The first Australian troops to depart in the 'Great War' are taken to their transport at Cockatoo Island aboard a Sydney ferry on 18 August 1914.

Australian War Memorial, negative H19497

Colonel Leonard Dobbin and Major Frederick Kindon, lived in the fashionable eastern waterside suburbs of Woollahra Point and Potts Point. Many of the other men down the ranks came from Balmain, Glebe, Leichhardt, Milsons Point, North Sydney and Mosman. A labourer called Charles Yule put his address as Goat Island where the Sydney Harbour Trust docked its dredges. There were clerks and skilled workmen – boilermakers, patternmakers, machinists. As a 'canvas cutter' from waterfront Pyrmont, Private William Egan was more familiar with sails and fishing nets than a rifle. Several of the newly trained infantrymen were professional sailors. James Logan was a lighthouse keeper of no declared address. A Scotsman by birth, he may have been living temporarily in the port city, like many other British men who joined the Australian Imperial Force as soon as war was declared.

The enthusiasm was maintained through 1915 – after many of the passengers of the *Afric* and the *Suffolk* lay dead at Gallipoli. Milsons Point ferrymaster John Leaver joined the 19th Battalion in August of that year and shortly after posed for a photograph under a recruiting banner which read 'Ferries to Gallipoli. Plenty of room at the Front'. Laconic humour and sense of place were not lost amidst the mud and blood of the trenches. One Australian soldier, presumably from Sydney, painted 'Circular Quay' on the wall of a ruined boathouse on the river Somme.[2]

Joe Summers left on 11 February 1915 with the *Seang Choon*, one of two troopships sailing that day with reinforcements for the 1st, 2nd, 3rd, 4th and 13th battalions. He was a Scottish Boer War veteran who had already lived a life such as might have been imagined by Jack London: left for dead on a South African battlefield, prize boxing and prospecting in North America, starting a new life in Sydney. When war was declared he was managing Dind's Hotel at Milsons Point. It was a favourite stop for Henry Lawson on the road down to the ferry arcade and Summers looked out for the poet when he had drunk too much. Joe survived Gallipoli only to be captured at Bullecourt in northern France. Memories of family life by the harbour sustained him as he wrote to his daughter from a prison camp in Germany: 'Tell grandma daddy will be home soon to take you to see the birds and the flowers, ride in the car, sail in the boat, and swim in the sea ...'[3] He sailed back through the Heads in March 1919 and set about establishing some form of normality.

Those returnees who could not overcome their traumas were sent on to a one-time gentleman's estate called Callan Park at Iron Cove. It had opened as a mental hospital in 1884 with landscaped gardens and water views that were thought to be therapeutic. In 1919 it was the largest military psychiatric institution in the country. Physical injuries were treated at another military hospital built on defence land at Georges Heights, and disease was monitored and treated at the North Head quarantine station. Hundreds waited in limbo before they could finally rejoin family. Many, of course, never came back. The social and economic toll of a war that had soaked up so much of the harbour's life, talent and skill was incalculable.

'[W]hat a' the cost?'

Sydneysiders, it seems, never tired of military arrivals and send-offs. After the 1885 Sudan Detachment, there were contingents heading for the Boer War in 1899 and 1900. Imperial loyalty was also accompanied by an underlying sense of vulnerability. So the appearance of the American Great White Fleet in 1908 saw unprecedented numbers flock to the foreshores. Many welcomed the United States as a nation of fellow 'Anglo-Saxons' and a potential protector in the context of the rise of Japanese naval power and the apparent indifference of the British. Australia's unilateral invitation to the touring American fleet may well have annoyed a complacent 'mother country' enough to assist with the creation of an Australian navy. Seven ships for the new naval fleet, including the first cruiser to be named *Sydney*, were built in Scotland and received in the harbour with enthusiasm and relief in October 1913. It was an understandably irresistible spectacle. 'Nowhere in the world', trumpeted the *Sydney Mail*, 'could there be found a more beautiful setting for the historic picture presented by the fleet as it slowly passed up the Harbour to its moorings in Farm Cove.'[4]

Warships had anchored there since the earliest days of the colony, supplied by boats from the same waterside stairs that Archie Barwick and the 1st Battalion would step off. The resident watermen William and Albert Stannard would do well as the war increased the busyness of the harbour. They operated five motor launches from the steps by war's end.[5] The huge ironclad cruiser HMS *Powerful* was a familiar sight to them and the users of the Botanic Gardens – it was the flagship of the Royal Navy's Australia station, which had operated on nearby Garden Island since 1859. Thirty years later the British had cut down one of the island's two distinctive hills in order to create level ground for upgraded facilities. By 1914 it resembled a small town.

The establishment of the Royal Australian Navy (RAN) in 1911 necessitated the rearrangement of naval sites in the harbour. Garden Island became the RAN's base. Cockatoo Island, which had serviced British warships since the 1850s, was now transferred from the State to the Commonwealth government and its facilities improved to accommodate the new ships and build others. The Sutherland Dock, designed in 1886 to fit the biggest masted steamships of the day, was enlarged for the 18 500-ton battle cruiser and flagship HMAS *Australia*, which was bigger than the *Powerful* and needed more than 30 metres of water depth to navigate safely.

The launch of the HMAS *Warrego* from Cockatoo in 1911 was an occasion for men and women to dress up and row out to cheer. The ship had been assembled from sections and parts manufactured on the Clyde River in Glasgow and went on to serve off New Guinea and in the Mediterranean during the war. The first modern warship built in the new Commonwealth ended its days where its service began. The *Warrego* sank beside the island before it could be towed out of the Heads for scuttling in 1931 – a downpour of winter rain filled the stripped hull and sent it to the bottom.[6]

American Fleet in Sydney Harbour, 1908. This view was taken
from the north shore. Note Fort Denison in the background.
North Sydney Heritage Centre, Stanton Library

The war substantially increased the pace of work at Cockatoo. The
workers there rapidly converted the P&O Steam Navigation Company's
passenger steamer SS *Berrima* into an armed transport. Within three
weeks of being requisitioned for military service at the beginning of
August 1914, it left the harbour with the 1500-strong Australian Naval
and Military Expeditionary Force bound for New Guinea.[7] The force
confronted German colonial forces in September, seven months before
the landing at Gallipoli was etched on the national consciousness.
Much of the wartime work was on transports. But repair and fitting
of warships was undertaken as well and the construction program
continued. The cruiser HMAS *Brisbane* was completed in 1916, the
same year as three torpedo-boat destroyers, the *Huon, Torrens* and
Swan, which served with the *Warrego* blockading the Adriatic Sea.

Despite its few trees, Cockatoo Island bore little resemblance to
anything created by nature. By 1914 it was simply a humped platform

213

covered with a complex of machine, fitting, joinery and turbine shops. Some of the buildings dated back to the first convict occupation, others were very recent. There were cranes and foundries, a powerhouse, a smithy and sawmill. In 1918 workers there assembled a floating crane called *Titan*. It was able to lift 150 tons and was the biggest in the southern hemisphere. The old Fitzroy Graving Dock was like an incision from the southeast, matched by the larger Sutherland Dock from the west. A shipbuilding slip flanked by cranes also faced the west. There were another four slips along the southern shore, a long wharf for cruisers on the eastern shore and a destroyer wharf around from that. The island was defined by straight lines.

The workforce was substantial before the war, but it grew by nearly nine hundred men to 2800 in 1915. By 1919 there were more than four thousand people working there.[8] The numbers had been bolstered by the recruitment of British shipbuilders to supplement the local workforce. The flat caps that typically topped men from the river Tyne could be seen among the rumpled, rabbit-felt fedoras preferred by Australian workers from forest to foreshore. The drawing office was built during the war and well lit with windows all around for the benefit of the draughtsmen, who sat in shirtsleeves and waistcoats at long trestle tables. The overwhelming majority of the Cockatoo workers were employed in the shipyards and shops. Welders were equipped with goggles, but few who toiled in the slips, docks or the vast workshops wore protective clothing more substantial than an apron. In the dark and smoky smithy they stripped down to undershirts and braces. At Garden Island the workforce increased from 950 in 1914 to 3000 by war's end. That was the main facility in the harbour for refitting transports, troopships and the ships of allied navies. By 1918 more than 850 vessels had been serviced at the island.[9]

War fervour and common purpose dissipated as the war dragged on and the threat of conscription loomed. Class solidarity, by contrast, rarely faltered. Before thousands of strikers in the Domain, the president of the Sydney Waterside Workers – a returned soldier himself – described 'kings, governors, bosses and parliamentarians' as 'parasites fattening off the backs of the workers'.[10] WM 'Billy' Hughes had defended waterside workers and their community at Milsons Point as the local member of parliament and then as leader of the Waterfront Workers Federation (WWF). Now, as prime minister, he was one of the 'parasitic' parliamentarians. With his energies devoted towards prosecuting the war, Hughes's old waterfront constituents expelled him from the federation for his support of conscription, which threatened to make soldiers out of wharfies and, in the minds of some, introduce cheap foreign labour to the docks in their absence.

In 1917 the waterside workers joined a general strike in support of tram workers protesting the introduction of new 'scientific' management methods. Workers at Cockatoo and Garden islands went on strike. Even the 'militarised' Naval Coaling Battalion went out. That unit had been formed in the wake of an earlier strike by Sydney coal-lumpers in 1915. On that occasion the minister for the navy suggested the union's leaders should face the firing squad. But a less dramatic solution was found and a 'battalion' that was both part of the military and affiliated with the Sydney Coal Lumpers Union (SCLU) was created to ensure the uninterrupted flow of troops to the front. The union men worked in uniform and under naval discipline in return for better pay and exemption from any possible conscription call.

The void created by the withdrawal of organised labour around the waterfront was filled by 'scabs' and volunteers. The North Coast Company, which ran steamers up to the outports, from Port Macquarie to Byron Bay and down the Nambucca and Bellinger rivers, continued its operations with the help of shareholders, loyalist students and customers who came down from the coast to work on the Sydney wharves. They, and others from out of town, were billeted at Dawes Point and Taronga Zoo.[11] The city was bitterly divided and so was the harbour. Loyalist coal-lumpers were housed at the Garden Island naval dockyard, presumably for their own protection.

Where the demands of war had earlier helped to improve the bargaining power and conditions of the waterfront workers, the unsuccessful general strike damaged their standing and influence.

Both the Coaling Battalion and SCLU were deregistered in 1917 and the latter had to fight bitter opposition to regain its recognition. Those who went on strike during the war found it difficult to get work shifting coal on the postwar waterfront. The strike adversely affected the finances of the WWF, and its power in Sydney was challenged by the newly formed Permanent and Casual Wharf Labourers Union. The economic depression that began in the late 1920s further sapped its ability to bargain. Through the 1930s men trudged up and down The Hungry Mile competing with each other for selection in the 'bull rings' where the biggest and strongest were chosen first. When employed, they worked long, hard and fast. They had little choice:

> the steam winches would rattle their cogs through the day
> with scarcely a two-minute stop. If there was a longish pause,
> you'd hear a roar from the foreman ... One gang was known
> to discharge, truck away and sort five thousand sacks of
> potatoes between eight am and five pm.[12]

The effect of war and its aftermath was obvious in the rates of pay. Where wharf labourers earned 1s 6d per hour in 1911, this increased to 2s 9d by 1921. But 18 years later, in 1939, they were receiving just a shilling more. Waterfront families would not have been eating much meat in those lean years. Even the cost of cheap cuts had doubled. Some, like the Brothers family who relied on the wages of a coal-lumper, supplemented income and meals by fishing – but one needed access to a boat to do that successfully.[13] It was not until the consolidation of a militant communist leadership, and the beginning of another world war at the end of the decade, that conditions improved again. By 1941, a wharfie could expect more than 3s 4d an hour for his labour.[14]

The Cockatoo and Garden island workers were also weakened by the 1917 general strike. And they then had to contend with the postwar downturn in available work: contracts that had come with war vanished with peace. In 1921 sixteen hundred men lost their jobs at Cockatoo. 'The Royal Australian Navy has fallen on evil days' was the conclusion of one contemporary observer.[15] There may have been little interest in maintaining a peacetime navy on a wartime footing, but Cockatoo Island's place as 'the only naval establishment of its kind in the Commonwealth' was acknowledged.[16] It was Garden Island that felt the greatest impact. By the early 1930s the workforce there was less than four hundred.[17] The sacked dockyard workers competed for jobs with each other and returned servicemen. Some may have found work in one of the smaller yards along the north shore or with Mort's at Balmain or Woolwich. In the late 1920s there was also hope of employment at the giant Dorman Long workshops set up at Milsons Point to fabricate steel for the Sydney Harbour Bridge.

But there was steady work on military and civilian vessels for those who stayed on. The Australian government ordered 19 steamers for the newly created but short-lived Commonwealth Line. The contracts were divided up among shipyards at Sydney, Newcastle, Williamstown, Adelaide and Maryborough. Two steamers and two refrigerated liners were launched from the Cockatoo slips between 1919 and 1924. But the British could always build cheaper ships. Labour costs in Australia were a factor, but so too was the sheer economy of scale that could be achieved by large British firms and the integrated industries that had developed over a century of maritime supremacy. When the Commonwealth liner *Forsdale* was inspected by British shipwrights on the Clyde, they acknowledged that they could not better the quality, but asked 'what a' the cost?' Subsequent contracts for two new RAN cruisers went to a firm at Clydebank.[18] Ironically, the difference between the Cockatoo tender and the British price was so great that the navy decided to build a seaplane carrier with the savings. Cockatoo workers got that job. It was one of more than 30 vessels built there before the outbreak of World War II.

Fifteen of the Australian-built Commonwealth Line steamers were eventually bought by Australian shipping firms that were slowly re-establishing the coastal trade disrupted by war and strikes. Most of the 32 other new freighters used in Australia in the 1920s and 1930s were built in Britain.[19] So too were the luxurious passenger liners that plied Australia's coastal routes. In the 1930s 10 000-ton ships such as the *Manunda, Manoora* and *Westralia* were regular visitors to Sydney's harbour and to the docks at Cockatoo, by then leased to a private company. The age of the steamer was giving way to that of the motor ship, just as sail had been replaced by steam. 'Coals have departed' was the conclusion of one writer as early as 1921.[20] The new vessels burned oil, but so strong were aesthetic conventions that funnels were retained despite their irrelevance to the exhaust system. The *Manunda's* was low and sleek whereas the motor ship *Westralia* kept the familiar tall stack of a steamer.[21] In the years before the primacy of air and road transport, these liners competed successfully with rail to carry people in comfort and style between towns and cities spread out around the vast coastline. Their lounges and dining rooms were as well appointed as the best hotels on shore. Then, in the 1940s, they were refitted and armed to carry Australian troops to and from another war.

'A wet weeping Sunday'

The second cruiser to be called HMAS *Sydney* sailed up the harbour in early February 1941, as it had done many times previously. It passed the remains of its earlier incarnation at Bradleys Head: a forward mast placed there as a memorial by the floating crane *Titan*. The old *Sydney* had gone the way of many other fighting vessels in the interwar years as international agreements forced a reduction in naval forces. It was broken up at Cockatoo in the early 1930s. That was when the mast was saved. The bow too was preserved for posterity and set into the sea wall beneath the Bridge at Kirribilli. Many small pieces were salvaged for the Naval Museum collection housed on nearby Snapper Island. Other bits were sold off to the public, presumably to find pride of place on mantelpieces and shed walls around the state. The ship had been so honoured in its namesake city because it was the first RAN unit to sink an enemy vessel. The destruction of the German raider *Emden* in the

Indian Ocean in 1914 was a rarely recognised naval triumph in a war dominated in the popular memory by the heroism of soldiers.

The second *Sydney* also arrived to a hero's welcome. During 1940 it had been bombarding positions and sinking merchant ships around the Mediterranean before sending an Italian cruiser to the bottom in a dramatic battle off Calabria. That victory provided a welcome boost to home-front morale at a time in the war when all else seemed bleak.

For Petty Officer John Ross it was a special homecoming – his family lived above Lavender Bay. As the ship neared the harbour, Ross sent a telegram to his wife and told her to 'put ice in the chest for Sunday'. The day – 11 February – was declared a holiday and the Ross children joined thousands of others lining George Street to cheer as their father and rest of the ship's company marched past. The *Sydney* was refitted at Cockatoo and then sailed for Western Australia. There it escorted a troopship part way on its journey to reinforce Singapore. On the return trip, it was sunk by a German raider with all hands in the Indian Ocean. The loss of the second HMAS *Sydney* had a tragic symmetry with the triumph of the first, and its disappearance would be seared into the national consciousness for decades. Back in Sydney Harbour, the Ross family must have received the news with a mix of horror and relief: Petty Officer Ross had disembarked at Fremantle and not rejoined the cruiser for its last voyage.

World War II affected the harbour more profoundly than the earlier conflict. Cockatoo and Garden islands were set on a war footing of course. A redundant waterfront gasworks at Neutral Bay was also taken over by the Commonwealth and turned into a naval torpedo factory. Various islands were used for storage. Private contracts and work flowed to businesses up and down the waterway. The biggest graving dock in the harbour was owned by Mort's Dock and Engineering Company on the harbour at Woolwich, where it had been cut into the sandstone headland in 1901. Passenger ships were converted to troop carriers there. At the company's original slipway in Balmain, they built warships. In front of a suburb of tiny timber and brick cottages, in less than two years between 1941 and 1942 workmen constructed

219

12 corvettes. They were named after regional towns and used for patrol and anti-submarine work.

Harry West's sail-making business nearby had catered for Sydney's vibrant yachting fraternity and its professional boatbuilders. West's also refilled, steam-cleaned and deloused hundreds of mattresses each week for the coastal passenger liners in port. The sail-making stopped during the war and the workshop set about sewing tarpaulin tents and hospital marquees for the armed forces. By 1945 there were 150 people employed there. A new floor added then to the workshop allowed both tarpaulins and sails to be made – the latter for the United States Navy, which had commandeered square riggers as well as motor boats for the war effort.[22]

Another contributor to the war effort was the Halvorsen family. They had been building boats in Sydney since the 1920s, having migrated from Norway via Cape Town. Moving from riverside Drummoyne to Careening Cove near Neutral Bay, they received contracts for yachts and motor launches from the waterway's elite. The ocean-going cruiser *Miramar II*, built for the commodore of the Royal Motor Yacht Club, was described as 'a floating palace'. Demand remained constant despite the Great Depression. On the eve of war in 1939, Lars Halvorsen and Sons moved to huge premises back up the harbour very near the site of James Squire's old orchard and Bennelong's grave. There they mass-produced air–sea rescue boats to their own design and many other craft besides. By the end of the conflict the company had completed more than 250 vessels for the Australian, United States and Dutch forces. Several of their prewar pleasure cruisers were commandeered from private owners by the navy to become known as the 'Hollywood Fleet'.[23] Occasionally the navy had to bargain. Racing-car driver Hope Bartlett had only bought *Sea Mist* in 1939 and he wanted £5500 for the boat. Based upon a Lloyd's valuation, the navy paid £4000.[24] The price was still at least 13 times the fulltime annual wage of a wharf worker.

At Cockatoo Island there were more than 20 defence-related building jobs completed from the outbreak of war to its end in August 1945. These ranged from the construction of target-towing launches to the completion of three tribal-class destroyers.[25] Nine ships from the

Royal Navy and 15 from the United States Navy docked there in need of repairs. The USS *New Orleans* had had its entire front end blown off. There was also conversion on passenger ships and preparatory work for others. The *Manunda* was turned into a hospital ship. It was a minnow compared with the passenger liners *Queen Mary*, *Queen Elizabeth*, *Aquitania* and *Mauretania,* which were converted to troopships by men from Cockatoo. The two *Queens* were longer than the *Titanic* and nearly twice as heavy and so conversion work was undertaken 'mid-stream' for all the city to see. The *Queen Mary* was bigger than an aircraft carrier and anchored off Bradleys Head where there was sufficient 'swinging room' from its single anchor line. The *Queens* appeared in the harbour one at a time for fear their bulk would block both channels of the waterway, but on at least one occasion they slipped passed each other at the Heads.[26]

In May 1940 ferries from Pyrmont took five thousand Australian soldiers out to the *Queen Mary*. Much of the ship's sumptuousness had gone, but Lieutenant Michael Clark was still 'staggered by the luxury' of the accommodation.[27] As a war correspondent, Kenneth Slessor was ferried with the soldiers from Darling Harbour to Circular Quay where the *Mauretania* waited. It was wet, like the day of Archie Barwick's departure a quarter of a century earlier. But it was also cold and wintery and the mood was sombre: 'A wet weeping Sunday, sky full of smoke and rain, greasy clouds, puffs of smoke, and rain blowing in drifts like a Turner print … On the other side of Sydney Cove, crowds, mostly women, stood in rain, clinging to iron railings, and staring through them.' The tension broke as the ship left and songs, cries and 'cooees' were sent across the water to the soldiers. On board, the mood of exuberance gave way to quiet awe at the 'sudden magnificence' of the interiors.[28] As the ships sailed across the Indian Ocean, Germany invaded Belgium and Holland. They arrived at the Clyde six weeks later in similarly awful weather – despite now being in a northern summer.

The departing troops might well have carried with them a copy of the *Australian Soldiers' Pocket Book*. It contained useful survival tips, exchange rates and a series of 'talking points on Australia' to ease conversation and satisfy the curiosity of foreigners. Among the general facts about cities, sheep farming and the country's unusual wildlife were the specifications of the Sydney Harbour Bridge, the 'colossal span' straddling the harbour 'claimed to be the finest in the world'.[29] The huge transports returned to the harbour on several occasions. The *Aquitania* took Australians from the Woolloomooloo finger wharf to north Africa, where they would make history as the 'Rats of Tobruk'. The *Queen Elizabeth* and the *Queen Mary* carried thousands of American servicemen to and from Sydney. Ferries took the men from the anchored liners to Glebe Island, where the main American base had been established in the shadow of huge grain silos built after the World War I. While in port they brought Australia face to face with modern America – fighting, charming and outspending the locals in the process.

It was the threat from Japan that drew the Americans to the harbour and, indeed, turned the waterway into one big naval base. The war in Asia and the Pacific had brought conflict for the first time to the Australian mainland. Darwin was bombed in February 1942, just two months after the Japanese had attacked the United States Navy at Pearl Harbour. That the planes had flown from aircraft carriers highlighted the reality that this was a naval conflict. Accordingly, Sydney Harbour assumed a strategic significance, and a vulnerability, that was unprecedented. The racism that motivated the earlier fear of Japan was compounded by its policy of 'southern expansion'. Billy Hughes had retained his interest in foreign policy and in 1934 recognised both the Japanese threat and the need for better naval air defence: 'Japan is no longer our ally ... The East, roused from its age-long slumbers, has awakened.'[30] He resigned two years later because of his forthright views on appeasement. In late 1938 waterfront workers in Port Kembla to Sydney's south refused to load pig-iron bound for Japanese factories because of its potential military use. Attorney-general and future prime minister Robert Menzies condemned the boycotters and earned the nickname 'Pig-iron Bob' for ever more.

Unable to understand, or at least accept, the moral or tactical logic of the wharfies' position, the Commonwealth nonetheless approved the construction of a new naval graving dock at Garden Island in 1940. The facility would, in Menzies' words, 'make Australia a fit base for a powerful fleet'.[31] The dock required filling the harbour between Potts Point and Garden Island so that it, like Glebe, Darling and Berry islands, would be joined to the foreshore. Despite protests from residents of Potts Point, concerned that they were now targets in any bombing raid, the site was chosen over the alternative location upstream at Woolwich. The *Sydney Morning Herald* helpfully explained the strategy behind the decision: 'Successful bombing of the Bridge and consequent blocking of the fairway would render the dock idle for a period upwards of three months.'[32] In engineering terms, it would be bigger than the Bridge, although the result was far less obvious or iconic. Balls Head gave up 382 500 cubic metres of sandstone for the initial work begun in late 1940, and the plant was shipped from Britain despite the danger posed by submarines.[33] The writer Nancy Keesing, then a young clerk on the island, described working conditions during the construction in terms of constant bombardment: 'Nearly continuous showers of little pebbles and grit rattled the roof ... we acquired a kind of instinctive sense of impending "rain" and whether one heard the sound of a blast, or picked up its shudder through one's boot-soles, one knew exactly when to duck into a sheltered doorway.'[34]

The excavations inadvertently uncovered some of the natural history of the harbour. A tree stump, subsequently estimated to be 8500 years old, was found in its original position some 15 metres below the current water level.[35] When completed, the dock was named to honour Captain James Cook, the man who brought the British to Australia – if not directly to the waterway. At its opening in 1945, the chief of naval staff Admiral Sir Guy Royle declared the decision to build the Captain Cook Graving Dock 'was a recognition of the extent to which the defence of the Commonwealth depends, and must always depend, upon seapower'.[36] Its construction, more than the facilities at

Cockatoo Island, ensured that the harbour remained a major naval base into the 21st century.

Defending these assets was more important than ever before. Armaments at the 19th-century headland forts had been improved at various times since their establishment. In the early 1930s there were three 9.2-inch guns installed at South Head, Bondi and Coogee, supplementing smaller weapons there and at Bradleys, Georges and Middle heads. The old guns had a range of 8 kilometres, less than that of a heavy cruiser. A battleship could sit well beyond and lob shells at the city. To discourage this, newer guns with longer ranges were placed at North Head in 1938. Small 'pill boxes' dotted the cliffs. There were searchlights for aircraft and patrol boats on the harbour. In January 1942 an anti-submarine boom was stretched across the waterway from Greens Point near Watsons Bay to Georges Head. It was fastened to the harbour floor at 49 points and three gates allowed arrivals and departures. The boom net joined a rather more sophisticated system of electrical loops laid down in eight lines to detect the passage of metal ships. One curved in deep water outside the Heads from Dover Heights in the south to Curl Curl on the northern beaches. Another two formed barriers within the harbour between South Head and North and Middle heads.

The electrical loops were monitored from South Head by staff of the Port War Signal Station who watched and interpreted the wavy line drawn on a stylograph with each passing vessel. It required concentration and judgment. Each Manly ferry, for instance, left at least one signature, maybe more. The net was inspected by civilian watchmen rowing a small wooden Maritime Service Board 'boom boat' and patrol boats from the Hollywood Fleet. On 31 May 1942, a cold, wet Sunday night, the outer loop failed and a Japanese midget submarine crossed it and then passed over the two inner loops without creating a significant blip on the stylograph – only to get tangled in the boom. A wooden boom boat and two patrol boats were on duty along the net. The crew of the rowboat first saw an object in the net after 8 pm but it took two hours for the incongruously named patrol

Raising one of the midget
submarines on 10 June 1942.
Australian War Memorial,
Negative 305046

boat *Lolita* to engage the submarine and release its depth charges.
When these failed to explode, the submariners detonated their own
scuttling charges and died beneath the harbour. Two more submarines
followed, guided through the Heads, ironically, by the brilliance of the
Macquarie and Hornby lighthouses. Remarkably enough, they slipped
through the boom gates. The destruction of the first submarine and
the delayed detonation of the depth charges raised the alarm in the
harbour. The large cruiser USS *Chicago*, the target for the Japanese
raiders, began firing at one of the submarines, which had looped
around the harbour and surfaced twice. That vessel then released two
torpedoes at the *Chicago*. The first hit Garden Island near the ferry
Kuttabul, which was lifted out of the water and sunk by the blast. The
second hit the island's shore. The attacker navigated back out of the
harbour, only to sink on Newport Reef just to the north. The third

submarine had meandered around Bradleys Head where the troopship *Westralia* was anchored and had been fired upon, but it was the patrol boat *Sea Mist* – Hope Bartlett's reluctant requisition – that found the submarine and sank it with depth charges in Taylors Bay just after 5 o'clock on Monday morning.[37] In the following days the two sunken submarines were pulled from the harbour like great black fish.

There was understatement and some censorship in the brief description of the 'exciting experience' of 'harbourside residents' that appeared in the *Sydney Morning Herald* the morning after the attack. The paper quoted the first official communiqué from General Head-quarters in Melbourne: 'The enemy's attack was completely unsuccessful. Damage was confined to one small harbour vessel of no military value.'[38] In fact the battle cost 27 lives: six Japanese submariners and 21 sailors who were billeted on the *Kuttabul*. It did not take long for that reality to be appreciated. By way of memorial, Garden Island was commissioned as HMAS *Kuttabul* in January 1943. The Japanese sailors were buried with military honours.

'[A] city of pleasure'

Within a week of the harbour raid, the Japanese lost four aircraft carriers at the Battle of Midway in the mid Pacific. It was a turning point in the war and fear of attack began to subside. A month later the satirical *Australian National Journal* was dismissing the drama with black humour: 'Sydney has not been able to complain so bitterly of gloomy Sundays, as the Japs have been doing their best to brighten things up. Harboursiders found themselves with ringside seats for the first show.'[39] The second may have been the shells sent into Vaucluse and Rose Bay a few days later by a larger Japanese submarine off the coast. Not everyone was amused. Desirable harbourside properties suddenly became available for sale and rent. Joyce Batterham moved quickly to secure a lease on an otherwise unaffordable large house at

Castlecrag with views of the water: 'it was a beautiful location even if some people thought it was a bit risky'.[40]

In the early months of the conflict Sydney remained, in the eyes of one correspondent, 'a city of pleasure'.[41] But while the Japanese attacks were sudden and shocking, the everyday reality of war was already very obvious to those who lived around the harbour. By 1942 the diversion of materials to wartime industry and the rationing of food, fuel and clothing were all pervasive. Lights were dampened at night for fear of air raids. Security around the headland forts was more rigidly enforced. And many people were dealing with the loss of friends and loved ones.

There were restrictions on recreational sailing east of the Bridge and therefore no organised races. However, while the established yacht clubs had ceased activities, workers and locals still sailed their skiffs to the west in between shifts around Cockatoo Island. Indeed, the protected wartime industry fostered many of the boatbuilders and sailors who had grown up on a waterfront where making and racing wooden boats had deep generational roots. Bill Barnett was a shipwright at the Shell Oil terminal at Gore Cove. He had lived near Berrys Bay, where he watched his father and others race skiffs and the peculiar 60-centimetre handcrafted model 'Balmain bugs' that were shepherded around their course by men in rowing boats. After the conflict Barnett won world sailing championships and helped to build yachts such as the 1967 America's Cup challenger *Dame Pattie*. George McGoogan started as an apprentice shipwright at Cockatoo Island just before the war. He was born in nearby Balmain and had known the boatsheds there since he could walk. McGoogan remained a resident of Balmain and stayed working at Cockatoo, where he finished up as the docking superintendent. In the meantime he became one of the most respected sailors and boatbuilders on the harbour. Ironically, in the 1990s he supervised the reconstruction of one of the salvaged midget submarines for display at the Australian War Memorial.[42]

In the lower harbour, Mosman sailor Peter Luke worked on the Volunteer Coastal Patrol, in and outside the Heads. In 1944, as the

Model yacht racing in Berrys Bay before the war. The sport continued until the 1950s.

North Sydney Heritage Centre, Stanton Library

tide ran against Japan, he formed the Cruising Yacht Club of Sydney with a small group of friends. The following year, with the enemy desperately defending its own home islands, a visiting Royal Navy engineer suggested turning a planned club pleasure cruise to Hobart into a competition.[43] The first Sydney-to-Hobart ocean race was run in December 1945 with nine boats and a few spectators. It was a modest return to normalcy after six years of war. The field grew quickly and by 1951 there were up to fifty thousand people crowding the foreshores to watch the boats' departure – reconfirming for many the identity of Sydney as a city of pleasure.[44] Two decades after that, the Sydney-to-Hobart was a blue-water race of international standing. The annual Boxing Day send-off became a spectacle symbolising the city and the nation. Sponsorship money grew with the crowds and coverage and in 1976 the Hitachi Company became the major commercial supporter. That year, Peter Luke relinquished his life membership of the club he had founded, now the Cruising Yacht Club of Australia. Commercialism was part of the problem. But the 'unpardonable crime' in his eyes was the association with a Japanese company. Like some others who remembered the war and the harbour attack, Luke's emotions remained raw.[45]

NINE

MODERN HARBOUR

'AUSTRALIA'S VERY
GOOD! DON'T
WORRY.'

When the aircraft carrier HMS *Formidable* docked at Sydney Cove in October 1945, it carried prison-camp survivors rather than warplanes. Women and children again pressed against the old guard rail at Campbells Cove – this time to welcome rather than farewell loved ones. They waved signs bearing the names of those they strained to see. One of the placards read: 'Welcome home, Tom Uren!' It really was a harbour homecoming for the young bombardier. He had lived at Balmain and Manly before the war and his father helped build the huge grain silos on Glebe Island where the old abattoirs once stood. Uren's Auntie Mary might not have recognised him had he not regained lost weight eating American chocolate bars after his liberation in Japan. He had endured three and a half years of malnutrition, malaria and beatings on the Thai–Burma Railroad and elsewhere. Stepping back on land, Uren was so moved by 'the beauty of Australia and that intangible feeling called freedom' that he 'felt like kissing the ground'.[1] Within a decade he had embarked on a political career that would see him become one of the country's most respected parliamentarians and environmentalists.

Soldiers, sailors, nurses and airmen were still returning to Australia in 1946 and, for many of them, Sydney Harbour was their first sight of home. They were followed two years later by refugees from Europe – human waves flowing from the aftermath of a hot war and the beginnings of a cold one. More than fifty thousand 'Displaced Persons' had come to the country by 1950. The government's motives were both humanitarian and 'practical'. 'If Australians have learned one lesson from the Pacific War', announced immigration minister Arthur Calwell as that conflict neared conclusion, '... it is surely that we cannot continue to hold our island continent for ourselves and our descendants unless we greatly increase our numbers.'[2] The idea that the country had to 'populate or perish' was older than the 'White Australia policy', introduced at the time of Federation to keep out Black and Asian people, but the two were motivated by a similar anxiety: the vulnerability of an island of white people sitting in an 'Asiatic sea'. In the late 1940s Europeans were welcome but many others still were not.

And so on 26 September 1949 a young Slovenian girl, Rozalia Cetinich, left Naples with her family in the Italian liner *Castel Bianco* bound for Melbourne. When the ship arrived contagion had broken out at their intended migrant camp so the passengers sailed on to Sydney. The entire journey took less than three weeks – a fraction of the eight months endured by the original European immigrants. But with the last-minute change of destination there was something of the surprise that had characterised that first entry into an unexpected harbour. Rozalia announced the sight of land to her family and others with an excitement that echoed the cries of countless shipborne arrivals who preceded her:

> We came through the Sydney Heads in the morning. Some people were still in their beds and they popped up their heads when I shouted, 'We can see the land; we can see the land'. Everybody ran up on deck to see.
>
> We had to wait until another boat left the port ... it was 12 when we docked. New Australians that had come years before asked, 'Which country did you come from?' From the deck we called, 'How do you like living here?' [They replied] 'Australia's very good! Don't worry.'[3]

The refugees were followed by other immigrants. They joined small networks established by earlier generations in a predominately Anglo-Celtic city. The impact of demographic change upon the broader culture was most immediately apparent in the realm of architecture and the arts, as professionals and intellectuals brought new ideas from Europe. But there were clear cultural shifts in localised areas such as Woolloomooloo and Leichhardt. Italian-born fishermen continued to practise the skills they had learned in the sea around Calabria and Sicily where buff-coloured villas crowded the cliffs around small harbours. As late as the 1960s, 45-metre nets were being laid out and mended along the quiet weekend roads of Woolloomooloo. Clubs, cafés and related food shops sprang up around there and in the western harbour. Gina Bortolin-Papa arrived with her mother and siblings to join a father and extended family already living in Leichhardt. Her 14-year-old brother went 'straight' into the fishing business that her uncles had helped to consolidate at Iron Cove. These fishermen could still trawl the Hawthorne Canal running from the Parramatta River to Marion Street, Haberfield, created when the Long Cove Creek was widened for barge traffic. Prawns, Australian salmon, mackerel and garfish were being caught around the nearby bays and in the eastern harbour. But the stocks were always precarious so boats also went out past the Heads for the deep sea.[4] When the fish were scarce, Gina's family found boat repair work at Woolloomooloo and Colonial Sugar's huge waterfront sugar refinery at Pyrmont.[5] Gradually the

Woolloomooloo fishermen themselves migrated west to join the fleet at Iron Cove.

Not everyone came by sea. The war had both depleted shipping stocks and improved the range and efficiency of aircraft. Kingsford Smith Airport, near Botany Bay, was enlarged to increase its capacity to five hundred movements per day.[6] The city's other international 'terminal' was in the harbour itself. Since 1938, the flying boats at Rose Bay had delivered mail and those few passengers who could afford an express ten-day trip from England. Twenty years later British-made Comet jets reduced the travelling time between Sydney and London to 33 hours and the Boeing 707 was introduced by Qantas, the first airline outside the United States to do so. New York was now just 20 hours away.[7] Air travel would eclipse passage by water in the following decade.

In the late 1940s shipborne arrivals docked at either the east or west side of Sydney Cove or at Walsh Bay. Two more berths for passengers were opened at Pyrmont in 1951 and shortly after international liners began berthing at the long Woolloomooloo finger wharf – where waterfront workers had wrestled bales of wool for export and Australian troops had left for war. By then there were rather too many migrants from the continent arriving for those who cherished the country's British roots. So the 'Bring out a Briton' campaign was launched in 1957. Ships such as the *Himalaya* and *Orontes* carried clerics from Bristol and farm workers from Dorset to the harbour to make new lives in Australia.

The traffic was not all one way. The cruise liners returned, trailing veils of streamers from the wharves. In 1959 Australians could sail for a three-month European holiday aboard the SS *Orion*. The all-inclusive cost of £409 prevented most working-class people, but affluence was spreading and the once-exclusive ocean cruise was a possibility for many.[8]

The increased size of the cruise ships, in turn, put pressure on harbour authorities to again upgrade Sydney's port facilities. Two P&O vessels, the 40 000-ton *Oriana* and the 45 000-ton *Canberra*, set a new benchmark. To accommodate them a passenger terminal was built on

West Circular Quay. It was a modern, functionalist and ultimately uninspiring building that extended long and low in front of the buildings of the old Victorian-era Rocks behind: the Sailors Home, the Rawson Institute for Seaman and the landmark Australian Steam Navigation Company Building designed in the Anglo-Dutch style by one of Sydney's leading architects, William Wardell, in 1884. The terminal was another element in a new blankly horizontal waterfront that had emerged with the replacement of the old Sydney Harbour Trust-era ferry wharves and the long-awaited completion of the quay's railway station (touted in 1909, agreed to in 1926 but not completed for another 30 years because of economic depression and war). The severance of the foreshore from the water by Circular Quay station and the elevated railway line was criticised as a 'master stroke of vandalism' then, just as its prospect had outraged Robert Hickson years earlier.[9]

The ferries still came to the quay, giving Sydney a sense of place as they glided like 'gondolas' along 'grand canals' formed by nature. For the returned war correspondent Kenneth Slessor, who conjured that image, they were 'one of the city's peculiar enchantments'. The ferries made Sydney a 'kind of dispersed and vaguer Venice'. Town planners too recognised their cultural significance keeping 'city workers in touch with shipping and with nature as they steam up the fairway or thread their way through sylvan coves'.[10] But they were also unprofitable and in 1951 the State government took over the operation of the inner harbour boats from Sydney Ferries Ltd so that they might keep running. From then on their quintessential presence on the harbour depended upon public subsidy.

It was the Bridge that had first devastated ferry-boat patronage and since World War II cars were carrying more people across the water than trains. So the concrete had hardly dried on the harbour-front train station when a roadway – the Cahill Expressway – was begun to be built on top. JJC Bradfield had anticipated the rise of the automobile as soon as his Bridge was opened. There were now so many people and cars that the approaches to the great arch were choked with traffic at peak hour. The waterfront expressway was the first of many vain attempts to alleviate the new problem of congestion across the harbour. The solutions highlighted the potential of engineering rather than the application of good social and environmental planning. In 1964 the Parramatta River would be spanned at Gladesville with a huge concrete curve – the largest then constructed – as part of an American-style expressway scheme that was never fully realised. Four years later a canyon of bitumen and concrete was carved out of the suburbs immediately to the north of the Sydney Harbour Bridge to create the Warringah Expressway. In time this often-clotted artery would feed a second harbour crossing, but one hidden from view – the Sydney Harbour Tunnel.

'A House is Built'

The displacement of liners such as the *Canberra* was such that Sydney Cove had to be dredged again – this time to a minimum depth of 10.7 metres. Over three weeks in 1960 some 69 000 cubic metres of harbour floor were dug and dumped outside the Heads. In the process small treasures were uncovered from the days of the first wharf: cannonballs, fish hooks and a 1787 coin from the Dutch East India Company.[11] They were no more than curios that emphasised the march of progress. Still, the changes that had swept across the harbour and foreshores with the construction of the Bridge and the redesign of the cove coincided with, and no doubt encouraged, a new interest in the history of Sydney and its waterway. Charles Bertie's beautifully illustrated booklet *Old Colonial By-Ways* appeared in 1928 with images of colonial-era buildings, the Rocks and 'Old Houses' at Blues Point. The historical novel *A House is Built* by 'M Barnard Eldershaw' was set in the cove and told the story of the rise of a waterfront family empire in the first half of the 1800s. It reflected the real-life stories of the Lords, Underwoods, Campbells and Morts and won the Bulletin Prize for best Australian novel when it was published in 1929. Five editions were printed within two years.

The remarkable writing partnership of Marjorie Barnard and Flora Eldershaw produced several more works of popular history, including *Phillip of Australia: An Account of the Settlement at Sydney Cove 1788–92* in 1938 and *The Life and Times of Captain John Piper* the following year. *A House is Built* had reached its 15th reprint as the new Overseas Passenger Terminal was welcoming its first arrivals.

But the sense of history and heritage rarely overcame the urge to redevelop in postwar Sydney. As Barnard and Eldershaw were finalising their book on John Piper, plans were being completed for the replacement of the 1812 Commissariat Building he must have known intimately. It was one of the most significant buildings of the early colonial era and a landmark of the old Sydney Cove. Just two years after the celebration of Australia's sesquicentenary, the great stone pile – its foundation stone inscribed with the arcane script of Macquarie's time – was demolished to build an enlarged headquarters for the new Maritime Services Board (MSB), which had just superseded the Sydney Harbour Trust. The historical significance of the Commissariat Building was recognised by some and there had been attempts to save it as a museum. However, its very convict-era origins counted against preservation in the minds of others. For one former lord mayor, the presence of the initials of a convict stonemason on each carved stone was 'a damn good reason why we should forget them'.[12] In the end the foundation stone was kept and displayed.

The construction of the MSB Building had been delayed by war. It was not completed until 1949. The new structure was designed by government architects WH Withers and WDH Baxter. It had its own undeniable presence and sense of place due, in part, to the use of high-quality Sydney sandstone – but also to its administrative connection to the waterfront. It followed the footprint and symmetry of the old store with its protruding wings, but added a monumental stepped Art Deco design that matched the pylons of the Bridge behind. Sydney-born sculptor and war artist Lyndon Dadswell executed a carved granite relief panel above the entrance, which celebrated maritime workers in a stylised social realism that recalled the earlier work of Isamu Noguchi and Nils Hanson in the United States and reiterated artistic odes to labour that had reached a zenith in the 1940s.

Somewhat ironically, half a century later the MSB Building itself would be saved from demolition and refurbished as the Museum of Contemporary Art. But at the time of its realisation, it was considered something of an anachronism. Within seven years, glass-and-steel oblongs were appearing on the east side of Sydney Cove. The construction of two head office blocks – ICI House designed by the firm Bates, Smart and McCutcheon and Unilever House by Stephenson and Turner – heralded a new corporate era of development around the area.[13] The postwar boom in commerce and property prices was apparently irresistible. There were £3 million worth of buildings erected in the city in 1956, and this had increased 17-fold just eight years later.[14] Although it was still scruffy and clogged with trams, Circular Quay was becoming a prestigious corporate address. The pressure to maximise real estate returns dramatically altered the scale of development, and between 1958 and 1962 the AMP Building rose 26 storeys behind the new train station and expressway. It was the first building to take advantage of the removal of absolute height restrictions and stretch up beyond 46 metres to become the city's first skyscraper.[15]

These new buildings had no working relationship to their harbour-front location – it was centrality, the availability of redundant waterfront sites and the desirability of harbour views that placed them there. Unilever and ICI houses became the first blocks in a wall of offices that would eventually screen the greenery of the Domain from Sydney Cove. Sandwiched between these blocks of glass and steel, the surviving stone bond stores that Joseph Conrad had known began to look incongruous. There was remarkably little concern over the barrier that was being created between the quay and the Botanic Gardens behind. The new buildings were more than twice the height of the bond stores.

The Australian Mutual Providence, or AMP, Building was intended to serve as a 'prestige' and 'distinctive' head office for the insurance firm for 50 years, although it too was superseded within three decades.[16]

In this instance, the building's qualities were such that it ultimately survived the wrecker's hammer. It was not quite the symmetrical 'carton' shape that characterised the other two buildings. The front and rear façades curved to form a concave 'H'. Its windows featured glass treated with gold dust. These glazed curtain walls afforded majestic views of the harbour but they also made temperature control difficult. To cool and heat the offices, sea water was sucked in from the cove and fed through heat exchangers in a basement dug deep in the sandstone. Similar technologies had been used for years in the harbourside power stations and the Olympic pool at North Sydney. Yet neither this nor the gold glazing was apparently adequate, for the fit-out included the largest order for venetian blinds yet filled in the country.

Like the designers of the ICI and Unilever buildings, the AMP architects – Peddle, Thorp and Walker – were among the first Australian architects to adopt postwar International Style modernism. All had designed in ornamented idioms in the interwar years. But the new architecture eschewed decoration and unnecessary adornment and sought to use modern materials in the most efficient way possible. By breaking with historical 'fashions', it was the ideal architecture for those who wanted to identify with progress and the future. SG Thorp had visited North America to view the most recent developments in office design there before finalising plans for the AMP Building. The multinational Unilever Company had embraced the International Style in their monumental New York headquarters, Lever House designed by Skidmore, Owings and Merrill and completed in 1952. Directly opposite it the Seagram Building – by Mies van der Rohe with Philip Johnson – was just being finished. The symbolism was particularly apparent with the AMP Building because it replaced Thomas Mort's grand old woolstore. That landmark building had grown over the years to resemble an Italian palazzo. By 1957 it was apparently obsolete as the quay was given over to office work and the cargo the woolstore once housed left from Darling Harbour and Pyrmont.

Perhaps because it spoke so emphatically of the future, postwar modernism did not age well in the eyes of the companies that had embraced it. Steel and glass rarely wears the patina of time as gracefully as sandstone and copper. Thirty years after they were started, the cycle of renewal and corporate image dictated the replacement of the East Circular Quay office blocks. When they were pulled down in the 1990s the public saw a quay opened to the Botanic Gardens for the first time in well over a century. There was an immediate backlash against any redevelopment and calls for the creation of park space by those who had come to hate the ever-increasing scale of office buildings at the quay. Resuming such sites may have been feasible at the beginning of the 20th century, but at its close the cost was untenable. However, such was the public scrutiny of the proposals that a compromise was arrived at whereby the new building was lower than those it replaced and incorporated a gap through which Government House could be glimpsed from the west side of the cove.[17]

In postwar Sydney the papers were full of high-rise stories. Opinions were expressed but rarely with the massed anger of later years. A front page 'artist's impression' of the AMP Building in late 1958 did trigger public and professional debate in articles and letters. It was obvious to any who saw the illustration that 'every part' of the towering structure would have a view, but the planning practitioner and academic Peter Harrison was shocked at the 'splendid disregard' for the scale of the surrounding buildings, the lack of integrated planning and the implications for congestion that such dense development entailed. He argued that the examples of 'building anarchy' in New York and Chicago were to be avoided rather than emulated. With rhetorical optimism, Harrison hoped that the illustration was 'a caricature of city development rather than an illustration of a serious proposal'.[18]

The building was erected much as it had appeared. Some regretted the loss of another piece of history and wrote letters to the papers outlining their concerns. But even those polite expressions of heritage consciousness were enough to annoy supporters of development. 'Too many Australians prefer to think of the achievements of our past rather than create for the future,' complained one correspondent. Sydney should be an international symbol of 'our vitality and maturity' and the AMP Building, along with the train station, the expressway and the offices at East Circular Quay, would encourage a 'spirit to achieve a greater history than our past holds'.[19] The missive was, in itself, a perfect expression of the spirit of modernism.

The letter-writer looked forward also to a fifth element in the 'new Quay' – the Sydney Opera House. The competition for such a building on Bennelong Point had been called in 1956 and decided the following year, but the site's suitability was recognised as early as 1951. It was suggested by the Viennese-born planning consultant Karl Langer and championed soon after by the conductor of the Sydney Symphony Orchestra Eugene Goossens, who got a bird's eye view of the waterway when he arrived by flying boat from England after the war.[20] Labor premier Joe Cahill, after whom the waterfront expressway was named, combined a utilitarian approach to transport planning with a democratic vision of aesthetics and so supported the construction of 'facilities' that would 'add grace and charm to living and which help to develop and mould a better, more enlightened community …'[21]

Nearly 900 competitors from 45 countries registered and 222 entries were received. The winner was a relatively inexperienced Danish architect, Jørn Utzon. Like the designer of the neo-Gothic Government House which survived behind, Utzon completed his drawings from afar. Yet he was familiar with living by the sea and with waterfronts and relished the opportunity to design an opera house for a peninsula he understood had a special place – in a harbour long renowned for its beauty.

Denmark is a country dominated by coastline and waterways. The young Utzon grew up around Alborg where his father worked as a marine architect. During the war he fled occupied Denmark to live in Sweden and there became familiar with the Stockholm Town Hall, built three decades earlier to reclaim the working waterfront for civic use.[22] By the 1950s Utzon had returned to work near the small coastal town of Helsingør, where Kronborg Castle looks across to Sweden and dominates the narrows of Øresund from its peninsula. When he finally arrived in Sydney in July 1957 he remarked, 'I had no difficulty in visualising Bennelong Point because we have the castle of Helsinger on the point just like your tram depot at Fort Macquarie.'[23] The influence of location was real – for any building on Bennelong Point would, like the Danish castle, be visible from the water on three sides. The reference to the tram shed was humorous because the presence of that castellated transport depot on the point had long been recognised as an 'absurdity'. With a rail loop, the closure of the city's tram network and plenty of cars, it was obsolete as well.

Utzon's modernism could not have been more different to that expressed in the oblongs of glass farther along the quay. The shell-like shapes of his original drawings were organic, or at least highly naturalistic in the manner of stones worn smooth by the action of water. They resonated immediately with one of the judges, Eero Saarinen, who had been working on expansive curved forms with his TWA airport terminal design in New York. Where that building perfectly expressed the moment of lift-off – and through that the new age of air travel – Utzon's resonated with its historic shoreline setting. The roof could be understood as a series of shells, a set of waves or a flotilla of sails. Utzon himself attributed some influence to the family of white swans that graced the lake near his architectural office.[24]

But the realisation of this vision depended upon geometry no less than the office buildings nearby. The architect explained this himself after years spent considering the practicalities of construction:

> Mies van der Rohe orientates himself and defines his shapes from a 90° grid system ... In a similar way I, for instance, subdivide space by grids of converging plans fanning out from a point at even angles ... [however] instead of making a square form, I have made a sculpture ...

Whereas the original drawings had shown variously flattened and upright 'shells' – a proposition that was unworkable – the roof sections that were ultimately built derived their proportional relationship by cutting large and small segments from a spherical timber block. The solution only came after the exasperated engineer Ove Arup insisted that the curves have a consistent geometry. The lines were first drawn on a beach ball then transferred to the wooden model after considering the shape of ships' hulls. The idea was later explained by reference to a segmented orange.[25] The shapes 'come from the same sphere with the same radius', Utzon wrote, 'and therefore when they are built up in space, we know they will intersect in accordance with a certain law – therefore the composition is in equilibrium'.[26] It would sit in equilibrium also with the great arch to create the twin icons of the waterway. The Bridge declared its masterful engineering quite openly, the Opera House disguised its technical brilliance as a work of art. Unlike the modernist blocks behind, it did not age.

The sombreness of the harbour's architecture had struck Utzon upon his arrival. Colonial-era whitewash and light yellow sandstone had given way to brick-and-tile flats and houses that seemed to negate nature's brightness: 'Sydney is a dark harbour,' he wrote. 'The colours of the waterfront are dull and the homes are of red brick. There is no white to take away the sun and make it dazzle the eyes – not like the Mediterranean countries or South America and other sunlit countries.'[27] So the building's 'colour' was decided: 'A roof of white tiles would emphasise the sculptural character of the building ... The sun, the light and the clouds will make it a living thing.'[28] A million glazed ceramic tiles were made in Sweden, in a factory just across from Helsingør, and shipped to Sydney to be stuck to tile-lids prefabricated on site and fitted into the great fan-like rib sections that were also cast on the harbour's edge.[29] Once mounted, the zigzag patterning of the tiles added another subtle geometry to the curve of the 'sails'. With the sheen of the glaze giving the impression of a scaly skin, it did indeed look like a living thing.

'A natural setting that nobody could undo'

Sydney's revolutionary Opera House immediately caught the attention of the architectural world, just as it would capture the popular imagination and become one of the most recognised buildings on the planet. It prompted Sigfried Giedion, the renowned Swiss historian and critic, to update his survey of the new architecture and enthusiastically describe a 'third generation' of modernism.[30] Mies van der Rohe, who had emerged in the first, hated it. There was hardly a 90-degree angle to be seen.[31]

Sydney's own up-and-coming prophet of the modern, Harry Seidler, had entered the Opera House competition with a wide colonnaded rectangular design that anticipated the National Library of Australia, one of the great civic buildings of the national capital, Canberra. Yet he graciously deferred to Utzon's winning entry, describing it as 'a magnificent piece of poetry'. Indeed, Seidler led the public protest when the Danish architect was forced to leave the project after the New South Wales government had frozen payments. Such a radical design had, not surprisingly, led to delays and increased costs. When a sympathetic Labor government lost to a conservative coalition, already antagonistic towards the project, Utzon's position became difficult, if not untenable. He left in 1966 and his Opera House was completed by a committee of others. Utzon was not invited to the opening in 1973 and, indeed, never returned to see his finished building. For Seidler, as for many others, the treatment of Utzon and his masterpiece represented the triumph of mendacious mediocrity after such a promising start.

Seidler's arrival in Sydney was no less a result of the upheaval of war as that of young Rozalia Cetinich and the other shipborne exiles. His uncle had fled Jewish persecution in Nazi-occupied Austria and travelled to Australia to relocate the family's textile business in 1939. Seidler's parents and brother arrived in 1946. Now he was visiting. Seidler's own introduction to the city was not a happy one. He had come by air rather than ship in 1948. His first impressions

This aerial photograph by Arthur Hamilton shows the Sydney Opera House on the day of its opening, 20 October 1973.

North Sydney Heritage Centre, Stanton Library

were formed, therefore, by the sparsely settled 'fibro frontier' around Kingsford Smith Airport and his parents' home at Maroubra rather than the breathtaking harbour vistas that had greeted generations of immigrants previously. Seidler's stay in the 'godforsaken place' was not meant to be permanent, but he was awestruck by the harbour's beauty: 'It was just wonderful, the fantastic panorama of the harbour, a natural setting that nobody could undo.'[32] And then his parents asked him to design them a house – so he stayed on. The first impressions never left him and over the next decade Seidler rarely lost an opportunity to condemn both the suburban sprawl he had witnessed on the day of his arrival and inappropriate development of the harbour he undoubtedly loved.

Seidler had studied and worked in the United States with Walter Gropius and Marcel Breuer, and briefly in South America with Oscar Niemeyer, whose planned developments in Brazil owed much to the theories of Le Corbusier. They, and Seidler, applied an uncompromising rationalism to architecture and planning. At best, their approaches were grounded in democratic and utilitarian principles: the production of well-designed buildings without excessive ornamentation in order to efficiently house as many people as possible in good urban communities. The MSB Building had immediately caught Seidler's eye as an example of regressive design. By 'copying old Greece and Rome' it was 'utterly decadent'.[33] A decade later he thought that the 'battle for modern architecture' was finally being won in a city characterised by a jumble of 19th- and early 20th-century styles: 'stripped clean logical building' was 'a necessary cleansing technique' for an industry 'steeped in traditional wasteful methods of construction, and stylistic architectural decoration'.[34]

Seidler might well have been optimistic. In 1951 he had won the Australian architectural prize named after John Sulman for the Breuer-inspired house he designed for his parents in Turramurra. And there was no shortage of work, much of it around the harbour. He began designing Ithaca Gardens Flats at Elizabeth Bay in 1950. Light-coloured bricks, concrete and large windows differentiated it from the dour red blocks that had been built along the foreshores in the previous decade. Still, when it was finally finished in 1960, it was likened to a 'biscuit factory'.[35] The new modernist style and materials were ideal for single dwellings on Sydney's steep foreshores previously considered 'unsuitable for home building'.[36] The T Meller House was designed for a Viennese family at Castlecrag in 1950. Built over a sandstone boulder, its three split-level floors all had water views. But the construction contravened the original building covenant and Seidler was compelled to seek permission to continue from the aging Marion Mahoney Griffin who had designed the suburb with her husband Walter. By the end of 1951 the Williamson House sat like a 'concrete sandwich' on top of the escarpment overlooking Middle Harbour.[37] In 1958 Seidler was designing a concrete shell-roofed dwelling at Clifton Gardens.[38] The following year he completed a house at Cammeray with reinforced concrete columns and simple geometric lines that perched on an incline with views over Long Bay in Middle Harbour.[39]

Seidler was not alone in exploiting the steep slopes around parts of the still undeveloped harbour front. At Castlecrag also, architects Bill and Ruth Lucas built themselves a similarly elevated house using glass, timber, steel and lightweight fibre cement. The 'Glass House' was also very different to the Griffin-designed homes of the 1920s but, in their minds, complied with the original covenant by respecting its bushy foreshore setting.[40] In 1963 Stan Symonds finished the futuristic Schuchard House at Seaforth in Middle Harbour. It was a remarkable example of organic modernism that made full use of the plasticity and affordability of concrete to cling to the edge of a cliff and provide 180-degree views. Five years earlier Hungarian immigrant Lazlo Peter Kollar completed the Creswell House on a steep lot near Quakers Hat Bay in Mosman. He shared a contempt for 'the degenerate, tasteless, and spineless squalor of XIXth Century eclecticism' with the European masters. The Creswell House featured massed whitewashed brick forms and asymmetrical windows in the manner of Le Corbusier's Chapel at Ronchamps, France, completed eight years earlier.[41]

The influence of the Swiss master was also noticeable to the west. By then Seidler and others had planned an extensive harbourside precinct around the cluttered waterfront at Blues and McMahons points – where two generations earlier Lawson had yarned and Streeton painted and chatted to the little boy and his pond yacht. The plan epitomised the idea of Le Corbusier's 'Radiant City' whereby urban densities might be increased and congestion simultaneously lessened by building well-planned tower blocks that maximised the open spaces around. Seidler pointed to its implementation in Marseilles, Roehampton and the city of Brasilia, built to replace the unplanned sprawling port of Rio de Janeiro as the Brazilian capital.[42] In the minds of the young

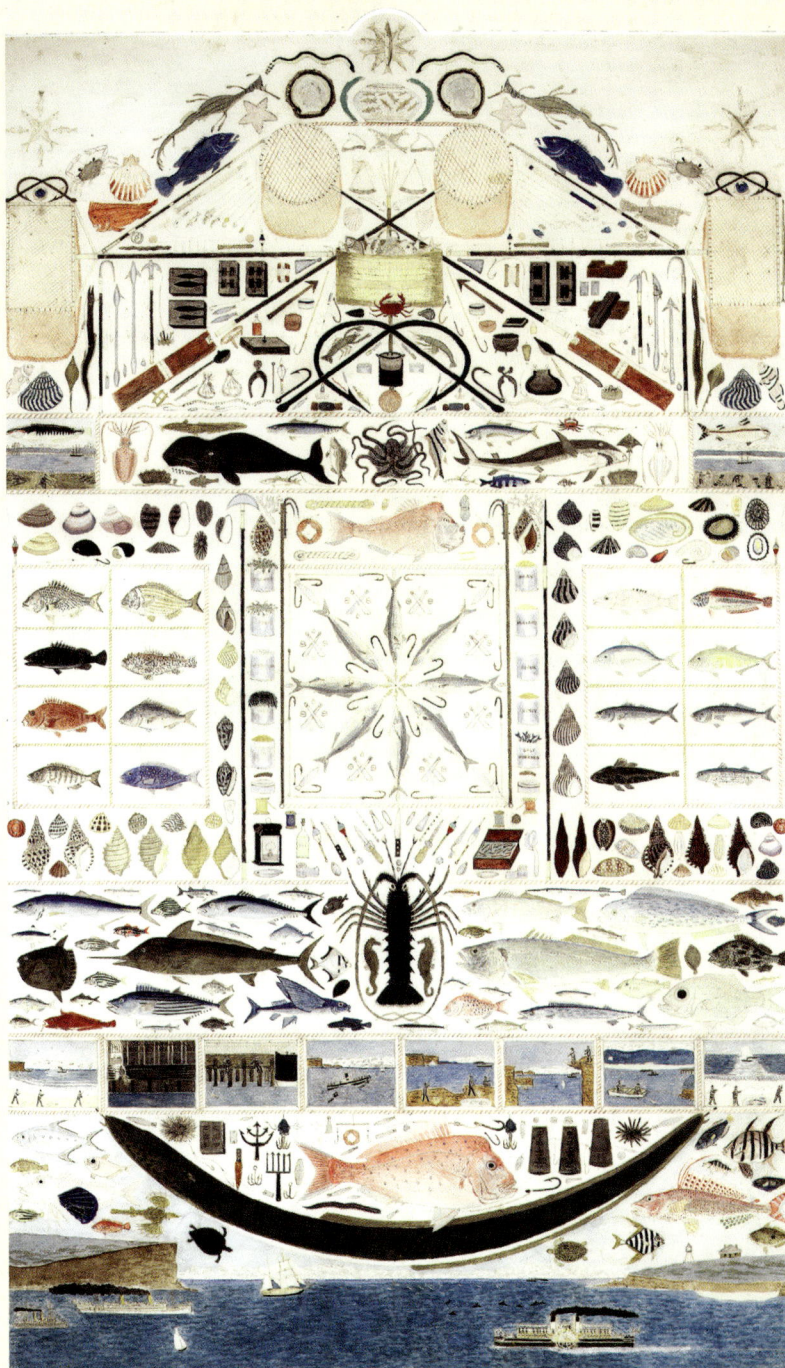

J Pearson, the creator of this watercolour chart of *The Fish of Sydney Harbour*, was obviously intimately involved in fishing and harbour life. It illustrates the variety of marine life from whales to shellfish along with fishing tackle and harbour scenes. The inclusion of the royal yacht *Ophir*, which visited in 1901, helps to date the image.

Australian National Maritime Museum

Above Montagu Scott's large 1870 oil, *A day's picnic on Clarke Island, Sydney Harbour* was both a landscape painting and a character study of the recreational habits of the harbour city's middle class. On the far left two women wait with plates ready for the fresh oysters being chiselled from the rocks by a plainly dressed man, possibly the waterman who ferried the party to the island. Champagne is being enjoyed by men and women alike. An interest in nature is suggested by the woman poking at a rock pool with her parasol and the field glasses worn by the gentleman in grey. Clarke Island was declared a public reserve nine years later. Shark Island followed in 1905.

Mitchell Library, State Library of New South Wales

Top right Arthur Streeton's 1895 oil painting *Cremorne Pastoral* was both a celebration of the beautiful harbour and an artistic argument for the preservation of natural beauty against the depredations of industries such as coal mining.

Art Gallery of New South Wales

Below right This oil painting, by an unknown artist from around 1870, shows the working waterfront of Millers Point and Darling Harbour in the two decades before the foreshore became intensively lined with commercial wharves. The windmill that gave the point its name is long gone but the observatory and signal station are prominent.

State Library of New South Wales

A. H. Fullwood.

AH Fulwood imagined this aerial view of Sydney and its bustling harbour in 1888, five years after he arrived from England. It both celebrates 100 years of British colonisation and shows the harbour city in all its guises, with green headlands to the east and an intense coal-blackened waterfront to the west around Darling Harbour, now given over to coastal shipping. St Andrew's Cathedral and the Sydney Town Hall rise up disproportionately as symbols of civic development.

Beat Knoblauch Collection. Historic Houses Trust of NSW

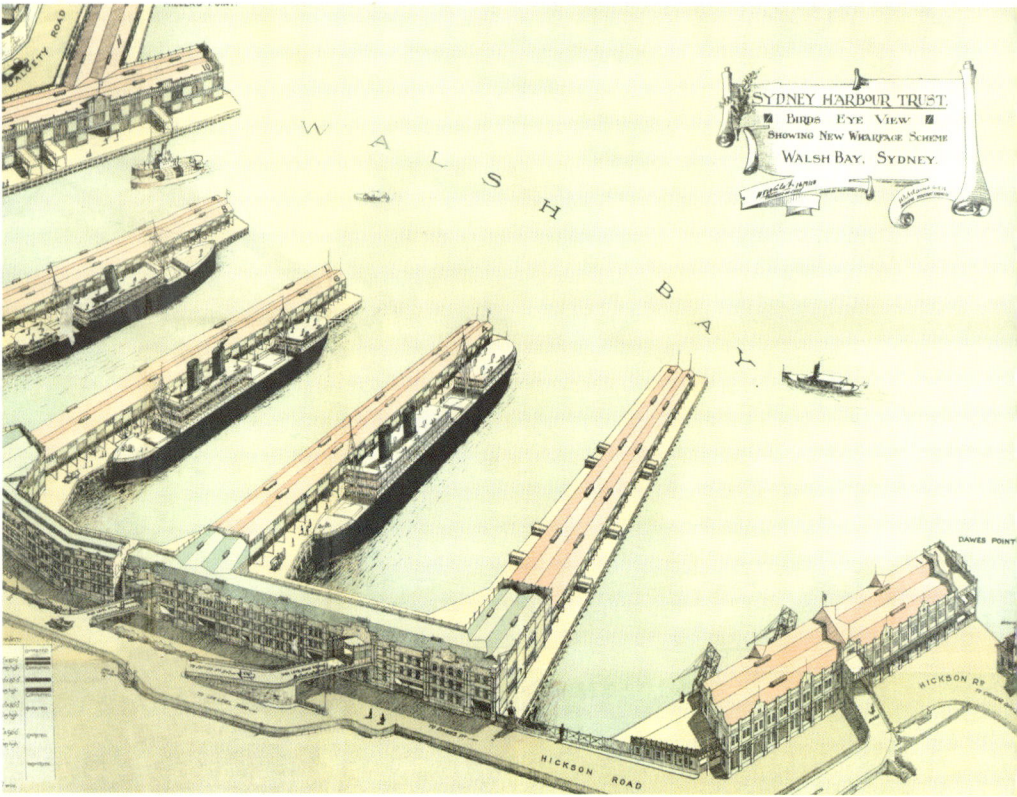

Above This detail from *Bird's Eye Viewing Showing New Wharfage Scheme, Walsh Bay Sydney*, embodies the ideals of cleanliness and efficiency that underpinned the resumption of the waterfront. The reality of work there was often different. It was signed by HD Walsh and dated '16.9.18'. The image appeared in the *Port of Sydney Official Handbook* published by the Sydney Harbour Trust Commissioners in 1924.

Research Library Collection, Powerhouse Museum, Sydney

Right Herbert McClintock painted the huge Captain Cook graving dock under construction at Garden Island in 1943–44. McClintock was employed as a war artist to document the work of the Civil Construction Corp. He was also a member of the Communist Party. Both roles explain the focus on workers in this work.

Australian War Memorial, Negative ART30255

Max Dupain's photograph shows Sydney's working western waterfront around 1965. The huge Colonial Sugar Refinery plant on Johnstones Bay can be seen in the foreground. Beyond is Darling Harbour with the Jones Bay wharves on the Pyrmont side and the finger wharves that would be demolished for container facilities on the city side. Pyrmont power station is still generating electricity.

Max Dupain and Associates

Eric Sierens's 1995 photograph shows the Darling Harbour
concourse with water features, the Marketplace and the
Australian National Maritime Museum.

Max Dupain and Associates

Ken Done's crayon and gouache *Sydney* was first published in a 1986 calendar.
It was reprinted on the cover of the *Hanako: Tokyo Women's Weekly* in 1988.

Permission of Ken Done Gallery

Peter Kingston's drawing of the demolition of 6/7 Wharf at Walsh Bay was titled *A Night to Remember*, a reference to the sinking of the *Titanic*.

Permission Peter Kingston, Art Galleries, Sydney

Above A model of the Hill Thalis Architects, Paul Berkemeier Architects and Jane Irwin Landscape Architecture design that won the 2005 competition for the design of the East Darling Harbour precinct that became Barangaroo.

Courtesy of Hill Thalis. Photograph Michael Nicholson

Left The Crown Resort tower at Barangaroo, 2022.

Photograph Ian Hoskins

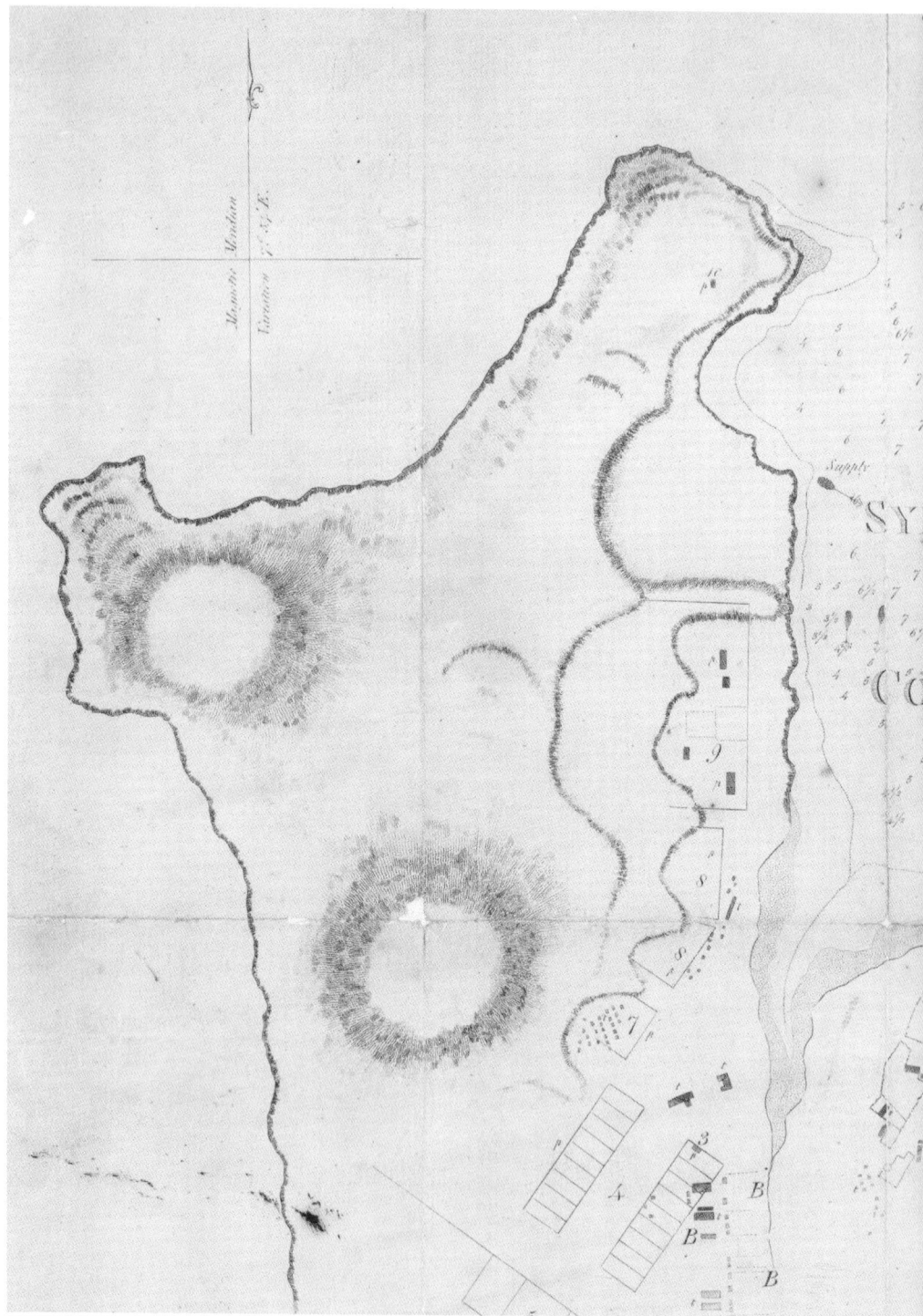

Magnetic Meridian

Variation 7° 3′ E.

Supply

SY

CO

16
B

9

8

7

3
4
B

B

B

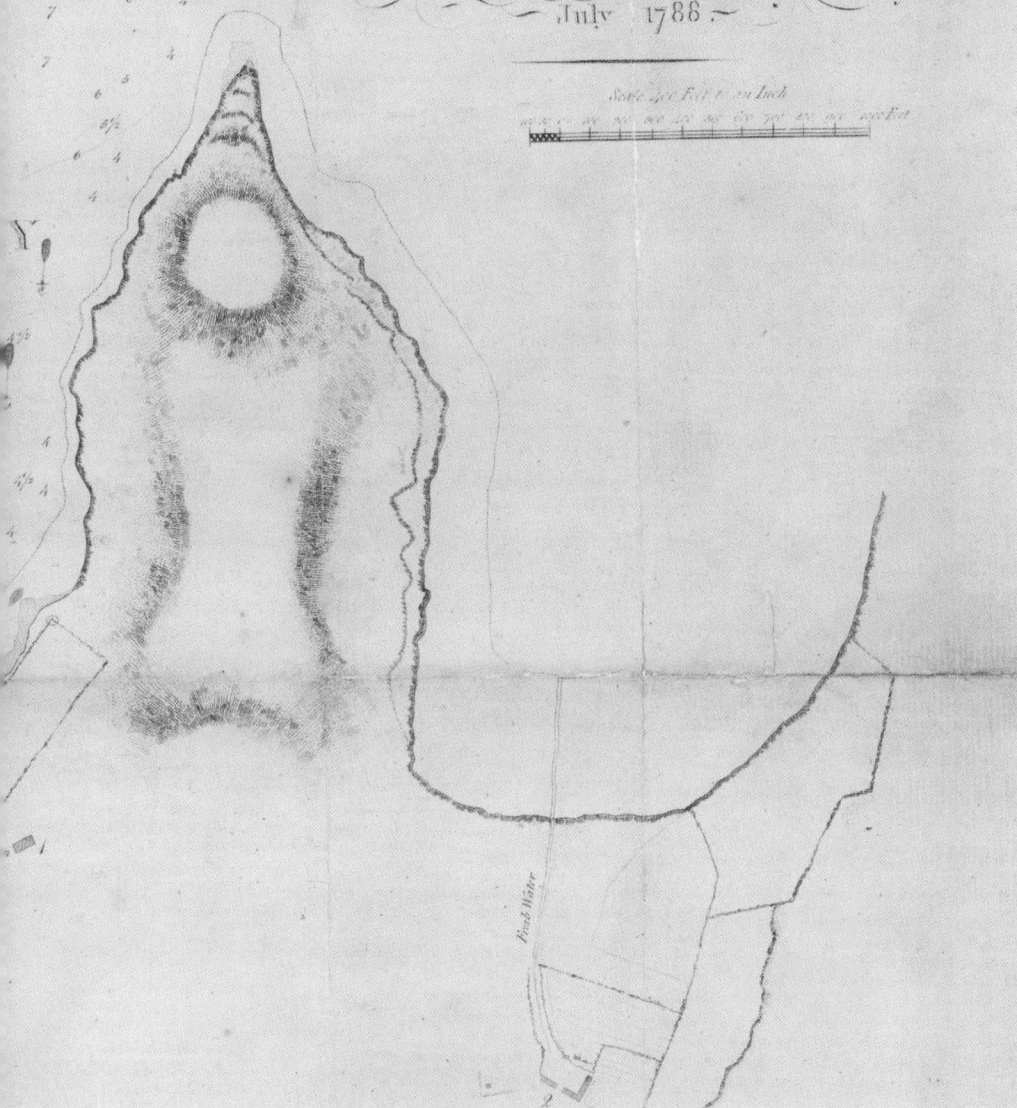

The 'naturalistic' foreshore of the headland park at
Barangaroo championed by Paul Keating, 2015.

Photograph Ian Hoskins

modernists, Sydney Harbour too was becoming an illogical mess: 'This superb amenity is slowly being spoilt by the type of development that is taking place around its foreshores. One of the finest headlands on this harbour, McMahons Point, had been zoned for industry!'[43] The editor of the *Daily Telegraph* concurred: 'Save what's left of our Harbor' it pleaded.[44]

That zoning had recently been enshrined by the Cumberland County Council (CCC), a new body whose task was to bring integrated development to greater Sydney. Dismissive though Seidler was of the CCC's competence, its huge plan was by no means the work of philistines and fools. It began poetically with Erasmus Darwin's 'Sydney Cove' and went on to acknowledge that 'nothing so completely identifies Sydney to the outside world as Sydney Harbour'. Later it quoted TS Eliot's bleak 1934 critique of modernity and alienation, *Choruses from The Rock,* by way of challenging readers to consider the reason for urban reform: [45]

> When the stranger says: 'what is the meaning of this city?
> Do you huddle close together because you love each other?'
> What will you answer? 'We all dwell together
> To make money from each other'? or 'this is a community'?

The Cumberland County Plan also acknowledged that 'life and beauty' had frequently been replaced by 'a discordant mass of buildings, often to the water's edge'.[46] It estimated that about a third of the industry currently located by the harbour did not need to be there and recommended that industrial foreshore areas should be established only if 'the use of waterfront facilities is essential to their operation'. However, although it gave special recognition to Balls Head as a beauty spot, the council generally adhered to the east–west divide that characterised earlier recommendations for harbour development. Industry at McMahons Point was acceptable, presumably because the area had accommodated it for much of the previous century with boatbuilders, a timber yard and, more recently, a line of oil tanks

An impression of the McMahons Point scheme as it appeared
in the booklet *Urban Redevelopment Concerns You!*
By permission Penelope Seidler. North Sydney Heritage Centre,
Stanton Library

set into the sandstone cliffs on the western side of neighbouring
Berrys Bay.[47]

But for Seidler this was no way to treat 'the finest harbour in the
world'.[48] The polemical booklet that accompanied his own scheme
included photographs of a chaotic working waterfront with boatsheds
and train tracks blocking access and beauty. The apparent stupidity was
compounded by the spectre of the sprawl beyond. In a city such as Sydney,

it seemed obvious that people should be living around the harbour, not in the 'wastes of suburbia'. The hilly topography around the point – and elsewhere for that matter – was far better suited to accommodating high-density residences with harbour views than it was to hauling out material on steep congested roadways.[49] McMahons Point was the ideal place to demonstrate the veracity of urban consolidation.

Seidler's plan received widespread publicity and almost universal approval. Its futurism was exciting. One 1957 newspaper article used it to illustrate how a 'Clean and Atomic Powered' Sydney would look in 50 years. A year later the architect suggested that the plan could be equally well applied to the 'hodge podge of slums' around the waterfront at Glebe and Balmain. That idea was endorsed by the CCC chief planner as well as the leading academic commentators Professor Denis Winston and JH Shaw.[50]

For architects Ian McKay and Phillip Jackson, who had just attended the influential 1956 International Congress of Modern Architecture (CIAM) conference in Dubrovnik, the scheme epitomised the new direction in modernist planning whereby stark functionalism was softened by consideration of 'habitat', with its accompanying emphasis on 'the heritage of nature' and the needs of community.[51] There was little in the scale and uncompromising order of the plan that differed from earlier modernist dreams. But Seidler's scheme would certainly have maximised views of the waterway and, amidst the towers, it allowed plenty of public open space, foreshore access and a variety of cultural and social facilities.

It was significant also as an example of a new collaboration between expert and the community. For the project had been sponsored by local residents in the McMahons Point and Lavender Bay Progress Association, who had sought Seidler's help in overturning the industrial zoning. Here was an idea that seemed to come from the bottom up rather than the top down. Such common purpose appeared to confirm the democratic appeal and rationalism of modernist planning – and the architect emphasised his plan's community roots as often as possible. Most others in the press applauded the project because they too disagreed with the industrial zoning of the point. For a while Harry Seidler was both a champion of common sense and a protector of the harbour.

The McMahons Point scheme achieved its first objective when the area was rezoned residential. In 1958 Gerardus Dusseldorp, a Dutch immigrant who had developed the Ithaca Gardens flats at Elizabeth Bay with Seidler, bought almost a hectare of land near the end of Blues Point and the implementation of the scheme seemed possible. Despite having a 'singular ugliness', Blues Point Tower was approved by both North Sydney Council and the CCC as 'a precedent for future development of the living areas immediately adjacent'.[52] The cost of the entire scheme was estimated at £20 million. In the early 1960s there was an economic slump and selling the flats in Blues Point Tower alone was difficult. The rest of the scheme was never realised.

The Cumberland County Plan had recognised the significance of sensitive development on foreshores and ridges: 'because the Harbour is visible from many viewpoints'.[53] But it apparently took the completion of Seidler's tower to make this logic tangible. 'It had the effect of making us realise that the surrounds of the Harbour would now be a completely different place,' recalled the CCC chief planner Nigel Ashton. 'In many ways it's been a great blessing.' As a boy, Ashton had loved to watch the coasters and sailing ships arrive in Darling Harbour from his boarding school above Lavender Bay. By the mid-1960s he was chairman of the body that had superseded the CCC – the State Planning Authority – and in that capacity was trying to stop developments on foreshores and headlands after the epiphany of Blues Point: 'If you keep your points landscaped when you look up and down the harbour you tend to get a feeling of a city on a landscaped harbour.'[54] To this end, waterfront land was resumed and parks created at Kurraba, Long Nose and Clarks points.

But by then the waterfronts and rises at Kirribilli and Elizabeth Bay were lined with flats built with little regard for the aspects of those around. That lack of coordination, and the negation of site and community it entailed, was what Seidler had hoped to avoid at McMahons Point. Local councils attempted to control the size and appearance of buildings with 'flat codes' and later heritage-based development controls – but Seidler grew ever more contemptuous of the ability of local government to plan and guide development. The optimist of the 1950s, who never retreated from the need for European-style master planning, came to dismiss the Australian experience as 'misguided grass roots democracy'.[55]

In the end, his 'thin needle' at Blues Point was admired by some architects for its 'maturity of expression'.[56] Years later its historical and architectural significance was acknowledged in the local heritage inventory. The building did, at least, respond to the vista. At Balmoral a 1920s-era amphitheatre that had been built by spiritualists expressly to face the Heads was knocked down in 1951 to make way for a remarkably grim squat block with mean windows that seemed oblivious to the breathtaking location.[57] Elsewhere towers sprouted up between bungalows and villas. Atop Darling Point there grew a forest of high-rises. At Kirribilli and Elizabeth Bay flats formed a wall on the waterfront. Mosman became 'virtually a new suburb'.[58] But none was as singularly obvious as Blues Point Tower and so it simply came to epitomise for many the insensitivity of modern development and the arrogance of the quest for the best water view. It became 'Sydney's most selfish building'.[59]

'[W]e can't differentiate the buildings from the people'

So great was the earlier support for the residential zoning of McMahons Point that few thought to question the implications of clear-felling a mixed precinct that had developed organically over a century. Attachment to place was recognised but rarely respected. So much so that the truism 'progress knows no sentiment' was used with varying degrees of regret and fatalism. In any case, the existing building stock was dismissed as 'decayed and obsolescent' and the point was considered to be hardly more than 'a slum'. There were echoes of the earlier reasoning that surrounded the resumption of the Rocks and Millers Point, although Seidler and his colleagues were probably better acquainted with the writings of Le Corbusier: 'The great task incumbent on us is ... clearing away from our cities the dead bones that putrefy them.'[60]

The Cumberland County Council had recognised the value in preserving some of those old bones when it bought Elizabeth Bay House for the State in the late 1950s. At McMahons Point, some locals gathered to form the North Shore Historical Society in order to save a 19th-century cedar-and-stone villa, Bell'vue, that stood on the site of the forthcoming Blues Point Tower car park. The society was one of a number of such groups that joined with the National Trust, established a decade earlier, to preserve local heritage. Bell'vue was a rare example of domestic design by the architect of St Marys Cathedral, Edmund Blackett. The artist Sydney Ure Smith had captured the antiquarian charm of the site in 1929.[61] In the late 1950s the building was the somewhat decrepit home of another artist, Wallace Thornton. Lloyd Rees painted the house and a related line of terraces in a work that won the 1951 Wynne Prize. Surrounded by greenery, Bell'vue was a special place. Gerardus Dusseldorp offered its stones to the society for reassembling elsewhere but the cost was too great and Bell'vue was lost.

There were other historic casualties in the move to consolidate, and democratise, the waterfront. At Kirribilli, Miandetta was knocked down for a flat block. The big old house had been home and meeting place to Edmund Barton as he led the federation movement and became the country's first prime minister in 1901. Despite being free from the taint of convictism and rich with historical association, the villa went down with barely a comment. But where one family had lived before, its replacement, the nautically named Quarterdeck, offered 48 apartments – some big enough for families with three or four children. It was designed by Aaron Bolot, who came from eastern Europe in an earlier period of immigration in 1911 and had already completed an innovative curved-front block for a co-operative building society in Potts Point that stood as one of the first and purist expressions of the visual and social ethic of postwar modernism.[62]

Eyes turned again to that most reviled of waterfront precincts: the Rocks. Planners and politicians had wanted to sweep away those 'dead bones' for decades and the possibilities of modern architecture revived their dreams. After the success of the Opera House competition, another international invitation for plans to that end was announced in 1960. Harry Seidler put in a submission as did Unilever House's architects, Stephenson and Turner. All involved the near-complete erasure of the old buildings behind the Overseas Passenger Terminal and their replacement with towers, ribbon-like high-rises and neat open space. Cadman's Cottage, the small Georgian waterman's house, was generally recognised as a worthy historical remnant, but little else was to remain. Seidler must have relished the opportunity to demolish the despised MSB Building. It survived in some of the plans but not in his.

The winning scheme by Edwards, Madigan and Torzillo kept the MSB Building and placed four huge office towers behind it. Thirteen low apartment buildings extended northwards. There were gardens in between. Significantly, the architects stressed the need to provide 'an important visual introduction' for 'overseas visitors entering Sydney Harbour'. The audience was international rather than local, yet curiously this scheme gave the least priority to hotels. It also had the second lowest density of the nine plans considered. Around a third of the ten thousand people accommodated would be residents, the rest office workers.[63]

But offices and hotels were where the investment money lay and the scheme was not implemented. The urge to demolish and redevelop in the name of commerce became even stronger under the pro-development government of Robert Askin, whose reign would last a decade from 1965 and profoundly change the character of the Sydney. When the novelist Ruth Park was asked to write a travellers' guide to the city in the early 1970s, she responded with bewilderment: 'Are you aware that Sydney is being pulled down? ... In no time this will be an out of date guidebook.' Park relented, motivated by her love of the city she had adopted as her own in the 1940s, and placated by the idea that the work would at least be a record of the place as it still stood in the mid-1970s as hammers 'pecked away at Sydney's sandstone foundations' leaving the 'air full of fearful noise, the sky of dust'.

Even as she wrote, the most dramatic changes were being considered at the Rocks. Park had become fascinated with the place when she stumbled across the early 20th-century resumption photographs in the course of researching her novel of inner Sydney, *The Harp in the South*.[64] The body that was to be responsible for the most recent round of demolitions was the Sydney Cove Redevelopment Authority (SCRA), established in 1968. There would be three new hotels and a mix of high-rise and low-rise accommodation to maintain residential character. The SCRA was not totally antipathetic to retaining existing buildings, but the occupants – now tenants of the authority – were not initially consulted and suspicion grew with regard to their landlord's motivations. They were pensioners and 'non-professional' people. Few still had any working connection to the waterway but many were long-term residents – 18 to 20 years was the average in surveys conducted by the SCRA.[65] In reaction to the new regime, the tenants formed a residents' action group.

It was not the first time local people had organised there, but this was the most effective and co-ordinated. The action group's founder, Nita McRae, traced her ancestry back to French and Norwegian sailors visiting and living in the Rocks. She consciously placed herself in a continuum of community action, much of it stemming from local women: 'I've read a lot of old newspaper accounts about what's happened before in The Rocks. We're the fifth residents' group to get organized here in the last eighty years ... Why can't they just leave the bloody place alone?'[66] McRae also looked beyond the neighbourhood to find alliances with the other grassroots organisations now coalescing around the antipathy towards the development that flourished under the Askin government. The Rocks group joined more than 80 other local groups in the Coalition of Residents Action Groups (CRAG). They were the vociferous and interventionist successors to bodies such as the McMahons Point and Lavender Bay Progress Association. But where that group enlisted the functionalist ideal of modernism in the fight against industrial development, the new groups emphasised preservation and organic development. They were defiantly anti-modernist and, in this respect, set the tone for much of the resident action around the harbour in the following decades.

McRae and the Rocks residents also sought the support of the Builders Labourers Federation (BLF), a trade union that in 1971 had worked effectively with a small group of local women up the harbour at Hunters Hill to stop the residential redevelopment of a vestige of waterside scrubland called Kelly's Bush. That action and the union's intervention at the Rocks introduced a new term into Australian planning lexicon: the 'green ban'. The builders' labourers who ordinarily did much of the demolition and reconstruction simply refused to do so and picketed the sites slated for redevelopment. 'Green ban' was something of a misnomer because, although the fight at Kelly's Bush had been over a 'green' space, those at the Rocks and elsewhere were concerned with preserving the built environment. The definition of heritage had expanded since the days of proposed coal mines at Cremorne. The campaigns in the late 1960s and the 1970s also brought to prominence a campaigner who came to personify resistance to state-sanctioned redevelopment – Jack Mundey. His justification for direct action exemplified the disillusionment with the official custodians of the people's heritage that had grown under the Askin government: 'We had every right to have a say in the future of our habitat.'[67]

The BLF's ideology was an interesting manifestation of New Left thinking. They supported the Rocks residents and refused to demolish their homes in the context of a long-standing class solidarity. But the concern with 'habitat' was new. And while it echoed the goal of modernist architects such as McKay, Jackson and Seidler, Mundey and his colleagues infused it with an ecological sensibility that eschewed functionalism.[68] Where they worked with 'forward looking town planners and architects' to tame the 'concrete jungle', the emphasis on 'grassroots democracy' was a significant departure from the master planning of architects such as Harry Seidler.[69] The BLF wholeheartedly backed the 'People's Plan', an alternative but professionally devised scheme, commissioned by the local residents' action group, which presented the area as 'an integrated residential and historic area, separated from the functions of the central business district'.[70] A compromise was reached with the SCRA and in 1975 the Rocks green ban was lifted. It was a pivotal moment in the history of planning generally and foreshore development more particularly. A working-class precinct was to be saved because heritage, history and an organically formed sense of place were accepted as significant elements of the city.

Indeed, they quickly came to be seen as commercial imperatives. So the historic character of the Rocks became a feature in tourist promotion. Buildings were restored and historic monuments erected. The SCRA dropped 'Redevelopment' from its name and became simply the Sydney Cove Authority. But the acknowledgment of heritage brought with it other dilemmas and issues. Central to these was the question of 'whose past do we acknowledge?' The engineering achievements of George Barney were certainly worthy and an instructive monument in bronze was duly set in place in 1979. But there was little about the Aboriginal people of the area and some came to regard the restored buildings and costumed town criers as a somewhat sterile rendering of the past. The complexity of social conflict had been erased and so had the grit.

Elevation to the status of 'national heritage' also threatened to undermine the very sense of place – the community – that prompted the residents to take on the State.[71] Well before the remaining line of warehouses at Campbells Cove became waterfront restaurants – with a rigged ship's mast for added effect – Nita McCrae had sounded a note of caution:

> Sure, we favour preserving the historic buildings of the area! But we can't differentiate the buildings from the people who live in them! When you read about the history of The Rocks, you read about the people who lived in the neighbourhood. Since we're descendants, we are still part of that history ... Our local chemist had to move out because the rents got too high. Now we go downtown to do our shopping.[72]

As historic buildings assumed more importance than people, the Rocks came to belong more to outsiders than to the locals.

TEN

THE PEOPLE'S HARBOUR

'JACK AND I ... JUST COOKED LOCAL FISH AND CHIPS'

As a girl in the early 1960s, the writer Glenda Adams rode north shore ferries to Circular Quay and walked through the 'seedy waterfront … past pubs and derelicts' to her school on the ridge above the Rocks. On occasions she went down to the Darling Harbour docks and ate fish and chips at a little café there. When Adams left Australia for two decades to study and teach in the United States, these places remained vivid in her memories of youth – and while she was gone they changed. The Rocks was renovated and lost it seediness while the east Darling Harbour waterfront was swept away altogether.[1]

The Builders Labourers Federation green bans in the early 1970s preserved the residences and shops of the Rocks, but there was little interest as yet in the 'old bones' of industry. Engineers shaped the redevelopment, and the stark functionalism they installed exceeded anything an architect might have imagined. All of HD Walsh's finger wharves and the huge Dalgety woolstore at the very end of Millers Point were demolished and replaced by a concrete apron that extended to the south for more than a kilometre. For shipping containers were the way of the future, and by 1976 the Maritime Services Board had built a longshore wharf large enough to fit the huge vessels that carried them and the cranes and vehicles necessary for unloading. While the destruction of some nearby houses attracted protest from locals, the old Sydney Harbour Trust wharves went without much comment.[2] A similar fate faced the jetties at Walsh Bay, and the board hoped the old swing bridge across Darling Harbour would go as well.

Overlooking the modern waterfront was a concrete-and-steel observation tower, the Ports Operations and Communications Centre. It erupted incongruously from a 19th-century townscape of crowded terraced workers' houses. The locals came to know it as 'The Pill', an insider's pun on its official function of 'berth control'.[3] The operations centre stood as a counterpoint to Seidler's Blues Point Tower directly across the water. The latter symbolised a vision of a high-density residential harbour; the former was evidence of the apparent resilience of the working port.

Along with the new city-side facilities, there would be container terminals at the recently dredged Mort Bay at the site of the old slipway, at Glebe Island and at the adjacent White Bay where a new coal-loader was also completed. Two lines of concrete mooring platforms – poetically called 'dolphins' but looking more like wartime defences – were put in place in Snails Bay off Birchgrove.[4] The navy had recently commissioned a patrol boat base, HMAS *Waterhen* Base, at Balls Head Bay. With existing oil-storage tanks at Ballast Point, Gore Cove and Berrys Bay, and the huge waterside coal-fired power stations at Pyrmont, White Bay and Iron Cove completed in the first decades of the 20th century, the western harbour was, in anyone's eyes, an intensely industrial waterway.

Sydney was still Australia's leading port when the Darling Harbour redevelopment was being planned in the mid-1960s. Some four thousand ships a year carried finished products and bulk goods, such as coal, grain and oil, from around the coast and overseas. The '60-miler' colliers that brought coal from Newcastle to Sydney were familiar visitors. Some docked at Balls Head and Balmain, others went up the Parramatta River to the Mortlake Gas Works near Concord. Steam and motors had long ago defeated the capricious winds but the tide was still a determinant on the estuary. Ronald Thiele had worked on one of these, the *Mortlake Bank*: 'when we got into Sydney Harbour, we would have to anchor off Cockatoo Island, somewhere where there's a nice anchorage, good anchorage, and then at the right state of the tide go on up the river ...'[5]

That Sydney would remain 'the foremost commercial centre and port in Australia' was endorsed in the planning scheme that superseded the County of Cumberland Plan: the State Region Outline Plan of 1968.[6] However, this confidence belied concerns over the harbour's capacity for sustainable port activities and expansion. The container ships and tankers were getting bigger, but Sydney's topography, with its deep water and steep foreshores, made further reclamation of land for modern wharf platforms difficult. So too did the residential suburbs that now crowded the industrial foreshores. The shallow basin of Botany Bay, conversely, had flat foreshores, fewer people and cheaper land. Botany's potential relationship to Sydney Harbour was acknowledged as early as 1961 when the MSB took control of its management. With oil refineries already in place, plans were drawn up to unload containers there. Dredging turned the waterway that Arthur Phillip had dismissed in 1788 into the country's deepest harbour – at considerable cost to its ecology.[7] But by 1979 the Port of Botany was an entity in itself.

The economic foundations of Sydney too were shifting as the working foreshores of Darling Harbour and Balmain were being modernised. The port city was becoming the financial capital of the country. The first signs of change were seen at Circular Quay with the AMP Building and the office blocks along the eastern shore. But the real move came in the wake of a commodities boom of the 1960s, which flooded Sydney with capital, investment firms and the attendant legal, insurance and hospitality services. It was the accompanying increase in office development that had prompted the schemes to level the Rocks. By 1976 the city was ranked ninth in the listing of international investment centres. Melbourne was 20 places farther down the ladder.[8] Where wool, gold, wheat and meat from the interior had fuelled the economy in the 19th and early 20th century, now it was bulk minerals, from coal to iron ore and bauxite. And whereas the products of the farms and forests often left from wharves of Darling Harbour, Pyrmont and later Glebe Island, wealth-generating ore was shipped from ports as far away as Port Hedland and Dampier on the west coast and Gladstone in Queensland. As home to the country's Reserve Bank and its biggest stock market, Sydney more and more handled the flow of money rather than the movement of goods upon the water.

This position was consolidated through the 1980s and 1990s with financial deregulation and the removal of trade protection. In turn, these policies and a revolution in communication technology encouraged the centralisation of economic power. Where previously a corporation may have needed several head offices in a country, the trend was to consolidate. More often than not companies chose to locate in Sydney alone. The term that would be used was 'globalisation' and Sydney, as a major business hub in the Asia–Pacific region, became known as Australia's first 'global city'.[9]

In one sense Sydney had long been such a city by virtue of its status as a major port. Young Glenda Adams felt she could almost touch that 'wider world' as she watched the ocean liners coming and going from her back window in Mosman.[10] But the city on the harbour was still parochial – 'like a far outpost'. The poet Robert Adamson described a postwar youth spent scrambling around scruffy waterfronts from Luna Park to Taronga Zoo in search of a world he understood through Saturday matinees at the cinema:

> ... There wasn't much more to explore
> there was no Mexico
> no border to wheel across
> just before dawn there was Luna Park
> or the Ham & Beef shop
> the rest of the world
> hadn't even heard of Neutral Bay ...[11]

Thirty years later the 'rest of world' was coming to know the harbour first-hand. A tide of tourists followed the investors in the 1980s. The rate of international arrivals to Australia had jumped fivefold in the 1960s with the popularity of air travel. It leaped again in the 1980s as middle-class Asians, particularly the Japanese, started travelling in large numbers. Over 1 100 000 tourists came in 1985 and this doubled again in just five years. Sydney was the country's single most popular destination and harbour sites were the most visited attractions within the city.[12] Souvenir shops proliferated, as did images of the harbour's immediately recognised icons: the Opera House and the Bridge. The mood and market were captured by the artist, designer and one-time advertising executive Ken Done. His 'naively' rendered, brightly coloured juxtapositions of the two structures were reprinted on calendars, T-shirts and postcards while 'inspiring' many more cheaper variations. The Japanese loved them.

Done's crayoned harbour was typically filled with yachts, for it had become one of the most intensively used recreational waterways in the southern hemisphere. There had been a spectacular growth in boat ownership from the mid-1960s, mirroring the general affluence of the times. Then there had been under nineteen thousand boats registered in New South Wales. Three decades later there were thirty-six thousand in the Sydney region alone and 7500 of these were moored on the harbour.[13] Countless smaller craft were stored in boatsheds and garages on and around the water. The new tourist industry was also of a different scale. Captain Cook Cruises began touring the waterway in 1970, with sightseers crowded onto a single Fairmile cruiser of the type built by the Halvorsens during World War II. By the 1990s the company had nine purpose-built boats circling the harbour. It bought the small private ferry business ND Hegarty and Sons and secured a valuable berth at Circular Quay. By then its vessels competed with more than 13 other cruise boats and a myriad of charter craft.[14]

Local wealth and tourist dollars stimulated the catering business. Restaurants that served seafood near the water were especially popular. By the 1980s the humble Ozone café at Watsons Bay had become Doyle's on the Beach, one of the most desirable eateries on the harbour. The old café had fed daytrippers at Watsons Bay since 1908, although it was closed for a prolonged period during World War II and economic hard times. There diners could buy simply prepared fish, oysters and even bouillabaisse near the beach where whiting was netted and laid out for sale and the less palatable Australian salmon crated up to be turned into paste. The place had been home to novelist Christina Stead in the 1920s and she used the 'fish-smelling bay' with its 'poor and unpretentious' characters as a setting in *Seven Poor Men of Sydney*. Decades later Doyles on the Beach was crowded with business people and visitors. The family opened more restaurants: one at a redesigned Overseas Passenger terminal and another in the once-utilitarian Sydney Fish Market, which was rebuilt for the tourist trade.[15]

The fish market was the third largest of its kind in the world. Most of the fish came from beyond the Heads but 40 trawlers still worked the harbour from there. They carried such names as the *San Joyce* and *Galicia Star* and were crewed by men of Italian, Greek and Vietnamese ancestry. These boats trawled for prawns and a by-catch of bream, tailor and whiting. Over Biaggio de Pasquali's working life the season had been progressively shortened out of respect for vulnerable seagrass beds and the ever-precarious fish stocks until it only ran over summer and spring: 'We used to fish seven days a week. It was open all year round, then we were reduced to nine months fishing, then six months, then five months.'[16]

These men could not have known, but they were among the last to fish the waterway commercially. After a gradual reduction in the season, the end came abruptly in 2006. Then it was not the number of fish that was of concern but the level of toxins in them. Chemicals from the industries to the west and up the river had been contaminating the ecosystem for decades. And so the State government bought back fishing licences and from then on the small fleet that moored at the market only trawled past the Heads.

When the fish market moved to its dour waterfront at Blackwattle Bay in the 1960s, Sydney was still a city with a cuisine characterised by 'steak and eggs'. The Italians and Greeks retained their own culinary traditions, which included a wider range of seafood than was generally accepted. Little had changed since the young Arthur Cox caught squid with a 'bent pin' at a pre-war Darling Harbour to sell to the local Greek shopkeeper: 'They ate them, we didn't …' When fish was consumed it was typically fried or grilled at home or in milk bars and cafés. Late-closing Kitt's café was as much an institution for Pyrmont residents as Doyle's was for the daytrippers and the locals of Watsons Bay.[17] At the other end of the social ladder, the floating Caprice restaurant at Rose Bay anticipated later trends by offering glamour and water views to celebrities and visiting dignitaries. It continued this role as Catalina's in the 1990s. The cultural elite sought out the few gourmet establishments available: restaurants such as the French-inspired Hermitage, where one might order local snapper cooked in white wine rather than beef dripping.[18] By the 1980s such combinations were commonplace and the city had its own 'modern Australian' cuisine, which made much of fresh seafood. Squid became calamari and an elderly Alice Doyle remarked that sashimi had entered her family's menu – 'a far cry from when Jack and I … just cooked local fish and chips'. Mrs Doyle acknowledged that seafood had always been relatively expensive in Sydney for those who were not catching it themselves – and so it remained.[19] Now it perfectly symbolised the new culture of cosmopolitanism and consumption.

'[A] gift to the nation'

The growth of tourism coincided with the approach of the bicentenary of colonisation in 1988, and the pending 'celebration of a nation' created a new type of waterfront. Bicentennial-inspired projects undertaken at Circular Quay gave a variety of prominent Australian architects the opportunity to rework key postwar developments. In the process, the gateway site became as much a precinct for the arts and entertainment as it was a transport hub. The firm Allen, Jack and Cottier was responsible for redeveloping the cavities under the railway and expressway and filling them with restaurants and cafés. The space between there and the ferry wharves became a promenade for sightseers and city workers. As a result, the barrier between the city and the water was a little less absolute. At East Circular Quay, Andrew Andersons designed a new sea wall that was built below the line of the Opera House approach. It was not what Utzon had in mind, but then there were fewer tourists and no outdoor dining in the 1960s – so the second tier accommodated restaurants and a waterfront walk. The grim Overseas Passenger Terminal was renovated by Lawrence Nield and Partners and turned into something postmodern that referenced its nautical connections. There were portholes and conning tower-like accretions at each end, and a colour-coded emphasis on the steel framework. The building still fulfilled its original function of accommodating cruise liners but now it also housed fine restaurants with views of the Opera House. The extensive introduction of glass lightened the presence of the building on the waterfront and maximised the views.[20] But as one of the most expensive berths in the world cruise ships did not stay long and for much of the year it was diners who frequented the terminal.

The State government's biggest bicentennial project began around the point in Darling Harbour. There, from the southern end of the container terminal to Pyrmont, public and private enterprise consorted to build a cultural and commercial precinct filled with shops, restaurants, conference centres and water-themed attractions, including a maritime museum and aquarium. As it faced the adjacent longshore wharf on the east side and replaced redundant infrastructure to the west, the new Darling Harbour epitomised the shift in the identity and economy of the waterway. Much of the redevelopment took place along the old tangled tracks and sheds of the late 19th-century goods yards where wool and grain were once brought to the harbour for export.

The glamour that replaced the grit was mostly gleaming white. Spectacular buildings and large civic spaces echoed utopian designs from the previous century – in particular, the ephemeral White City that went up in weeks for the 1893 Columbian Exposition in Chicago. Darling Harbour's large glass barrel-roofed marketplace building was a distant relation to the Crystal Palace erected in London to display the commercial and industrial wares of mid-Victorian Britain at the 1851 Great Exhibition. The project's more recent antecedents, however, could be found on the revamped waterfronts of North America, where gentrification had been underway for some years. Indeed, the marketplace design owed much to Harborplace in Baltimore, a precinct designed by the Rouse Corporation. So ubiquitous did the Rouse schemes become that the somewhat derisive term 'Rousification' was coined. The American planning practitioner and academic Mort Hoppenfeld, who worked with Rouse, drew the first detailed designs. Implementation and development of these were carried out by Barry Young from an Australian firm, McConnel, Smith and Johnson.[21]

The maritime museum, aquarium and large exhibition halls were the creation of the Australian architect Phillip Cox. The intent was to create a sense of place and uniqueness by the water. The museum and the aquarium both made playful reference to the sea with their wavy sail-like roofs. The use of metal sheets – the cladding of water tanks, shearing sheds and outback homes across the country – had nationalistic overtones. These historical associations and the primary purpose of promoting leisure and consumerism contrasted with the austere civic intent that underlay much modernist planning. The new Darling Harbour was, in this respect, a postmodern place.

And yet the wholesale redevelopment of the site and the image of urban perfection that emerged were not unlike the goals that motivated architects such as Harry Seidler. It was master planning on a grand scale – the 'greatest urban redevelopment ever undertaken in Australia', in the words of the statutory body that orchestrated it.[22] So much so that the principle of collaboration between local and State governments, enshrined in the wake of the green bans within the *Environmental Assessment and Protection Act* (1979), was set aside and the area exempted from regular planning controls. The *Darling Harbour Act* also excluded provisions of the *NSW Heritage Act* (1977). It was excised from the control of the Sydney City Council, which had originally envisioned a residential precinct there, and the development entrusted to the Darling Harbour Authority working in collaboration with private developers who were seeking to emulate the new American waterfronts.

The project spread over 54 hectares and made a swathe of water-front accessible where before there were disused wharves and train tracks. And it provided a remarkable harbourside site for Australia's first National Maritime Museum which could collect and display the waterway's heritage in some context. The Heritage Council of New South Wales welcomed the building's 'bold design' as 'reminiscent of tall masts and billowing sails in steel and glass'.[23] The exhibits included the cedar wood 5.5-metre *Britannia*, a product of the renowned boatbuilder 'Wee' Georgie Robinson and one of the few craft of its kind to have survived years of racing on the harbour.

However, the development model and the outcome also stirred hostility in a sizable group of residents, professionals and comment-ators, including green ban campaigner Jack Mundey. People in neigh-bouring Pyrmont felt marginalised, arguing that they were 'briefed' rather than consulted on a project that would impact so profoundly upon their community.[24] There was particular dislike of the futuristic monorail 'people mover' that emerged from the precinct to snake around the city with little regard for façades, existing transport links and needs of residents and city workers. They distrusted the use of public money to bolster private enterprise, which was itself courting a fickle tourist market.

The State premier Neville Wran, who backed the project from the start, wanted 'a place where people could enjoy themselves, where families could come ... all for the price of a glass of lemonade and an ice cream' – and he was pleased with the result.[25] Darling Harbour's critics saw frivolousness and consumerism: the 'mobilisation of spectacle' to 'capture the consumption dollar' where there might have been homes.[26] That the project had been initiated by a Labor government rather than a typically pro-business Liberal administration added to the disquiet. The politicians had 'defeated' the planners and the result had little to do with the city's historic waterfront: there was 'no housing, no fishing, no swimming – nothing Sydney about it'.[27]

The New South Wales government had promoted Darling Harbour as its bicentennial 'gift to the nation'. That all the country might benefit from the transformation of a piece of waterfront was not a new idea. Niels Nielsen's resumptions earlier in the century had prompted similar Sydney-centricity. Now the State was also confident that the larger waterway would play a pivotal role in the 'celebration of a nation'. The harbour was Australia's 'birthplace' and as an arena on which to stage a televised pageant it was unsurpassed. There was some evidence for this in the annual Sydney-to-Hobart ocean race, which had grown in size and reputation through the 1970s and 1980s. For his part, the chairman of the Australian Bicentennial Authority was mindful of the need to ensure the event was not 'just a glorified celebration of Sydney Harbour' and so there were hundreds of events funded and organised in communities throughout the country.[28] But the harbour's pre-eminence was assured early on when the authority decided to support the voyage to Australia of sailing ships sent and funded by well-wishing nations from across the globe. The passage of the 'tall ships' would culminate with a parade on the harbour on Australia Day, 26 January 1988. Because of the international participation the event was guaranteed world-wide interest.

Like Darling Harbour, the progenitor for the tall ships was American: New York Harbour had hosted a similar flotilla in 1976 for the bicentenary of that country's independence. In Australia the involvement of ships from some 20 countries was symbolic of the relatively new pride in multiculturalism and inclusiveness. The director of the event, Rear-Admiral Rothesay Swan, made another claim for their relevance. 'Our history is inextricably linked to the sea,' he wrote as the ships arrived. '... As an island continent our economic growth and development has been and will continue to depend on shipping. We have a maritime tradition and a maritime heritage.'[29] The rear-admiral was undoubtedly right and his words echoed the reasoning behind the establishment of the National Maritime Museum at Darling Harbour. Ironically, as the role of the harbour itself slipped more and more towards accommodating recreation and spectacle rather than traditional port work, sentiment such as this would sound increasingly plaintive.

In the 1980s debates about the relevance of the working harbour were still some years away. Instead, bicentennial controversy oscillated around the public benefit served by Darling Harbour and the sensitivity of celebrating an occasion that had initiated the dispossession of the country's original inhabitants. Indeed, the decision to support the tall ships had been motivated in part by political concerns over an earlier proposal to re-enact the arrival of the First Fleet. That idea had been presented by Jonathan King, a historian, academic and descendant of Governor Philip King. The objections of Aboriginal people were hardly a consideration when the landing of Arthur Phillip and his companions and wards was replayed at Farm Cove back in 1938. Half a century later, awareness of the often awful history of Black–white relations was much greater within the white community, and Aboriginal reaction to such a re-enactment was certain to be less polite. Generic tall ships arriving from across the world, it was hoped, would only obliquely evoke the entry of the first Europeans while ensuring an impressive visual display.

The New South Wales government's bicentennial council disagreed. They chose to financially back a privately organised First Fleet voyage from Portsmouth to Sydney – on the understanding that there be no landing at the end of it. It was a concession to political sensitivities and a pragmatic assessment of the risk of confrontation.

And it also acknowledged the popularity of the idea. Some $900 000 in donations were later received through the Sydney radio station 2GB to ensure the venture succeeded. As a result Sydney got two fleets, one backed by the Australian Bicentennial Authority, the other by the State Council and a large section of the public.[30]

The distinction was hardly relevant for the Aboriginal community. They met the early tall ships in the harbour with a catamaran and a dinghy bearing flags of protest, just as they shouted at the 'First Fleet' re-enactment from a 'tent embassy' at the water end of the Domain on Australia Day itself. Some forty thousand people – Black and white – gathered in the middle of the city to listen to speeches about the need to acknowledge the dispossession. In the end, opinion divided among the participants of the contentious 'First Fleet'. Some still wanted to stage a defiant landing but others had a wreath made up in the Aboriginal colours of red, yellow and black, which was dropped by way of tribute into the harbour as the ships passed the protest camp. This group, which included the organiser Jonathan King, accompanied the gesture with a newspaper notice stating: 'The way in which Aboriginal society has been disregarded and almost destroyed since the arrival of Captain Phillip's fleet must now be recognised. Their needs must be acknowledged, their protests today must be heeded.'[31]

These gestures and debates were somewhat overwhelmed by the scale of the pageant. Two million people crowded around a still unfinished Darling Harbour in the days before 26 January to see the tall ships moored there. On Australia Day itself, a similar number lined the foreshore to watch both sets of rigged vessels pass by, accompanied by thousands of pleasure craft. The numbers of spectators at Farm Cove were so great that any re-enacted landing there would simply have been impossible. It was the harbour's biggest spectacle.

The organisational and popular success of the bicentenary undoubtedly encouraged the State government just two years later to consider competing for the greatest 'hallmark' event of all: the Olympic Games. The site chosen for a possible venue was up the river at Homebush Bay, 'a clapped out industrial wasteland' that had accommodated the relocated Glebe Island abattoir and a huge State-owned brick pit until 1988.[32] But it was the harbour that helped sell the bid in the early years. The influential General Assembly of International Sports Federations met at Darling Harbour in 1991 and there the bid team started marketing the 'spirit' of Sydney as 'a young colourful friendly, modern and informal place'.[33] Ken Done submitted a design for the logo. The winning image featured a streamer shaped like the sails of the Opera House and incorporating Aboriginal-style dots and the five colours of the Olympic rings. It was the work of Michael Bryce with the Goreng Goreng and Mununjali artist Ron Hurley, but the influence of Done's ubiquitous Opera House outlines was obvious.[34] Variations on that theme would serve as tourist logos into the next decade.

Sydney won the bid for the 2000 Olympics in 1993, beating Beijing by just two votes. The bid logo was replaced by another to promote the games themselves. It was an easily reproduced image that linked place and event – with the Opera House sails suggested by a streamer fluttering above a runner who has boomerang-like limbs. Development of the Homebush site was fast-tracked but hyperbole held that the 'real star of the Olympic Games will be the city of Sydney'.[35] The city's council was compelled to implement upgrades in anticipation of the influx and exposure. These included the refurbishment of Customs House, the decorative landmark of the working Circular Quay quit by the Commonwealth government's Customs Service in 1990 in favour of more practical premises at Neutral Bay and the airport. Now it was leased from the Commonwealth to become 'a new Sydney icon' with restaurant, exhibition and commercial space. There was hope that the hated railway would be placed underground to reunite the city and its waterfront. In the meantime, the forecourt paving was designed to symbolise 'waves meeting the shoreline'.[36]

While most of the Olympic events were held at the Homebush facilities, the sailing races were, not surprisingly, run on the harbour from Rushcutters Bay. The white buildings of Darling Harbour hosted other competitions. The hospitality programs were conducted at the

Rocks and Darling Harbour, with the 'vibrancy and natural beauty of Sydney Harbour' providing a visual backdrop, and the fireworks that streamed from the Bridge set an international standard for pyrotechnic spectacle.[37] With such a wealth of imagery, the waterway featured in countless aerial pans and still images for an audience of billions across the world.

Despite the critical success of the games, the predicted tourist boom did not eventuate. Sydney's already sizable share of Australia's international tourist market rose from 56 per cent to 58 per cent and then returned to its pre-games level as economic downturns in Asia and the spectre of terrorism after September 2001 flattened an already competitive tourism trade.[38] But twice as many continued to come to Sydney as visited the next most popular place, Melbourne. More than ever before, the harbour city represented the nation itself. The Australian Tourism Commission had acknowledged the trend as early as 1984 when it paid the actor Paul Hogan to star in a series of advertisements, which included him standing atop the Bridge with the Opera House behind, in an attempt to lure Americans to the country. It was one of the country's most successful tourist campaigns. In 1993 the Opera House and the Bridge were the only places featured throughout separate advertising campaigns across Asia, North America and Europe.[39]

There was, of course, a need to promote the remainder of the country. References to Aboriginal culture were increasingly common. And, as the century-old association of Australia's identity with the interior was deeply ingrained, there were plenty of images of kangaroos and the outback. Uluru was there for those who knew their geography well enough not to think of desert landscapes elsewhere. There were generic beaches and coral reefs. However, in their harbour setting the Opera House and Bridge were unique for only they did not require explanatory captions or narratives. They fulfilled the role of instant icons in the years following the Olympics when cities competed even more keenly for business and tourist attention, and 'city branding' became the goal of local and state governments courting tourists and business investment. In 2006 and 2007 Sydney was voted best 'city brand' ahead of London, New York and Paris in the international Anholt Index – not because of the numbers who had visited but because its 'overwhelmingly positive image', a general memorable impression formed over years of exposure to spectacles and iconic pictures.[40] It had as perfect a 'place brand' as any city could want.

'[B]its and pieces'

The Olympics had as little impact on Sydney's residential property market as it did on tourism – with one notable exception. Prestige harbourside houses and units in the eastern harbour waterway leaped in price in 2000: the average amount paid for waterfront flats increased by $1 million and that for houses went to over $6 million. The volatility seemed to reflect the global interest in the Sydney real estate market for the prices flattened and even declined suddenly at the end of the year.[41] But generally the prices were greater than they had been before the games. In any case, the trend in waterfront real estate had been heading upwards for years and the increases were much greater around the water than in other residential markets.

The obsession with harbour homes had begun well before the Olympics. David Williamson's hugely successful satire of acquisitiveness and social climbing in Sydney, *Emerald City*, premiered at the Opera House in 1987. The play worked because the fundamental premise, that proximity to the harbour symbolised success, was so widely understood and acknowledged. It opened with the observation that: 'No one in Sydney ever wastes time debating the meaning of life, it's getting yourself a water frontage. People devote a lifetime to the quest.'[42] Equally, the move to a 17th-floor office with water views symbolised a rising career: 'On a sunny day when the eighteen footers are out, the combination of striped spinnakers, sparkling blue water and sky is absolutely overwhelming'.[43] The commentary was partly autobiographical, as

Williamson's wife Kristin later acknowledged. They had moved from Melbourne to a harbourside home in the 'Emerald City' themselves in 1979: 'we began to understand how so many people we knew dreamt of a house on the waterfront. Sydney Harbour was alluring. In Sydney our lives changed.'[44]

Undoubtedly, the link between social status and a harbour view had long historical roots. Captain John Piper was probably the first to confirm the association back in 1817. The peninsula where Henrietta Villa had stood retained its exclusivity down through the decades, even as estates were subdivided and flats crowded the ridge and were squeezed between mansions. By 1971 a waterfront home at Point Piper could fetch $125 000, while a house in respectable Pymble might be obtained for a third of the cost. In the decade after the Olympics, the differentiation became much more extreme. Point Piper was touted as the most expensive suburb in the country, with its main waterfront street ranked ninth in the world. Heritage value had little currency. It was ostentation that prevailed. But then that had been the motivation for Captain Piper. Just as his villa was taken down for something grander in the mid-1800s, most newcomers to the place sought to remake or replace existing structures. In 2008 estimated values for the perpetually renovated homes ranged up to $80 million.[45]

Beyond prestige, proximity to the water provided beauty, recreation and an extraordinary sense of space in the increasingly congested metropolis. It gave easy access to the aquatic common. So the cost of waterfront rose also in the less desirable western harbour. There substantial but run-down residences such as Wyoming, overlooking Snails Bay, still stood as evidence of some respectability in previous times. That house had been built by the Colonial Sugar Refinery's manager QL Deloitte and was home in the mid-1880s to the heroic marine biologist Nicolai Miklouho-Maclay. In the intervening century, Balmain lost its appeal to the middle and upper classes and was 'owned' by the sailmakers, shipwrights and others who worked and lived cheek by jowl with the waterfront power stations and factories and put up with the noise and airborne soot that darkened their house fronts and the wet washing pegged behind. But by 1990 the affluence had returned and the place was characterised as a suburb 'where a four wheel drive vehicle is obligatory' – and the ability to handle a skiff less so.[46] The middle-class rediscovery of the western foreshores gathered pace over 30 years. In the 1960s affordability was important but a large part of the attraction seemed to reside in the diversity to be encountered there. It had a chaotic picturesqueness that distinguished it from the natural beauty of the eastern harbour and the suburban order in which many of the newcomers to the city had grown up. This quality had appeal in the face of the uncompromising scale and uniformity of much postwar architecture. It was part of what the contemporary American urban critic Jane Jacobs called the 'intricate order' of urbanism – and reflected an appreciation that the city should be respected as an organic entity rather than something that could emerge suddenly from a planner's blueprint. An 'emphasis on bits and pieces is of the essence', argued Jacobs in 1961, 'this is what a city is, bits and pieces that supplement each other and support each other'.[47]

At that time Lavender Bay was a decidedly unglamorous waterfront, bounded to the east by an aging amusement park and a rail shunting yard filled with red suburban train carriages, for the track that changed the waterfront there had become redundant after the Bridge was built. To the west were flats, houses, boatsheds and all that remained of the Neptune Engineering Company slipway and works that were mostly destroyed in a calamitous fire a few years earlier. In front were the old timber swimming baths that Barney Kieran had frequented – decrepit and soon to be demolished.

What had been single-family dwellings near the water were divided into low-rent flats in the postwar years. By the 1970s these were inhabited by artists, architects and others. Brett and Wendy Whiteley moved into the top half of an Edwardian-era villa there in 1969 after a decade travelling the world. They eventually bought the house and added a tower from where the harbour could be observed in near entirety. Brett Whiteley found studio space within the old, unused North Shore Gas Works building on the waterfront farther along in

Balls Head Bay. But it was the view of Lavender Bay that would recur in the paintings he executed from the mid-1970s to 1981 – sometimes as an interior glimpse through a window, sometimes filling a large canvas. At home, Whiteley was in a position to capture the waterway in all its different moods – from hot summer afternoons in *Big Orange* to rainy days in *Grey Harbour,* and then dazzling brilliance in *The Jacaranda Tree (on Sydney Harbour)* and *The Balcony 2* in which blue water dominates the canvas much as it had when Streeton painted the bay from McMahons Point. The works gave primacy to a celebration of nature, but did so while including dream-like, delicate treatments of the human-made forms that rimmed and filled the harbour: the finger wharves at Walsh Bay, the Bridge, the Lavender Bay ferry jetty and boats moored around it. Compared with the disturbing commentary of his earlier 'American Dream' series or the surrealism of the 'Alchemy' works, Whiteley's Lavender Bay paintings focused quite simply on the marvellous life of the harbour. They began from 'points of ecstasy, where romanticism and optimism overshadow any form of menace or foreboding'.[48]

Whiteley's friend and fellow artist Peter Kingston moved next door in 1974 – to a house divided into seven small flats. His passion for the harbour had been seeded long ago during a childhood at Parsley Bay to the east. His respect for heritage began by working with others refurbishing nearby Luna Park. Kingston's fascination with cartoons and Australian popular culture prompted etchings of Lavender Bay that were filled with a cheerful diversity of boats, characters and waterfront structures. As his relationship with the water matured over the next two decades, there were oils that gave prominence to the changing colours, textures and moods of the water itself.

This attraction was part of a well-established tradition of viewing urban and waterfront Sydney through the prism of the picturesque. Cazneaux had celebrated the working port in his photographs as Max Dupain had after him. Ephemeral ditties like 'Port O'Sydney' reflected the popular delight in the varied people and activity of the harbour:

… The grimy-hided collier and the dandy P.&O.,
the fussy little tug with the barquentine in tow,
The trader from the islands and the tramp from Callao –
They'll go dancing up the harbour in the morning …[49]

In the 1970s Peter Carey seemed to find charm in similar scenes. He had moved to Sydney from Melbourne in the early 1970s and rented 'a leaking ramshackle semi' in Wharf Road fronting Snails Bay in Birchgrove. From there he drove across the Bridge in a red Jensen sports car to the North Sydney advertising firm where he worked before taking up fiction-writing full time. The street at Birchgrove was bookended by Stannard's boatyard and the Caltex oil terminal on Ballast Point: 'In those years Balmain had a working waterfront and at the bottom of my neglected garden I could watch the low-riding brown working boats, oil tankers, container ships and smell the fuel oil.' At night the 'oily iridescent dark throbbed with the sound of ships' generators'.[50] The ambience had some attraction for when the time came to buy Carey chose nearby 'low-rent' Louisa Road. David Williamson acquired his piece of waterfront there in 1979. Lined with large Victorian-era homes awaiting renovation, it became one of the most fashionable streets on the western waterway.

The appreciation of 'bits and pieces' was shared by many who were moving into the old precincts along the western waterway – places such as Balmain, Annandale and Glebe. It formed part of their appreciation of the organic development and heritage of these suburbs. The Balmain Association was one of the first preservationist organisations formed by the newcomers. In 1965 it aimed to preserve the 'best in architecture, town planning and natural beauty'.[51] In later years it became part of the Coalition of Residents Action Groups that supported Jack Mundey and his green bans. Early on, the association tried to save the definitive Macquarie-era marine villa, Birchgrove House, from being turned into a block of flats. It lost that battle but went on soon after to document many other buildings of note.

It was the 'grace' of 19th-century architecture that appealed to the association: there was a distinct ambivalence about manifestations of the working harbour. Although the members had an appreciation of the remnants of Mort's slipway, it set itself against 'the noise, dirt and danger threatened by large scale industrial developments'. These included both early 'monstrous' waterfront developments, such as the power stations and soap factories, and the 'new threats of computer age industries like containerisation'.[52] Accordingly, the association determined early on to oppose these threats.[53] There were echoes of Harry Seidler's still-recent arguments against the place of industry on the harbour, although clearly none of his zeal for its replacement with high-rises.

The White Bay facility stayed to upset those who never reconciled to the new technologies. Twenty-five years after it arrived, one commentator argued that the container traffic had created 'an acoustic hell for the residents of the older maritime suburbs'. There was some hope in 1993 that the commercial intensity might end, for Sydney Harbour had 'had its day as a large-scale port ...'[54] The unpopular and impractical Mort Bay dock was indeed short-lived. In the 1970s and 1980s many other nearby waterfront work sites also closed, just as they had in other inner-city and harbour-front sites around the world. The vast Balmain power station, which had burned garbage and coal to supply power to local houses and industries for 60 years, shut down in 1972 after electricity was sourced directly from the coalfields of the Hunter Valley. Having lost its access to the waterfront when the White Bay terminal was built, Unilever moved its soap manufacturing to a purpose-built industrial zone on the outskirts of the city. The old Monsanto chemical plant next to the power station shut down in 1989 and Caltex, which operated a marine lubricant manufacturing and distribution facility on Ballast Point, was looking to do the same. Even Cockatoo Island, once the largest ship-building yard in Australia, closed. The place had been refitting Oberon-class submarines that were now obsolete and its facilities were deemed too old to warrant upgrading.

Technological change also affected activity in the small boatyards as aluminium replaced spruce for spars, synthetic sails displaced cotton, fibreglass cloth took the place of planking; as one veteran noted, 'it is more dressmaking than building'. The work was less interesting, there were fewer apprentices and, as in other Australian industries, there was competition in the boat-building business from cheaper imports.[55]

The departure of industry raised obvious questions about the future of the sites. Many, such as the CSR and Balmain power station sites, were freehold and by the 1990s their owners were keen to maximise the value with high-density residential development. The State government was equally enthusiastic about the possibilities for urban consolidation and the additional revenue derived from stamp duties and land tax on investment apartments. Local residents were often less impressed. Those around working-class Pyrmont were concerned about the loss of local jobs and the prospect of a reconstructed suburb. Around gentrified Balmain they were happier to see the industry go.

The spirit of Niels Nielsen and WA Notting had certainly been revived in the wake of the green bans: the popular wish was for parkland as each piece of foreshore became available for redevelopment or resumption. In some instances, this mood assumed an almost utopian fervour. When the public glimpsed an empty East Circular Quay in 1997, after the demolition of the postwar office blocks, forty-five thousand signed a petition to stop redevelopment and preserve the open space, despite a potential resumption cost of hundreds of millions of dollars.[56]

Where building at Balmain was inevitable, the campaigning residents wanted the retention of a low-rise 'village environment'. The difficulty lay in the balance, for the greater the area of open space demanded by the council, the higher the density that could be sought by developers.[57] There may have been some local nervousness at the outcome on the opposite shore at Waverton, where the North Sydney Council had rejected a development proposal on an old gas works site only to lose the case in the Land and Environment Court. Bulk, scale and character had largely been the issue there. The crowded resort-style unit blocks, named Wondakiah, were very different from the slender, spaced towers and maisonettes of Harry Seidler's scheme, although neither would have pleased opponents of waterfront apartments. Functional modernism had had its day and it was Wondakiah that presaged the design of subsequent industrial-site redevelopments, including at the old Balmain power station where the construction of 460 medium to high-density apartments and townhouses was underway by 2000.

The building of the Balmain Shores on the power station site came only after a protracted legal battle between the State government, local residents and the Leichhardt Council – one in which all three parties were sometimes in dispute. At stake was the right of local communities and their councils to influence planning decisions alongside, or in spite of, the will of the State government. Balmain residents such as David Williamson had given a high profile to what was already a well-funded and resourced community campaign to create parkland on the old sites. In the end, there was landscaped public foreshore fronting Balmain Shores but the architectural result behind was disappointing. Postwar modernism had given way to postmodern pastiche and the Georgian-style pediments and columns added little interest to the mass of balconies and windows. Commentator Elizabeth Farrelly put it as bluntly as any: 'even dirty industry is somehow cleaner … than the Balmain Shores-style bloatery jostling for its spot'.[58] In terms of scale it was more a town than a village, but the lifestyle it promised was obviously appealing for nearly half the properties were presold before the project itself was halfway completed. They were not inexpensive but neither were they aimed at millionaires. The resident campaigners and the local council were less willing to compromise on such a prominent harbour site as Ballast Point at the end of prestigious Wharf Road. As planner Nigel Ashton had realised in the 1960s, peninsulas are special places in any waterway, providing views for those who occupy them and profoundly influencing the sense of place from the water. As if in warning, Blues Point Tower sat diagonally across the harbour, the model of what should not happen in the minds of many. Somewhat optimistically, a trust was formed to take donations to buy the site, which had an unimproved value of $5 million and a developed potential of up to ten times that amount.[59] In 1993 this group paid for a full-page newspaper advertisement, addressed to the Liberal premier, that presented the case for resuming Ballast Point in terms of public interest: 'Only by creating a harbourside park can the entire community benefit.' It would be a waterside development that kept 'growing and growing'.[60] Some, however, questioned the motivation and effect of this civic spirit. It was Balmain residents, rather than the broader public, who stood to gain most from the enhanced property values that would follow.[61]

A change of government in 1995 and the election of the Labor premier Bob Carr promised hope to the Ballast Point campaigners. Carr had a penchant for bushwalking and history. In 1997 he delivered a 'vision statement' on the harbour, which committed the government to 'maximise public access to, and use of, land on the foreshore', foster development 'in the scale and character of its foreshore location' and consider the retention of 'key waterfront industrial sites'.[62] Ballast Point was duly resumed for the public in 2002. The acquisition was lengthy and complicated since Caltex had already sold the development option to Walker Corporation, which immediately demanded $60 million in compensation, a figure that was eventually dismissed in appeal. The ultimate cost to the public was $26 million.[63] By then the government had also turned over two formerly leased industrial sites at Berrys Bay – the BP oil terminal and the old coaling bunker that had upset Henry Lawson back in 1918 – to the local North Sydney Council for redevelopment as public space. Sixteen oil tanks were removed from the vacated BP terminal to create a parkway amidst the carved sandstone cliff. The coal-loader platform remained to be interpreted as a piece of industrial heritage.

Carr was also keen to regain control of harbour-front defence lands – resumed for the colony of New South Wales in the 1860s, passed to the Commonwealth after Federation and now slated for sale and residential redevelopment. Some of this had already been added to the islands and foreshore that comprised the 73-hectare Sydney Harbour

National Park in 1975. Fort Denison and Goat Island followed in 1995. Two years later the premier, in an attempt to forestall the sale of the remainder, evoked the vision of an earlier Labor government in wanting to 're-establish the Nielsen concept of a green belt around Sydney Harbour'.[64]

He was strongly encouraged in this by a growing band of community activists who had coalesced in an organisation called Defenders of Sydney Harbour Foreshores. Their patron was Tom Uren, the man who had 'felt like kissing the ground' when he returned to Sydney Harbour with other prisoners of war back in 1945. Uren had retired from Federal parliament after 40 years of public service and was living in a house that looked over to Ballast Point. It had been designed using recycled timber by another harbour lover, the architect Richard Leplastrier. Uren himself acknowledged Nielsen as the pre-eminent champion of public foreshore but his language recalled earlier battles over coal mining at Cremorne and Bradley's Head: 'the [Federal] Government is attempting to pilfer land which is part of our Sydney Harbour Heritage'.[65] The battle over the old defence sites was won by the advocates of public accessibility but the land did not come back to the State as Carr had wanted. Rather, the headland forts, the old Woolwich dock and Cockatoo Island were eventually handed over to a new federally established body, the Sydney Harbour Federation Trust, to be managed as heritage sites with their infrastructure in place.

The appreciation of industrial heritage had introduced another dimension to the increasingly frequent and heated fights over Sydney's foreshores. The debate splintered when demolition of the giant finger wharf at Woolloomooloo was proposed in the late 1980s. Like the other remnants of the old working waterfront, its original role had been usurped. A permanent conservation order was placed over the structure in the bicentennial year and consideration given to its reuse for cultural activities. There was, not unexpectedly, an outcry when this was revoked after a State government inquiry in 1990. The wharf had been there for 70 years. It was where wool had been exported, soldiers farewelled and immigrants welcomed. Architect Lawrence

Nield celebrated the wharf in terms of its social significance and the quality of the structure itself: 'A sense of place involves understanding our formative experiences and our present Woolloomooloo and its Wharf are such a record of our experience and provide such a sense of place.' Paraphrasing Ralph Waldo Emerson, he wrote: 'a city is a language to which every human being has brought a stone'.[66]

Had the place, in fact, been built of stone rather than timber, the then Federal treasurer Paul Keating might also have defended it. A man with a keen interest in aesthetics and city planning, he preferred the colonial architecture of sandstone to that which followed and, like some others, thought the wharf simply an eyesore, best demolished to return the foreshore to its natural state. 'The cost of restoring the decadent structure is too high', agreed the State Labor parliamentarian Bryan Vaughan, '... the western shore of Woolloomooloo Bay ought to be reclaimed and landscaped. The result would be in sympathy with idyllic Farm Cove. For 200 years the foreshores of Sydney Harbour have been alienated and spoliated. Let us rescue the western shore of the bay ...'[67] Keating felt vindicated in his original assessment by the compromise: a wharf preserved but converted to high-cost apartments, restaurants and a hotel surrounded by a flotilla of luxury power boats. It was, in his assessment, 'the sorriest and most shameful development in Sydney's long history'.[68]

Soon after, controversy surrounded the future of the Walsh Bay wharves. The longshore No. 1 had languished through the 1980s as a poorly designed commercial conversion. No. 4/5 wharves had been refitted more successfully for use as a theatre. In 1994 the State government sought private interest in the redevelopment of the remaining structures to enhance 'Sydney's image' for the year 2000 and the Olympics.[69] Where in 1988 the entire western side of Darling Harbour had been cleared for the construction of the Marketplace and the Maritime Museum, the intent here was to retain structures, despite their dilapidation after two decades of disuse. Best practice in heritage and architecture now embraced the concept of 'adaptive reuse'. It was altogether a more complex and ambitious project than Woolloomooloo for it involved the redevelopment of an entire precinct: 17 hectares with four wharves and the buildings behind, along and above Hickson Road.

The tender process was begun under a Liberal government but it mired the new Carr Labor government in controversy and counteracted the goodwill fostered by the stand on foreshore parkland. It was the presence of termites and marine borer that led to the problems. Even the hardwood that impressed Norman Selfe did not last forever. With the belated discovery of serious infestation, the successful proposal was revised by the developers to include the demolition of two of the structures in order to preserve the commercial viability of the project. The government rejected this, but instead of reopening the tender sought the advice of the French architect and 'adaptive reuse' expert Phillipe Robert. The alternative scheme involved the demolition of one wharf and its replacement by a pier of luxury apartments. Connecting sheds would also go in order to create a continuous public walkway.

The decision not to re-open the tender process was criticised by the Audit Office of New South Wales, which felt that it had locked the government into accepting removal of any of the wharves. The pending destruction incensed Tom Uren, Richard Leplastrier, Jack Mundey and others. What was being proposed, wrote Uren, was the destruction of a 'cathedral of timbers' and its replacement with 'vulgar' apartments for the wealthy. They were joined in a site protest by Peter Kingston, who had looked over to the wharves from his home in Lavender Bay for the past 20 years: 'We marvelled at the gigantic size of the hardwood trees that had formed each of the 34 columns ... Citizens of Sydney should demand access to witness what they are about to lose.'[70]

Wharves 6/7 were demolished and rebuilt as luxury apartments, with the most desirable dwelling at the end selling for a record $16 million in 2006. The previous high had only just been set for an apartment in the Woolloomooloo wharf. Like their peers on Point Piper, the new owners were rarely satisfied with the size of the homes, and the noise of jackhammers and drills knocking out walls resonated through the five floors as frequently as it did in other waterfront precincts.[71] However, the remaining wharves survived to be occupied by commercial firms. Neither they nor the luxurious 6/7 were 'sold off', as was frequently claimed. Rather, the property remained leasehold – as it had been when operating as working waterfronts. Although the controversial 6/7 was closed off to the public and surrounded by large motor yachts, access had been afforded around all the other jetties. The development became a stage in the creation of continuous waterfront access from Woolloomooloo to Pyrmont. Pedestrians interested in the history of the place could follow a heritage walk that took them past signage and exhibit, including whale bones excavated from the days of Robert Towns and his black whaling ships and displayed near the entrance to new units at Towns Place.

The history displays usefully put the place in some context and, in doing so, emphasised the extent of the gentrification. It was indeed, as the accompanying walking brochure suggested, 'a new way of life'. Proximity to the harbour and its icons – the Bridge and Opera House – had become so lucrative that the government could hardly afford to ignore the pay-offs it offered for providing access in other measures. Andrew Andersons, who worked on the Walsh Bay project as director of the firm Peddle, Thorp and Walker, defended the outcome by pointing to the million dollar annual maintenance bill paid by the Ministry of Arts for its Wharf Theatre at No. 4/5.[72] It was money that might have been spent on productions. Recycling had its costs too.

In 2005 the Walsh Bay project won the Royal Australian Institute of Architects' Lloyd Rees Prize for Outstanding Urban Design and the Walter Burley Griffin Urban Design Award.

Richard Leplastrier and his colleague Roderick Simpson had hoped for something different along the waterfront. Concerned at maintaining Sydney's character as a 'great maritime city', they imagined a foreshore retained as the functional interface between the population and water: 'The "working harbour" is losing infrastructure to residential development all the time … it doesn't make sense to demolish a wharf, construct a private marina for the well-heeled … and not provide any facilities for public water use at Walsh Bay.' For those redundant sites that still lined the river, they imagined a series of 'village ports' in the mould of Watsons Bay in which 'harbour culture' could be reinvigorated with water taxis, ferries, cafés and applied heritage activities such as the operation of 'historic boats'.[73]

Adaptive reuse preserved the infrastructure of the old port, even though some thought the compromises it entailed were unacceptable. In this respect it marked another step along in the debate about foreshore use – one beyond the creation of parkland on old industrial sites. But Leplastrier and Simpson had now begun to address the future function of the working harbour itself, even though the viability of building 'beautiful little port towns' up and down the waterway in the late 20th century was questionable. Huge residential developments, such as Cape Cabarita at Hen and Chicken Bay, were well underway as these ideas were being presented.

In 2003 the broader public also focused on the working harbour. The catalyst was Bob Carr's announcement that the government had a new ports growth plan in which leases on the major container terminals at White Bay, Glebe Island and Darling Harbour would not be renewed when they lapsed from 2006. Bulk cargo and the containers would continue to go south to Botany Bay but the growth in imports would be accommodated at Port Kembla and then Newcastle where, the premier argued, much-needed jobs would be created. The removal of containers from Darling Harbour would free up that land for an 'iconic' development to match the Opera House. Such was the suspicion of government and the disillusionment with architecture that the suggestion was met with derision. In time a consensus emerged that the place be reserved for parkland and a symmetry with Bennelong Point was established by naming the place Barangaroo. The future of White Bay and Glebe Island remained less certain.

Despite the significance of the ports growth plan, relatively few in the maritime industries had been informed and its announcement was a public relations disaster. Four years earlier Carr had unequivocally supported the retention of containers and this decision appeared to be politically rather than rationally based. Details of the plan were withheld and some questioned whether such a comprehensive document actually existed. The shipping industry expressed concern at the economic and logistical effects of the closure of White Bay, a facility with the one remaining commercial rail link on the harbour. Unions were worried about the loss of 150 stevedoring jobs and the flow-on effects for other jobs.

Because this was iconic Sydney Harbour, an industry debate immediately became a public debate. There was an outpouring of anger and emotion as the foreshadowed end of the container leases was equated with the end of the 'working harbour', the loss of Sydney's 'soul' and the inevitable release of more foreshore land for housing. In this context, even the White Bay facility, which had for so long been regarded as a nuisance, became something of a treasured harbour site. The National Trust convened a 'crisis' summit to discuss the implications and its director wrote an impassioned plea to save the 'colourful character' of the harbour – one which took a somewhat broad interpretation of the sentiments of the First Fleeters: 'When Phillip sailed into Sydney Harbour 215 years ago, he immediately recognised the potential of the port as a working harbour … Today there is still nothing so majestic as a huge container ship being guided by tugs to Millers Point or Glebe Island.'[74]

The debate was replete with complexity and irony. The premier's announcement coincided with a celebration of the working harbour in the Maritime Museum, itself situated at the white 'sanitised' Darling Harbour, which had erased that part of the city's working waterfront. Speaking at the exhibition launch, Richard Leplastrier argued that big ships were essential to the character of the city. To see a '10 storey ship' move past from the vantage of a waterside restaurant was unique: 'you watch it and you say "wonderful wonderful Sydney"'.[75] He was right, but those restaurants often occupied the waterfronts where once industry was carried on. And it was containers that had depleted the stevedoring workforce and led to the destruction of the finger wharves at Darling Harbour. Wharf workers, with whom broader Sydney had had such an ambivalent relationship in times of war and peace, became the representatives of Sydney's soul.

Letters and articles were published in abundance, but not all were critical of the decision. Jeremy Dawkins, who had served as the harbour manager for four years from 1998, argued that the removal of containers opened opportunities for a myriad of other port activities and dismissed the angst as 'nostalgia' for a working harbour that had, in any case, long disappeared. The columnist Adele Horin clearly thought she detected middle-class self-interest. The appeal of the picturesque seemed more important than the reality of economic need:

> A container ship entering Darling Harbour or White Bay is a gorgeous thing in its own way, providing we can view it from a harbourside cafe, or better still, a harbourside apartment. To most Sydneysiders a working harbour is an aesthetic concept. To many people in Newcastle and Wollongong, it is the promise of a decent living, at last.[76]

At the National Trust summit several spoke for the need for diversity. There was a desire to have a waterway around and upon which many things happened. None wanted a pond simply surrounded by high-density residences. It was a confirmation of Jane Jacobs's argument for the value of 'bits and pieces'. One could also detect a moral unease at the displacement of workplaces by apparent luxury. It was as if the cycle of empire that had occupied the minds of the harbour's colonisers were being realised. Sydney Harbour had become the industrious symbol of a rising nation, but now it was descending into 'bloatery' and decadence.

And yet underlying this there was still equivocation about the reality of large-scale modern port work. Containers remained anathema to those White Bay residents who carefully monitored the waterfront noise they created. The Defenders of Sydney Harbour Foreshores wanted a 'working harbour' but thought the fight for open foreshores was more important: 'It will be sad to see the end of Sydney Harbour as a working port but if that is to happen we must ensure that the freed foreshores are adequately preserved for the public.'[77] In

the years that followed the Summit, attempts to establish an import
and distribution facility for cement at White Bay were overwhelmingly
defeated on the grounds of residential amenity. There were five
submissions in favour and 1421 against. Similarly, a dry boat storage and
refuelling depot at nearby Rozelle was opposed by the local council and
residents concerned about visual impact, pollution, noise, public access
and danger to rowers. Alternatives considered for White Bay included a
facility for heritage vessels with complementary boat-building activities
or one for marine research. A maritime film set and a 'Sydney Harbour
Heritage Centre' were also suggested.[78] It sounded very much like the
village port idea suggested by Leplastrier and Simpson but it was a
long way from the muscular image of the working harbour evoked
by the National Trust. For its part, the Glebe Society, a counterpart of the Balmain Association, declared its preference for parks over
messy and inaccessible waterfronts:

> Patience and persistence, over three decades, has seen the
> foreshore turned from untidy timber yards to parkland and
> the bays remain, substantially, open water ... Blackwattle
> and Rozelle Bays must not be made 'places of last resort' for
> industries now housed in other harbour sites where local
> communities oppose them.[79]

As each community defended its own piece of liveable harbour it
became harder to maintain diversity. There were approvals, however.
Despite local opposition a slipway was allowed at Rozelle – at an
already cluttered site used for storing maritime equipment and zoned
for 'waterfront use' and 'port and employment'. It was to employ as
many as 140 people and cater for recreational and commercial vessels
up to 800 tons.[80] In the absence of a residential community, establishing
a balance between amenity, industry and heritage was perhaps a little
easier to achieve on Cockatoo Island – but the task was formidable
nonetheless, not least because of the pressures of commercial
sustainability. There, the Sydney Harbour Federation Trust hoped

to preserve heritage values through adaptive reuse, provide access and historical interpretation and 'revive the island by reintroducing maritime and related industry as well as a range of contemporary uses including cultural, entertainment, dining, education, recreation, retail, offices and studios'.[81]

Even with this laudable and all-embracing model, it was hard to escape the conclusion that the 'gritty' waterfront of old was receding into the past. Accessibility was one pay-off. With the decline of industry, and despite the residential and commercial development that sometimes replaced it, the foreshores of Sydney Harbour were more open than at any time since the wharves, boat slips, timber yards and power stations bustled with activity. But never had homes near the water been so unaffordable.

'[T]he bow of a boat'

By the time the working harbour debate unfolded, Lavender Bay had been gentrified and tidied up. There was a small foreshore park where once the swimming baths and boatsheds stood. The place retained a little bit of diversity and interest. The train viaduct still stretched across the head of the bay – now an industrial-era relic – and squeezed into one of its arches was Bob Gordon's boat-building workshop. Passers-by could find out what was happening by reading the answers

A museum dedicated to the preservation of Sydney's steam vessels was established in 1965. It evolved into the Sydney Heritage Fleet. Anthony Browell's 2007 photograph of part of the fleet in front of the disused White Bay power station recalls the work of Harold Cazneaux. It was taken as part of 'The Waterfront' series intended to 'document and interpret [the] disappearing industrial fairyland' of Sydney Harbour.

Courtesy of Anthony Browell

to 'frequently asked questions' written on a white board outside. Bob did not like interruptions.

Bob Gordon had been working in Lavender Bay intermittently since World War II, between bouts of fishing to make a living. He knew the great boatbuilders there: the Holmes, the Merediths, the Dunns. In the 1970s and 1980s he built steel fishing boats and slipped them from the old Neptune Engineering site – and then that property was bought and demolished to build residential units. The slip might have continued to operate out front but the prospect of noise was unacceptable and instead it became part of the park: 'We fought like mad to try and hold that area in Lavender Bay which had been waterfront activity for a hundred years but it was reserved open space.'[82]

There had been contests over land around the harbour since the Europeans had first 'taken possession' from the clans. In the intervening centuries, the newcomers continued the disputes among themselves. It was at Lavender Bay that William Tunks had challenged James Milson and reclaimed a patch of foreshore for the people. That little beach had long disappeared under the railway. Somewhat poignantly it was the viaduct that replaced it that gave Bob Gordon his last retreat. Unwilling to give up his passion, he continued to build wooden yachts beneath the train line. In an era of 'plastic boats' there were not many of this kind still being produced on the waterway. Bob made his for love rather than money, waiting until the right owner turned up to take the finished product. His last, created with the help of his son, was in 2005. The 28-foot *Ivy* was built to a design that first appeared in the 1930s and, with no slipway left, it had to be eased out of its arch and lowered into the bay by crane. Bob died the following year and on the closed doors of his workshop Peter Kingston left a quote from John Ruskin's 1856 book *Harbours of England* – one that had appeared in the eulogy printed for the funeral: 'But one object I never pass without the renewed wonder of childhood and that is the bow of a boat.' Bob Gordon's ashes were scattered on the little beach there. The workshop was closed and the spray-painted tribute was, in due course, erased

in an official 'clean-up'. All signs of the old boatbuilder were gone –
except the sand-covered slipway and Bob's little yacht *Away,* which still
rocked about among the plastic boats in the bay.

BARANGAROO

'[AN] ALLIANCE BETWEEN
EGO AND PHALLUS'

Apples never fall far from their tree. So says the enduring truism that explains traits and interests shared between parent and offspring. Having worked beside his father, Robert Gordon took over the lease for the viaduct workshop in which Bob had built wooden boats for decades. In 2022 the son was putting the finishing touches to a couta, the hull of which barely fit within the repurposed arch. Designed as a wind-powered fishing vessel in the 1870s, the boat was named after the species it chased, 'barracouta'. Three generations later, engines had replaced sail and the couta was obsolete as a working boat. But an appreciation of good design and beauty has created a loyal following. couta boats are now built and sailed as leisure craft.

As Robert Gordon went carefully about his business in Lavender Bay, another very different construction rose quickly in clear view across the water. The gleaming six-star casino, 'resort' and apartment building called 'Crown Towers Sydney' was completed well before Robert slipped his couta boat into the harbour. It stands just over 271 metres high, taller than anything else except the antennae on Centrepoint Tower. The reflective twist of glass can be seen well away from the waterway it now dominates, and from which the building takes its value and purpose. In 2022, a Harbour Bridge King Room could be booked for just under $1000 per night. An Opera Twin Room, with views over that other harbour icon, cost a little more. The precinct in which the luxury tower stands is named after Barangaroo, the Aboriginal woman who kept a wary distance from the naval officers with whom her husband, the canny Bennelong, consorted in the first years of colonisation. More of that strange pairing of glitz and memorialisation later.

Although branded with Crown Resort's golden logo – part coronet, part jester's hat, part champagne pop – the edifice is popularly associated with the man who initiated its construction, billionaire James Packer. Therein lies another story of fallen apples. James inherited vast wealth from his father Kerry who was, for many years, Australia's richest man. The family's fortune can, in turn, be traced back to Robert Clyde Packer, great grandfather to James, who bet a chance 10-shilling note on a horse and thereby funded his way to Sydney from far-flung Tasmania to begin a career in journalism and media ownership.[1] Gambling gained a lucky break, but media made the Packers. Robert's son Frank became immensely wealthy through newspapers and television and was duly knighted. Like many others in Sydney's business elite, he bought property in the harbour's eastern suburbs dress circle in 1935. One large house and garden – 'Cairnton' in Bellevue Hill – was expanded to become a 1.2-hectare family compound of huge homes and lawns by the 1990s.[2] Frank passed his money and interest in journalism to son Kerry, whose television and publishing firms were merged to form Publishing and Broadcasting Limited [PBL], earning James' father the sobriquet of 'media tycoon'.

Kerry was clever and lucky in business. Like his father he was blunt, even bullying, in his dealings. Winning was all-important. The wealth Kerry accrued allowed, or perhaps compelled, him to bet huge sums in casinos across the world. He was known to have won and lost fortunes in a night. The father introduced his son to the world of 'high-rollers', in which casinos offered packages of free luxury accommodation, air travel, meals and sex to big betters – or 'whales' as they are called in the industry. The reality that 'the house never loses', even with such largesse, became apparent to the younger Packer. 'I spent a lot of time in casinos with my dad', he recalled with a chuckle at a business dinner in 2012 as the Barangaroo casino gained momentum, 'and I ended up thinking "fuck this must be a good business"'.[3] James had bid for the licence of Sydney's first casino on behalf of his father in 1994. His conversation with the then Liberal Premier John Fahey included the following threat: 'The old man told me to ring ... this is the message. If we don't win the casino, you guys are fucked'.[4] Fahey took that risk and Packer's bid was unsuccessful. Nonetheless, it was James who convinced his sceptical father to invest in Crown Casino after it opened a venue on the revamped south bank of Melbourne's Yarra River in 1997. PBL took over Crown Melbourne in 1999. After Kerry's death in 2005, James moved away from the media which had underpinned his father's political influence and made the name Packer synonymous with gambling alone. Crown Resorts Limited was established in 2007. James Packer became its chairman and majority shareholder. In 2012 he privately, and this time successfully, lobbied another Liberal Premier for the licence to run a second Sydney casino.

Crown Towers at Barangaroo was built to house that establishment. The project would be something far more exclusive than the casino run with the licence that had eluded Kerry Packer in 1994. The Star was a ziggurat-like monolith which filled the site of the old Pyrmont Power Station across Darling Harbour when completed in 1997. The architect Philip Cox, who had designed the white exhibition halls and Maritime on west Darling Harbour, would later admit the building was his 'worst'.[5] Golden shuttle buses delivered suburban gamblers, the hopeful and the hopeless, to The Star. Its exclusive licence – effective until 2019 – cost $100 million, an indication of the profits to made from gambling and the huge revenue the industry paid to state government – money that was used to fund public services and build infrastructure. The figures, thereby, spoke of another form of dependency.

In contrast to The Star's 'small fry', Packer promised a world-class venue which would attract the new wealth of burgeoning China and bring the 'whales' of that country to Sydney Harbour. In the process the waterway would receive a third iconic landmark, to add to the Bridge and the Opera House.

However, before the building was complete, a NSW Independent Liquor and Gaming Authority inquiry into Crown's business practices judged the company unfit to hold a casino licence in Sydney. When connections to Chinese organised crime were laid bare in February 2021, Packer himself admitted to 'shameful' and threatening behaviour.[6] For a time, the tower was destined to be just a very expensive hotel; with a private penthouse apartment estimated to be worth $100 million – owned by Packer.

The British architectural firm that designed the building remained proud of their achievement despite its notoriety. In 2022 WilkinsonEyre's website told readers that the tower was inspired by nature in contrast to the mass of elongated oblongs elsewhere in the city; its 'form emanates from three petals that twist and rise together, and its sculptural shape maximises the opportunity for accommodation to make the most of the views of Sydney's famous bridge and harbour'.[7]

Not all welcomed Packer's benefaction or the appearance of his edifice, with or without its gaming rooms. In the decade after Jane Jacobs' critique of the hubris of Modernism, the influential urban theorist Henri Lefebvre borrowed from psychoanalysis, anthropology and semiology to equate the architecture of international capitalism with the monumental columns and fetish objects of earlier times. All made manifest the importance of their male designers and owners and all were, thereby, symbols embodying an 'alliance between Ego and Phallus'. This masculine potency drove 'political arrogance'.[8] The idea of the skyscraper as phallic symbol spread remarkably quickly from the realm of arcane discourse to the vernacular. Accordingly, as it took shape on Sydney's waterfront, the Barangaroo tower was soon nicknamed 'Packer's pecker'. Floral inspiration notwithstanding, the WilkinsonEyre design is particularly penile – something that cannot have been lost on designer or client. Possibly therefore the billionaire approved the design as an appropriate symbol of his potency.

Others might recognise a similarity between this edifice and the extraordinary waterfront buildings of Qatar and Dubai in the Middle East. The latter is an absolute monarchy, the former ruled by an Emir with near total authority. In both places patriarchal power, privilege and immense wealth find architectural expression with scant regard for anything else. In 2022 Dubai was home to the world's tallest tower. Sydney, however, is the largest city in a liberal democracy in which transparent process and public interest is supposed to determine development. But arrogance often accompanies power when humility is disregarded and supplicants abound – even in a democracy. Packer's tower is sculptural, as its designers maintain, and more intentionally suggestive than most of the office blocks which fill the city. Therefore, another reading of the column atop its podium, is as a clenched fist with an elongated middle finger held up to those who question its place on the harbour front.

The story of Barangaroo, the place, is indeed a lesson in the masculine arrogance of which Lefebvre wrote. The redevelopment laid bare the contest between public and private interest, power and process, global and local benefit. It raised questions over the definition of the harbour's heritage. The contests were bitter and protracted because, by the 21st century, Sydney's beautiful waterway was an amplifier of real estate value as never before.

'He's the king'

Barangaroo emerged from an international architectural competition; much as the plan to build the national capital Canberra had a century earlier, and the astonishing Opera House was decided 50 years after that. The call for entries was made by the New South Wales government in March 2005. The desire to redevelop East Darling Harbour, as the area was then called, was a natural extension of Premier Bob Carr's 1997 'vision statement'. The project was made possible, of course, by the end of the harbour container terminal leases announced in the 'ports growth plan' of 2003. Indeed, an iconic development at Millers Point, on the northern end of East Darling Harbour, had been given precedence in that document.

The 'message' from Carr, which prefaced the competition guidelines, prioritised the use of 50 per cent of the 22-hectare site as a 'foreshore parkland for the people of Sydney', and the promotion of the city as 'the premier business, cultural and living centre of the Asia-Pacific region'. The development had also to be self-funding. In those three mandatory principles – there were others – lay the tension that would characterise the project for the next 15 years. The balance swung dramatically in favour of the need to boost Sydney's status as a global city and the commercial viability of the place.

The 2005 brief was both challenging and open to interpretation. Among other stipulations were the provision of berths for cruise vessels, an 'appropriate scale of built form' and a consideration of 'the historic pattern of the development of the site' from pre-colonial times to present day.[9]

Two rounds of assessment and one year later, 137 entries had been whittled down to one winner. That was a plan developed by a partnership of the firms Hill Thalis Architecture + Urban Projects, Paul Berkemeier Architects and Jane Irwin Landscape Architecture (THBI). Remarkably, given the scale of the project and the international interest, all were Sydney-based.

They presented a scheme that retained the essential form of the longshore container facility: a straight waterfront with a squared headland. It was both cost-efficient and respectful of the 'historic pattern' as required in the brief and, indeed, as had been heritage best practice since the drafting of the Burra Charter, the quintessential set of guidelines for work on historic sites which first appeared in 1979 with a reiteration in 1999. The Charter stressed that historic landscapes should be 'conserved', a concept that entailed 'respect for the existing fabric, use, associations and meanings'.[10]

It was essentially the principle that underpinned adaptive reuse. But, whereas at Walsh Bay the early 20th century finger wharves presented a beautifully textured palate that made the case for conservation obvious, East Darling Harbour had been an expanse of concrete since the 1960s when its jetties were demolished to accommodate the new technology of shipping containers. The THBI scheme adapted that flat landscape, building it up in parts for small green hills but working with the space and simplicity of the existing fabric to create a long foreshore lined with a park. Four water features and harbour swimming baths were located along this green zone. This was more active community park than passive tourist precinct. It prioritised public space and access to the water and did so with many nuanced features. Heritage was retained by preserving the Harbour Control Tower and history was artistically interpreted in a series of kinetic sculptural cranes, activated by wind and tide evoking the erstwhile container facility. Cultural and commercial buildings stood back from the waterfront, increasing in size gradually as one moved away from the headland. The cruise ships were to be berthed beside that built up zone.

A similar scheme was submitted by the landscape architects McGregor Coxall. That firm had pioneered the design of post-industrial sites on Sydney Harbour with the landscaping of the former BP site at Berrys Bay, opened in 2005, and the Caltex site at Ballast Point, then in design. In both, elements of industrial history were retained in the landscape and incorporated into commissioned artworks. Another 'highly commended' scheme, from Lippmann Associates, Richard Rogers and others, maintained the straight long foreshore but with small boat harbour-like inserts and a crescent shaped beach at the headland. A third finalist, from Lendlease, proposed a curvaceous foreshore within which water featured heavily.

In the end the decision was unanimous. The jury noted that 'The winning [THBI] scheme comes from local Sydney talent who have a deep understanding of Sydney's urban and natural form'. The judges included heritage champion Jack Mundey, whose vision had saved the adjacent colonial-era Rocks precinct from high rise development in the 1970s, and former Prime Minister Paul Keating. Retirement from parliament in 1996 had given Keating the time to comment upon planning matters in his home city. That coincided fortuitously with Bob Carr's ascension as State premier. In 2001, Keating urged his Labor comrade to ensure Ballast Point was preserved as a park when Caltex departed. Carr readily agreed.

No fan of retaining industrial heritage for its own sake, Keating would come to loathe McGregor Coxall's landscaping of Ballast Point, completed in 2009, describing it as 'an archie park, done by an architect, or misdone by an architect'.[11] As competition juror, Keating's influence was apparent in the recommendation that accompanied the endorsement of the THBI scheme: 'A natural headland form which touches the water at the northern end of the site' should be developed along with a 'large northern cove located directly behind the headland to further define the headland'.[12] That essentially reiterated the natural form of the waterfront as depicted in the 1788 map that accompanied the contextual historical information provided to entrants.

There had been no assurance in the competition guidelines that the winner would be engaged to implement their scheme. THBI were invited to present amendments to the Sydney Harbour Foreshore Authority, which had assumed control of the process as the statutory body responsible for the state government's harbourside assets since 1999. They did so in 2006 but the consortium's involvement ended the following year. Philip Thalis recalled the termination: 'We were completely excluded soon after winning the competition … We never received a letter, a phone call, a meeting detailing any reasons …'[13]

There were echoes of the treatment of Canberra designer Walter Burley Griffin and Jørn Utzon. Both architects lost control of their winning schemes after submission and refinement. However, the exclusion of THBI was early and abrupt. Furthermore, in the previous cases, political and bureaucratic intervention was aimed at reining in expansive visions in the name of cost and expediency. At east Darling Harbour, Paul Keating replaced the architects' ideas with his own, even more ambitious, dream. As Chair of the Design Excellence Review Panel, established in 2008 to oversee the look of the park, he was well placed to do so. 'The fact is I've had my eyes opened by my imagination', he later declared.

Keating pursued, then justified, the idea of a naturalistic headland with the determination and invective that had characterised his parliamentary career: 'I was not going to be turned over by some group of architects who mostly do kitchen amendments'.[14] The principle of respecting existing fabric at east Darling Harbour had become ludicrous: 'there's no notion of heritage in that flat piece of concrete'. Despite its unanimous endorsement by the jury, the THBI scheme was implicitly dismissed as 'dull as dishwater'.[15]

Keating wanted a raised vegetated headland with a foreshore that resembled the pre-colonial shape depicted in early maps so that the aesthetic damage done by years of industrialisation would be reversed. The job of realising this Romantic vision went to a high-profile American who barely knew the site. Peter Walker was the New York-based landscape architect who had designed the 9/11 memorial park in lower Manhattan. He was commissioned in 2009 after Lendlease was appointed sole developer for the entire precinct by the Barangaroo Delivery Authority (BDA), the body created to manage the project from 2008.

The concrete was subsequently removed, and millions of tonnes of sandstone excavated to build up the headland. Stone was also cut into blocks to line the foreshore with terraces. More cubes and oblongs were used for the stepped gradient of the elevated ground, within which trees and shrubs were planted. Curiously, given the emphasis on naturalism, the result was an obviously artificial landscape. The park comprised six hectares of the 11 to be given to public space.

Unsurprisingly, the control tower was demolished. Gone, too, was the cruise ship berth; that was to be relocated at White Bay – useless to liners too large to sail beneath the Bridge. With that, Darling Harbour lost the last vestige of its maritime association.

Walker and Keating formed a close working relationship. The Australian made sure the American saw the harbour through his eyes. So much so that Walker seemed to regard Keating as both the client and project lead. 'He's the king', Walker once laughingly admitted.[16] That throwaway comment gives some insight into the force of Keating's personality and the significance of his input. Another came from an admiring Morris Iemma, the Labor Premier who had succeeded Bob Carr in 2005: 'We implemented what he wanted to do ... Nobody understood the site like Keating did.'[17]

Not everyone agreed. Former New South Wales government architect Professor Peter Webber thought rejection of the THBI scheme lost an opportunity to situate an above ground cultural centre – a suitable companion to the Opera House.[18] Architect Richard Leplastrier was particularly scathing of the pursuit of naturalism. The design should reflect the 'grittiness' of a maritime city, he mused, not install a 'green lawn park that you take your dog to crap on'.[19] The National Trust loathed the idea for similar reasons. After the headland was opened in 2015, Australia's pre-eminent urban historian, Graeme Davison admitted to being 'troubled' by the 'confected rather than organic sense of connection to the past' that the greenery embodied.[20]

A decade earlier it had been thought that the area might be called 'The Hungry Mile', the vernacular name for the adjacent strip of Hickson Road used by desperate wharf workers seeking casual employment in the first half of the 20th century. Having decided to divest the area of its industrial heritage, that was inconceivable.

Some just wanted to keep it as 'Millers Point'. Instead, the place became Barangaroo. There was poignance in that name, given the proximity to Bennelong Point. An Opera House stood where Arthur Phillip had built a stone house for the canny Wongal man who helped him mediate relationships with the harbour clans more than two centuries earlier. Where the truly beautiful architecture on Bennelong's point represented the best of modern Australia, Barangaroo's park was meant to evoke a time before the fall. And, of course, Barangaroo and Bennelong were wife and husband. It was also, therefore, a reunion of sorts. Davison acknowledged that the vision of reinstating a 'pre-European' landscape reflected Keating's respect for the harbour's first people. As prime minister in 1992, he had made an astonishingly candid admission that it was 'we', white Australians, who had dispossessed Aboriginal people and wrought havoc upon their culture. That was the so-called 'Redfern Address', one of the finest speeches in Australian history.[21]

Yet oddly enough, Sydney's Aboriginal community had little role in designing the area. Instead, the 'imagination' of one powerful white man came to determine the design of the public headland that commemorated an Aboriginal woman.

The Metropolitan Local Aboriginal Land Council, which formally represented Sydney's Aboriginal communities, boycotted the naming ceremony because the traditional Welcome to Country address was delivered by an outsider rather than someone whose ancestry was connected to the harbour.[22] It was an unfortunate error of protocol.

There had been talk of creating an Aboriginal Cultural Centre within the cavernous void left beneath the constructed headland hump, but no plans were settled before the park was opened. Instead, what was christened The Cutaway became a general-purpose arts venue. However, Lendlease subsequently consulted with members of the Aboriginal community to utilise the spaces already made. The offer to interpret the history of the site and the harbour was graciously accepted. One result was a video installation called 'Wellama', co-created by Walbanga and Wadi Wadi designer Alison Page. The title means 'to come back' in the language of the first harbour people and the dramatised sequences it shows recreate idyllic scenes of pre-colonial life derived from early colonial artworks of Watling, Lycett and others. It is a clever appropriation of European topographic art, which typically foregrounded Aboriginal people to illustrate the significance of the arrival of 'civilisation'. By contrast, 'Wellama' makes a powerful point about the world that ended with British invasion and the dispossession it unleashed.

That Aboriginal presence on the harbour will gain greater resonance in 2026 when nearby Me-Mel (Goat Island) is given back to Aboriginal people. The island was identified by Bennelong as his own land, if colonial accounts are accurate, and David Collins recorded the feasts enjoyed there by the Wongal man and Barangaroo. Announced in 2022, the return will realise that 'graceful act' of 'compensation' suggested by Edward Dowling back in 1878.[23] As Yvonne Weldon, the Deputy Chair of the Metropolitan Local Aboriginal Land Council, said in May 2022: 'It's so long overdue'.[24]

'An iconic representation of a bad process'

In the course of pressing his vision of the 'natural' headland, Paul Keating had been scathing of the Sydney Lord Mayor and member for Sydney, Clover Moore. His ire was raised in May 2011 by her tabling of a petition in State parliament bearing the names of 11 000 people demanding a review of the Barangaroo project. Keating characterised Moore as a meddling fool with a 'miserable microscopic view of world' and no grasp of complexity of town planning. She represented, in his words, Sydney's 'sandal wearing, muesli chewing, bike riding' community.[25] Moore was, what might otherwise be called, 'a progressive' politician. That, in itself, was anathema to someone from the right-wing of the Labor Party – as Paul Keating had been. A great many of Moore's constituents considered their Lord Mayor a champion against over-development. Since assuming office in 2004, she had defended the public realm in the country's largest city, while negotiating the interests and associated pressure from property developers and 'big business', both local and international. As well, there was the will of state government, which controlled the approval of large projects – 'state significant sites' – within Sydney's Local Government Area, such as Barangaroo. Moore would be returned to office several times subsequently.

In 2007, she commissioned the respected Danish-born planner Jan Gehl to reconceptualise the city's public spaces. Well before plans for the tram-like 'Metro' transport system were finalised by the state government, Moore supported the introduction of light rail to the city. She shared Keating's desire to remove the Cahill Expressway, which had blocked the waterfront Circular Quay since the 1950s, and argued for demolition of the elevated freeway that dominated Darling Harbour's southern end.[26]

Both Moore and Gehl worked with the BDA, the former as member and the latter as consultant. However, Moore resigned in 2010 and Gehl ended his association in 2013. The issue was the lack of transparency, public consultation and the encroachment of ever-growing buildings upon the public realm. While the THBI scheme had preserved the northern and middle sections of the site for the stipulated 50 per cent of parkland with a gradual increase in building size to the south, the BDA approved a 30 per cent increase in floor space and dramatic wall of high towers to the edge of the park; the new scheme presented by Lendlease in 2009. Of particular concern for Moore, and the 11 000 petitioners in 2011, was the accompanying approval for a large hotel to be built over the water.

Frustration and fury had been growing since images of the building standing on stilts above its own wharf-like protrusion were made public in the press in December 2009. The design came from a consortium led by the high-profile British architect Lord Richard Rogers and reflected his signature 'structural expressionism' whereby the skeletal support of a building was laid bare. Rogers had made his name 50 years earlier with the revolutionary Pompidou Centre in Paris. The over-harbour hotel resembled a set of glass boxes set within huge red girders. It was consequently nicknamed 'Big Red'.[27]

The *Sydney Morning Herald* described the reworked built landscape with its huge red hotel, as something 'more reminiscent of the excesses of Dubai than Sydney'.[28] The paper polled architects on their views. Just one third of respondents supported the addition. They thought it was suitably innovative design with a satisfactory precedent for an over-water location in the old finger wharves. Of major concern for objectors was the private intrusion into a public harbour in the form of a luxury hotel. Clive Lucas, one of the most respected heritage consultants in the country, made the dismal observation that 'the harbour is probably the only thing we haven't mucked up'. The hotel would do just that. Jack Mundey joined the debate stating that the plan bore 'no resemblance' to the winning concept approved in 2006.[29]

The state Labor government backed the building. In 2009, then premier Kristina Keneally reportedly equated the hotel with a 'tall ship' sailing into the harbour. It was 'bold and inspiring'.[30] The enthusiasm may have related, in part at least, to the realisation that Paul Keating's headland park had cost Lendlease some 250 million dollars more than initial projections. Increasing saleable real estate by creating more floor space and adding a luxury hotel would help offset the cost of the park for developer.[31] The redesign of the park was thereby directly linked to the pressure to build higher on the remainder of the site. That connection may also explain Keating's outburst against Clover Moore in 2011. As Lendlease 'necessarily' increased the size of buildings, opposition to the whole project grew – something that, in turn, jeopardised the completion of his beloved park.

The controversial hotel was approved in an amendment called Modification 4, at the end of 2010. Labor lost office in March 2011. It was the party's worst ever defeat in New South Wales. While the controversy at Barangaroo was not a major election issue, it added to an image of a party beholden to developers and special interests. Members of Labor's right-wing had long been tainted with allegations of corrupt real estate dealings, though not in relation to Barangaroo. Unbeholden by Labor loyalties or due deference, Brad Hazzard, the new Liberal Party planning minister, was quick to rebuke Paul Keating for the attack on Clover Moore two months later. Unwilling to accept that, or perhaps any criticism, Keating angrily resigned from the Design Excellence Panel.

Hazzard's rebuke was soon followed by a review of planning at Barangaroo to date, conducted by Melbourne-based consultants

Meredith Sussex and Shelley Penn. In August they concluded, among other things, that Modification 4 had been given appropriate consideration. However, they recommended that the hotel be relocated on land, rather than over the harbour. The state government immediately requested that Lendlease consider another site. Many welcomed the change.

With the uncertainty of the over-water hotel development, James Packer saw an opportunity to build a different facility – a hotel and casino. He approached the radio broadcaster Alan Jones to broker a private meeting with the Premier Barry O'Farrell. Jones was another who had perfected the use of invective and intimidation as a radio shock jock. He pioneered an Australian version of the right-wing populism already influential in the United States with figures such as Rush Limbaugh, and that would catapult Donald Trump to power in 2016. Veracity and transparency were irrelevant, just as opinionated anger attracted loyal listeners. In 1999 Jones was exposed for making undeclared commercial endorsements for payment on air, but the 'cash for comment' affair had no impact on his ability to demand huge salaries or his appeal to audiences. Politicians defied him at their peril. In his 2006 exposé of the man, respected investigative reporter Chris Masters labelled the harbour city 'Jonestown' – such was the broadcaster's sway in the global capital of Australia and the second official home of the nation's leader, harbourside Kirribilli House.[32] When, in 2012, Jones' publicly said Labor prime minister Julia Gillard should be put in a chaff bag and dumped at sea like an unwanted cat, he demonstrated his familiarity with the geography of his city, political power and sense of invincibility to which he was willing to take his intimidation.

In February 2012, Jones introduced Packer to O'Farrell in his luxury apartment with views over the Opera House and west to the Bridge. It was a perfect location for Packer to present the argument for a third harbour landmark – his six-star hotel casino. The premier left that intimate lunch having 'embraced' Packer's 'vision', in Jones' recollection. Plans for a casino appeared in the sympathetic Murdoch media that month. The premier publicly backed the proposal on

26 February. The following day, on Jones' radio program, Packer welcomed the support but denied that any private discussions with O'Farrell had taken place. The broadcaster knew that was untrue but kept silent. Similarly, the premier overlooked the lunch when asked about contact with Packer in parliament the following year. Jones would tell all to an ABC reporter and camera crew for an investigative report on the process in 2021, when the tower was completed.

It was a remarkable revelation. Having reluctantly resigned from radio station 2GB the previous year after publicly insulting the New Zealand prime minister, Jacinda Ardern, Jones' candour seemed driven by a need to demonstrate his relevance as political powerbroker. But then there were many who sought to benefit from Packer's reflected power.

The first news of the casino in 2012 shocked Clover Moore, as she confessed to the same investigative reporter: 'having represented Sydney for a while, I'm used to being taken by surprise, but I think that took the breath away'.[33] Chris Sidoti, the state's Independent Liquor and Gaming Authority chairman, was doubly surprised when O'Farrell announced his support for Packer's plan without consultation. That, of course, was the body that would find Crown unworthy of a casino licence in 2020.

For O'Farrell there was clear alignment between the interests of Packer and those of the public. Taxes gleaned from the multi-billion dollar market in high roller gambling justified the price of forgoing the foreshore public land Crown wanted for their resort, and the potential damage to public trust in government. The pathway towards realising the plan was progressively cleared of obstacles. Packer's unorthodox 'unsolicited proposal' for a hotel and casino was formally made on 6 September 2012, and accepted. O'Farrell announced approval of the submission, with further detail to follow, on 25 October. In November, Cabinet approved the granting of a second casino licence, to commence from the end of Star's monopoly in 2019. The *Casino Control Act 1992* was amended to allow the facility to be built at Barangaroo. Remarkably there would be no tender required. Labor provided bipartisan support, led by its right-wing faction and convinced by former party powerbrokers employed by Crown to lobby old friends. Packer would duly thank both parties for keeping politics out of their assessments. In parliament it was left to the Greens party and independent members to voice opposition. Clover Moore was forced to resign from parliament that year when legislation was passed preventing her retaining state and local government positions.

Having lost one luxury hotel, Lendlease happily partnered with Packer to build another, with the added attraction of a casino. The amendment that laid out the location of the building, called Modification 8, was presented in 2015. It was endorsed, with some changes, by the Barangaroo Design Advisory Panel, comprised of the government architect and Meredith Sussex and Shelley Penn who had conducted the 2011 review.[34] There was, then, some professional support for the radical change. Paul Keating had already praised Crown's plan when the over-water hotel he preferred was abandoned – something he blamed on the 'vile campaign' against that development conducted by the City of Sydney and public action groups.[35] The tall tower was an effective delineator between his park and the rest of Barangaroo.

Conversely, the president of the NSW chapter of the Australian Institute of Architects described the result as a 'diabolical mess'.[36] Apart from the near complete abandonment of the original concept, concern centred on the loss of a deep inset cove and prime foreshore park land in central Barangaroo – the site of the Crown hotel casino. By way of compensation, another green space called Hickson Park would be created on the eastern side of the tower. The local resident action group dismissed that as 'a landscape frontage' for Crown's casino.[37] The NSW Planning Assessment Commission, which was asked to advise the minister for planning on Modification 8, was sympathetic to these and other public concerns but stated that parliament had 'effectively settled the issue' in 2013 when it legislated for the Casino's foreshore location.[38] Modification 8 was approved in June 2016.

All was finalised without Barry O'Farrell. He had resigned two years earlier amidst controversy over an undeclared gift: a $3000 bottle of wine from the director of a water infrastructure company seeking a partnership with the state government. The premier had forgotten about that gesture, just as he had the lunch with James Packer and Alan Jones. Apparently sanguine about the benefits of gambling, O'Farrell became the CEO of Racing Australia in 2016, the year that work began on the casino he facilitated as premier.

Crown's gambling licence was conditionally reinstated in June 2022 shortly before the company was bought by the US private equity firm, Blackstone. Having confessed to 'shameful' behaviour as Crown's chair, Packer sold his share in Crown for a reported $3.3 billion.[39] The billionaire's gift to his city stands, therefore, as intended – a casino resort. It glitters in the afternoon light that best illuminates the harbour, yet many think the tower's aesthetic qualities will never justify the ill-will and distrust that the project generated. One of the most pessimistic summations came from Kerry Clare, the architect who represented the City of Sydney as one of two women on the seven-person BDA board during the period of the tower's proposal and approval: 'it's not an iconic building, it's an iconic representation of a bad process'.[40]

Icon or not, the building is replete with symbolism. It sits on the harbour's edge as an architectural twin to the Opera House; a house of avarice and privilege where the other is a democratic temple of creativity and beauty. The pairing says much about the identity of Sydney and modern Australia. As I have suggested, the tower epitomises the phallic fetishism identified by Henri Lefebvre and is colloquially recognised as such. That is regrettable as the form rises over a headland dedicated to an Aboriginal woman. And it is only from within Crown's tower that one can actually discern the naturalistic outline of the headland – the manifestation of Paul Keating's singlemindedness which began the saga. One wonders if the occupants of the luxury suites and apartments know or care.

Of cutters and coutas

Beneath the glass and recreated greenery lay something wonderful. In 2018, workers excavating a cavity for Barangaroo's Metro station discovered the remains of a boat. The ribs and planks of the vessel lay where it fell apart to be preserved within compacted sand and clay – when the headland and foreshore really was a natural landscape. It looked for all the world like a Viking long boat recovered on some European coast. Experts identified a vessel made from local timbers: Sydney blue gum, spotted gum and stringy bark. It was colonial, possibly even harbour-built; a descendant of Daniel Paine's local boats with timbers using the natural curves of carefully chosen tree limbs to maximise strength and minimise labour. The wide hull suggests a cutter – a fast craft with a single mast and large sail area. It may have fished the harbour but, at nine metres long, the vessel could also have negotiated waters beyond the heads and even sailed between Sydney, Pittwater or Newcastle.

The remains were found near the stone walls and flagging of William Langford's boatyard. Whether the cutter was built by the convict-turned-artisan is unclear. It likely pre-dates Langford's arrival in the harbour in the 1850s. More probably the cutter ended its days at his slip, beyond repair and abandoned. As the Darling Harbour waterfront was given over to busy wharfage, Langford moved his business across the water to quieter shores, first Berrys then Lavender Bay. Of course, it was there that Robert Gordon would build his single-masted couta boat 160 years later – keeping the skills of boatbuilding alive.

Continuity is sometimes the secretive companion of change in Sydney Harbour.

ACKNOWLEDGMENTS

I have necessarily relied heavily on the research of others. The work of Alan Atkinson, Val Attenbrow, Tim Bonyhady, James Broadbent, Inga Clendinnen, Robert Dixon, Shirley Fitzgerald and Peter Spearritt has been especially useful. A doctoral thesis by Sacha Jenkins alerted me to the significance of a bifurcated harbour, one divided into a beautiful east and a working west. These and other authors are included in the endnotes for further reference. Thanks are due specifically to Val Attenbrow, Peter Cochrane, Bronwyn Hanna, Jon Isaacs, Peter Kingston, Mark McGrouther, David Morris, Julian Pepperell, Peter Spearritt and Tom Uren for their advice and help. Thanks also to Phillipa McGuinness at the University of New South Wales Press for her invaluable suggestions and encouragement, and my editor Mary Trewby for her careful eye. Thanks to Philip Thalis, Laura Harding and Michael Nicholson for their help with the 2nd edition.

North Sydney Council has a long and proud history of encouraging historical research and interpretation. The council supported this project despite its scope beyond local boundaries. Without that this book would not have been written. The opinions expressed here, however, are entirely my own. I would like to thank my colleagues at Stanton Library for their help and, in particular, Martin Ellis and Helen Sutherland for their support. Thank you also to the various collecting institutions and individuals for permission to reproduce the images used, and staff at the National Library of Australia for their help and patience.

NOTES

Introduction

1 Craig Munro, *Inky Stephensen: Wild Man of Letters*, University of Queensland Press, Brisbane, 1992, p. 263.

2 PR Stephensen, 'Author's Note', [1966], in PR Stephensen with Brian Kennedy, *The History and Description of Sydney Harbour*, Reed, Sydney, 1980.

3 Kenneth Slessor, 'The Harbour through My Window', in Laurence Le Guay, *Sydney Harbour*, Angus and Robertson, Sydney, 1966, p. 5.

Chapter 1

1 WD Campbell, *Aboriginal Carvings of Port Jackson and Broken Bay*, Department of Mines and Agriculture, Government Printer, Sydney, 1899, pp. 7, 8, 11, 13, 14, 20.

2 Ruth Park, *Fishing in the Styx*, Penguin, Melbourne, 1994, p. 176.

3 The reference to Birra Birra comes from the Tribal Warrior Association. The Metropolitan Local Aboriginal Land Council recognises 29 clans of the Eora Nation. Quotes from the ceremony from the author's notes, 28 June 2008.

4 Spellings varied over time. I have used the current preference for a soft 'G' over the hard 'C' for clan names as often used by colonists. The 'C' has been retained in the spelling of Aboriginal territories. See Val Attenbrow, *Sydney's Aboriginal Past: Investigating the Archaeological and Historical Records*, UNSW Press, Sydney, 2002, pp. 22–26. For Eora discussion, see pp. 35–36.

5 David Collins, *An Account of the English Colony in New South Wales*, vol. 1 [1798], AH and AW Reed/Royal Australian Historical Society, Sydney, 1975, p. 465.

6 Campbell, *Aboriginal Carvings*, p. 3

7 Gerry Bostock interview with Bill Cope and Mary Kalantzis, in Bill Cope and Mary Kalantzis, 'Harbourside', George Papallinas (ed.), *Harbour: Stories by Australian Writers*, Pan Macmillan, Sydney, 1993, p. 301.

8 Attenbrow, *Sydney's Aboriginal Past*, pp. 112–24.

9 *The Voyage of Governor Phillip to Botany Bay with an Account of the Establishment of the Colonies of Port Jackson and Norfolk Island*, [1789], Library Board of South Australia, Adelaide, 1968, p. 64; James L Kohen, *Aboriginal Environmental Impacts*, UNSW Press, Sydney, 1995, pp. 39–40.

10 John Hunter, *An Historical Journal of Events at Sydney and at Sea 1787–1792*, [1793], Angus and Robertson/Royal Australian Historical Society, Sydney, 1968, p. 44.

11 Collins, *The English Colony in New South Wales*, pp. 495, 462.

12 Ibid., pp. 461, 499.

13 Ibid., p. 457.

14 Attenbrow, *Sydney's Aboriginal Past*, pp. 64–66.

15 *The Voyage of Governor Phillip*, p. 136.

16 Watkin Tench, *Sydney's First Four Years: Being a Reprint of A Narrative of the*

Expedition to Botany Bay and A Complete Account of the Settlement at Port Jackson, Library of Australian History/Royal Australian Historical Society, Sydney, 1979, pp. 226, 230. The encounter was recorded in Tench's journal, *A Complete Account of the Settlement at Port Jackson*, on 11 and 14 April 1791. For an overview of the debates about language, see Attenbrow, *Sydney's Aboriginal Past*, pp. 3–36.

17 Collins, *The English Colony in New South Wales*, p. 458.

18 Ibid., p. 485.

19 Ibid., p. 483.

20 Ibid., p. 453.

21 *Sydney Gazette*, 24 November 1832, quoted in Eric Russell, *The Opposite Shore: North Shore and its People*, North Shore Historical Society and North Sydney Council, Sydney, 1990, p. 56.

22 *Freemans Journal*, 12 October 1889.

Chapter 2

1 Denis Mahoney, *Botany Bay: Environment under Stress*, Charden Publications, Sydney, 1979, pp. 13–14.

2 Paul Brunton (ed.), *The Endeavour Journal of Joseph Banks: The Australian Journey*, Angus and Robertson with State Library of New South Wales, Sydney, 1998, p. 22.

3 Ibid., p. 20.

4 Evidence of Mahroot in 'Minutes of Evidence taken before the Select Committee on Aborigines', *New South Wales Legislative Council Votes and Proceedings*, Sydney, 1845, p. 947. See also Keith Vincent Smith, 'Voices on the Beach' in *Lines in the Sand: Botany Bay Stories from 1770*, Hazelhurst Regional Gallery, Gymea, 2008, pp. 13–21.

5 Brunton, *The Endeavour Journal of Joseph Banks*, p. 31.

6 Cook claimed the coast on 22 August 1770, *Cook's Endeavour Journal 1768–1771*, National Library of Australia, Manuscript 1, 2004, p. 287.

7 James Matra, 'A Proposal for Establishing a Settlement in New South Wales', 23 August 1783, *Historical Records of New South Wales (HRNSW)*, vol. 1, pt. 2, 1783–92, pp. 1–6.

8 Lord Sydney to the Lords Commissioners of the Treasury, 'Heads of a Plan', 18 August 1786, *HRNSW*, vol. 1 pt. 2, 1783–92, p. 18. Like Alan Atkinson I take this plan and subsequent announcements by the king at face value. The absence in these of declared strategic or commercial motives seems to me evidence that the colony was established as a means of relocating convicts. See Alan Atkinson, *The Europeans in Australia:*

A History, vol. 1, The Beginning, Oxford University Press, Melbourne, 1997, pp. 58–59.

9 Alan Frost, 'Towards Australia: The Coming of the Europeans 1400–1788', in DJ Mulvaney and J Peter White (eds), *Australians to 1788*, Fairfax, Syme and Weldon Associates, Sydney, 1987, pp. 398–400. For a detailed account of the preparation and voyage, see Alan Frost, *Arthur Phillip: His Voyaging 1738–1814*, Oxford University Press, Melbourne, 1987, pp. 141–64.

10 See Roger Knight, 'The First Fleet: Its State and Preparation 1786–1787', in John Hardy and Alan Frost (eds), *Studies from Terra Australis to Australia*, Australian Academy of the Humanities, Canberra, 1989, p. 126; Anthony Farrington, *Trading Places: The East India Company and Asia 1600–1834*, The British Library, London, 2002, p. 10.

11 The instructions were addressed to 'our trusty and well-beloved Arthur Phillip Esq …', 25 April 1787, in *HRNSW*, vol. 1, pt. 2, 1783–92, p. 91.

12 Frost, *Arthur Phillip*, p. 142.

13 From 'The Convict's Farewell to Old England', Windmill Tavern, Newgate Street, 6 January 1787, quoted in Frost, 'Towards Australia', p. 401.

14 Collins, *The English Colony on New South Wales*, vol. 1, p. lxvi.

15 Ibid., p. lxxxvi. Phillip still felt himself to be 'out of the world' some eight months after arriving at Sydney Cove; see Frost, *Arthur Phillip*, p. 135.

16 *The Voyage of Governor Phillip*, p. 47.

17 William Bradley, *A Voyage to New South Wales: The Journal of Lieutenant William Bradley of HMS Sirius 1786–1792*, Trustees of the Public Library of New South Wales/Ure Smith, Sydney, 1969, p. 59.

18 George Worgan to Richard Worgan, 12 June 1788, in George B Worgan, *Journal of a First Fleet Surgeon*, [1788], Library Council of New South Wales/Library of Australian History, Sydney 1978, p. 1.

19 Collins, *The English Colony in New South Wales*, vol. 1, p. 5.

20 Ibid.

21 JF Campbell, 'The Valley of the Tank Stream', *Journal of the Royal Australian Historical Society*, vol. 10, pt. 1, 1924, pp. 66–69.

22 John Fidlon and RJ Ryan (eds), *The Journal and Letters of Lt. Ralph Clark*, Australian Documents Library/Library of Australian History, Sydney, 1981, p. 95.

23 John White, *Journal of a Voyage to New South Wales*, [1790], Angus and Robertson/Royal Australian Historical Society, Sydney, 1962, p. 112.

24 In Bernard Smith, *European Vision and the South Pacific*, Oxford University Press, Melbourne, 1989, p. 180.

25 Collins, *The English Colony in New South Wales*, vol. 1, p. 4.

26 Fidlon and Ryan, *The Journal and Letters of Lt. Ralph Clark*, p. 94.

27 White, *Journal of a Voyage to New South Wales*, p. 113.

28 Helen Proudfoot, 'Fixing the Settlement upon a Savage Shore: Planning and Building', in Graeme Aplin (ed.), *A Difficult Infant: Sydney before Macquarie*, UNSW Press, Sydney, 1988, pp. 55–71.

29 Bradley, *A Voyage to New South Wales*, p. 104–05.

30 Collins, *The English Colony in New South Wales*, vol. 1, p. 17.

31 The ecological impact of wharf structures is referred to in *Port Survey for Introduced Marine Species: Sydney Harbour, Final Report*, Australian Museum Business Services, Sydney, 2002, p. 2.

32 In Helen Heney (ed.), *Dear Fanny: Women's Letters to and from New South Wales, 1788–1857*, Pergamon Press, Sydney, 1985, p. 2.

33 Worgan, *Journal*, p.11.

34 Penny Olsen, *Feather and Brush: 300 Years of Australian Bird Art*, CSIRO Publishing, Melbourne, 2001, p. 26.

35 Ibid., p. 19.

36 *The Voyage of Governor Phillip*, p. 286.

37 Collins, *The English Colony in New South Wales*, vol. 1, p. 6.

38 White, *Journal of a Voyage to New South Wales*, p. 113.

39 Bradley, *A Voyage to New South Wales*, pp. 79–80.

40 Tench, *Sydney's First Four Years*, p. 272.

41 Ibid., pp. 69, 272.

42 *The Voyage of Governor Phillip*, p. 59.

43 Quoted in WS Campbell, 'Use and Abuse of Stimulants in the Early Days of the Settlement of New South Wales', *Journal of the Royal Australian Historical Society*, vol. 18, pt. 2, 1933, p. 78.

44 Worgan, *Journal*, p. 12

45 White, *Journal of a Voyage to New South Wales*, p. 118.

46 In Heney, *Dear Fanny*, p. 2.

47 Lois Davey et al, 'The Hungry Years: 1788–1792: A Chapter in the History of the Australian and His Diet', *Historical Studies*, vol. 3, no. 11, October 1945, pp. 193–98.

48 White, *Journal of a Voyage to New South Wales*, p. 124.

49 Ibid., p. 128.

50 Arthur Phillip to Right Hon. WW Grenville, 17 June 1790, *Historical Records of Australia (HRA)*, series 1, vol. 1, 1788–96, p. 182.

51 Tench, *Sydney's First Four Years*, p. 258.

52 'Instructions for our trusty and well-beloved Arthur Phillip Esq.', p. 89.

53 Collins, *The English Colony of New South Wales*, vol. 1, p. 6.

54 In Henry Reynolds, *The Law of the Land*, Penguin, Melbourne, 1987, p. 25.

55 Matra, 'A Proposal for Establishing a Settlement', p. 1.

56 In Reynolds, *Law of the Land*, pp. 31–32.

57 *The Voyage of Governor Phillip*, pp. 49–50.

58 Hunter, *An Historical Journal*, p. 57.

59 Tench, *Sydney's First Four Years*, p. 48.

60 See White, *Journal of a Voyage to New South Wales*, p. 113, and Collins, *The English Colony of New South Wales*, vol. 1, p. 12.

61 *The Voyage of Governor Phillip*, p. 138.

62 Tench, *Sydney's First Four Years*, pp. 135, 187.

63 Bradley, *A Voyage to New South Wales*, p. 115.

64 Ibid., p. 107.

65 See also Attenbrow, *Sydney's Aboriginal Past*, p. 83.

66 *The Voyage of Governor Phillip*, p. 132.

67 Ibid., p. 139.

68 White, *Journal of a Voyage to New South Wales*, p. 110.

69 *The Voyage of Governor Phillip*, p. 139.

70 Tench, *Sydney's First Four Years*, p. 142.

71 Ibid., p. 143.

72 Collins, *The English Colony in New South Wales*, p. 496.

73 Ibid., p. 53.

74 Bradley, *A Voyage to New South Wales*, pp. 182–83.

75 Ibid., p. 497. It is unclear whether Bennelong conceived of this notion of singular ownership after his involvement with the Europeans as it sits counter to the system of communal territory that apparently operated elsewhere around the harbour.

76 For a close reading of the encounters between Phillip and Bennelong [Baneelon] and other harbour people, see Inga Clendinnen, *Dancing with Strangers*, Text, Melbourne, 2003.

77 John Easty, *Memorandum of the Transactions of a Voyage from England to Botany Bay 1787–1793: A First Fleet Journal* [1786–96], Trustees of the Public Library of New South Wales/ Angus and Robertson, Sydney, 1965, p. 117.

78 Tench, *Sydney's First Four Years*, p. 176.

79 Clendinnen, *Dancing with Strangers*, pp. 124–28.

80 Collins, *The English Colony in New South Wales*, vol. 1, pp. 126–27.

81 Ibid., p. 296.

82 Brian Fletcher, *Landed Enterprise and Penal Society: A History of Farming and Grazing in New South Wales before 1821*, Sydney University Press, Sydney, 1976, p. 48.

83 Collins, *The English Colony in New South Wales*, vol. 1, p. 367.
84 Ibid., p. 362.

Chapter 3

1 CH Currey, *The Transportation, Escape and Pardoning of Mary Bryant*, Angus and Robertson, Sydney, 1963, pp. 1–4.
2 Tench, *Sydney's First Four Years*, p. 272. Joseph Bishop and the volatile William Boggis were the only other First Fleeters with such qualifications.
3 Collins, *The English Colony of New South Wales*, vol.1, p. 92.
4 Ibid., pp. 44–45.
5 Letter from a 'young man at Port Jackson', in John Cobley (ed.), *Sydney Cove 1789–1790*, Angus and Robertson, Sydney, 1963, p. 166.
6 Collins, *The English Colony of New South Wales*, vol. 1, p. 96.
7 Rev R Johnson to Mr Thornton, July 1730, in *HRNSW*, vol. 1, pt. 2, 1783–92, p. 386.
8 Collins, *The English Colony of New South Wales*, vol.1, pp. 99–100.
9 Governor Phillip to the Right Hon. WW Grenville, 13 July 1790, *HRA*, series 1, vol. 1, 1788–96, p. 188.
10 Collins, *The Colony of New South Wales*, vol. 1, p. 98.
11 Letter from W Hill to Jonathan Watham Esqr. of Bond Court, Walbrook, London, dated Sydney Cove, Port Jackson, 26 July 1790, Mitchell Library MLMSS 6821.
12 Davey et al, 'The Hungry Years,' p. 201.
13 Clendinnen, *Dancing with Strangers*, p. 198.
14 Easty, *Memorandum*, p. 127; Currey, *Mary Bryant*, p. 14.
15 Currey, *Mary Bryant*, p. 44.
16 Tench, *Sydney's First Four Years*, p. 219.
17 Easty, *Memorandum*, p. 127.
18 See Atkinson, *The Europeans in Australia*, vol. 1, pp. 48–58.
19 See Gov Phillip to Under Secretary Nepean, 10 July 1790, *HRA*, series 1, vol. 1, 1788–96, p. 187.
20 In AGL Shaw, *Convicts and the Colonies: A Study of Penal Transportation from Great Britain and Ireland to Australia and Other Parts of the Empire*, Faber and Faber, London, 1966, p. 57.
21 JT Bigge, *Report of the Commissioner of Inquiry into the State of the Colony of New South Wales*, [1822], Libraries Board of South Australia, Adelaide, 1966, p. 33.
22 Collins, *The English Colony of New South Wales*, vol. 1, p. 175.
23 Ibid., p. 131.
24 See Phillip to Secretary Stephens, 28 September 1788, *HRA*, series 1, vol. 1,

1788–96, p. 89; Phillip to Under Secretary Nepean, 22 August 1790, *HRNSW*, vol. 1, pt. 2, 1783–92, p. 393; Collins, *The English Colony of New South Wales*, vol. 1, p. 169.
25 Reverend Johnson to Mr Henry Fricker, 9 April 1790, in Cobley, *Sydney Cove 1789–1790*, pp. 167–68.
26 Collins, *The English Colony of New South Wales*, vol. 1, p. 63.
27 White, *Journal of a Voyage to New South Wales*, p. 119.
28 Tench, *Sydney's First Four Years*, p. 263.
29 RJB Knight and Alan Frost (eds), *The Journal of Daniel Paine 1794–1797*, National Maritime Museum/Library of Australian History, Greenwich/Sydney, 1983, pp. 38, 68.
30 Collins, *The English Colony of New South Wales*, vol. 2, p. 73.
31 Brian Fletcher, 'The Development of Small Scale Farming in New South Wales under Governor Hunter', *Journal of Royal Australian Historical Society*, vol. 5, pt. 1, June 1964, p. 4.
32 Captain Waterhouse, 'Memorandum on the Timber of New South Wales', [March 1802], in Knight and Frost, *Journal of Daniel Paine*, pp. 78–79.
33 'Return of Labour at Sydney, Parramatta and Toongabbe 1797', in *HRA*, series 1, vol. 2, 1797–1800, p. 337.
34 Sir Ernest Scott, *The Life of Captain Matthew Flinders RN*, Angus and Robertson, Sydney, 1914, pp. 87, 104.
35 Ibid., pp. 104–22.
36 François Péron, *Voyage of Discovery to the Southern Lands*, books 1–3 (trans. Christine Cornell), [1824], Friends of the State Library of South Australia, Adelaide, 2006, p. 294.
37 Scott, *The Life of Matthew Flinders*, pp. 173–74.
38 The names Australia and Australasia had been applied to imagined lands and regions before this. The continent had generally been called New Holland before Flinders' popularisation of the alternative name. See ibid., pp. 420–25.
39 'Government and general order', 18 July 1796, *HRNSW*, 1796–99, vol. 3, p. 59.
40 'Government and general order', 9 October 1797, *HRNSW*, 1796–99, vol. 3, pp. 303–4.
41 Scott, *The Life of Matthew Flinders*, p. 113.
42 The link between the abandoned convicts and the *Sydney Cove* comes from Collins, *The English Colony of New South Wales*, vol. 2, p. 56. Scott suggests that the abandoned convicts were the political prisoners who took the *Cumberland* (*The Life of Matthew Flinders*, pp. 111–12). Collins clearly states, however, that they were part of the crew of one the subsequently stolen 'settler's boats'.

43 Margaret Steven, *Merchant Campbell, 1769–1846*, Oxford University Press, Melbourne, 1965, pp. 23–24.
44 *The Voyage of Governor Phillip*, p. 142.
45 Collins, *The English Colony of New South Wales*, vol. 2, p. 84.
46 Joseph Holt, *Memoirs of Joseph Holt: General of the Irish Rebels, 1798*, vol. 2, Henry Culburn, London, 1838, pp. 56–58.
47 Collins, *The English Colony of New South Wales*, vol. 2, p. 92.
48 Steven, *Merchant Campbell*, pp. 38–39.
49 In JEB Currey (ed.), *Reflections on the Colony of New South Wales: George Caley Explorer and Natural History Collector for Sir Joseph Banks*, Lansdowne Press, Melbourne, 1966, pp. 78, 68.
50 Collins, *The English Colony of New South Wales*, vol. 1, p. 251.
51 The description comes from William Smith, a destitute missionary who enjoyed Campbell's hospitality and help in 1799. Quoted in Steven, *Merchant Campbell*, p. 39.
52 John Bach, *A Maritime History of Australia*, Book Club Associates/Thomas Nelson, Melbourne, 1976, p. 27.
53 Captain Colnett to Secretary Nepean, 14 September 1803, *HRNSW*, 1803–05, vol. 5, p. 209.
54 Stevens, *Merchant Campbell*, p. 188; CET Newman, *The Spirit of Wharf House*, Angus and Robertson, Sydney, 1961, pp. 17–18; Susanna De Vries, *Historic Sydney as Seen by its Early Artists*, Angus and Robertson, Sydney, 1987, p. 16.
55 WC Wentworth, *Statistical, Historical and Political Description of the Colony of New South Wales, and its Dependent Settlement in Van Diemen's Land*, [1819], Griffin Press, Adelaide, 1978, p. 7.
56 'Regulations to be observed by all masters or commanders of English or foreign merchant vessels arriving in Port Jackson ...' 10 September 1800, *HRNSW*, vol. 4, 1800–02, pp. 144–46; 'Orders regarding passage boats between Sydney and Parramatta', *HRA*, series 1, vol. 4, 1803–04, p. 344.
57 Péron, *Voyage of Discovery*, pp. 298–99.
58 The East India Company monopoly meant that the only British ships that could trade between New South Wales and China were 'company' owned. That monopoly did not apply to foreign vessels. However the Navigation Acts that had operated since the mid-1700s restricted all trade between Britain and its colonies and between these colonies themselves to British or colonial ships. American and other foreign ships selling goods in Sydney were breaking British law (Bach, *A Maritime History of Australia*, p. 46).
59 Hunter to the Duke of Portland, 25 June 1797, *HRA*, series 1, vol. 2, 1797–1800, p. 30.
60 King to Lord Hobart, 1802, in DR Hainsworth, *The Sydney Traders: Simeon Lord and his Contemporaries 1788–1821*, Melbourne University Press, Melbourne, 1981, p. 130.
61 Hainsworth, *The Sydney Traders*, p. 133.
62 Ibid., p. 131.
63 *Sydney Gazette*, 19 February 1804, quoted in Max Kelly, *Anchored in a Small Cove: A History and Archaeology of The Rocks*, Sydney Cove Authority, Sydney, 1997, p. 43.
64 DD Mann, *The Present Picture of New South Wales*, [1811], John Ferguson, Sydney, 1979, pp. 19–20.
65 Now called Port Hacking; see *Sydney Gazette*, 14 December 1806.
66 Steven, *Merchant Campbell*, p. 149.
67 Governor King to Lord Hobart, 1 March 1804, *HRA*, series 1, vol. 4, 1803–04, p. 491.
68 Hainsworth, *The Sydney Traders*, p. 139.
69 Ibid., p. 155.
70 Robert McNab, *Murihiku: A History of the South Island of New Zealand and the Islands Adjacent and Lying to the South from 1642–1835*, Whitcombe and Tombs, Wellington, 1909, p. 209. See also Rhys Richards, '"The Uplands Seal" of the Macquarie and Antipodes Islands: A Historian's Perspective', *Journal of the Royal Society of New Zealand*, vol. 24, no. 3, September 1994, pp. 289–95.
71 'Proclamation', 17 January 1814, *HRA*, series 1, vol. 3, pp. 98–100.
72 Marc Serge Riviere (ed.), *The Governor's Noble Guest: Hyacinthe de Bougainville's Account of Port Jackson, 1825*, Miegunyah Press, Melbourne, 1999, pp. 73–74.
73 Mrs Charles Meredith, *Notes and Sketches of New South Wales*, [1844], Penguin, Melbourne, 1973, p. 36.
74 Peter Cunningham, *Two Years in New South Wales*, [1827], ed. by David S Macmillan, Angus and Robertson, Sydney, 1966, quoted in Alan Birch and David S Macmillan (eds), *The Sydney Scene 1788–1960*, Melbourne University Press, Melbourne, 1962, p. 27.
75 Governor Darling noted as much to the colonial secretary W Huskisson in 1828; see *HRA*, vol. 14, p. 130.
76 Cunningham, *Two Years in New South Wales*, p. 41.
77 Meredith, *Notes and Sketches*, p. 43.
78 RM Hartwell, 'Australia's First Trade Cycle', *Journal of the Royal Australian Historical Society*, vol. 7, pt. 2, 1957, pp. 57–58.
79 *Sydney Herald*, 25 April 1831.
80 Bach, *A Maritime History of Australia*, p. 76.
81 James Jervis, 'Notes on the North Shore and the Whaling Establishments', *Journal of the*

Royal Australian Historical Society, vol. 21, pt. 5, 1936, p. 287.

82 JSN Wheeler, 'Old Millers Point, Sydney', *Journal of the Royal Australian Historical Society*, vol. 48, pt. 4, August 1962, pp. 308–13.

83 Quoted in Birch and Macmillan, *The Sydney Scene*, pp. 79–80.

84 *Sydney Record*, 17 October 1843.

Chapter 4

1 Charles Darwin, *Voyage of the Beagle,* [1839], Penguin, Harmondsworth, 1989, pp. 317–27.

2 This figure includes repeat visitations by steamers and small vessels. See Charles Bateson, *The Convict Ships 1788–1868*, Brown, Son and Ferguson, Glasgow, 1959, pp. 310–12; Ian Hawkins Nicholson, *Shipping Arrivals and Departures, Sydney 1826–1840*, Roebuck, Canberra, 1964, pp. 141–60.

3 *Australian*, 17 February 1825.

4 See Robert Dixon, *The Course of Empire: Neo-Classical Culture in New South Wales 1788–1860*, Oxford University Press, Melbourne, 1986, pp. 1–5.

5 In Smith, *European Vision*, pp. 284–85.

6 William Kent, quoted in Atkinson, *The Europeans in Australia*, vol. 1, p. 291.

7 Bigge, *Report into the State of the Colony of New South Wales*, pp. 28–30.

8 John R. Stillgoe, *Common Landscapes of America, 1580–1845*, Yale University Press, New Haven, 1982, pp. 109–11.

9 Helen Proudfoot, 'Captain Piper and Henrietta Villa', *Journal of the Royal Australian Historical Society*, vol. 59, pt. 3, September 1973, p. 169.

10 M Barnard Eldershaw, *The Life and Times of Captain John Piper*, Ure Smith, Sydney 1973, p. 125.

11 Proudfoot, 'Captain Piper and Henrietta Villa', p. 169.

12 Quoted in Eldershaw, *The Life and Times of Captain John Piper*, p. 130.

13 For descriptions and analysis of Henrietta Villa, see James Broadbent, *The Colonial House: Architecture and Society in New South Wales 1788–1842*, Hordern House, Sydney, 1997, pp. 96–102.

14 Joseph Lycett, *Views in Australia*, J Souter, London, 1824, [no page number].

15 Ibid., p. 14.

16 Edward West Marriott (ed.), *The Memoirs of Obed West: A Portrait of Early Sydney,* Barcom Press, Bowral, 1988, pp. 32–33.

17 Governor Macquarie to Earl Bathurst, 12 December 1817, *HRA*, vol. 9, 1816–18, p. 720.

18 Joan Kerr and James Broadbent, *Gothick Taste in the Colony of New South Wales*, David Ell Press/Elizabeth Bay House, Sydney 1980, p. 43.

19 Riviere, *The Governor's Noble Guest,* p. 72.

20 Augustus Earle, *Views in New South Wales and Van Diemen's Land: Australian Scrapbook*, J Cross, London, 1830, p. 5.

21 Ralph Darling to colonial secretary W Huskisson, 27 March 1828, *HRA*, vol. 14. 1828–29, p. 47.

22 In 1819 Earl Bathurst made clear: 'Not having been established with any view to territorial or commercial advantages, they [settlements in New Holland] must chiefly be considered as receptacles for offenders, in which crimes may be expiated, at a distance from home, by punishments sufficiently severe to deter others from the commission of crimes, and so regulated as to operate the reform of the persons by whom they had been committed.' *A Copy of the Instructions Given by Earl Bathurst to Mr Bigge on his Proceeding to New South Wales,* Australian Facsimile Editions No. 68, Libraries Board of South Australia, Adelaide, 1966, p. 3.

23 WC Wentworth, *Australasia: A Poem Written for the Chancellor's Medal at the Cambridge Commencement, July 1823*, Whittaker and Co, London, 1873, p. 22.

24 Ibid., pp. 3, 10.

25 Ibid., pp. 1–2.

26 See Broadbent, *The Australian Colonial House*, p. 155.

27 The idea is from John Skinner Prout and John Rae's *Sydney Illustrated,* [1843], see Broadbent, *The Australian Colonial House*, p. 340.

28 See Susan Hunt and Graeme Davison, *Sydney Views 1788–1888 from the Beat Knoblauch Collection*, Historic Houses Trust, Sydney, 2007.

29 *Australian*, 31 July 1835, quoted in Elizabeth Ellis, *Conrad Martens: Life and Art*, State Library of New South Wales Press, Sydney, 1994, p. 20.

30 Conrad Martens, *Journal of a Voyage Aboard HMS Hyacinth,* [1833–35], quoted in Ellis, *Conrad Martens*, p. 15

31 Ellis, *Conrad Martens*, pp. 23, 50–51.

32 Ibid., pp. 51–52.

33 See RHW Reece, *Aborigines and Colonists: Aborigines and Colonial Society in New South Wales in the 1830s and 1840s*, University of Sydney Press, Sydney, 1974, pp. 172–73.

34 'Minutes of Evidence taken before the Select Committee on the Aborigines', pp. 944–45.

35 Collins, *The English Colony of New South Wales*, vol. 2, pp. 161, 162.

36 Keith Vincent Smith, *King Bungaree: A Sydney Aborigine Meets the Great South Pacific Explorers, 1799–1830*, Kangaroo Press, Kenthurst, 1992, p. 53. This is the most comprehensive account of Bungaree's life and much of the following detail is derived from it.
37 Governor Macquarie to Earl Bathurst, 24 March 1815, *HRA*, vol. 8, 1813–15, p. 467.
38 The term is Inga Clendinnen's; see *Dancing with Strangers, p. 273.*
39 Bellingshausen, quoted in Glynn Barrat, *The Russians at Port Jackson 1814–1822*, Aboriginal Institute of Aboriginal Studies, Canberra, 1981, p. 34.
40 In Barrat, *The Russians at Port Jackson*, p. 52.
41 The term was used by Earle himself in his 1830 book of lithographs, *Views of New South Wales*. Earle also painted a third portrait at this time – of the governor, Thomas Brisbane. See Tim Bonyhady, *The Colonial Image: Australian Painting 1800–1880*, Australian National Gallery, Ellsyd Press, Sydney, 1987, pp. 16–21.
42 He said that the Captain had 'an ingenious and indefatigable mind', in Earle, *Views of New South Wales.*
43 Earle, *Views of New South Wales.*
44 In Russell McGregor, *Imagined Destinies: Aboriginal Australians and the Doomed Race Theory, 1880–1939*, Melbourne University Press, Melbourne, 1997, p. 13.
45 Her name was also recorded as Kaaroo, Carra, Caroo, Car-roo or Ba-ran-gan. See Smith, *King Bungaree*, pp. 145–46.
46 There was genuine respect for Caroo in some quarters. After she died in 1852, a gravesite was purchased for her in the public 'Sandhills' cemetery on the south side of town.
47 George French Angas, *Savage Life and Scenes in Australia and New Zealand*, vol. 1, [1847], AH and AW Reed, Wellington, 1968, p. 274.
48 Darwin, *Voyage of the Beagle*, p. 322.
49 *Sydney Morning Herald*, 23 November 1878.
50 See Maria Nugent, *Botany Bay: Where Histories Meet*, Allen and Unwin, Sydney, 2005.

Chapter 5

1 Henry Kendall, 'Sydney Harbour', in TT Reed (ed.), *The Poetical Works of Henry Kendall*, Libraries Board of South Australia, Adelaide, 1966, p. 394.
2 Frank Fowler, *Southern Lights and Shadows*, [1859], Sydney University Press, Sydney, 1975, p. 96.
3 Sir Thomas Brisbane to Earl Bathurst, 25 May 1825, *HRA*, series 1, vol. 11, 1823–25, pp. 616–17.

4 Alan Barnard, *Visions and Profit: Studies in the Business Career of Thomas Sutcliffe Mort*, Melbourne University Press, Melbourne, 1961, pp. 26–31.
5 William Shaw, *The Land of Promise or My Impressions of Australia*, Simpkin, Marshall and Co., London, 1854, p. 3.
6 Norman Selfe, 'A Century of Sydney Cove and the Genesis of the Circular Quay', *Journal of the Royal Australian Historical Society*, vol. 1, pt. 4, 1901–02, pp. 63–66.
7 'Report of the Commission Appointed to Inquire into the Condition of the Harbour of Port Jackson', *New South Wales Legislative Assembly Votes and Proceedings*, vol. 2, 1866, p. 96.
8 Mrs Eliza Walker, 'Old Sydney in the Forties', *Journal of the Royal Australian Historical Society*, vol. 16, pt. 4, p. 302.
9 *Heads of the People*, 13 November 1847, p. 35.
10 *Sydney Morning Herald*, 11 June 1849.
11 Captain WAB Greaves, 'Recollections of Old Sydney in 1852 and Since', *Journal of the Royal Australian Historical Society*, vol. 3, pt. 9, 1916, p. 404.
12 *Sydney Morning Herald*, 13 June 1849.
13 Ibid., 11 June 1849.
14 See Peter Cochrane, *Colonial Ambition: Foundations of Australian Democracy*, Melbourne University Press, Melbourne, 2006, pp. 203–10, for a fuller discussion of the events.
15 *Sydney Morning Herald*, 12 June 1849.
16 The governor had ruled with the assistance of an appointed council since 1826.
17 Carol Liston, *Sarah Wentworth: Mistress of Vaucluse*, Historic Houses Trust, Sydney, 1988, pp. 103–7.
18 Cochrane, *Colonial Ambition*, p. 341.
19 The museum was established in 1827. The permanent building where the ball was held opened in 1857.
20 See Bach, *A Maritime History of Australia*, pp. 98, 110–11.
21 Ibid., pp. 110–13.
22 *Sydney Morning Herald*, 23 June 1851, quoted in Cochrane, *Colonial Ambition*, p. 287.
23 Shirley Fitzgerald, *Sydney 1842–1992*, Hale and Iremonger, Sydney, 1992, p. 225.
24 Shaw, *The Land of Promise*, pp. 3–4.
25 Cochrane, *Colonial Ambition*, pp. 285–86.
26 Quoted in Graeme Davison, 'The Unsociable Sociologist: WS Jevons and His Survey of Sydney, 1856–8', *Australian Cultural History*, 1997–98, no. 16, p. 145.
27 'Report from the Select Committee on the Condition of the Working Classes of the Metropolis', *New South Wales Legislative Assembly Votes and Proceedings*, vol. 4, 1859–60, pp. 1272, 1380, 1402.

28 Ibid., p. 1295.
29 See Shirley Fitzgerald, *Red Tape, Gold Scissors: The Story of Sydney's Chinese*, State Library of New South Wales, Sydney, 1997, pp. 19–23; Andrew Markus, *Fear and Hatred: Purifying Australia and California, 1850–1914*, Hale and Iremonger, Sydney, 1979, p. 34.
30 *Port Regulations Laws and Regulations to be Observed in the Harbour of Port Jackson New South Wales*, Office of the Marine Board of New South Wales, Geo. Lindeman RN Secretary, 1899, pp. 23–24.
31 'Report on the Condition of the Working Classes of the Metropolis', p. 1275.
32 Ibid., p. 1272.
33 'Report from the Select Committee on the Proposed Nautical School', *New South Wales Legislative Council Votes and Proceedings*, vol. 2, 1854, p. 144.
34 DI McDonald, 'Henry Parkes and the Sydney Nautical School', *Journal of the Royal Australian Historical Society*, vol. 52, pt. 3, September 1966, pp. 212–27; John Ramsland, 'Life Aboard the Nautical School Ship *Sobraon*, 1891–1911', *Great Circle*, vol. 3, no. 1, April 1981, pp. 30–32.
35 James Semple Kerr, *Cockatoo Island: Penal and Institutional Remains*, National Trust of Australia (NSW) Sydney, 1984, p. 3; RG Parker, *Cockatoo Island: A History*, Thomas Nelson, Melbourne, 1977, p. 2.
36 Parker, *Cockatoo Island*, p. 10.
37 Peter Oppenheim, *The Fragile Forts: The Fixed Defences of Sydney Harbour 1788–1963*, Department of Defence, Canberra, 2004, p. 30.
38 Instructions to Captain Freemantle of the *Juno*, 1854, quoted in John Bach, 'The Royal Navy in the South West Pacific: The Australia Station 1859–1913', *Great Circle*, vol. 5, no. 2, October 1983, p. 118.
39 Oppenheim, *The Fragile Forts*, p. 20.
40 Ibid., p. 27.
41 James Semple Kerr, *Admiralty House: A Conservation Plan Prepared for the Department of Housing and Construction*, National Trust of Australia (NSW), Sydney 1987, p. 11.
42 James Semple Kerr, *Fort Denison: An Investigation for the Maritime Services Board of NSW*, National Trust of Australia (NSW), Sydney, 1986, pp. 101–4.
43 See Ward L Havard, 'The Beacon in Port Jackson', *Journal of the Royal Australian Historical Society*, vol. 20, pt. 3, 1934, p. 272; Oppenheim, *The Fragile Forts*, p. 28.
44 John Dunmore Lang, *An Historical and Statistical Account of New South Wales*, vol. 2, Longman, Brown Green and Longman's, London, 1852, pp. 153–54.
45 See *Sydney Morning Herald*, 23 June 1849, for an extensive coverage of the issue, and Oppenheim, *The Fragile Forts*, pp. 39–40.
46 In Oppenheim, *The Fragile Forts*, p. 55.
47 The Port Master to the Secretary to the Treasury, 26 August 1857, quoted in RV Pockley, *Ancestor Hunt: The Pockley Family and Descendants in Australia 1842–1976*, Wentworth Books, Sydney, 1977, p. 26; see also *Sydney Morning Herald*, 22 August 1857.
48 *Sydney Morning Herald*, 22 August 1857.
49 Quoted in Tom Mead, *The Fatal Lights: Two Strange Tragedies of the Sea*, Dolphin Books, Sydney, [no date], p. 18.
50 Kendall, 'Drowned at Sea', in Reed, *The Poetical Works of Henry Kendall*, p. 51.
51 *Sydney Morning Herald*, 24 August 1857.
52 The crews of the pilot boats of Watsons Bay did not benefit from the rush to improve the harbour's navigation. The recommendation that they be supplied with schooners was ignored and the crews continued to use whaleboats powered by oars and sails – technology that had changed little since Phillip's time. Six were drowned fighting bad weather in a pilot's whaleboat in 1868. It was not until 1871 that the pilots got a steamer that could counter the swells and winds.
53 Henry Kendall, 'Sydney Harbour', in Reed, *The Poetical Works of Henry Kendall*, p. 394.
54 Pockley, *Ancestor Hunt*, p. 24.
55 *Sailing Directions for the Harbour of Port Jackson (Rendered Necessary by the Erection of a New Lighthouse and Additional Beacons. Survey by Captain Denham of the* Herald *and Compiled by Robert F Pockley, Harbour Master Under Supervision of the Light Pilot and Navigation Board)*, Government Printer, Sydney, 1858, p. 6.
56 Gavin Souter, *Mosman: A History*, Melbourne University Press, Melbourne, 1994, pp. 87–95.
57 PR Stephenson, *Sydney Sails: The Royal Yacht Squadron, 1862–1962*, Angus and Robertson Sydney, 1962, p. 29.
58 Ibid., p. 16.
59 See Leone Huntsman, *Sand in Our Souls: The Beach in Australian History*, Melbourne University Press, Melbourne, 2001, pp. 19–21.
60 Lachlan Macquarie Journal, entry for 13 April 1821, Mitchell Library A786.
61 Cunningham, *Two Years in New South Wales*, vol. 2, p. 208.
62 Earl Bathurst to Sir Thomas Brisbane, 1 January 1825, *HRA*, series 1, vol. 11, p. 437.
63 Reference to a government order of 21 August 1828 reserving 100 feet [30 metres] above high water was made by the surveyor-general Walker Rennie Davidson in the 'Report from the Select Committee on the Reserve, Lavender Bay', *New South Wales*

Legislative Assembly Votes and Proceedings,
vol. 5, 1866, p. 13. The above quote comes
from instructions sent by Colonial Secretary
Viscount Goderich to Governor Darling,
14 February 1831; see *HRA*, p. 851.

64 'Report from the Select Committee on the
Reserve, Lavender Bay', *New South Wales
Legislative Assembly Votes and Proceedings*,
vol. 5, 1866, pp. 3–4. For Manly baths, see
Pauline Curby, *Seven Miles from Sydney:
A History of Manly*, Manly Council, Sydney,
2002, p. 60.

65 Fred Cavill, quoted in Curby, *Seven Miles
from Sydney*, p. 126.

66 See John Ramsland, '"He is a fish, not
a man!" Barney Kieran, North Sydney
Amateur Swimming Club's First World-
champion Swimmer', unpublished paper,
2007.

67 *Illustrated Sydney News*, 3 February 1877.

68 Ibid., 7 January 1887.

69 Ramsland, 'He is a fish, not a man!'

Chapter 6

1 Tim Bonyhady, *The Colonial Earth*,
Miegunyah Press, Melbourne, 2000, p. 320.

2 The testimony is quoted at length in Eric
Russell, *The Opposite Shore: North Sydney and
its People*, North Shore Historical Society/
North Sydney Council, Sydney 1990,
pp. 173–78.

3 Michael Jones, *North Sydney 1788–1988*, Allen
and Unwin, Sydney, 1988, pp. 148–49.

4 Bonyhady, *The Colonial Earth*, p. 310.

5 Russell, *The Opposite Shore*, pp. 193–94.

6 Ibid., p. 193.

7 In Bonyhady, *The Colonial Earth*, p. 334.

8 Anthony Trollope, *Australia and New
Zealand*, George Robertson, Melbourne,
1873, p. 135.

9 *Freemans Journal*, 15 February 1896, quoted in
Russell, *The Opposite Shore*, p. 198.

10 Virginia Spate, *Tom Roberts*, Lansdowne
Press, Melbourne, 1978, p. 34.

11 Letter to Theodore Fink, undated, quoted in
Ann Galbally and Anne Gray, *Letters from
Smike: The Letters of Arthur Streeton 1890–
1943*, Oxford University Press, Melbourne,
1989, p. 17.

12 Ibid.

13 Mary Eagle maintains that Streeton was
almost certainly unaware of Curlew Camp
in 1890. Barry Pearce and Linda Slutzkin
suggest that he was painting from there in
that year. Much of the uncertainty stems from
the undated correspondence from Streeton
to Theodore Fink, quoted above. Pearce
and Slutzkin follow Galbally and Gray in
dating that to mid-1890. Eagle subsequently

suggested September 1891. I have followed
Eagle's chronology. See Mary Eagle, *The Oil
Paintings of Arthur Streeton in the National
Gallery of Australia*, National Gallery of
Australia, Canberra, 1994, p. 60; and Barry
Pearce and Linda Slutzkin, *Bohemians in
the Bush: The Artists Camps of Mosman*, Art
Gallery of New South Wales, Sydney, 1991,
p. 50.

14 Letter to Frederick Delmer [1891], in Galbally
and Gray, *Letters from Smike*, p. 34.

15 Letter to Tom Roberts April 1890, in ibid.,
p. 18.

16 In Eagle, *The Oil Paintings of Arthur Streeton*,
p. 66.

17 See Margaret Molloy, *A Century of Sydney's
Flying Sailors*, Sydney Flying Squadron,
Sydney, 1991, p. 9; John Ferguson (ed.),
*The Amateurs: The Second Century Begins
1972–1992*, Maritime Heritage Press, Sydney,
1997, pp. 1–6.

18 Frank Hutchinson and Francis Myers,
*The Australian Contingent: A History of the
Patriotic Movement in New South Wales*,
Government Printer, Sydney 1885, p. 59.

19 Quoted and carried forward in Bonyhady,
The Colonial Earth, p. 326.

20 *Australasian Star*, 26 September 1895, quoted
in Bonyhady, *The Colonial Earth*, p. 332.

21 *Bulletin*, 11 August 1900, quoted in Bonyhady,
The Colonial Earth, p. 327.

22 In RH Croll (ed.), *Smike to Bulldog: Letters
from Sir Arthur Streeton to Tom Roberts*, Ure
Smith Pty Ltd, Sydney, 1949, p. 90; Eagle, *The
Oil Paintings of Arthur Streeton*, p. 153.

23 Leigh Astbury, *City Bushmen: The Heidelberg
School and the Rural Mythology*, Oxford
University Press, Melbourne, 1986, p. 68.

24 Richard Twopeny, *Town Life in Australia*,
[1883], Penguin, Melbourne, 1973, p. 247.

25 Andrew Garran (ed.), *Picturesque Atlas of
Australasia*, vol. 1, Sydney, 1886, p. 66.

26 Vice Admiral N Bowden-Smith, 'Two Years
in Australian Waters', privately circulated
paper, speech given before Lord Hopetoun,
15 April 1896, p. 7.

27 James Inglis, *Our Australian Cousins*,
Macmillan and Co., London, 1880, p. 140.

28 Trollope, *Australia and New Zealand*, p. 141.

29 Francis Myers, *The Coastal Scenery, Harbours,
Mountains and Rivers, of New South Wales*,
Government Printer, Sydney, 1886, p. 8.

30 EJ Brady, *Sydney Harbour*, Builder Printing
Works, Fine Art Printers, Sydney, 1903, p. 14.

31 EJ Brady, *The Ways of Many Waters*, The
Bulletin Newspaper Co Ltd, Sydney, 1899,
p. 40.

32 In Colin Roderick (ed.), *Henry Lawson,
Collected Verse: 1885–1900*, Angus and
Robertson, Sydney, 1967, p. 349.

33 Olive Lawson, *Henry Lawson's North Sydney*, North Shore Historical Society, Sydney, 1999, p. 3.

34 'The Old Horse Ferry', [1914], in ibid., p. 93.

35 'The Kids', [1905], in ibid., p. 39.

36 Henry Lawson, 'Kerosene Bay 1914' and 'Balls Head', in Lawson, *Henry Lawson's North Sydney*, p. 79.

37 Henry Lawson, 'The Sacrifice of Balls Head', in ibid., p. 96.

38 'Report of the Commission Appointed to Inquire into the Condition of the Harbour of Port Jackson', *New South Wales Legislative Assembly Votes and Proceedings*, vol. 2, 1866, pp. 5, 9.

39 Ibid., p. 9.

40 Dan Huon Coward, *Out of Sight: Sydney's Environmental History, 1851–1981*, Australian National University, Canberra, 1988, p. 29.

41 'Report into the Condition of the Harbour of Port Jackson', p. 8.

42 'Final Report from the Select Committee on the Sydney Sewerage and Water Appropriation Bill', *New South Wales Legislative Council Votes and Proceedings of Legislative Council*, vol. 1, 1854, pp. 923–24.

43 Ibid., p. 924.

44 Ibid., p. 898.

45 Coward, *Out of Sight*, pp. 160–64.

46 Shirley Fitzgerald and Hilary Golder, *Pyrmont and Ultimo under Siege*, Hale and Iremonger, Sydney, 1994, p. 39.

47 Twopeny, *Town Life in Australia*, pp. 63–64

48 Coward, *Out of Sight*, p. 161.

49 *Illustrated Sydney News*, 29 November 1888.

50 Evidence to 'Select Committee on the Abattoir, Glebe Island', 1902, in Max Solling and Peter Reynolds, *Leichhardt: on the Margins of the City*, Allen and Unwin, Sydney, 1997, p. 152.

51 'Report on the Royal Commission to Inquire into and Report upon the Actual State and Prospects of the Fisheries of this Colony', *New South Wales Legislative Assembly Votes and Proceedings*, 1880, p. 1206.

52 'Glebe Island Abattoir Inquiry: Final Report', *New South Wales Legislative Assembly Votes and Proceedings*, vol. 5, 1879–80, p. 880.

53 'Report upon the Actual State and Prospects of the Fisheries', p. 1167.

54 *Country Gentleman's Newspaper*, December, 1876, quoted in *The Good Old Days? Historical Insights into New South Wales Coastal Fishing Populations and their Fisheries, Report to the New South Wales Recreational Fishing Trust Expenditure Committee*, Pepperell Research and Consulting Pty Ltd, p. 47.

55 'Report upon the Actual State and Prospects of the Fisheries', pp. 1217, 1237.

56 RB Walker, 'Fauna and Flora Protection in New South Wales, 1866–1948', *Journal of Australian Studies*, no. 28, March 1991, p. 17.

57 'An Act to Protect the Fisheries of New South Wales [1st June 1865] 28 Vic No. 10', in *Public General Statues of New South Wales 1862–1874*, Government Printer, Sydney, 1874, pp. 3630–31.

58 From a series of articles in the *Sydney Mail*, 1874, reprinted in *Royal Commission 1880*, p. 1288.

59 Alexander Oliver MA, *The Fisheries of New South Wales*, Government Printer, Sydney 1871, p. 2.

60 Peter Stanbury and Julian Holland (eds), *Mr Macleay's Celebrated Cabinet: The History of the Macleays and their Museum*, Macleay Museum, Sydney, 1988, p. 47; Robyn Stacey and Ashley Hay, *Museum: The Macleays, their Collections and the Search for Order*, Cambridge University Press, Melbourne, 2007, pp. 32–33.

61 The Marine Biological Station operated from 1881 to 1886 and was then turned over to the Department of Defence.

62 See *Proceedings of Linnean Society of New South Wales*, vol. 5, 1880–81.

63 'Report on the Actual State and Prospects of the Fisheries', 1880, p. 1161.

64 Ibid., pp.1219–23.

65 Ibid., pp. 1189, 1184.

66 Ibid., pp. 1240, 1254–56.

67 Ibid., p. 1161.

68 Ibid., p. 1244.

69 Ibid., p. 1131.

70 TA Coghlan, *The Wealth and Progress of New South Wales, 1894*, Government Printer, Sydney 1896, p. 901. This figure is calculated by adding the populations of the North-western, Western, Eastern and Northern districts given in Coghlan. Not all the suburbs in these districts had waterfronts.

71 Warwick Gullet, *Fisheries Law in Australia*, LexisNexis Butterworth, Chatswood, 2008, pp. 60, 82–83.

72 Many years later the depletion of the finite resources of the common places such as the sea would be called 'the tragedy of the commons'. See Garrett Hardin, 'The Tragedy of the Commons', *Science*, 162, 1968, pp. 1243–48.

73 'An Act to Provide for the Development and Regulation of the Fisheries of the Colony', [6 April 1881], in *Public Statues of New South Wales 1879–1885*, Government Printer, Sydney, 1886, pp. 293–311.

74 Lindsay G Thompson, *History of the Fisheries of New South Wales*, Government Printer for the New South Wales Commissioners for the World's Columbian Exposition, Sydney, 1893, p. 39.

75 'Report of the Royal Commission to Report on the Best Means of Developing the Marine and Other Fisheries of New South Wales', *New South Wales Legislative Assembly Votes and Proceedings*, vol. 6, 1894–95, p. 213.
76 Brady, *Sydney Harbour*, p. 4.

Chapter 7

1 *Daily Telegraph*, 17 November 1893, quoted in Bonyhady, *The Colonial Earth*, p. 314.
2 William Allen, 'Australia Federata: A Cantata', in *Sydney Morning Herald,* 1 January 1901.
3 *Sydney Morning Herald*, 2 January 1901.
4 Kerr, *Admiralty House: A Conservation Plan*, pp. 32–34.
5 Jean Duncan Foley, *In Quarantine: A History of Sydney's Quarantine Station 1828–1984*, Kangaroo Press, Sydney, 1994, pp. 96–99.
6 Angas, *Savage Life and Scenes*, vol. 1, p. 201.
7 Peter Curson and Kevin McCracken, *Plague in Sydney: The Anatomy of an Epidemic*, UNSW Press, Sydney, [no date], pp. 118–30, 147–48.
8 *Port Laws and Regulations for Port Jackson*, 1899, p. 23.
9 Fitzgerald, *Red Tape Gold Scissors,* pp. 83–84; Curson and McCracken, *Plague in Sydney*, pp. 174–76.
10 WM Hughes, *Crusts and Crusades*, Angus and Robertson, Sydney, 1947, p. 174. See also Shirley Fitzgerald and Chris Keating, *Millers Point: The Urban Village*, Hale and Iremonger, Sydney, 1992, pp. 65–73.
11 Curson and McCracken, *Plague in Sydney*, pp. 163, 157.
12 Fitzgerald and Keating, *Millers Point*, p. 76.
13 Curson and McCracken, *Plague in Sydney*, p. 59; Fitzgerald and Keating, *Millers Point*, p. 73.
14 Joseph Conrad, *The Mirror of the Sea: Memories and Impressions*, JM Dent and Sons, London, 1968, p. 121. The ship was the *Otago*. See Norman Sherry, *Conrad's Eastern World*, Cambridge University Press, London, 1966, p. 33.
15 There were 292 213 tons in 1860 and 2 716 651 in 1900. See HD Walsh, 'Notes on Harbour Engineering', in *Sydney University Engineering Society Journal and Proceedings for 1911*, vol. 14, p. 76.
16 Norman Selfe, 'The Quays, Wharves and Shipping of Port Jackson, Past, Present and Prospective', paper presented to Engineering Association of New South Wales, 9 July 1908, p. 100.
17 Kimberley Webber and Ian Hoskins, *What's in Store? A History of Retailing in Australia*, Powerhouse Publishing, Sydney, 2003, pp. 31–33.
18 TA Coghlan, *Wealth and Progress of New South Wales 1894*, pp. 30–32.
19 Alan Roberts, 'Planning Sydney's Transport 1875–1900', in Max Kelly (ed.), *Nineteenth Century Sydney: Essays in Urban History*, Sydney University Press/Sydney History Group, Sydney, 1976, pp. 25–29, 32.
20 *Sydney Morning Herald*, 11 December 1913, quoted in Margo Beasley, 'Sarah Dawes and the Coal Lumpers: Absence and Presence on the Sydney Waterfront 1900–1917', PhD thesis, Department of History and Politics, University of Wollongong, p. 111.
21 Walsh, 'Notes on Harbour Engineering', p. 79.
22 Ibid., pp. 90–96; Fitzgerald and Keating, *Millers Point*, p. 81; Chris Pratten and Robert Irving, 'Pier One, Sydney', *Fabrications*, 6 June 1995, pp. 1–8.
23 'Report on the Condition of the Working Classes of the Metropolis', p. 1275.
24 Beasley, 'Sarah Dawes', p. 111; 'Report of the Royal Commission into the Improvement of the City of Sydney and its Suburbs', *New South Wales Parliamentary Papers,* vol. 5, 1909, p. 180.
25 *Waterside Worker*, 22 March 1952, p. 6. See also Winifred Mitchell, 'Sydney's Wharfies: The First Fifty Years of Unionism', in Garry Wotherspoon (ed.), *Sydney's Transport: Studies in Urban History*, Hale and Iremonger, Sydney, 1983, pp. 31–32.
26 Lillian Kent, born in Millers Point in 1912, quoted in Fitzgerald and Keating, *Millers Point*, p. 80.
27 *Sydney Morning Herald*, 1 February 1901, 5 February 1901.
28 'Report into the Improvement of the City of Sydney and its Suburbs', p. xxxix.
29 Ibid., pp. xxxv, 123.; see also Sacha Jenkins, 'Our Harbour: A Cultural History of Sydney Harbour, 1880–1938', PhD thesis, Department of History, University of Sydney, 2002.
30 Selfe, 'The Quays, Wharves and Shipping of Port Jackson', p.121.
31 'Report into the Improvement of the City of Sydney and its Suburbs', p. 150.
32 *Sydney Morning Herald*, 21 July 1911.
33 Julie Petersen, 'Nielson Park: The Bush Beach', *Locality*, Autumn 2001, p. 14.
34 Jo Anne Pomfrett, 'New Reflections on an Old House: Vaucluse House and its History as a Museum', *Public History Review*, vol. 3, 1994, pp. 148–66.
35 Peter Spearritt, *Sydney's Century*, UNSW Press, Sydney, 1999, p. 68.
36 Caroline Butler-Bowden and Charles Pickett, *Homes in the Sky*, Miegunyah Press, Melbourne, 2008, p. 58.

37 Slessor, 'The Harbour through my Window', p. 5.
38 Lloyd Rees, *The Small Treasures of a Lifetime: Some Memories of Australian Art and Artists*, Collins, Sydney, 1989, pp. 63, 64.
39 John Gunter, *Across the Harbour: The Story of Sydney's Ferries*, Rigby, Sydney, 1978, pp. 17–21.
40 Graeme Andrews, *Ferries of Sydney*, Sydney University Press/Oxford University Press, Sydney, 1994, pp. 42, 49, 52–57.
41 DH Lawrence, *Kangaroo*, [1922], Penguin, Melbourne, 1976, p. 5.
42 In Lianne Hall (ed.), *Down the Bay: The Changing Foreshores of North Sydney*, North Sydney Council, Sydney, 1997, pp. 20–21.
43 Quoted in Souter, *Mosman*, p. 140.
44 Lawrence, *Kangaroo*, p. 5.
45 Advance Australia, September 1927, in Spearritt, *Sydney's Century*, p. 33.
46 Walter Burley Griffin, quoted in Esther Leslie (ed.), *The Suburb of Castlecrag: A Community History*, Willoughby Municipal Council, Sydney, 1988, p. 73.
47 See Peter Harrison, *Walter Burley Griffin: Landscape Architect*, National Library of Australia, Canberra, 1995, p. 77.
48 In John Slater, *Through Artists' Eyes: Australian Suburbs and Their Cities 1919–1945*, Miegunyah Press, Melbourne, 2005, p. 183.
49 Deborah Edwards, *Margaret Preston*, Art Gallery of New South Wales, Sydney, 2005, p. 82.
50 Section 313 of the 1919 Local Government Act in Denis Winston, *Sydney's Great Experiment: The Progress of the Cumberland County Plan*, Angus and Robertson, Sydney, 1957, p. 28.
51 William Beard, *'Neath Austral Skies*, J. Bell and Co., Sydney, 1948, pp. 58–59.
52 Quoted in A. James Hammerton and Alastair Thompson, *Ten Pound Poms: Australia's Invisible Migrants*, Manchester University Press, Manchester, 2005, p. 125.
53 In Peter Spearritt, *The Sydney Harbour Bridge: A Life*, UNSW Press, Sydney, 2007, p. 27.
54 Ray Wedgwood and Caroline Mackaness, 'An Engineering Marvel', in Caroline Mackaness (ed.), *Bridging Sydney*, Historic Houses Trust of New South Wales, Sydney, 2006, pp. 63–64.
55 Rees, *Small Treasures of a Lifetime*, p. 63.
56 Unidentified newspapers dated 1925 and 28 July 1924, in Watson Press Clippings, vol. 25, pp. 25, 1, Royal Australian Historical Society Research Library.
57 *Sydney Morning Herald*, 11 February 1925, in Mackaness, *Bridging Sydney*, p. 140.
58 Quoted in Mackaness, *Bridging Sydney*, p. 147.
59 JJC Bradfield, 'The Sydney Harbour Bridge', paper read before the Institute of Architects,

Architecture, 15 October 1921, in Mackaness *Bridging Sydney*, p. 111.
60 *Great Northern*, 15 April 1935.
61 In Daina Fletcher, 'Swimmers, Sharks and Social Control', *Signals*, June–August 2004, p. 10.
62 Eleanor Dark, *Waterway*, FH Johnston Publishing Co., Sydney, 1946, pp. 12–13.
63 *Sydney Mail*, 2 February 1938, p. 5.
64 Ibid., p. 6.

Chapter 8

1 Diary of No. 914 AA Barwick C Company 1st Battalion, Mitchell Library, MLMSS 1493. See also memories of Signaller RJ Kenny of the 4th Battalion, in Patsy Adam Smith, *The Anzacs,* Nelson, Melbourne, 1978, pp. 30–31.
2 See Australian War Memorial photograph E04795.
3 In Ian Hoskins, '*Was thinking of home today …': North Sydney and the Great War*, North Sydney Council, Sydney 2008, p. 49.
4 *Sydney Mail*, 8 October 1913.
5 Graeme Andrews, *The Watermen of Sydney: Memories of a Working Harbour*, Turton and Armstrong, Sydney, 2004, p. 21.
6 John Jeremy, *Cockatoo Island: Sydney's Historic Dockyard*, UNSW Press, Sydney, 1998, p. 184.
7 Parker, *Cockatoo Island*, pp. 22, 31.
8 Ibid., p. 29; Jeremy, *Cockatoo Island*, p. 30
9 TR Frame, *The Garden Island*, Kangaroo Press, Kenthurst, 1990, pp. 173–74.
10 In Margo Beasley, *Wharfies: the History of the Waterside Workers' Federation,* Halstead Press/Australian National Maritime Museum, Sydney, 1996, p. 50.
11 See Richard Morris, 'Australia's Naval Coaling Battalion 1916–17: The Brief Militarisation of the Sydney Coal Lumpers', *Great Circle*, vol. 22, no. 2, 2000, pp. 44–45; Bach, *A Maritime History of Australia*, p. 328.
12 Captain James Gaby, *The Restless Waterfront*, Antipodean Publishers, Sydney, 1974, pp. 33–34.
13 Beasley, 'Sarah Dawes', pp. 205–6.
14 SR Carver, *Official Year Book of New South Wales 1945–1946*, Government of New South Wales, Sydney, [1948], p. 801; Beasley, 'Sarah Dawes', pp. 105–25.
15 Garden Island Chaplain Vivian Thompson, quoted in Frame, *The Garden Island*, p. 180.
16 *Report of the Royal Commission into the Cockatoo Island Dockyard*, 1921, quoted in Parker, *Cockatoo Island*, p. 33.
17 Frame, *The Garden Island*, p. 179.
18 Parker, *Cockatoo Island*, p. 35.
19 Barry Pemberton, *Australian Coastal Shipping*, Melbourne University Press, Melbourne, 1979, p. 165.

20 G Thow, 'Oil Tankers of the Future', *Sea, Land and Air*, 1 February 1921, p. 724.
21 Pemberton, *Australian Coastal Shipping*, pp. 148, 166.
22 Jack West, Sydney Maritime Museum Interviews, Mitchell Library MLOH 134/27.
23 Randi Svenson, *Wooden Boats, Iron Men: The Halvorsen Story*, Halstead Press, Sydney, 2007, pp. 44, 79–89.
24 Peter Grose, *A Very Rude Awakening: The Night Japanese Midget Subs Came to Sydney Harbour*, Allen and Unwin, Sydney, 2007, p. 48.
25 See list in Parker, *Cockatoo Island*, pp. 76–77.
26 Peter Plowman, *Across the Sea to War: Australian and New Zealand Troop Transports from 1865 through Two World Wars to Korea and Vietnam*, Rosenberg, Dural, 2003, pp. 118, 212, 215.
27 Ibid., p. 124.
28 Ibid., pp. 125–26.
29 William Keays (ed.), *The Australians Soldiers' Pocket Book*, 9th edition, April 1943, pp. 88–89.
30 William Morris Hughes, *The Price of Peace*, Defence of Australia League, Sydney, 1934, pp. 70, 78.
31 Frame, *The Garden Island*, p. 190.
32 In Oppenheim, *The Fragile Forts*, p. 250.
33 Frame, *The Garden Island*, p. 190.
34 Nancy Keesing, *Garden Island People*, Wentworth Books, Sydney, 1974, p. 38.
35 Attenbrow, *Sydney's Aboriginal Past*, p. 38.
36 In Frame, *The Garden Island*, p. 200.
37 An in-depth account of the raid can be found in Grose, *A Very Rude Awakening*.
38 *Sydney Morning Herald*, 2 June 1942.
39 In Spearritt, *Sydney's Century*, p. 78.
40 In Joanna Penglase and David Horner, *When the War Came to Australia*, Allen and Unwin, Sydney, 1992, p. 129.
41 *National Geographic Magazine*, March 1943, quoted in Macmillan and Birch, *The Sydney Scene*, pp. 348–50.
42 Bruce Stannard, *The Blue Water Bushmen: The Colourful Story of Australia's Best and Boldest Boatmen*, Angus and Robertson, Sydney, 1981, p. 19; Fred Thomas, *Boating Legends of Sydney Harbour*, Lothian, Melbourne, 2006, pp. 31–34, 99–108.
43 See obituary in *Sydney Morning Herald*, 18 October 2007.
44 Lou d'Alpuget, *Let's Go Sailing*, Ure Smith, [Sydney], 1951, p. 34.
45 *Sydney Morning Herald*, 18 October 2007.

Chapter 9

1 Tom Uren, *Straight Left*, Vintage, Sydney, 1995, pp. 55–56.
2 In Klaus Neumann, *Refuge Australia: Australia's Humanitarian Record*, UNSW Press, Sydney, 2004, p. 28.
3 *Belongings: Post World War Two Migration Memories and Journeys*, database, Migration Heritage Centre NSW.
4 In the early 1950s TC Roughley was still decrying the overfishing of estuary and harbour waters in Australia. See his *Fish and Fisheries of Australia*, Angus and Robertson, Sydney 1951, p. 168.
5 *Belongings*. See also Heather George, 'The Australian Scene', *Walkabout*, November 1962, pp. 23–25; Annette Salt, *The Fishermen of Iron Cove*, Leichhardt Council/Public Centre for Public History, University of Technology, Sydney, c. 2006, p. 22.
6 *Report of the Planning Scheme for the County of Cumberland Council New South Wales*, 27 July 1948, Cumberland Country Council, Sydney, 1948, p. 156.
7 *Sydney Morning Herald*, 17 July 1959.
8 Ibid., 28 January 1959.
9 See Paul Ashton, *The Accidental City: Planning Sydney since 1788*, Hale and Iremonger, Sydney, 1993, p. 76.
10 Kenneth Slessor, 'A Portrait of Sydney', in Gwen Morton Spencer and Sam Ure Smith (eds), *Portrait of Sydney: A Photographic Impression*, Sydney, [1950], p. 11; *Report of the Planning Scheme for the County of Cumberland Council*, p. 195.
11 'Preparations for the New Passenger Ships', *Port of Sydney*, September 1960, pp. 104–7.
12 Sir Archibald Howie, in Robert Freestone, 'Preserving Sydney's Built Heritage in the Early Twentieth Century', *Australian Historical Studies*, no. 112, April 1999, p. 57.
13 Shirley Fitzgerald, *East Circular Quay 1788–1998*, City of Sydney, Sydney, 1998, p. 9.
14 Ashton, *The Accidental City*, p. 78.
15 This came in 1957; see ibid., pp. 77–78.
16 'AMP Head Office Sydney', *Architecture in Australia*, June 1962, pp. 108–9, 147.
17 See Fitzgerald, *East Circular Quay*, pp. 19–29.
18 *Sydney Morning Herald*, 25 October 1958.
19 Ibid., 31 October 1958.
20 Thomas Shapcott, 'The Man who Proposed Bennelong Point', *Sydney Review*, August 1995, p. 3; Anne Watson, 'An Opera House for Sydney: Genesis and Conclusion of a Competition', in Anne Watson (ed.), *Building a Masterpiece: The Sydney Opera House*, Powerhouse Publishing, Sydney, 2006, pp. 40–43.
21 From Joe Cahill's speech at the conference 'to consider the establishment of an Opera House in Sydney', 1954, quoted in Watson, 'An Opera House for Sydney', p. 43.
22 Philip Drew, 'Poetic Paradox: Utzon's Sources

for the Sydney Opera House', in Watson, *Building a Masterpiece*, pp. 73–74.

23 In Françoise Fromonot, *Jørn Utzon: The Sydney Opera House*, Gingko Press, Corte Madera CA, 1998, p. 64.

24 Drew, 'Poetic Paradox', p. 74.

25 Philip Drew, *The Masterpiece: Jørn Utzon, A Secret Life*, Hardie Grant Books, Melbourne, 1999, pp. 194–97.

26 Jørn Utzon, 'The Sydney Opera House', *Architecture in Australia*, December 1965, pp. 79–80.

27 In Andrew Metcalf, *Architecture in Transition: The Sulman Award 1932–1996*, Historic Houses Trust, Sydney, 1997, p. 128.

28 Utzon, quoted in Fromonot, *Jørn Utzon*, pp. 113, 123.

29 Ibid., pp. 114–123.

30 Sigried Giedion, 'Jørn Utzon and the Third Generation', [1967], in Ann Stephen, Andrew McNamara and Philip Goad (eds), *Modernism and Australia: Documents on Art Design and Architecture 1917–1967*, Miegunyah Press, Melbourne, 2006, pp. 967–82.

31 See Drew, *The Masterpiece*, p. 157.

32 Alice Spigelman, *Almost Full Circle: Harry Seidler, A Biography*, Brandl and Schlesinger, Sydney, 2001, p. 169.

33 Ibid., p. 191.

34 *Sydney Morning Herald*, 1 April 1958.

35 The comment came from architectural academic and critic George Molnar, quoted in Caroline Butler-Bowden and Charles Pickett, *Homes in the Sky: Apartment Living in Australia*, Historic Houses Trust of New South Wales/Miegunyah Press, Sydney/Melbourne, 2007, p. 105.

36 *Sydney Morning Herald*, 10 September 1959.

37 Kenneth Frampton and Philip Drew, *Harry Seidler: Four Decades of Architecture*, Thames and Hudson, New York, 1992, pp. 48–49, 50–51.

38 *Sydney Morning Herald*, 1 April 1958.

39 Ibid., 10 September 1959.

40 WE Lucas and Ruth Lucas, 'Lucas House: Castlecrag', *Architecture in Australia*, October–December 1958, p. 61.

41 L Peter Kollar, 'The Problem of Duality: Function or Beauty', *Architecture in Australia*, October–December 1958, p. 78.

42 Harry Seidler, Lyle Dunlap et al., *Urban Redevelopment Concerns You!*, [McMahons Point and Lavender Bay Progress Association], Sydney, 1957, p. 10; Peter Hall, *Cities of Tomorrow: An Intellectual History of Urban Planning and Design in the Twentieth Century*, Basil Blackwell, Oxford, 1988, p. 215.

43 *Sydney Morning Herald*, 10 September 1957.

44 *Daily Telegraph*, 22 October 1958.

45 *Report of Planning Scheme for County of Cumberland*, p. 192.

46 Ibid., p. 190.

47 Ibid., pp. 193–94.

48 *Sydney Morning Herald*, 12 January 1957.

49 Seidler, Dunlap, et al., *Urban Redevelopment Concerns You!*, pp. 4–7.

50 *Sun Herald*, 26 October 1958.

51 McKay and Jackson were writing in 1957, see Stephen, McNamara and Goad, *Modernism and Australia*, pp. 901–9.

52 'Report on the Projected Development of 14–28 Blues Point Road, McMahons Point, January 19, 1959', Cumberland Council Minute Paper, in Sigelman, *Almost Full Circle*, p. 207.

53 *Report of Planning Scheme for the County of Cumberland*, p. 198.

54 Merle Coppell Oral History Collection, OH 206, North Sydney Heritage Centre/Stanton Library.

55 Coppell Collection, OH 245.

56 Robin Boyd, *The New Architecture*, Longmans, Sydney, 1963, p. 22.

57 The block was built as a co-operative venture, see Jill Roe, 'Three visions of Sydney Heads from Balmoral Beach', in Jill Roe (ed.), *Twentieth Century Sydney: Studies in Urban and Social History*, Hale and Iremonger with Sydney History Group, Sydney, 1980, p. 104.

58 Gavin Souter and George Molnar, *Sydney Observed*, Angus and Robertson, Sydney, 1968, p. 128.

59 The description came from Max Kelly, one of the city's most respected historians and heritage campaigners. See his 'Sydney Icons', *Sydney Review*, March 1989, p. 3.

60 Le Corbusier, *The City of Tomorrow and its Planning*, [1929] Architectural Press, London, 1971, p. 244.

61 See Charles Bertie, *Old Colonial By-Ways*, [1928] Ure Smith/National Trust of Australia (NSW), Sydney, 1974, p. 24.

62 These are the Wylde Street Cooperative Apartments; see Butler-Bowden and Pickett, *Homes in the Sky*, pp. 108–12.

63 'Reality on the Rocks', *Architecture in Australia*, June 1963, pp. 51–71.

64 Park, *Fishing in the Styx*, pp. 62–64, 279–80, 282. Her subsequent book about childhood in the Rocks, *Playing Beattie Bow*, became a classic of Australian children's literature.

65 Richard J Roddewig, *Green Bans: The Birth of the Australian Environmental Politics*, Hale and Iremonger, Sydney, 1978, p. 21.

66 Quoted in ibid., p. 22.

67 Quoted in Meredith Burgmann and Verity Burgmann, *Green Bans, Red Union: Environmental Activism and the New South Wales Builders Labourers' Federation*, UNSW Press, Sydney, 1998, p. 47.

68 Indeed the goals and effectiveness of the movement directly inspired the development of 'green politics' in Europe; ibid., pp. 9–10.

69 Bob Pringle and Jack Mundey, Foreword, in Pete Thomas, *Taming the Concrete Jungle: The Builders Laborers' Story*, NSW Branch of Australian Building Construction Employees and Builders Laborers' Federation, Sydney, 1973, p. 3.

70 Quoted in Roddewig, *Green Bans*, p. 25.

71 See George Morgan, 'History on the Rocks', in John Rickard and Peter Spearritt (eds), *Packaging the Past: Public Histories*, Melbourne University Press, Melbourne, 1991, pp. 78–87; Tony Bennett, 'History on the Rocks', in John Frow and Meaghan Morris (eds), *Australian Cultural Studies: A Reader*, Allen and Unwin, Sydney, 1993, pp. 231–34.

72 Quoted in Roddewig, *Green Bans*, p. 27.

Chapter 10

1   Glenda Adams, 'Beyond the Turkey Gobblers', in Drusilla Modjeska (ed.), *Inner Cities*, Penguin, Melbourne, 1989, pp. 18–19.

2   Fitzgerald and Keating, *Millers Point*, p. 107.

3   Ibid., p. 91.

4   *A Ten Year Port Redevelopment Plan*, Maritime Services Board, Sydney, September 1966, pp. 7–19.

5   Ronald Thiele interviewed on 27 August 1984, Sydney Maritime Museum Oral History Project, Mitchell Library, MLOH 134/17.

6   *Sydney Region Outline Plan Review*, New South Wales Planning and Environment Commission, Sydney, 1980, p. 4.

7   Mahoney, *Botany Bay*, pp. 65–77.

8   MT Daly, *Sydney Boom, Sydney Bust: The City and its Property Market 1950–1981*, Allen and Unwin, Sydney, 1982, p. 5.

9   Maurie T Daly and Bill Pritchard, 'Sydney: Australia's Financial and Corporate Capital', in John Connell (ed.), *Sydney, Emergence of a World City*, Oxford University Press, Melbourne, 2000, p. 167.

10 Adams, 'Beyond the Turkey Gobblers', p. 18.

11 'The Difference Looking Back', in Robert Adamson and Juno Gemes, *The Language of Oysters*, Craftsman House, Sydney, 1997, p. 59.

12 See Sant and Waitt, p. 206; Jim Davidson and Peter Spearritt, *Holiday Business: Tourism in Australia since 1870*, Melbourne University Press, Melbourne, 2000, p. 330.

13 Morgan Sant, 'Accommodating Recreational Demand: Boating in Sydney Harbour, Australia', *Geoforum*, vol. 21, no. 1, p. 100; WM Widmer and AJ Underwood, 'Factors Affecting Traffic and Anchoring Patterns of Recreational Boats in Sydney Harbour, Australia', *Landscape and Urban Planning*, 66, (2004), p. 174.

14 Andrews, *Ferries of Sydney*, p. 179.

15 Alice Doyle, *Doyle's Seafood Cookbook: Recipes and Memories from Australia's First Family of Seafood*, HarperCollins, Sydney, 2005, pp. 13–23.

16 In Christopher Sweeney, *Sydney Harbour*, Collins, Sydney, 1989, p. 200.

17 Arthur Cox and Mollie Peel in *Doors were Always Open: Recollections of Pyrmont and Ultimo*, City West Development Corporation, Sydney, 1997, p. 38.

18 Hal Missingham, *Good Fishing: A Handy Guide for Australia: How to Catch and How to Cook Them,* Dymocks Book Arcade, Sydney, [1953], p. 65.

19 Doyle, *Doyles Seafood Cookbook*, pp. 18, 21.

20 See Francoise Fromonot and Christopher Thompson, *Sydney: History of a Landscape*, Vilo Publishing, Paris, 2000, pp. 122–29.

21 For a discussion of the Darling Harbour design and its critics, see John Docker, *Postmodernism and Popular Culture: A Cultural History,* Cambridge University Press, Melbourne, 1994, pp. 93–102; and Mark Aarons, *A Place for People: The Transformation of Sydney's Darling Harbour*, Sydney Harbour Foreshore Authority, Sydney, 2009, pp. 14–23.

22 *Darling Harbour Authority Annual Report 1986*, quoted in Margo Huxley, 'Making Cities Fun: Darling Harbour and the Immobilisation of Spectacle', in Peter Carroll et al. (eds), *Tourism in Australia*, Harcourt Brace Jovanovich, Sydney, 1991, p. 143.

23 *Heritage Conservation News*, vol. 4, no. 1, 1986, p. 4.

24 Fitzgerald and Golder, *Pyrmont and Ultimo Under Siege*, p. 115.

25 Quoted in Aarons, *A Place for People*, p. 8.

26 See Huxley, 'Making Cities Fun', p. 149.

27 Max Kelly, 'Gateway to the Ordinary', *Sydney Review*, September 1990, p. 3.

28 John Reid quoted in Peter Spearritt, 'Celebration of a Nation', in Susan Janson and Stuart Macintyre (eds), *Making the Bicentenary*, Melbourne University Press, 1988, p. 5.

29 *Sydney Morning Herald*, 20 January 1988.

30 Paul Ashton, *Waving the Waratah: Bicentenary New South Wales*, New South Wales Bicentennial Council, Sydney, 1989, pp. 109–13.

31 *Sydney Morning Herald*, 26 January 1988.

32 The description was from the state minister for the Olympics, Michael Knight.

33 Rod McGeogh and Glenda Korporaal, *Bid: How Australia Won the 2000 Games*, William Heinemann, Melbourne, 1994, p. 66.

34 Ibid., pp. 61–68.

35 *Sun Herald's Olympic Games Countdown Calendar*, September 1999–October 2000.
36 *City of Sydney Annual Report, 1997–1998*, City of Sydney, Sydney, 1998, p. 19.
37 *Olympic City: Central Sydney Celebrations for the 2000 Games*, OCA, Sydney, 1999, pp. 3–11.
38 *International Visitors to Australia: Annual Results of the International Visitor Survey, 1999–2002*, Survey Research Section, Bureau of Tourism Research, Canberra, 2003, p. 47.
39 See Gordon Waitt, 'Selling Paradise and Adventure: Representations of Landscape in the Tourist Advertising of Australia, *Australian Geographer*, April 1997, vol. 35, no. 1, p. 56.
40 *Anholt City Brands Index*, 3rd edition, 2007, p. 5; *Sun Herald*, 2 March 2008.
41 See Chris Eves and Alastair Adair, 'An Analysis of the Sydney Prestige Waterfront Property Market: 1991–2002', *Pacific Rim Property Research Journal*, vol. 11, no. 1, March 2005, pp. 53–56.
42 David Williamson, *Emerald City*, Currency Press, Sydney, 1987, p. 2.
43 Ibid., p. 60.
44 Kristin Williamson, *David Williamson: Behind the Scenes*, Penguin Books, Melbourne, 2009, p. 298.
45 Daly, *Sydney Boom, Sydney Bust*, p. 191; *Sydney Morning Herald*, 10 January 2008, 9–10 August 2008.
46 Meg Stewart, 'Denizens of Balmain', *Sydney Review*, March 1990, p. 9.
47 Jane Jacobs, *The Death and Life of Great American Cities: The Failure of Town Planning*, [1961], Pelican Books, Harmondsworth, 1972, pp. 404–5.
48 Brett Whiteley exhibition note, quoted in Sandra McGrath, *Brett Whiteley*, Bay Books, Sydney, 1979, p. 168.
49 WA Tainsh, 'Port O'Sydney', *Shell Cruises for Boat Owners: Sydney Harbour*, [Sydney, 1930], p. 26.
50 Peter Carey, *30 Days in Sydney: A Wildly Distorted Account*, Bloomsbury, London, 2001, p. 3.
51 Peter Reynolds and Robert Irving, *Balmain in Time: A Record of a Historic Suburb and Some of Its Buildings*, Balmain Association, Sydney, 1971, p. 40.
52 Ibid., p. 40.
53 Solling and Reynolds, *Leichhardt*, p. 240.
54 Jim Colman, 'The Baby and the Bathwater', *Sydney Review*, March 1993, p. 3.
55 Ken Beashel in Fred Thomas, *Boating Legends of Sydney Harbour*, pp. 58–59.
56 J Punter, 'Urban Design in Central Sydney 1945–2005: Laissez Faire and Discretionary

Traditions in the Accidental City', *Progress in Planning*, no. 63, 2005, p. 103.
57 Tim Bonyhady, 'The Battle for Balmain', in Patrick Troy (ed.), *Australian Cities: Issues, Strategies and Policies for Urban Australia in the 1990s*, Cambridge University Press, Melbourne, 1995, pp. 130, 134.
58 *Sydney Morning Herald*, 21 October 2003.
59 Bonyhady, 'Battle for Balmain', p. 122.
60 *Sydney Morning Herald*, 1 December 1993.
61 Michael Bounds, 'Property Values and Popular Politics', *Australian Planner*, March 1991, p. 17.
62 'Sydney Harbour Foreshore, A Statement by the Premier of New South Wales, August 1997', quoted in *New South Wales Auditor-General's Report Performance Audit: Disposal of Sydney Harbour Foreshore Land*, Audit Office of New South Wales, Sydney, 2003, p. 10.
63 *Sydney Morning Herald*, 6 October 2005.
64 Ibid., p. 31.
65 See letters to the *Sydney Morning Herald*, 11 September 1996, 5 November 1996.
66 Lawrence Nield, 'That Wharf Again', *Sydney Review*, December 1990, p. 3.
67 BH Vaughan MLC, 'Woolloomooloo Finger Wharf Redevelopment', *NSW Parliamentary Hansard*, 22 April 1993.
68 *The Sydney Magazine*, November 2003, p. 42.
69 *Performance Audit: Walsh Bay*, Audit Office of NSW, Sydney, 1998, p. 16.
70 *Sydney Morning Herald*, 5 August 1998.
71 Ibid., 13 August 2008.
72 Andrew Andersons, 'Pressures on the Designer', *Proceedings of Adaptive Reuse: Continuity and Creativity*, National Trust (NSW), 9–10 November 2000, p. 64.
73 Richard Leplastrier and Roderick Simpson, 'Redundant Industrial Sites: Catalyst for a Reworking of the Harbour', unpublished discussion paper, 1999, North Sydney Heritage Centre Research Collection.
74 *Sydney Morning Herald*, 13 October 2003.
75 Quoted in ibid., 11–12 October 2003.
76 Ibid.
77 'The Future of Sydney Harbour', *Proceedings of the Working Harbour Summit*, 24 October 2003, National Trust of Australia (NSW), Sydney, 2003, pp. 15, 35–6; letter to *Sydney Morning Herald*, 7 October 2003.
78 Phil McManus, 'The Changing Port-city Interface: Moving towards Sustainability', *State of Australian Cities Conference Proceedings*, Vol. 3, 2007, Adelaide, pp. 427–433.
79 The quote comes from the society's website <www.glebesociety.org.au/AboutTGSI/BaysAndForeshores/the-bays>, accessed May 2009.

80 *Major Project Assessment: Sydney Slipway Marine Maintenance Facility, Rozelle Bay*, Director General's Environmental Assessment Report, 2006, p. 6.

82 Quoted in Lianne Hall, *Down the Bay*, North Sydney Council, Sydney, 1997, p. 44.

Afterword

1 Paul Barry, *Who Wants to be a Billionaire?: The James Packer Story*, Allen and Unwin, Crows Nest, 2009, p. 4.

2 Lucy Macken, 'How very Sydney: City's ultra-rich don't live in houses, they build mega-compounds', *Domain*, 30 March 2018, <https://www.domain.com.au/news/how-very-sydney-citys-ultrarich-dont-live-in-houses-they-build-megacompounds-20180330-h0y3v2/>, accessed 2 April 2022.

3 'Packer's Crown Casino Gamble: A Tale of big money, lobbying and political influence', *Four Corners*, ABC TV broadcast 31 May 2021, <https://www.abc.net.au/4corners/packer%E2%80%99s-crown-casino-gamble/13366976>, accessed 30 May 2022.

4 Quoted in Barry, *Who Wants to be a Billionaire?*, p. 54.

5 *Sydney Morning Herald*, 13 September 2013.

6 *Guardian Australia*, 9 February 2021.

7 WilkinsonEyre, One Barangaroo, Sydney, Australia, <https://www.wilkinsoneyre.com/projects/one-barangaroo>, accessed 8 April 2022.

8 Henri Lefebvre, *The Production of Space*, [1974], Blackwell Publishers, Oxford, 1995, p. 261.

9 *East darling harbour, Sydney, urban design competition*, New South Wales Government, 2005, pp. 1, 8.

10 *The Burra Charter: The Australia ICOMOS Charter for Places of Cultural Significance*, Australia ICOMOS, Melbourne, 2000, p. 3.

11 'Quoted in Kate Legge, 'It's Fun Being a Bastard', *Australian Weekend Magazine*, 3–4 October, 2015, p. 14.

12 *East darling harbour, Sydney, urban design competition*, Stage 2, Jury's Report, March 2006, p. 6.

13 Quoted in Guy Allenby, 'The Good, The Bad, The Ugly', *Sydney Magazine*, June 2010, p. 47.

14 Quoted in Kate Legge, 'It's Fun Being a Bastard', *Weekend Australian Magazine*, 3–4 October 2015, pp. 14, 16.

15 Legge, 'It's Fun Being a Bastard', p. 15.

16 Ibid., p. 13.

17 Quoted in Troy Bramston, *Paul Keating: The Big-Picture Leader*, Scribe, Melbourne, 2016, pp. 654–55.

18 *Sydney Morning Herald*, 10–11 September 2011.

19 Quoted in Allenby, 'The Good, The Bad, The Ugly', p. 51.

20 Graeme Davison, *City Dreamers: The Urban Imagination in Australia*, NewSouth, Sydney, 2016, p. 266.

21 Ibid., p. 265.

22 *Sydney Morning Herald*, 4 February 2015.

23 David Collins, *An Account of the English Colony in New South Wales*, vol. 1 [1798], AH and AW Reed/Royal Australian Historical Society, Sydney, 1975, p. 497; *Sydney Morning Herald*, 23 November 1878.

24 Housnia Shams, 'NSW government takes first step to returning Me-Mel/Goat Island to Indigenous community', ABC, <www.abc.net.au/news/2022-05-29/nsw-me-mel-goat-island/101108566>, accessed 17 September 2022.

25 *Sydney Morning Herald*, 6 May 2011.

26 *Sydney Morning Herald*, 26 March 2008.

27 *Sydney Morning Herald*, 21 December 2009.

28 *Sydney Morning Herald*, 22 December 2009.

29 *Sydney Morning Herald*, 10 March 2010.

30 *Sydney Morning Herald*, 21 December 2009.

31 Mike Harris, 'Barangaroo: Machiavellian megaproject or erosion of intent?', in Kristian Ruming (ed.), *Urban Regeneration in Australia: Policies, Processes and Projects or Contemporary Urban Change*, Routledge, Abingdon, 2018, pp. 120–21.

32 Chris Masters, *Jonestown: The Power and Myth of Alan Jones*, Allen and Unwin, Sydney, 2007.

33 'Packer's Crown Casino Gamble'.

34 NSW Planning Assessment Commission, *Determination Report of Section 75W Modification Application for the Barangaroo Concept Plan*, 28 June 2016, p. 5.

35 *Sydney Morning Herald*, 7 November 2013.

36 Ibid.

37 NSW Planning Assessment Commission, *Determination Report*, p. 17.

38 NSW Planning Assessment Commission, *Determination Report*, p. 12.

39 *Guardian Australia*, 6 October 2020; *Sydney Morning Herald*, 23 June 2022.

40 'Packer's Crown Casino Gamble'.

BIBLIOGRAPHY

Primary and unpublished sources

Australasian Star.

Australian.

The Burra Charter: The Australia ICOMOS Charter for Places of Cultural Significance, Australia ICOMOS, Melbourne, 2000.

Bradley, William, *A Voyage to New South Wales: The Journal of Lieutenant William Bradley of HMS Sirius 1786–1792*, Trustees of the Public Library of New South Wales/ Ure Smith, Sydney, 1969.

Brady, EJ, *Sydney Harbour, Builder Printing Words Fine Art Printers*, Sydney 1903.

—— *The Ways of Many Waters*, The Bulletin Newspaper Co Ltd, Sydney, 1899.

Campbell, WD, *Aboriginal Carvings of Port Jackson and Broken Bay*, Department of Mines and Agriculture, Government Printer, Sydney, 1899.

Cobley, John, (ed.), *Sydney Cove 1788*, Hodder and Stoughton, London, 1962.

—— *Sydney Cove, 1789–1790*, Angus and Robertson, Sydney, 1963.

—— *Sydney Cove 1791–1792*, Angus and Robertson, Sydney, 1965.

Collins, David, (1975), *An Account of the English Colony in New South Wales*, Vol.1 [1798], AH and AW Reed and Royal Australian Historical Society, Sydney, 1975.

Daily Telegraph.

Earle, Augustus, *Views in New South Wales and Van Diemen's Land: Australian Scrapbook*, J Cross, London, 1830.

Fidlon, John, and RJ Ryan (eds), *The Journal and Letters of Lt Ralph Clark*, Australian Documents Library/ Library of Australian History, Sydney, 1981.

Freemans Journal.

'The Future of Sydney Harbour', *Proceedings of the Working Harbour Summit*, 24 October 2003, National Trust of Australia (NSW), 2003.

Greaves, Captain WAB, 'Recollections of Old Sydney in 1852 and Since', *Journal of the Royal Australian Historical Society*, vol. 3, Pt. 9, 1916, pp. 404–28.

Heads of the People.

Historic Records of Australia [HRA].

Historic Records of New South Wales [HRNSW].

Hunter, John, *An Historical Journal of Events at Sydney and at Sea 1787–1792*, [1793], Angus and Robertson/ Australian Historical Society, Sydney, 1968.

Illustrated Sydney News.

Jenkins, Sacha, 'Our Harbour: A Cultured History of Sydney Harbour, 1880–1938', PhD thesis, Department of History, University of Sydney, 2002.

Knight RJB and Alan Frost (eds), *The Journal of Daniel Paine 1794–1797*, Library of Australian History, Sydney, 1983.

Lycett, Joseph, *Views in Australia*, J Souter, London, 1824.

Marriott, Edward West (ed.), *The Memoirs of Obed West: A Portrait of Early Sydney*, Barcom Press, Bowral, 1988.

Meredith, Mrs Charles, *Notes and Sketches of New South Wales*, [1844], Penguin, Melbourne, 1973.

'Minutes of Evidence taken before the Select Committee on Aborigines', *New South Wales Legislative Council Votes and Proceedings*, 1845.

Oliver, Alexander, *The Fisheries of New South Wales*, Government Printer, Sydney, 1871.

Rees, Lloyd, *Small Treasures of a Lifetime: Some Memories of Australian Art and Artists*, Collins, Sydney, 1989.

'Report of the Commission Appointed to Inquire into the Condition of the Harbour of Port Jackson', *New South Wales Legislative Assembly Votes and Proceedings*, vol. 2, 1866.

'Report of the Royal Commission to Inquire into and Report upon the Actual State and Prospects of the Fisheries of this Colony', *New South Wales Legislative Assembly Votes and Proceedings*, 1880.

'Report of the Royal Commission to Report on the Best Means of Developing the Marine and other Fisheries of New South Wales', *New South Wales Legislative Assembly Votes and Proceedings*, vol. 6, 1894–95.

'Report of the Select Committee on the Reserve, Lavender Bay', *New South Wales Legislative Assembly Votes and Proceedings*, vol. 5, 1866.

Seidler, Harry et al., *Urban Redevelopment Concerns You!*, McMahons Point and Lavender Bay Progress Association, Sydney, 1957.

Sydney Gazette.

Sydney Herald.

Sydney Mail.

Sydney Morning Herald.

Sydney Review.

Tench, Watkin, *Sydney's First Four Years: Being a Reprint of a Narrative of the Expedition to Botany Bay and a Complete Account of the Settlement at Port Jackson*, Library of Australian History/Royal Australian Historical Society, Sydney, 1979.

Thompson, Lindsay G, *History of the Fisheries of New South Wales*, Government Printer for the New South Wales Commissioners for the World's Columbian Exposition, Sydney, 1893.

The Voyage of Governor Phillip to Botany Bay with an Account of the Establishment of the Colonies of New South Wales and Norfolk Island, [1789], Library Board of South Australia, Adelaide, 1968.

Walker, Mrs Eliza, 'Old Sydney in the 'Forties', *Journal of the Royal Australian Historical Society*, vol. 16, pt. 4, pp. 292–320.

Wentworth, WC, *Statistical Historical and Political Description of the Colony of New South Wales, and its Dependent Settlement in Van Diemen's Land*, [1819], Griffin Press, Adelaide, 1978.

White, John, *Journal of a Voyage to New South Wales*, [1790], Angus and Robertson, Sydney, 1962.

Secondary Sources (see Notes on pages 314–30 for articles)

Aarons, Mark, *A Place for People: The Transformation of Sydney's Darling Harbour*, Sydney Harbour Foreshore Authority, Sydney, 2009.

Andrews, Graeme, *Ferries of Sydney*, Sydney University Press/Oxford University Press, Sydney, 1994.

—— *The Watermen of Sydney: Memories of a Working Harbour*, Tutton and Armstrong, Sydney, 2004.

Aplin, Graeme (ed.), *A Difficult Infant: Sydney Before Macquarie*, UNSW Press, Sydney, 1988.

Aplin, Graeme, and John Storrey, *Waterfront Sydney 1860–1920*, Allen and Unwin, North Sydney, 1984.

Atkinson, Alan, *The Europeans in Australia, A History: Vol. 1, The Beginning*, Oxford University Press, Melbourne, 1997.

Attenbrow, Val, *Sydney's Aboriginal Past: Investigating the Archaeological and Historical Records*, UNSW Press, Sydney, 2000.

Bach, John, *A Maritime History of Australia*, Book Club Associates and Thomas Nelson, West Melbourne, 1976.

Barnard, Marjorie, *Sydney: The Story of a City*, Melbourne University Press, Melbourne, 1956.

Paul Barry, *Who Wants to be a Billionaire?: The James Packer Story*, Allen and Unwin, Sydney, 2009.

Beasley, Margo, *Wharfies: the History of the Waterside Workers' Federation*, Halstead Press and Australian National Maritime Museum, Sydney, 1996.

Birch, Allan, and David S Macmillan (eds), *The Sydney Scene 1788–1960*, Melbourne University Press, Melbourne, 1962.

Blaxcell, Gregory, *The River: Sydney Cove to Parramatta, Brush Farm Historical Society*, Eastwood, 2004.

Bonyhady, Tim, *The Colonial Earth*, Miegunyah Press, Melbourne, 2000.

Bowen, Jan, *The Sydney Sailors' Home 1859–2009*, The Australian Mariners' Welfare Society, Sydney, 2009.

Broadbent, James, *The Australian Colonial House: Architecture and Society in New South Wales 1788–1842*, Hordern House, Sydney, 1997.

Burgmann, Meredith, and Verity Burgmann, *Green Bans, Red Unions: Environmental Activism and the New South Wales Builders Labourers Federation*, UNSW Press, Sydney, 1998.

Butler-Bowden, Caroline, and Charles Pickett, *Homes in the Sky: Apartment Living in Australia*, Historic Houses Trust of New South Wales / Miegunyah Press, Sydney/ Melbourne, 2007.

Clendinnen, Inga, *Dancing with Strangers*, Text Publishing Company, Melbourne, 2003.

Cochrane, Peter, *Colonial Ambition: Foundations of Australian Democracy*, Melbourne University Press, Melbourne, 2006.

Corbin, Alain, *The Lure of the Sea: The discovery of the seaside 1750–1840*, Penguin Books, Harmondsworth, 1995.

Curby, Pauline, *Seven Miles from Sydney: A History of Manly*, Manly Council, Manly, 2002.

Currey, CH, *The Transportation Escape and Pardoning of Mary Bryant*, Angus and Robertson, Sydney, 1963.

Curson, Peter, and Kevin McCracken, *Plague in Sydney: The Anatomy of an Epidemic*, UNSW Press, Sydney, [no date].

Davies, Simon, *The Islands of Sydney Harbour*, Hale and Iremonger, Sydney, 1984.

Graeme Davison, *City Dreamers: The Urban Imagination in Australia*, NewSouth, Sydney, 2016.

Dixon, Robert, *The Course of Empire: Neo-Classical Culture in New South Wales 1788–1860*, Oxford University Press, Melbourne, 1986.

Eagle, Mary, *The Oil Paintings of Arthur Streeton in the National Gallery of Australia*, National Gallery of Australia, Canberra, 1994.

Eldershaw, M Barnard, *A House is Built*, Australasian Publishing Company, [1929], Sydney, 1961.

—— *The Life and Times of Captain John Piper*, [1939], Ure Smith, Sydney, 1973.

Ellis, Elizabeth, *Conrad Martens: Life and Art*, State Library of New South Wales, Sydney, 1994.

Emmett, Peter, *Sydney Vistas: Panoramic Views 1788–1995*, Historic Houses Trust of New South Wales, Sydney, 1995.

Farrer, KTH, *A Settlement Amply Supplied: Food Technology in Nineteenth Century Australia*, Melbourne, University Press, Melbourne, 1980.

Fitzgerald, Shirley, *Sydney 1842–1992*, Hale and Iremonger, Sydney, 1992.

Fitzgerald, Shirley, and Keating Chris, *Millers Point: The Urban Village*, Hale and Iremonger, Sydney, 1992.

Fitzgerald, Shirley, and Hilary Golder, *Pyrmont and Ultimo Under Siege*, Hale and Iremonger, Sydney, 1994.

Foley, Jean Duncan, *In Quarantine: A History of Australia's Quarantine Station 1828–1984*, Kangaroo Press, Sydney, 1994.

Frame, Tom, *The Garden Island*, Kangaroo Press, Kenthurst, 1990.

Fromonot, Francoise, and Christopher Thompson, *Sydney: History of a Landscape*, Vilo International, Paris, 2000.

Gaby, James, *The Restless Waterfront*, Antipodean Publishers, Sydney, 1974.

Grose, Peter, *A Very Rude Awakening: The Night the Japanese Midget Subs Came to Sydney Harbour*, Allen and Unwin, Sydney, 2007.

Hainsworth, DR, *The Sydney Traders: Simeon Lord and his Contemporaries 1788–1821*, Melbourne University Press, Carlton, 1981.

Hall, Leanne (ed.), *Down the Bay: The Changing Foreshores of North Sydney*, North Sydney Council, Sydney, 1997.

Hunt, Susan, and Graeme Davison, *Sydney Views 1788–1888 from the Beat Knoblauch Collection*, Historic Houses Trust of New South Wales, Sydney, 2007.

Huntsman, Leone, *Sand in Our Souls: The Beach in Australian History*, Melbourne University Press, Melbourne, 2001.

Jeremy, John, *Cockatoo Island: Sydney's Historic Dockyard*, UNSW Press, Sydney, 1980.

Karskens, Grace, *The Colony: A History of Early Sydney*, Allen and Unwin, Sydney, 2009.

Keesing, Nancy, *Garden Island People*, Wentworth Books, Sydney, 1975.

Kelly, Max, *Anchored in a Small Cove: A history and archaeology of The Rocks, Sydney*, Sydney Cove Authority, Sydney, 1997.

Kerr, Joan, and James Broadbent, *Gothick Taste in the Colony of New South Wales*, David Ell Press, Sydney, 1980.

Lefebvre, Henri, *The Production of Space*, Blackwell Publishers, Oxford, 1994.

Le Guay, Laurence, *Sydney Harbour*, Angus and Robertson, Sydney, 1966.

McCormick, Tim et al., *First Views of Australia, 1788–1825: A History of Early Sydney*, David Ell Press / Longueville Publications, Sydney, 1987.

Mackaness Caroline (ed.), *Bridging Sydney*, Historic Houses Trust of New South Wales, Sydney, 2006.

Molloy, Margaret, *A Century of Sydney's Flying Sailors*, Sydney Flying Squadron, Sydney, 2001.

Oppenheim, Peter, *The Fragile Forts: The Fixed Defences of Sydney Harbour 1788–1963*, Department of Defence, Canberra, 2004.

Parker, RG, *Cockatoo Island: A History*, Nelson, Melbourne, 1977.

Proudfoot, Peter, *Seaport Sydney: The Making of the City Landscape*, UNSW Press, Sydney, 1995.

Riviere, Marc Serge, *The Governor's Noble Guest: Hyacinth de Bougainville's Account of Port of Jackson, 1825*, Miegunyah Press, Melbourne, 1999.

Salt, Annette, *The Fishermen of Iron Cove*, Leichhardt Council and Australian Centre for Public History, University of Technology, Sydney, 2006.

Smith, Bernard, *European Vision and the South Pacific*, Oxford University Press, Melbourne, 1989.

Smith, Keith Vincent, *Bungaree: A Sydney Aborigine Meets the Great South Pacific Explorers 1799–1830*, Kangaroo Press, Kenthurst, 1992.

Solling, Max, *Grandeur and Grit: A History of Glebe*, Halstead Press, Sydney, 2007.

Solling, Max, and Peter Reynolds, *Leichhardt: On the Margins of the City*, Allen and Unwin, Sydney, 1997.

Souter, Gavin, *Mosman: A History*, Melbourne University Press, Melbourne, 1994.

Spearritt, Peter, *Sydney's Century: A History*, UNSW Press, Sydney, 1999.

—— *The Sydney Harbour Bridge: A Life*, UNSW Press, Sydney, 2007.

Stannard, Bruce, *Blue Water Bushmen: The Colourful Story of Australia's Best and Boldest Boatmen*, Angus and Robertson, Sydney, 1981.

Stephenson, PR, with Brian Kennedy, *The History and Description of Sydney Harbour*, Reed, Sydney, 1980.

Steven, Margaret, *Merchant Campbell, 1769–1846*, Oxford University Press, Melbourne, 1965.

Sweeney, Christopher, *Sydney Harbour*, Collins Publishers, Sydney, 1989.

Sydney Opera House in its Harbour Setting, New South Wales Department of Urban Affairs and Planning, Sydney, 1996.

Terry, Martin, *Maritime Painting of Early Australia 1788–1900*, Miegunyah Press, Carlton, 1988.

Watson, Anne (ed.), *Building a Masterpiece: The Sydney Opera House*, Powerhouse Publishing, Sydney, 2006.

INDEX

2GB 270, 309
150th Anniversary celebrations 206

A House is Built 235–6
A Study in Curves 200, *200*
abattoir at Glebe Island 166–7
Aboriginal carvings 5, 13, 107
    Aboriginal peoples
    at 150th anniversary
        re-enactment 206
    at Bicentennial re-enactment
        269–70
    before European settlement
        7–11
    captured for liaison purposes
        41–7
    cultural remains 4–5
    dwindling numbers of
        99–108
    early European contact
        33–40
    housed at La Perouse 108
    in artworks 99
    little regard for 257
    on Cockatoo Island 122
    role in tourism 272
    sealers and 72
    settled at Elizabeth Bay 90
    use of harbour by 10–15
    violent clashes with 40, 45,
        102–3
accountability 147
*Act to Protect the Fisheries of New
    South Wales* 1865 167–8
Adams, Glenda 258, 261
Adamson, Robert 261
Admiralty House 126, 178
Afghan 119
Afric 208
alcohol use 66–7, 72
Alderton, George 144
Allen, Jack and Cottier 265
AMP Building v, 237–40
Andersons, Andrew 265, 285
'Andy's Gone with Cattle' 158
Angas, George French 106–7,
    179
Anholt Index 273
Ann Jameson 110–11
Anna Josepha 70
Anniversary Day regattas 110,
    139, 151
anti-submarine boom 224
Anzacs 208–11, 222
Aquitania 222
Arabanoo 41–2
Argyle Cut 126
Arrowanelly (Homebush) 32
Art Society of New South Wales
    151, 153
Arup, Ove 242
asbestos sheeting 187

Ashton, Julian 155, 161
Ashton, Nigel 251, 280
Asia, tourism from 261
Askin, Robert 254
Atlantic 45
Australasia iv, v, 94–5
Australasian Star 154
Australia 212
Australia, Federation of 177
Australian Gas Light Company
    81, 162
Australian Museum 117, 168
Australian National Journal 226
Australian Naval and Military
    Expeditionary Force 213
Australian (racing yacht) 134
Australian Soldiers' Pocket Book
    221
Australian Steam Navigation
    Company
    building for 234
    employs Chinese 180
    facilities built by 124
Australian Tourism Commission
    272
Australian Workman 157
Australian Yacht Squadron 134

Ba-ing-hoe (Garden Island) 106
Bal-loo-der-ry 7, 43
Balcony 2, The 276
Ball, Lidgbird 41
Ballast Point
    Caltex oil terminal 277
    redevelopment of 280–1, 301
    storage tanks 259
Balls Head 1–3, 159–60
    Aboriginal carvings 5–7, 6, 9
    as beauty spot 247
    coal loader at 15
    planned remodelling 192
    Waterhen base 259
Balmain
    in World War II 219
    power station 278
    redevelopment of 274–5,
        279–80
    waterfront at 147
Balmain Association 277
Balmain Shores 280
Balmain, William 70, 138
Balmoral 251
Banks, Joseph 17–18, 34
Barangaroo (person) 11–12,
    43, 46
Barangaroo (development) 286,
    294–312
Barangaroo (ferry) 196
Bare (Pinchgut) Island 25, 127,
    see also Fort Denison
Barnard, Marjorie 235–6
Barnett, Bill 197, 227
Barnett, Walter 149

Barney, George 126–7, 129, 257
Barrack Square 114
Barrett, Thomas 25
Barry, WJ 77
Bartlett, Hope 220
Barton, Edmund 253
Barton, Mr 54
Barwell 64
Barwick, Archie 208
Bass, George 59–60, 62–3
Bass Strait, naming of 59
bathing areas 92, *137*, 139
Bathurst, Earl 92, 102
Batterham, Joyce 226
Baudin, Nicholas 60
Baughan, John 68
Baxter, WDH 236
Beach, William 139
Beagle 80
Beard, William 201
Bell'vue 252–3
Ben Bolt 136
Bennelong 7, 43
    death and burial 46
    England trip 45
    marriage 11
    on Gamaragal people 13
    saves Bryant boat 51
Bennelong (ferry) 196
Bennelong Point
    Bennelong housed at 43
    fort built at 84
    Opera House 240–1
    sewerage facilities 162, 165
    tram depot 189
Bentham, Jeremy 54
Berrima 213
Berrys Bay
    Aboriginal peoples at 108
    boat building at 196
    model yacht racing *228*
    oil tanks at 248, 259
    redevelopment of 281
Bertie, Charles 235
Bicentennial projects 265–70
Big Orange 276
Bigge, JT 92
Biloela (Cockatoo Island) 122
Birchgrove House 277
bird species 28, 31, 63
Birra Birra (Sydney Harbour) 5
Birrabirragal people 7
black bream 3
Black Swan 131, 134
Blackett, Edmund 252
Blackwattle Bay 264
Blackwattle Creek 166–7
Bligh, William 73–4, 84–5
Bloodworth, James 27
Blore, Edward 96
Blue, Billy 91, 138
blue groper 3
Blue Mountains 80, 94

Blues Point 4, 193
Blues Point Tower 251–2, 259, 280–1
boat building
associated industries 165
early 54–60
private 61
technological change in 278–9
Boer War 211
Bolot, Aaron 253
Bondi 165, 224
Booragy (Bradleys Head) 7
Borogegal people 7
Boromedegal people 7
Bostock, Gerry 8–9
Boston, Mr 71
Boswell, James 52
Botanic Gardens v, 171, 206, 239
Botany Bay
Aboriginal name for 16
European discovery of 17
fishing in 29
MSB takes over 260
settlement of proposed 19–20
Bowes, Arthur 23
Boyes, George Thomas 88
Bradfield, JJC 202, 204, 207, 234
Bradley, William 29, 42
Bradleys Head 191
Aboriginal name for 7
coal mining at 147
gun battery at 127
Taronga Zoo at 193–4
waterfront leased 146
Brady, EJ 157, 165, 175
Bramble 206
Brasch, Reuben 148
Brazier, John William 169
Breuer, Marcel 245
Bridge in Curve, The 200
Brighton (ferry) 196
'Bring out a Briton' campaign 233
Brisbane 213
Brisbane House 135, 136, 203
Brisbane, Thomas 111, 141
Britannia 67, 267
Broad, Mary 48–9, 51–3
Brooklyn Bridge 202
Brothers family 216
Bryant, William 48–9, 51–3
Bryce, Michael 271
bubonic plague 120, 179–81
Buffalo 64
Builders Labourers' Federation 255–6, 258–9
Bulletin, The 148, 154, 157, 180
bumboats 65
Bungaree 101–6
Bungaree (ferry) 196
Buruberongal people 12

Cadi territory 7
Cadman's Cottage 253
Cahill Expressway 234, 306
Cahill, Joe 240
Caire, Nicholas 147
Caley, George 67
Callan Park 211
callarr (fishing spear) 11
Calwell, Arthur 231
Cammeray 4, 7
Camp Cove 35
Campbell Island 72
Campbell, John 63
Campbell, Robert 63–4, 68–9
as naval officer 85
Milson–Campbell dispute 134–5
sealing by 72–3
trading by 66–7
Campbell, Robert Jr 115
Campbell, WD 4–5
Campbells Cove 68
Canberra 233
Cape Barren Island 72
Cape Cabarita 286
Caprice restaurant 264
Captain Cook Cruises 262
Captain Cook Graving Dock 223
Carey, Peter 277
Caroo 105–7
Carr, Bob 281–2, 284, 286, 299, 301
Carter, Jane 97
Cash, Frank 202
Castel Bianco 231
Castle of Good Hope 70
Castlecrag 198, 245
Casuarina 60
Catalina's 264
Catherine Adamson 133, 167
Cattle Point 22, 27
Cavill, Dick 139
Cavill, Fred 139
Cazneaux, Harold 200, 276
Cetinich, Rozalia 231–2, 243
Charlotte 48
Chicago 225
Chinese immigrants 119, 180–1
Choruses from The Rock 247
Chowder Bay 129
'Chusan waltz' 117
Circular Quay 111–12, *197*
Aboriginal peoples at 108
new buildings 237–40
new sea wall 265
passenger terminal 234
planned remodelling 190
redevelopment of 260–1, 271, 279

City Beautiful 190–1
city council 163–4, 181–2, *see also* local government
City Iron Works 165
Clare, Kerry 311
Clark, Edward M 145
Clark, Michael 221
Clark, Ralph 22
boat built by 56
on early Sydney 24
on Port Jackson 23
Clarke, WB 145
clay for building 27
Clayton, Joseph 119
coachwood 57
coal
from Hunter Valley 61
mining at Balmain 147
mining at Bradleys Head 147
mining at Cremorne 145
shipping 260–1
unionisation in industry 187–8, 215–16
Coal (Hunter) River 62
Coalcliff 59
Coalition of Residents Action Groups 255, 277
Cockatoo Island
as naval base 213–4
building on 122
closure of 278
Commonwealth takeover 178, 212
in World War II 219–20
Nautical School at 121
redevelopment of 289
silos on 126
workforce at 214–17
Cohen, Philip 172
Colbee 12, 42
Cole, Thomas 83
Collins, David
on Aboriginal peoples 13, 42
on Bennelong 45, 51
on boat accidents 56
on Bungaree 102
on convict labour 24
on escape attempts 62
on First Fleet 21
on fishermen 49
on land claims 33–4
on Second Fleet 50
Colnett, James 69
colonial era 48–78
Colonial Sugar Refinery 166
Commissariat Building 66, 236
commodities boom 260–1
Commonwealth government
Royal Australian Navy 211–12, 259
shipping line 215–16

takes over Cockatoo Island 178, 212
takes over Garden Island 178
Commonwealth Line 217–18
Congdon, Samuel 170
Conrad, Joseph 184
Considen, Denis 31
container terminals 259–60, 286
convicts
  Aboriginal peoples clash with 40
  departure of emancipists 54
  disciplining 25
  escapes by 51–4, 61
  Francis Morgan 64
  marooned by shipwreck 63
  on Second Fleet 50
  transportation of 19–20, 96, 116
Coogee, gun battery at 224
Cook, James 17
Cooper, William 93
Cornish, Muriel 199
Cornwall 64
'Course of Empire' series 83
couta (boat) 294, 312
Cox, Arthur 264
Cox, Phillip 266, 296
Cox, Sarah 95
Craigend 96
Cremorne 143–6, 148, 153, 191, 199
Cremorne (painting) 199
Cremorne Pastoral 153
Creswell House 246
Cronin, Thomas 112
crown land 138, *see also* land grants and sales
Crown Sydney 294–7, 309–11
Crows Nest Cottage 90
Cruising Yacht Club of Sydney/ Australia 228–9
Crystal Palace 266
CSR 166
Cumberland 61–2
Cumberland County Council 247, 251
Cunningham, Peter 75
Curlew Camp 148
Curtis, Robert Emerson 202
Curve of the Bridge, The 200
Customs House 111, 190, 271
cutter (boat) 35, 51, 52, 60, 312

Dadswell, Lyndon 236
Daily Telegraph 247
Dalgety woolstore 259
Dame Pattie 227
Daringa (Da-ring-ha) 13, *14*
Dark, Eleanor 205
Darling Harbour

Aboriginal name for 7
flour mill at 81
goods loaded at 185
pollution in 162
redevelopment of 258, 260, 265–8
whaling ships in 77
Darling Harbour Act 267
Darling Harbour Authority 1984 267
Darling Island 185
Darling Point 252
Darling, Ralph 92, 93, 136
Darwin bombing 222
Darwin, Charles
  friends with Martens 97
  on grandfather's poem 83–4
  social observations 108
  Sydney visit 79–81
Darwin, Erasmus 81–3, 94
Davison, Graeme 303, 304
Dawes Point 3, 22, 158–9, 215
  Aboriginal name for 4
  gun battery at 84, 91, 129, 204
Dawes, William 7
Dawkins, Jeremy 288
de Bougainville, Hyacinthe 74, 91
de Castelnan, Comte 169
de Pasquali, Biaggio 263
Defenders of Sydney Harbour Foreshores 282, 288
defensive works 122–30, 224–5, 282
Deloitte, QL 274
Denison, William 129
Dharug language 12
Dickson, John 81
Dilboong 7
disease
  bubonic plague 120, 179–81
  djee-ball djee-ball disease 10
  galgalla disease 8, 41
  impact on Aboriginal peoples 8
  scurvy and dysentery 29, 31
'Displaced Persons' 231
djee-ball djee-ball disease 10
Dobbin, Leonard 208–9
Domain, The 84–5, 91–2, 129, 138, 148, 237, 270
Done, Ken 262, 271
Dorman Long workshops 217
Dowling, Edward 108, 305
Doyle, Alice 264
Doyle's on the Beach 264
'Dripping Rocks' 110
Dudley, Thomas 179
Dunbar, Duncan 130
Dunbar wreck 130–3
Dupain, Max 276
Dusseldorp, Gerardus 250, 253

Dwyer, Catherine 187
dysentery 29

Earle, Augustus
  on Fort Macquarie 91
  paintings of Bungaree 104–5
  portrait of Piper 88
East Australian Current 3
East India Company
  cooperation with Royal Navy 19–20, 56
  monopoly held by 62
Easty, John 43, 51–3
Edwards Beach 147
Egan, William 210
El Niño Southern Oscillation 39
Eldershaw, Flora 235–6
electric telegraph 133
electrical loops 224
Eliot, TS 247
Eliza 64
Eliza Point 87
Elizabeth Bay 90, 251
Elizabeth Bay House 96, 169
  bought for State 252
  land subdivided 195
Elizabeth Farm 58
Elliott Brothers 165–6
emancipists, departure of 54
Emden 218
Emerald City 273
Emma 133
Empire Games 205
Endeavour 17–18
engineer officer position 126
Environmental Assessment and Protection Act 1979 266
Eora people 7
Euripides 208
European refugees 231
evaporation works 73
Evening, Sirius Cove, Athol Bay 199
Eyre, John 99

'Faces in the Street' 158
Fahey, John 296
Farm Cove
  Aboriginal name for 12
  cattle herded to 23
  initiation ceremony at 12–13
  tidal flat filled 171
Farrelly, Elizabeth 280
Faulkner, Alderman 205
Federation celebrations 176–8
Feez, Adolph 96
Female Factory, Parramatta 85
ferries *209*
  carry troops to ships 208–9, 222

double-ended 195
paintings of 150
State takes over 234
terminal buildings 190
to North Shore 198
to Parramatta 55
Field, Barron 105
financial deregulation 261
finger wharves, *see* wharves,
quays and jetties
First Fleet
1938 re-enactment 206
Bicentennial re-enactment
269–70
voyage and arrival 21–2
fishing
by Aboriginal peoples 10–11,
35, 38
by early European settlers
39–40
declining stocks 29–31, 71
enquiries into 1880,
1894–95 169–70, 174–5
ethnic shifts in 232
in Botany Bay 17
markets regulated 174
net 168, 171, 173
new technology in 10
permanent station established
55
pollution and 167–8
range of 3
regulations for 173–4
species described 28
Sydney Fish Market 264
Woolloomooloo Fish Market
169, 172
Fitler, WC 147, 155
Fitzgerald, JD 202
Fitzroy, Charles 115, 124, 128
Fitzroy Dock 122, *123*, 177, 214
Flagstaff Hill 113, 152
flax plants 74
fleas, plague and 179
Flinders, Matthew 59, 60, 102
flying boats 233
foreshores, *see* waterfront
Formidable 230
Forsdale 217
Fort Denison 129
after Federation 178
in National Park 282
navigation lights 133
Pinchgut levelled for 126
Fort Macquarie
after Federation 178
construction of 91
decommissioned 129
demolished 189
improvements to 129
Fort Phillip 91

Forth Bridge 202
Fowler, Frank 110
*From McMahon's Point – Fare One
Penny* 150
Fullwood, AF 148, 155
*Funeral of Rear-Admiral Phillip
Parker King* 97
fur seals 71–2, *see also* sealing
industry
Gadigal people 7, 13
Galicia Star 263
galgalla disease 8, 41
Gamaragal people 13
Game Protection Act 1866 168
Gameygal people 16–18
Garden City 190–1
Garden Island
becomes naval base 212
Bungaree carried to 106
handed to Admiralty 126
handed to Commonwealth
178
in World War II 219
new graving dock 223
workforce at 214
Garling, Frederick 96
Gayamaygal people 7
Gehl, Jan 306
General Assembly of
International Sports
Federations 271
General Synopsis of Birds (Latham
1781–86) 28
Georges Head 102
foreshores reclaimed 139
gun battery at 129
Georges Heights 211
Giedion, Sigried 243
Gill, ST 96
Gipps, George 96, 125,
163–4
Gladesville Bridge 235
Glass House 246
Glebe Island
abattoir at 166–7
bridge connecting 200
container terminals 259
Glebe Society 289
globalisation 261–2
Goat Island 43, 46, 108, 305
gold discoveries 117–19
Goond, James 171–3
Goosens, Eugene 240
Gooweebahree (Lavender Bay)
135
Gordon, Adam Lindsay 148
Gordon, Bob 290–3, 294
Gordon, James 127
Gore Cove 259
Gothic architecture 84, 92, 95–8,
126

government, *see* Commonwealth
government; local government;
State government
Government House 92
Governor King (schooner)
72–3
Governor's Domain, *see* Domain,
The
grain-handling facility, Darling
Island 185
Grantham 96, 203
grass trees 9
'Great Protest meeting' 114–15
Great War 207–11, *209*
Great White Fleet 211, *213*
green bans 256, 258–9
Greenoaks 96
Greenway, Francis 86, 87, 89,
91, 134
Grey, Earl 114, 128
Grey Harbour 276
Greycliffe (ferry) 195
Griffin, Marion Mahoney 198,
245–6
Griffin, Walter Burley 198,
245–6, 301
'grog', *see* alcohol use
Gropius, Walter 245
Grose, Francis 46
Guardian 50
Guringai language 11
Gweagal people 16–18

habitat concerns 256
Halvorsen family 220
Harborplace in Baltimore 266
Harbour Foreshores Vigilance
Committee 193
Harbour from Craigend, The
98
'Harbour Impressions' 203
harbour regulations 65, 69
Harbour tunnel 189
Hardy, Alderman 205
Harnett, Richard 134, 148
Harp in the South, The 254
Harris, John 138
Harrison, Peter 239
Hashemy 114, 177
Hasty, Charles 171
Haswell, H Atchison 169
Hawkesbury River, land grants
on 58
Hawthorne Canal 232
Heads of the People 113
Heidelberg School 149, 154
Hen and Chickens Bay 286
Hen and Chickens Islands 122
Henrietta Villa 84, 87, 89–90, 93,
195, 274
Hercules 111, 112

Heritage Council of New South
  Wales 267
heritage issues 142, 257, 282–3
Hermitage 264
Hickson Road 188, 284
Hickson, Robert 186, 189–90
Hill, Edward Smith 168
Hill Thalis Architecture + Urban
  Projects 299–301, 303, 306
Hill, Thomas 25
Himalaya 233
Hine, Lewis 202
Hitachi Company 229
Hixson, Francis 170
Hogan, Paul 272
'Hollywood Fleet' 220
Holt, Joseph 65
Homebush 32
Homebush Bay 270–2
*Hope, Art, Labour and Peace at
  Botany Bay* 81
Hopetoun, Lord 177
Hopkins, Livingston 147
Hoppenfeld, Mort 266
Horin, Adele 288
Hornby Lighthouse 133
Hospital Wharf 50, 69, 111
House is Built, A 235–6
housing
  built by Mort 120
  by Sydney Harbour Trust 187
  for Aboriginal peoples 90, 108
  for convicts at the Rocks 25
  property prices 273–4
Hudson, Captain 124
Hungry Mile, the 188, 216, 303
Hughes, William Morris 215, 222
Hulk Bay (Lavender Bay) 135
Hunter 64, 66
Hunter, John
  Aboriginal survey by 35
  becomes Governor 58
  navigation instructions by 64
  on Aboriginal fisheries 10
  on alcohol abuse 67
  on First Fleet 21
  plan drafted by 36–7
  port regulations 69
  timber regulations 57
  trade regulations 66
  watercraft regulations 61
Hunter River 61
Huon 213
Hurley, Ron 271

ICI House 237
Iemma, Morris 303
Illustrated Sydney News 139, 154,
  167
Immigration Restriction Act 1861
  119

industrial heritage 282–3
Industrial School for Girls 121
Inglis, James 156
initiation ceremonies 12–13, 46
Inner South Head 129
introduced species 26, 179
Investigator 60
Iron Cove 201, 211, 259
Ithaca Gardens Flats 245
Ivy 292

*Jacaranda Tree (on Sydney
  Harbour)* 276
Jackson, Phillip 250
Jacobs, Jane 275, 297
Jane Irwin Landscape
  Architecture 299–301, 303, 306
Japan
  military threat from 222, 226
  submarine attacks 224–6
Jerrowan (Eliza Point) 87
jetties, see wharves, quays and
  jetties
Jevons, William Stanley 118
Jones, Alan 308–9, 311
Johnson, Richard 25, 50
Johnston, George 41, 85
Jordan, John 202

Ka-may (Botany Bay) 16, 22
Kable, Henry 68, 72–3
Kangaroo 196
kangaroos 31–2
Kay-ye-my (Manly Cove) 7
Keating, Paul 283, 301–3, 304,
  305, 307, 310
Keesing, Nancy 223
Kelly's Bush 255
Kendall, Henry 110, 132–3
Keneally, Kristina 307
Kerosene Bay 159
Kieran, Barney
  at Federation 177
  at Nautical School 122
  swimming career 139–40
Kill van Kull bridge 202
Kindon, Frederick 210
King George 73
King, Jonathan 269–70
King, Philip
  on sealing industry 71
  presentation to Nicholas
    Baudin 60
  supports trade and sealing 74
  warns of sharks 135
King's Wharf 111
Kingsford Smith Airport 233
Kingston, Peter 276, 284, 292
Kirribilli
  flats in 251
  gun battery at 129

land claims 138
  redevelopment at 253
Kirribilli House 96, 178
Kissing Point 58
Kitchen, Henry 89
'Kitten' (Aboriginal man) 102
Kitt's café 264
Kogerah (Rushcutters Bay) 26
Kollar, Lazlo Peter 246
Koree Bay (Georges Head) 102
Kulgoa 209
Kuring-gai (ferry) 196
Kuttabul 225

La Perouse, Aboriginal peoples
  relocated to 108
Lady Barlow 74
Lady Juliana 50
Land Appeal Court 146
land grants and sales 99
  Aboriginal dispossession by 13
  after plague 181–4
  at Robertsons Point 141
  by Phillip 33–4
  for Aboriginal peoples 99
  Milson–Campbell dispute
    134–5
  of foreshores 138, 193
  on Hawkesbury River 58
  to raise revenue 80
*Lands for Public Purposes
  Acquisition Act* 1900 181–2
Lang, John Dunmore 128, 204
Langer, Karl 240
Langham, William John 172
Lars Halvorsen and Sons 220
Latham, John 28
Lavender Bay 135
  baths at 139
  boat building at 193
  industrial development 144–5
  Lawson on 159
  redevelopment of 204–5,
    275–6, 290–3
  waterfront buildings 147
Lawrence, DH 196–7
Lawrence Nield and Partners 265,
  282–3
Lawson, Henry 158–61, 198,
  203, 210
Lawson, Louisa 158
Laycock, Thomas 138
'Laying on the Screw' 157
Le Corbusier 252
leatherjackets 167
Leaver, John 210
Lefebvre, Henri 297, 298, 311
Legislative Council and
  Legislative Assembly, see State
  government
Leichhardt, ethnic shifts in 232

Lendlease 300, 302, 304, 306, 307, 310
Leplastrier, Richard 282, 284, 285–7, 303
Lever House 238
Liberty Plains 58
lighthouse buildings 84, 86–7, 133–4
Little Sirius Cove 148–9, 152, 193
local government
  building controls by 199
  Cumberland County Council 247, 251
  North Sydney Council 281
  Seidler contemptuous of 251
  Sydney City Council 163–4, 181–2
Locke, John 34
Logan, James 210
Lolita 225
London, pollution in 165
Long Cove 23, 25–6
Lord, Simeon 68, 70, 92
Lowe, Robert 115
Lucas, Bill and Ruth 246
Luke, Peter 227–8
Luna Park 205–6
Lycett, Joseph 89

Macarthur, John 58, 73, 89
Macleay, William 169–70
Macquarie Island 72
Macquarie, Lachlan
  building program 84–7
  on Bungaree 102–3
  promotes trade 74
  protects Pacific Islanders 75
  return to Britain 97
  warns of sharks 136
Macquarie Place 92, 95, 114
mahogany 57
Mahroot 100–1
Mallard, Henri 203
mammal species, *see* wildlife
Mangles 81
'Manly' (captive Aboriginal), *see* Arabanoo
Manly Cove
  Aboriginal name for 7
  ferries to 196
  named after Aboriginal inhabitants 34
Manoora 218
Manunda 218, 221
Maori people 75, 105, 125
marine invertebrates
  introduced species 26
  oysters 3, 29–30, 86, 151, 172
  scarcity of shells 86
Maritime Museum 267, 269, 287

Maritime Services Board
  building for 236–7, 245, 254
  manages Botany Bay 260
  wharf built by 259
Martens, Conrad 96–9
Mat-tew-na-ye (Pinchgut Island) 25
Matora 103
Matra, James Mario 18–19, 34
Mau-ber-ry 7
Mauretania 221
Mayall Creek massacre 99
Mazeppa 134
McConnel, Smith and Johnson 266
McDaniel, Michael 6
McGoogan, George 227
McKay, Ian 250
McMahons Point
  development plan 247–51, 248–9
  Lawson at 159
  paintings done at 150
  zoned for industry 247
McMahons Point and Lavender Bay Progress Association 250, 255
McMahons Point Ferry 150
McRae, Nita 255, 257
Me-Mel (Goat Island) 43, 46, 108, 305
Menzies, Robert 223
Meredith, Louisa 75–6
Metropolitan Local Aboriginal Land Council 304, 305
Meudon 195
Miandetta 253
Middle Harbour v, 1, 4, 8, 15, 32, 46, 131, 148, 198, 246
Middle Head 129, 139
midget submarines 224–6, *225*
Mies Van der Rohe, Ludwig 238, 241, 243
Miklouho-Maclay, Nicolai 169, 274
Military Road 129
Millers Point 181, 259
Milson, James 134–5
Milson, James Jr 134–5, 141–2
Milson, John 135
Milsons Point
  demolitions at 203
  Dorman Long workshops 217
  terminus at 196
Miramar II 220
Mirror of the Sea 184
Mitchell, Thomas 164
monorail 267
Monsanto chemical plant 278
Moore, Clover 305–7, 309, 310

Moorooboora 106
mooting 10–11
Morgan, Francis 64
Mort Bay 259, 278
Mort, Thomas
  buys Martens paintings 98
  dock built by 124, 138
  housing built by 120
  woolstore building 111
Mortlake Bank 260
Mortlake Gas Works 260
Mosman
  Aboriginal carvings 5, 8
  post-whaling 191–2
  suburbanisation of 198, 252
Mosman, Archibald 76–7
Mosmans Bay 77
Mrs Macquarie's Chair 129
Mrs Macquarie's Point 148
MSB, *see* Maritime Services Board
mud oysters 3, 29–30
Muir, Thomas 13, 54
Mulhall, Thomas 170
Mundey, Jack 256, 267, 284, 301, 307
Murro-ore-dial clan 106
mutton birds 63
Myers, Francis 157

National Maritime Museum 267, 269, 287
National Trust 287–9, 303
nationalism 140
native bread 10
native sarsaparilla 31, 51, 52
natural history, *see* wildlife
Nautical School 121
Naval Coaling Battalion 215
Naval Museum 218
naval officer position 70
Naval works 126
Navigation Acts (UK) 62, 70
navigation laws rescinded 117–18
ND Hegarty and Sons 263
neo-Gothic architecture, *see* Gothic architecture
Neutral Bay
  Aboriginal carvings 5
  anchorage created at 53
  bushland around 110
  in World War II 219
New Left ideology 256
New Orleans 221
New South Wales, *see also* State government
  Aboriginal peoples in 99–108
  self-government 116–7
  settlement of proposed 18–19

New South Wales Corps 66–7
New Zealand, Maori immigrants
    from 75
Newcastle Harbour 186
Nielsen, Niels 268
Nielsen Park 194
Niemeyer, Oscar 245
Niland, D'Arcy 5
Norfolk Island 33
Norfolk Island Pine 57
North Coast Company 215
North Head
    gun battery at 224
    quarantine station 178–9, 211
    trees at 4
North Head Port Jackson 98
North Shore Gas Works 276
North Shore Historical Society
    252
North Sydney Council 281
Norval 76
Notting, William Albert 193–4
Nowland, James 171
NSW Heritage Act 267
nullius tempus 143

observatory at Flagstaff Hill 113
ocean liners, *see* passenger liners
ochre stencils 4–5
O'Farrell, Barry 308–9, 310–11
Ogilby, James Douglas 169
Old Colonial By-Ways 235
old wife (fish) 28
Oliver, Alexander 168, 170
Olympic Games 270–2
Olympic Pool at North Sydney
    205
O'Neill, Thomas 90
Oriana 233
Orontes 233
Otter 54
Overseas Passenger Terminal 266
oysters 3, 29–30, 86, 151, 172
Ozone café 264

Packer, James 295–8, 308–11
Packer, Kerry 295–6
Pacific Islanders 75
paddle steamers 109
Page, Alison 304
Paine, Daniel 57–8, 61, 312
panopticon prison 53
paperbark leaf tea 31
Parbury's wharf 184
Park, Ruth 5, 254
Parkes, Henry
    allocates Milson foreshores 142
    early career 116
    on the Rocks 118
    reaction to immigration 119
    supports Nautical School 121

work on Federation 177
Parliament, *see* State government
Parramatta
    Aboriginal name for 7
    first ferry to 55
    foundation of 33
    governor's house at 85
    land grants 58
Parramatta River bridge 235
passenger arrivals 233–4
passenger liners 218
    berths for 233–4
    converted to troopships 221
    Harbour dredged to
        accommodate 235
Pat-ta-go-rang 7
Paterson, William 46
Paul Berkemeier Architects 299–
    301, 303, 306
paymaster bills 66
Payne, Arthur 179
Peacock 125
Pearl Harbour 222
Peddle, Thorp and Walker 238
Peel, Don 188
People's Advocate 114
'People's Plan' 256
Permanent and Casual Wharf
    Labourers Union 216
Péron, François 60, 70
Perseverance 72, 74
Phillip, Arthur
    account of the settlement 28–9
    chooses Sydney Cove 22–3
    chosen to head First Fleet 20
    early contact with Aboriginal
        peoples 33–40
    first night in Sydney 25
    journal of 81–2
    on Aboriginal trails 11
    on Second Fleet 50
    on tree density 10
    plans for Sydney 26
    relations with Bennelong
        42–3
    search for crop lands 32–3
    speared by Aboriginal man 45
pictograph carvings 4–5
Picturesque Atlas of Australasia
    154–5
Piddington, AB 176
Pier Hotel 131
Pinchgut Island 25, 127, *see also*
    Fort Denison
Piper, John 274
    bankruptcy 93
    house built by 87–9
    land acquisitions 138
    paintings of 104
Pitcairn, Mrs 204
Pitt 55

*Plan of Port Jackson New South
    Wales* 36–7
Pockley, Robert 130–1, 133–4
Point Maskelyne 22
Point Piper 5, 8, 138, 274
Police Offences Act 162
political protests 114
pollution
    in fish 264
    industrial 165–6
    Victorian era 161–6
Porpoise 64, 85
Port Hacking 59
Port Jackson
    Darwin's account of 79–81
    First Fleet arrives at 22
    geography of 1–3
    naming of 18
    steering into 64
Port Jackson and Manly Steamship
    Company 196
Port Jackson shark 28
Port Kembla 223
'Port O'Sydney' 276
Port War Signal Station 224
ports growth plan 286–9
Ports Operations and
    Communications Centre 259
Powerful 212
Preservation Island 63
Preston, Margaret 199
Priory 126
Prout, John Skinner 96
public baths 92, *137*, 139
Pyrmont
    bridge connecting 190, 201
    passenger arrivals 233
    power station 259, 296

quarantine station 178–9, 211
Quarterdeck, The 253
quays, *see* wharves, quays and
    jetties
Queen Elizabeth 222
Queen Mary 221
Queen's Wharf 111
Queensboro Bridge 202
Quiberee (Lavender Bay) 135

'Radiant City' 246
railways
    at Circular Quay 234
    loop proposed 189
    to Hornsby 144
Ramsay, EP 169
rats and plague 179, 181
Raven, William 67, 72
red rock cod 3
Reeks, Walter 196
Rees, Lloyd 195–6, 203, 253
Reid, George 146

Reliance 58–9
residents' action groups 255
restaurants and cafés 263–4
'Retired Seaman, The' 155–6
'right of discovery' 34
Robert, Phillipe 284
Roberts, Tom 148, 152, 155
Robertson, John 141
Robertsons Point 141–2
Robinson, Georgie 267
Rockleigh Grange 97
Rocks, The
    Chinese settlement in 180
    convicts housed at 25
    poor conditions in 118
    public acquisition of 181–2
    redevelopment of 253–8
    remodelling schemes 189
    whaling crews in 66
Rodd, Brent 143
Rodius, Charles 96
Rogers, Lord Richard 306
Rose Bay 106, 233
Rose Hill 33, *see also* Parramatta
Rose Hill Packet 55
Ross, John 218
Rouse Corporation 266
Royal Australian Navy 211–12, 259
Royal Commissions 169–70, 189–90
Royal Navy, Australian squadron 126
Royal Sydney Yacht Squadron 134
Royal Yacht Squadron 152
Royle, Guy 223
Rozelle 289
Rushcutters Bay
    convicts killed in 40
    Olympic yacht races 271–2
    rushes from 26
Russia, war with 129

Saarinen, Eero 241
'Sacrifice of Balls Head, The' 161
Sadler, James 139
Sailing Directions for the Harbour of Port Jackson 1858 133
sailors, desertions by 77
Sally 64
salt manufacture 73
San Joyce 263
sandstone
    Aboriginal carvings 4–5, 6, 15
    use as abrasive 9

use for building 27, 86, 122, 236
Sandy Cape feast 102
sanitation 164, *see also* sewerage facilities
Schell, Frederick 155
Schuchard House 246
Scots Church 203
scurvy 29, 31
sea dragons 3
sea lions 72
Sea Mist 220, 225
Seagram Building 238
sealing industry 71–2
Seang Choon 210
Second Fleet 50
Seidler, Harry
    architectural work 240, 245–6
    on grassroots democracy 256
    on Opera House 243–4
    urban planning by 246–7, 253
Selection Acts 156
Selector's Hut: Whelan on the Log 150, 156
self-government 116–7
Selfe, Norman 184–7
    designs bridge 189–90
    designs steam ferry 195
    on Balmain 191
    on Royal Commission 189
Semi-Circular Quay 111, *see also* Circular Quay
Seven Poor Men of Sydney 263
sewerage facilities 112, 161–6
sharks 135–6, *163*
    increasing numbers 167
    Port Jackson shark 28
Shaw, JH 250
Shaw, Shadrach 67
Shaw, William 111, 117–18
sheep 58, 75, 76, 166
shells, scarcity of 86
Shipping, Circular Quay 155, *160*
Ship's Cat, The 183
Shortland, John 61
Sidney Barnett *163*
signal station at Flagstaff Hill 113
Siminov, IM 103–4
Simpson, Roderick 286
Sirius 21, 49
skyscrapers v, 237, 297
Slaughterhouse Bay 135
slaughterhouses in the Rocks 119
Slessor, Kenneth 195, 221, 234
Smedley, WT 155
Smith, Grace Cossington 199
Smith, HG 81

Snails Bay 259
snapper 3, 11, 168
Snapper Island 218
Sobraon 122
Solander Island 74
Sophia Jane 81
South Head
    Aboriginal carvings 5
    communications with 113, 133
    gun battery at 224
    lighthouse building 87
    road to 86
Southwell, Daniel 44
Sow and Pigs Reef 81, 110, 127
Speer, William 162
spotted wobbegong 28, *30*
Squire, James 46–7, 89
St Leonards 98
St Phillip's Church 91
Stannard, Albert 212
Stannard, William 212
Star, The 296–7, 309
State government
    first Parliament of 116
    ports growth plan 286–9
    property holdings after Federation 178
    State Planning Authority 251
    State Region Outline Plan 260
    Sydney Cove Authority 257
    Sydney Harbour Federation Trust 282, 289–90
    Sydney Harbour National Park 281–2
    Sydney Harbour Trust 182, 185–8
    takes over ferries 234
    under Askin 254
    urban planning by 279, 281–2
State Planning Authority 251
State Region Outline Plan 260
Stead, Christina 263
steam power 81, 116–17, *291*
Stephenson and Turner 253
Streeton, Arthur
    bush camping by 149
    paintings by 149–54
    return to Cremorne 198–9
    strikes by waterside workers 214–5
Study in Curves, A 200
Sudan war 152, 211
Suffolk 208
Sulman, John 189–90, 245
Summers, Joe 210–11
Supply 49, 51, 52, 55, 57, 59,
    in First Fleet 21

replica of 206
Surprise (steamer) 81
Sutherland Dock 124, 212, 214
Swan 213
Swan, Rothesay 269
Sydney, *see also* local government
  increasing population 117,
    173–4, 195
  Royal Commission into
    improvement 189–90
Sydney Amateur Sailing Club 152
Sydney City Council 163–4, 181–2
Sydney Coal Lumpers Union 215
Sydney Cove, *see also* Circular
  Quay
  chosen for settlement
    22–3
  dredging operations 111
  passenger arrivals 233
  pollution in 161–6
Sydney Cove Authority 257
Sydney Cove from Fort Phillip 112
Sydney Cove Redevelopment
  Authority 254–5
Sydney Cove (ship) 62–3
Sydney Ferries Ltd 196
Sydney Fish Market 263–4
Sydney Flying Squadron Yacht
  Club 151–2
Sydney Gazette 72, 73, 76, 106
Sydney Harbour 2
  Aboriginal name for 7
  as national treasure 176
  defensive works 122–30, 224–5,
    282
  dredged to accommodate liners
    235
  illustrations of 153–4
  maritime trade 184–5
Sydney Harbour Bridge 83
  effect on ferries 234–5
  landmark status 200–6
  role in tourism 272–3
Sydney Harbour Collieries Ltd
  145–7, 147
Sydney Harbour Federation Trust
  282, 289–90
Sydney Harbour Foreshore
  Authority 301
Sydney Harbour National Park
  281–2
Sydney Harbour Trust 182, 185–8
Sydney Heritage Fleet *291*
Sydney, Lord 20
Sydney Mail 206, 212
Sydney Morning Herald
  on Barangaroo development
    304
  on *Dunbar* disaster 132–3
  on gold discoveries 117–18
  on new graving dock 223

on resumption of transportation
    115
  on submarine attack 226
Sydney Opera House 240–4, *244*,
    272–3
Sydney Rowing Club 152
Sydney (schooner) 57
Sydney scorpionfish 4
Sydney-to-Hobart yacht race 228,
    268
Sydney I (HMAS) 212
Sydney II (HMAS) 218–19
Symonds, Stan 246

T Meller House 245
tall ships display 268–70
Tank Stream 22
  early pollution of 46
  exclusion zone around 29
  mud from 110
Tar-ra (Dawes Point) 4
Taronga Zoo 193–4
Tarwood, John 53
Taylor, James 126
Tench, Watkin
  on Aboriginal fisheries 35
  on Bryant escape 52
  on fishermen 49
  on native timber 56–7
  on seafood 30–1
  on Sydney Cove 33
  on theft from Aboriginal
    peoples 38
  relations with 'Manly' 41
Tennison-Woods, Julian Edmund
  169
terra nullius doctrine 34
The Balcony 2 276
The Bridge in Curve 200
The Bulletin 148, 154, 157, 180
The Curve of the Bridge 200
The Domain 84–5, 91-2, 129, 138,
    148, 237, 270
The Harbour from Craigend 98
The Harp in the South 254
*The Jacaranda Tree (on Sydney
  Harbour)* 276
The Quarterdeck 253
'The Retired Seaman' 155–6
The Rocks, *see* Rocks, The
'The Sacrifice of Balls Head' 161
*The Selector's Hut: Whelan on the
  Log* 150, 156
The Ship's Cat 183
'The Visit of Hope to Sydney Cove'
    82–3
Therry, Roger 105–6
Thompson, Ashburton 181
Thompson, Lindsay George 174
Thornton, George 162
Thornton, Wallace 253

Thorp, SG 238
Thrupp Estate 88, 93
'Thunderbolt' 122
timber
  around Sydney Cove 23–4
  commercial use of 57
  overseas trade in 63
  problems with 29
Titan crane 214
Toft Monks 191, *192*
Tom Thumb I & II 59
tooth evulsion 12–13
Torrens 213
tourism
  after Olympics 272
  Bicentennial and 265
  in 1980s 261
Town Planning Association of New
  South Wales 205
Towns, Robert 121
trade
  Corps monopoly on 66–7
  emancipation of 67–70
  growth of 75
  in timber 63
  with Aboriginal peoples 38–9
Traill, Jessie 203
trains, *see* railways
tram depot, Bennelong Point 189,
    241
treasury bills 66
trees and plants, *see also* timber
  around Sydney Cove 4, 23–4
  medicinal 31
  tree stump on Garden Island
    223
  use in building 9
Trickett, Edward 139
Trollope, Anthony 146, 157
Tubow-gule (Bennelong Point)
    4, 43
Tumbalong (Darling Harbour) 7
Tunks, William 136, 138, 142, 162,
    292
Twofold Bay 185
Twopeny, Richard 166

Underwood, James 68, 72–3
Underwood, John 84
Unilever House 237, 238
United States
  Great White Fleet 211, *213*
  Japanese attack on 222
  vessels from 54, 70, 125
urban planning
  by Arthur Phillip 26
  by Harry Seidler 246–7, 253
  by Sydney Harbour Trust
    185–8
  preparation for Sydney Harbour
    Bridge 203–4

Royal Commission into
(1909) 189–90
State involvement 279
Victorian era 119–20
Ure Smith, Sydney 253
Uren, Tom 230–1, 282, 284
Utzon, Jørn 240–3, 301

Vaucluse 93, 95–6, 116, 194,
201
Vaucluse (ferry) 195
Vaughan, Bryan 283
Vernon 121
View from the Window 96
Views in Australia 89
'Visit of Hope to Sydney Cove'
82–3
von Bellingshausen, Thaddeus
103
Vostok 103

Wa-rea-mah (Cockatoo Island)
122
Waaksamheyd 51, 52
Wakelin, Roland 200
Walker Corporation 281
Walker, Peter 302–3
Wallumede territory 7, 10
Wallumedgal people 7
Walsh Bay
cargo wharves 187
jetties 259
redevelopment of 283–5
whaling ships in 77
Walsh, Henry Deane 186
Wane territory 7
Wangal people 7
Ward, Frederick 122
Wardell, William 234
Warrane (Sydney Cove) 4, 22
Warrego 212
Warringah Expressway 235
Warrungareah (Blues Point) 4
water police 77
watercraft, *see also* boat
building; *names of craft*
bumboats 65
naval vessels 212
paddle steamers 109
passenger liners 218, 221
whaleboats 59
waterfront
land grants and sales 136,
138, 142, 193–4
social status and 273–7
Waterhen base 259
Waterhouse, Henry 58
waterside workers
early 1900s 214–16
heritage value of 287
strikes by 223

working conditions 187–8
Waterview Bay 124
Waterway 205
Watling, Thomas *14*
Watson, Robert 86
Watsons Bay 5, 191, *192*
Watt's Shark 28, *30*
Waverton, redevelopment of
279–80
Webber, Peter 303
Wedgwood, Josiah 81
Welch, Patrick 90
Wentworth, WC
birthday celebrated 194
departure and death 116
founds Vaucluse 93–6
supports transportation of
convicts 114
West, Harry 220
Westmacott, Robert 96
Westralia 218
whaleboats 59
whales 44, 77
whaling industry
Aboriginal workers dislike
101
crews visit Rocks 66
growth of 76–78
sperm whaling 71
Wharf House 69
wharves, quays and jetties, *see
also* Circular Quay
development of 184–7
early 26
finger wharves 186, 259
industrial heritage 282–3
Walsh Bay redevelopment
283–5
While the Billy Boils 158
White Australia Policy 231
White Bay
closure of 286–7
container terminals 259,
278, 288
power station 259
'White City' projects 191, 266
White, John
account of the settlement
27–9
land grants to 138
on early Sydney 23–4
on eating emu 31
on fishing stocks 29
on native timber 57
search for crop lands 32
Whitelegge, Thomas 169
Whiteley, Brett 275–6
Whiteley, Wendy 275–6
White's seahorse 1
whiting 3
Wia Wia 135

wildlife, *see also* fishing; trees
and plants
bird species 28, 31, 63
early accounts of 28
introduced species 26, 179
mammal species 31
marine invertebrates 3, 26,
29, 86, 152
rats 179, 181
seals and sealions 71–2
sharks 28, 135–6, *163*, 167
Victorian era 169
whales 44, 77
WilkinsonEyre 297, 298
William IV 81
Williams, Robert 74
Williamson, David 273, 277
Williamson, Kristin 274
Wilson, Reverend Canon 155
Windeyer, Richard 99–100
Windmill Hill 91
Winston, Denis 250
Withers, WH 236
Woggan-ma-gule (Farm Cove)
12, 23
Wollstonecraft, Edward 90
Wondakiah 280
wool industry 75
Woollahra (ferry) 195
Woollahra House 93, 195
Woolloomooloo
ethnic shifts in 232
finger wharves 187, 282
fish market 169, 172
pollution at 162
woolstore building 111
Woolwich dock 219
Worgan, George 22, 27, 31
World War I 207–11, *209*
World War II 218–26
Wotonga 126
Wulworra-jeung (Robertsons
Point) 141
Wyoming (house) 274
Wyreepi *137*

yacht ownership 134, 262
Yem-mer-ra-wan-nie 45
Yoolangh 12
Young, Barry 266
Younger, Henry 144
Yule, Charles 210

zoology, *see* wildlife